IN DEFENCE OF DEMOCRACY

Dynamics and Fault Lines of Nepal's Political Economy

IN DEFENCE OF DEMOCRACY

DYNAMICS AND FAULT LINES OF NEPAL'S POLITICAL ECONOMY

RAM SHARAN MAHAT, Ph.D

ADROIT PUBLISHERS

Published by
ADROIT PUBLISHERS
4675/21, Ganpati Bhawan, Ansari Road,
Daryaganj, New Delhi-110 002
Phones : 011-23266030

Distributors
AKHIL BOOK DISTRIBUTORS
e-mail: akhilbooks@yahoo.com
akhilbooks@hotmail.com

ISBN : 81-87392-67-3

Layout
Sudhir Vatsa

Laser Typeset by
Arpit Printographers
E-mail : arpitprinto@yahoo.com

Printed in India on behalf of
M/s Adroit Publishers by Arpit Printographers
Phones : 09350809192, 011-22825424

Dedicated
to all countrymen
truly committed to hard work and sacrifice
for the nation's pride, prosperity and democracy.

Contents

PART II
DEMOCRACY AND DEVELOPMENT

PART III
CRITICAL ISSUES & FAULT-LINES

Foreword

Sir Winston Churchill once famously said that democracy was the worst form of government... except for all the rest.

Ram Sharan Mahat illustrates this point vividly through his analysis of the dynamics and fault-lines of Nepal's political economy.

In Defence of Democracy is a timely and valuable contribution to understanding why democracy has been so fragile in Nepal, and why more democracy, not less, is the ultimate answer to overcoming the current tragic impasse.

Currently, political debate in Nepal is highly polarized because of a murderous insurgency and an autocratic monarchy bad-mouthing the deficiencies of liberal democracy. Dr. Mahat frankly acknowledges the shortcomings of Nepal's recent democratic experiment, while pointing out the many significant achievements.

Those bad-mouthing the performance of democracy point out the rampant corruption, maladministration, and inequitable development that has characterized the post-1990 multi-party parliamentary democracy. Mahat puts these negative features in a historical perspective of Nepal's feudal past, its oligarchic polity and its donor-dependent economy that has distorted some of Nepal's development priorities.

Yet, democracy tends to be a self-correcting system, and given a fair chance the distortions can and will have been rectified.

Moreover, the value of democracy should be measured not only by the performance of political leaders but also by the vibrancy of civil society, the freedoms enjoyed by people to express their views and pursue their dreams.

Though far from perfect, the advent of democracy in 1990 did usher in a new era of unprecedented openness and freedom to Nepal. Socio-economic progress too—though inadequate and inequitable—was not insignificant in Nepal's historical context.

And while the pace of progress was not fast enough to meet people's rising expectations for economic development and social justice, Mahat documents how people were beginning to be empowered as globalization in all its dimensions began to penetrate the mountains and valleys of the kingdom.

Dr. Mahat was personally a key player in the politics and economic policy-making of the post-1990 dispensation. Hence some might doubt the objectivity of his analysis. Yet, he has presented his analysis in a refreshingly frank, and even self-critical, manner. And as such, this book is a valuable contribution to students and policy-makers who care deeply about peace, prosperity and democracy in Nepal.

New York
20 May 2005

Kul Chandra Gautam
Deputy Executive Director, UNICEF
Assistant Secretary-General, United Nations

Preface

The post-1990 was a period of transition in many ways. The People's Movement brought about a polity based on political plurality and broad freedom. The state-imposed conformity and authoritarianism under the *Panchayat* gave way to diversity and innovations. The period was accompanied by new paradigms and ideas in many aspects of national life. A variety of concepts, idioms, and clichés of the contemporary world found their expressions in various forms. In a sense, the period was a laboratory of various constitutional exercises and application of new economic thinking and development paradigms—partly indigenous and partly in response to emerging contemporary thinking.

The twelve years of democracy have been hailed both for its successful democratic experiment and economic progress and criticized as a failure on all fronts. Especially after the Royal takeover of 1st February 2005, there is a new rush of well-crafted campaign to discredit the period and prove that the country was not yet ready for a liberal democracy. The period has been blamed for politics of personal and partisan interest, mal-governance, and economic failure that created circumstances for the growth of Maoist insurgency. The period in fact was a learning experience for an adolescent democracy. The objective of this book is to review the post-1990 democratic dispensation in a proper perspective, by evaluating its strength and weaknesses, successes and failures. The book summarizes the political events and facts of the period, and in parallel provides a full account of economic policies, processes, and performances. It has also attempted to capture some of the critical issues and controversies which dominated the period, and will continue to be debated with implications for public policy.

What was this period like in Nepal's own historical context? Was the post-1990 democratic era better or worse compared to other periods?

Was the development performance in keeping with the rising expectations of the people? In providing a historical perspective, the evolution of the political economy through various stages of Nepali history since the time of national unification till the *Panchayat* era has been analyzed. The objective is not to test any hypothesis and postulates, or theorize the process of economic and political development and changes, but to describe, explain, and analyze the events and facts from a practical perspective. In the narration, I have tried to cast aside my own personal and partisan biases to offer a detached evaluation of evidences.

Historically speaking, the Nepali people were never ruled by an elected government before 1990, except for a short-lived government under B.P Koirala. Barring the 1950s, the country was practically under autocracy throughout its history. The autocracy in the earlier era after the birth of the Nepali nation was in keeping with the contemporary trends. All resources, attention, and energy were devoted to military preparation and territorial expansion. The peasantry formed the foundation of the political economy during this phase. The emergence of the Ranas as ultimate rulers and their oligarchic order introduced a different form of autocracy unique only to Nepal. The common man who had inevitably borne the high cost of geo-political expansion and unbridled militarism under the early Shah rule continued to suffer. When liberal political values, expansion of railway network and industrial development were becoming the new national themes in the neighbourhood, the Nepali people still suffered from exploitation and political oppression. On the external front, the Ranas maintained extreme closeness with British India which provided the protective umbrella for their rule. What ensued was over a hundred years of unprecedented family enrichment through a variety of methods.

The end of the Rana Shogunate brought new hopes and optimism for the people who were suppressed for centuries. The people enjoyed new freedom that found their creative expressions in education, art, culture, and other activities. Political parties started functioning. Reforms were started to fight the feudal order, create modern state institutions, and initiate modern economic policies. But the era was marked by political instability, confusion, and the intense power struggle around personalities, with the monarch ultimately getting the upper hand. The first general election in 1959 brought relief and optimism, but the impatience shown by the new government for progressive reforms and modernization brought it into conflict with the conservative forces and a powerful king. The parliamentary polity was brought to an abrupt end. The *Panchayat* period was an era of executive monarchy, devoid of pluralism and political freedom.

Therefore, in the historical perspective, the post-*Panchayat* era of over a decade represented a period in the Nepali history when the country was served by elected governments and enjoyed full political freedom. It brought a new set of political leaders with rural middle-class backgrounds. Despite the shortcomings and weaknesses of the political elite, this period empowered the rural population and their representatives. This shifted the focus of state attention from urban centres to villages with increased investment. All social and human development indicators including education, literacy, life expectancy, child mortality, and maternal mortality have shown significant improvements during the period. There was an unprecedented development and growth of the press, media, and civil society with increasing maturity. The expansion of physical infrastructure like roads, communications, bridges, irrigation, and drinking water facilities has never been more impressive. The macro-economic indicators including the growth rate, production structure, trade, and balance of payments also point out a better development performance under democracy. It is in the nature of democratic political process that compels an elected government to address the concerns of its electorate. Resources were dispersed and the benefits widely distributed.

But the achievements were short of the popular expectations that had been unleashed after being stifled under the previous decades of autocracy. Schematic weaknesses and distortions in political life were also seen. Conflicts of inter-personal, intra-party, and inter-party nature surfaced in an agonizing manner. Actors in general, whether in government or in opposition, showed weaknesses. The period exposed the weaknesses and fault-lines in the national polity, social system, and economic order, which called for urgent prescriptions. This was perhaps natural in the early phase of democracy and part of the process of a growing pain. A section of the intelligentsia even attributes the rise of the Maoists to the shortcomings of the democratic rule. Others blame the lack of visible economic changes as the reason for their growth. It is generally agreed that the unmet expectations from democracy, the country's economic backwardness, poverty, and unemployment provided fertile grounds for Maoist recruitments. The rugged terrain and formidable geography offered further facilitating conditions. The Maoists also used the breathing space provided by the post-1990 democracy for organizational expansion.

The Maoists were, however, preparing for their 'revolution' ever since 1984 when their party became the founding member of Revolutionary International Movement. In 1985, their party adopted the doctrine of violent movement to instigate mass uprising. After the

1990 Peoples' Movement, when the party under the banner of Unity Centre created a political front to participate in the parliamentary election of 1991 to "expose the hypocrisy" of the parliamentary system, the hardcore leadership remained underground. The political line of "protracted people's war to start a new democratic revolution with a Marxist-Leninist and Maoist perspective" was passed in 1991 under Prachanda's leadership. The Maoists blame the monopoly of political and economic power since 1768 as the root cause of the present ills, which the post-1990 democratic rule could not address. The principal goal of their struggle is an end to the institution of monarchy.

Under democracy, feelings that had been suppressed for centuries found their expressions. The regional disparities, the urban-rural dichotomy, gender discrimination, the problem of exclusion and neglect of the various caste and ethnicities emerged as major concerns of national debate and discussion. These have now been manifested in the demands for radical socio-economic and political reforms from the minorities, the discriminated and excluded communities. The Communist Party of Nepal (Maoists) shrewdly exploited these fault-lines to their advantage to make a case for one-party republican utopia as the ultimate solution.

Other issues of developmental and political nature also dominated the nineties. The issue of Arun III was one such case. Apart from the intensive campaign by a global network of NGOs and the political failure to properly grasp the intricacies of aid dynamics, the project typified the case of a small nation falling victim to the changing mood and attitude of powerful global organizations. The donor perception of priorities does not always conform to that of the recipients. The foreign assistance responding to the recipient priorities in form and content is an ideal and theoretical proposition. But practice does not always follow this precept. Based on my first-hand experiences, I have highlighted the divergence in perception that at times occurred in Nepal. The recipient country desperately in need of assistance everywhere finds it hard to resist the temptation of accepting the aid even in areas not treated as priorities.

No other subject has received as much concern and attention as the issue of corruption since 1990. The democratic era is often criticized for corruption and malpractices. Draconian measures have been put in place to mitigate this menace with strong and unique laws being legislated which led to the prosecution of some leading public figures and officials. People who piloted the bill in the parliament became its first targets. This speaks of the strength of democratic institutions and its superiority over other systems. Under autocracy, the target of anti-corruption drive is often the group of political opponents and those who do not subscribe to the official line. The donor community has a tendency to put the entire blame on the recipient state for corruption in development projects, ignoring the partnership nature of the process. The procurement beneficiaries of the major development projects are the multi-national companies of the industrialized countries whose propensity to bribe public officials of the recipient countries for favourable treatment is well known. The annual reports and surveys by such organizations as Transparency International bear testimony to this fact.

The impasse on the refugees question is a subject of great concern to Nepal. Unfortunately, due to Nepal's internal problems, this problem has not yet received the priority it deserved in foreign policy agenda. Bhutan has shrewdly manipulated this situation to its favour through quiet diplomacy. It has succeeded in avoiding international condemnation for its outrageous ethnic policy, and stalled any progress towards repatriation. The royal takeover of political power since 4 October 2004, which reached its climax on February 1st, 2005 resulted in a political deadlock and the country is now embroiled in a triangular struggle for power. This has added a new dimension to Nepal's political crisis, which already was suffering from the violent insurgency. Not by design, but in terms of impact, the insurgency and the regression have complemented each other. By crippling the democratic process, the Maoist insurgency has given an alibi for the king's direct rule. On the other hand, the king's actions have given validity to the Maoist theory that the ultimate power in the present political order lies with the king.

This book is divided into three parts. The first part contains the evolution of Nepal's political economy in a historical perspective. This has been divided into four distinct political phases: the period of national unification, a century of Rana oligarchy, the 1950s, and the *Panchayat* era. The second part of the book covers the development performance of the democratic era, the post-Panchayat period. I have tried to capture major political developments of the period that had a bearing on the economy. Major economic reforms, policy initiatives, and departures have been highlighted and statistics about development performance, at macro and sectoral levels, have been recorded. Data on poverty, human development indicators, and other macro and sectoral performance have been drawn from the latest nation-wide surveys and those published by authoritative sources.

The third and last part of the book attempts to deal with major controversies and critical issues that dominated the national debate in the nineties and afterwards. These ranged from the hotly discussed subject of exclusion and discrimination to dependence on foreign aid and the rising cost of security. Before concluding the book with a few observations, I have tried to flag off a few major fault lines of our society, which, if not addressed properly in time, could weaken the nation and destroy democracy. The education system, which is becoming increasingly dualistic, has reinforced the foundation for further economic disparities. A weak state system characterized by all the symptoms of a soft state is another fault-line afflicting the Nepali society. Politics instead of the economy has always assumed centre stage in the national agenda. The violence of the Maoist insurgency that has already taken a heavy toll constitutes the primary state problem. There is a clear imperative for a strong democratic innovation that can bring all forces to commit themselves to a true multi-party democracy without the threat of violence.

The country's economic future would depend on how soon and how effectively the critical issues and fault lines are corrected. The country has a resource base, which can provide the basis for sustained growth and development. But mere resource endowment is not a sufficient condition for a country's prosperity. Recent economic history is replete with instances where resource-poor countries with the right policy and high quality manpower have been star performers. In the absence of enabling economic environment and creative manpower, natural resource in itself will be of no use. Economic development is a process, which will involve the creative harnessing of all human and material resources to generate production and wealth. This is a political process for which democratic institutions are essential. People's participation in the political and economic process is possible only in a democracy. Even in dealing with a conflict situation, democratic institutions provide more effective mechanisms. Nepal's own experience shows that democracy provides a better facilitating environment for economic growth, human development, and poverty alleviation. It gives greater voice to the rural population and those at the margin. Development and growth process should not accentuate disparities and punish the neglected as injustice and exclusion provide fertile ground for radical movements. That is where the national priority should be. There is no alternative to inclusive, decentralized, and liberal democracy capable of assuring equity and economic justice.

Ram S. Mahat

Acknowledgements

This book resulted largely from the use of my free time in the last one year. Relieved of official responsibilities after my resignation as Finance Minister following the House dissolution of 22nd May 2002, and the restricted political activities due to the changed political and security situation, I used my free time to collect and compile materials for the work. My desire to work on a book such as this goes back to my Hubert Humphrey fellowship days in 1987/8. The genesis of the first four chapters can be traced to that period when I frequently visited the Library of Congress, Washington D.C. for studying, and preparing notes. A large part of this book is devoted to the economy and political aspects of the post-1990 period with which I myself was fortunate to be closely associated. Thus, I have taken the liberty to record my own personal experience with respect to various events and facts. I express my gratitude to my party Nepali Congress and the three Prime Ministers I worked with for the opportunity to serve in various capacities that exposed me to the country's myriad problems and enabled to contribute to the best of my ability. In preparation to some chapters under part III of the book, I have liberally drawn from the seminar papers I presented at various forums, and from my articles published in the *Kathmandu Post*, and the *Himalayan Times*.

I also take this opportunity to acknowledge with my appreciation the support I received from numerous hands in bringing this work to this shape. It is not possible to name them all, particularly those who helped me by providing useful materials and information. In particular, my son Raxak and a promising young man who prefers to remain anonymous spent considerable time going through the whole draft manuscript and making editorial improvements. Dr. Rabindra Shakya provided some useful inputs and comments. Dr. Shyam Thapa and Chakra Bastola also offered their insights and suggestions.

Support was received from Raju Babu Shakya (Sarav) in cover design, Indra K.C in graphics, Min Bajracharya of Himal Media, Gopal Chikrakar and his colleagues of Kantipur Publications, Devendra Pratap Shaha, Kathmandu University and Bhaktapur Municipality for the photographs. Sarad Bikram Rana, Arun Mahat and Pralhad Dhakal assisted by offering computer skills at different times while Ramesh Mahat through his assistance freed me from various constituency-related responsibilities. My daughter Agya was indulgent with a father who spent time mostly with his computer even when she was at home for holidays. Appreciation is due to my wife Roshana who not only released me from all responsibilities at home, but was a unceasing source of encouragement, inspiration and advice.

Lastly, I am grateful to Kul C. Gautam, presently Deputy Executive Director of UNICEF and Assistant Secretary General of the United Nations for sparing time to go through the manuscript and write a foreword for the book.

I remain, however, solely and personally responsible for any lapses, shortcomings and errors that may have crept in this undertaking.

List of Tables

List of Photographs

LIST OF CHARTS

PART I
HISTORICAL PERSPECTIVE

Chapter One

Political Economy of National Unification

The territorial foundation of Nepal as we know it today was laid down by King Prithvi Narayan Shah through a process of military expeditions, expansion, and unification. The House of Gorkha, to which the Shah dynasty belonged, grew and expanded from a small hill kingdom into a viable modern nation with the unification and consolidation of various small, scattered, and independent states. In particular, the Chaubisi of the Gandaki region, the basin of the Karnali region, Makawanpur, the Kingdoms of Chaudandi and Bijayapur in the east, and several *tarai* districts were annexed through a series of military expeditions. It was only after the conquest of the three states of the Kathmandu Valley between 1760 and 1769, however, that the Kingdom of Nepal came into existence.

The foundation laid down by Prithvi Narayan showed extraordinary political foresight for his time. The high quality of his leadership and diplomatic skills, backed adequately by military prowess, unrelenting determination and at times ruthlessness, contributed significantly to the success of his missions. The national boundary underwent further expansion under his successors, particularly during the regency rule of Bahadur Shah. Under Bahadur Shah, the country graduated from the status of a small kingdom to a major power in the subcontinent. Its borders extended from the Tista river in the east to Kangra in the West.

But the national preoccupation with territorial expansion during that period resulted in the concentration of efforts solely to military preparations, expeditions, and conquests. As all resources—human and material—were mobilized for military purposes, the consideration of the country's modernization, reforms and welfare of the people received little attention. Land was the principal national resource and provided a source of livelihood to almost the entire population, except to those living in the harsh geographic and climatic conditions of the northern

Himalayan region. Trade, rather than agriculture, was the principal economic activity for the people living in this region where food deficit exacerbated the already adverse living conditions. Trade centres were developed at various Himalayan passes to facilitate trade with Tibet. Commodities such as rice, ghee, paper and iron were exchanged for Tibetan salt, sheep and wool. The cereal requirements of this region had to be supplemented with foodgrains from the lower region which were exchanged with salt and other goods procured from the Tibetan traders.[1] The people in the Himalayan region also relied on sheep and yak husbandry for their income. There are also some historical references to the clothes made out of sheep wool. Some areas like Baglung in the western hills were noted for producing minerals, particularly copper and iron, which were also exported.

The *tarai* region of Nepal, with its rich agricultural land and favourable terrain had intimate trade relations with India. It produced rice, oil seeds, cotton, jute, sugar cane and tobacco. Large qualities of rice were exported to Bihar, Bengal and other parts India. It also exported other foodgrains, timber, elephants, musk, herbs and drugs to India in large quantities. Agriculture in the hilly region was largely at a subsistence level. The distribution of land was unequal and the production relations between the tenants, landlords and the state were exploitative, as will be discussed in later paragraphs. Animal husbandry supplemented the income from farm produce. Because of enormous transportation difficulties, villages were physically separated from each other and were largely self-sufficient in meeting most of their consumption requirements, which were themselves rather modest.

The Kathmandu valley, on the other hand, was rich not just in fertile agricultural land but also in the artistic excellence of its inhabitants engaged in various handicraft occupations. The Newars who inhabited the valley were renowned as skilled architects and goldsmiths, accomplished artisans in woodcarving and in copper, bronze and brass works. The description of the proud valley architecture can be found in the travel accounts of early Chinese travellers.[2] The extraordinary richness in wood and stone carvings, sculpture works and paintings was reflected in the architecture of palaces, temples and even individual houses. The magnificence and grandeur of copper, bronze and stone craftsmanship of the valley can be seen even today in the palaces and temples built under the Malla kings who ruled Kathmandu valley before the Gorkha invasion.

ENTREPOT TRADE AND NEW PROTECTION

Apart from thriving agriculture and advanced craftsmanship of its people, the prosperity of Kathmandu valley owed significantly to its location as the entrepot for Indo-Tibetan trade—a position which was strengthened by various treaties with the Tibetan authorities at different times. From the emergence of Tibet in the seventh century to the opening of the Gangtok route in 1902, Nepal was the most dominant centre for entrepot trade[3]. Kathmandu's proximity to the Kuti and Kerung passes which channelled most of the trade between South and Central Asia provided it with the strategic advantage in the trans-Himalayan trade structure. There are historical evidences of the struggle between Kathmandu and Gorkha to control the Himalayan trade routes to Tibet for strategic and economic reasons. The Gorkha incursion of Tibet under Ram Shah (1606–1641) was subsequently followed by a Nepali expedition around 1630. The ensuing treaty between Kathmandu and Tibet helped restore and preserve the near monopoly status of the Kathmandu route for Tibetan trade. It was this treaty that sustained the prosperity of the valley for more than a century. Things started to change towards the mid-eighteenth century with the increasing ascendancy of the military might of the Kingdom of Gorkha under Prithvi Narayan. By 1757 and prior to the conquest of Kathmandu Valley, Gorkha commanded all trade routes between Kathmandu and Tibet and eventually forced a treaty with Kathmandu entitling Gorkha to an equal share of the benefits from entrepot trade with Tibet.[4]

The exports from Bengal to Tibet at that time consisted of *Malda* cloth, *Rangapur* leather, tobacco, indigo, coral, spices, sandal wood and precious stones and the imports consisted of gold dust, tinkle and musk.[5] The cheap gold from Tibet also attracted the British. The Kathmandu valley exported silver species, coarse linen cloth, rice, copper and spices to Tibet and imported gold dust, diamonds, pearls, coral tinkle, woollen cloth and animal skins. At that time Tibet did not have its own currency and Nepali currency was used for both internal and external exchange purposes. Tibet paid Nepal a fixed quantity of silver each year in exchange for this facility—an arrangement which continued for a long time.[6]

Prithvi Narayan Shah was very suspicious of the motives of the East India Company and therefore, followed a very protective economic and trade policy with them. After his conquest of Kathmandu, he banished all Capuchin missionaries who had taken up abode in the valley after their expulsion from Tibet, and prevented more Europeans from entering Nepal. During the Malla reign of Kathmandu the entrepot trade between India and the Tibetan region in Kathmandu was conducted mainly by Kashmiri Muslims and *Gosains* (Hindu merchants-cum-pilgrim mendicants) in Kathmandu. Deeply suspicious of their activities and loyalty, Prithvi Narayan expelled some of these traders while significantly curtailing the activities of those that were allowed to stay. He not only resisted all British efforts to establish regulated trade relations with Nepal, but also attempted to prevent the British from gaining an ascendancy over the commerce of Tibet. In a letter to the Dalai Lama, he advised that in return for free access of Indian goods to Tibet, the Lamaic government should join him in forbidding the entry of anything and everything associated with the gravely suspect ambitions of the East India Company in Bengal.[7] Furthermore, he patronized local crafts and restricted the import of goods in general and luxury items in particular.

After his conquest of Kathmandu valley, Prithvi Narayan anticipated that the East India Company might try to open new trade routes to Lhasa through the eastern hills. This consideration led him to push for eastward military expansion after 1770. He desired to control and close all the access routes between India and Tibet in the sub-Himalayan hill areas, in a bid to preserve Kathmandu's monopoly as entrepot for the Indo-Tibetan trade.[8] Unsatisfied with the trading arrangements of the Mallas, he attempted to introduce a new trading system by starting trade marts in Parsa Gadhi in the *tarai* for trade with India, and along some points at Tibetan border for Tibetan trade. However, the new system did not evoke a favourable response from Tibet and led to an eventual decline in trade with Tibet. Prithvi Narayan also wanted to circulate his own new currency in Tibet, but not on the same exchange rate as the debased coins of the Malla rulers. However, complications arose when Tibet refused to accept them for circulation until Nepal agreed to buy back all the debased coins of the Malla kings at face value. Prithvi Narayan refused to accept the responsibility for the coins of the vanquished rulers.[9]

After the passing away of Prithvi Narayan, his successor, Pratap Singh Shah, made attempts to improve relations with both Tibet and the British. The Panchen Lama wrote to the new ruler proposing the resumption of trade for mutual advantage of the two sides and a trade treaty was signed to this effect with Tibet in 1775. The contentious issue about the circulation and exchange rate of the Nepali coin remained unaddressed in this treaty.

Meanwhile, the British, in keeping with their mercantilist policy, continued their efforts to revive and expand the old trade by sending numerous missions to Nepal and Tibet in quick succession. The British interest in the possibility of trade with Tibet and West China had been aroused initially after the Kinloch mission of 1767 dispatched by the East India Company at the behest of Jaya Prakash Malla when the Gorkha king had laid siege to the Kathmandu valley. Warren Hastings who came as Governor General of Bengal in 1772 was instructed by the East India Company to explore the prospect of Himalayan trade. Hastings dispatched the Bogle mission in 1774 to open trade communications with Bhutan, Nepal and Tibet. This was followed by the mission of Captain Samuel Turner in 1782. But there was little progress.[10]

Nepal went to war with Tibet in 1788 over the issue of circulation of Nepali coins in Tibet and the imposition of taxes on goods traded between India and Tibet through Nepal. The war ended in Nepal's favour with Tibet committing to four clauses: pay 300 ingots of silver every year to Nepal, accept the use of Nepali coins on Nepali terms, host a Nepali trade representative in Tibet, and grant Nepal a monopoly in Tibetan trade by closing alternative routes in the east and west. War broke out with Tibet for the second time in 1791 on account of Tibet's failure to honour the treaty and make the annual payments of silver. This time, the war ended with the Chinese invasion of Nepal. Nepal not only lost the war but suffered major reverses which resulted in the loss of some important economic benefits from Tibet.

The reverses suffered in the north prompted the Nepali rulers to turn towards East India Company for assistance. Nepal offered the British to sign a commercial treaty in the hope of obtaining military assistance. A commercial treaty was concluded in 1792 with Nepal that laid the foundation of trade relations between the two countries for the first time. The treaty, among others, provided for commercial traffic between the two countries at the rate of 2.5 per cent as duties on a reciprocal basis and the protection of merchants on both sides against oppression and violence. Aware of the paramount British interest in preserving Chinese friendship and cooperation, the Governor General sent Captain William Kirkpatrick to mediate between Nepal and China. Kirkpatrick arrived in Kathmandu in 1793 after the war had ended.[11] Kirkpatrick's other objective to pursue commercial interest also did not achieve anything concrete. This treaty, forged strictly on economic and political considerations, did little to change the prevailing attitude of suspicion towards the British. However, the mission was successful in gathering enough information about Nepal that was later published in the form of a book. Nepal became better known to East India Company through Kirkpatrick's accounts.

The Company persisted in its efforts and decided to send the Kadir

Khan mission in 1795 to leverage trade on the basis of the 1792 treaty. After initial hiccups, the mission was received by the Court of Nepal. Kadir Khan had himself brought with him merchandise worth Rs.15,000 to gain practical knowledge of trade prospects with Nepal. His estimate of the total value of prospective export was Rs.400,000 to Rs. 500,000 annually. Khan's assessment was that if Nepal could be convinced to accept the import of manufactured European articles such as broad clothes—which were in high demand in all hilly countries—their imminent popular demand here would force the rulers to remove all obstacles to trade with the Company. Khan also estimated that there was higher profit in trade with Tibet than with Nepal. He identified a large number of products for sale in Nepal and Tibet, and suggested warehouses in five locations in Indian territories close to Nepali borders where the Tibetans would come to purchase these articles. The purpose was to circumvent Kathmandu for Tibetan trade.[12] These suggestions were, however, not immediately followed up.

Taking advantage of the court feud in Nepal when King Rana Bahadur Shah had withdrawn to Varanasi, the British made one more attempt to pressurize Nepal for concessions in trade and other treaty matters. They were successful in negotiating the treaty of 1801 which provided, among others, the exchange of diplomatic representatives between the two counties. This paved the way for the stationing of British residency in Kathmandu. Captain Knox was appointed the first British representative. In addition to securing the implementation of the 1792 commercial treaty, he was asked to assess trade and transit prospects with Nepal and Tibet, and ascertain the possibility of securing a belt of the *tarai* forest in exchange for equivalent company territory or cash. The East India Company had strong interest in Nepal's forest resources, particularly timber.

PRITHVI NARAYAN'S ECONOMICS

Prithivi Narayan Shah stressed the importance of tilling every available acre of land. He went even to the extent of planning the demolition of buildings, if erected on land suitable for agriculture. He favoured the construction of multi-storeyed buildings to save land. He preferred shifting of settlements from locations with mine deposits. An uncompromising proponent of self-reliant, *swadeshi* economy, he issued instructions to promote domestic products, art, music and culture. He opposed import of clothes for domestic consumption, and believed in exporting farm and forestry products to earn revenue. He was also opposed to the contractual system of collecting revenue. Prithvi Narayan was not just a strong champion, but a real practitioner of fairness and justice in administration and governance. He considered both bribe-takers and bribe-givers as the enemy of the state and deserving of capital punishment. He believed in disencumbering soldiers of economic worries, but strongly opposed high earnings and wealth creation, since that would make them lazy.[13]

Prithvi Narayan's concept of the state was based on two sturdy pillars—a contended peasantry and a loyal army.[14] Land remained the principal national resource, not only as a source of livelihood for the bulk of the population, but also as a source of public revenue and the economic basis for the country's defence requirements. During Nepal's territorial expansion, the importance of land soared as peasants gave it their highest loyalty. In practical terms, the state could not survive unless peasants retained enough of their crops after taxes to support themselves and their families in modest security. But the need of the expanding state and the attendant proliferation of administrative units tended to increase the burden of taxes on the peasantry. This was despite the fact that the peasants in the Hills were already committed to paying half of their annual yields. Recognizing this reality, Prithvi Narayan Shah decreed simplicity in the lifestyle of administrators and court officials and emphasized honesty and fairness in tax administration. Stiller writes:

> Concretely, he suggested that the salaries of the court officers be kept low, with rewards for superior work being given in terms of honour rather than wealth; that taxes be collected, not by taxing farmers on a contract basis, but by government officials; that the taxes accounts be strictly audited at regular intervals. The court itself be expected to be a nobility of service, not an arena where affluence and prestige could become the goal of political striving and the cause of factionalism. To further protect the peasants, the king himself was to see that justice be fairly administered, and that bribery, which is the death of justice, be strictly punished.[15]

To make the soldiers free from the worries of family welfare, land provided to them was exempt from major taxes. Furthermore, in case of death in battle, land was to be provided to their sons for support. Land assignment to military personnel was also necessitated by the fact that the total government revenue in cash was simply insufficient to cover all the expenses of the Nepali fighting machine of the time. The size of the army in those days has been varyingly estimated. Kirkpatrick estimated the number to be between 7,500 to 9,000 in 1792. The estimates by Hamilton in 1802 put the figure between 9,000 to 10,000. The total strength of approximately nine thousand men in 1792 at the prevailing salary would cost about 45 lakhs rupees a year, against a total annual revenue of 25 to 30 lakhs rupees around that time.[16]

LAND, PEASANTRY AND EXPANSION

All land belonged to the State. But various kinds of land tenure existed in the form of *Raikar, Birta, Jagir, Rakam, Sera* and *Kipat*. Of them, *Raikar* was the only system under which the tenants made direct payments to the State. The *Birta* land was gifted by the state to private individuals for their subsistence and enrichment primarily based on political, economic and religious considerations. *Jagir* land was assigned as emoluments to government officials for their civil and military functions in place of regular cash payments. *Rakam* land was used as remuneration for the performance of specific functions of manual nature, such as carpentry, masonry, woodcutting and charcoal supply as required by the state or the royal palace. Land assigned for religious and charitable purposes was known as *Guthi*. *Kipat* land was a form of communal tenure. Members of certain ethnic groups—such as the Rais and Limbus in the East—were permitted to own *Kipat* land.

The Government enjoyed unlimited power to grant *Raikar* lands to individuals as *Birta* and to temples and monasteries as *Guthi*, thereby enabling the beneficiaries to not only directly appropriate the payments from the cultivators but also to dispense justice and exact unpaid labour from them. Furthermore, these beneficiaries could also supplement their income through other sources such as litigation fees and local levies on commercial goods in transit. In return for the land assignments, the *Jagir* and the *Birta* grantees were normally under obligation to supply troops, weapons and ammunitions, and logistical support to the state during war times. In effect, all these obligations were ultimately passed on to the tenants and cultivators under their jurisdiction when the need arose. Regmi writes:

> Land grants and assignments under the *Birta* and *Jagir* systems, therefore, formed the bedrock of the political and administrative set-up introduced after political unification. Large areas of lands were appropriated as rewards or emoluments to civil and military officials, members of the nobility, chieftains of vanquished principalities and others.[17]

The expansion of defense in the process of territorial expansion, which necessitated new recruitment, was, therefore, governed by the availability of new land for the purpose of assignment as *Jagir*. The government was therefore compelled to convert vast chunks of private *Raikar* land and communal land such as *Kipat* into *Jagir*. But in the process, the interest of the peasantry was neglected leading to the elimination of small owner-cultivator farmers, the vanishing of the direct relationship between the state and the peasantry. The rentier class in the forms of *Birtawals* and *Jagirdars* expanded. This superstructure of agrarian relations very well served the immediate administrative and military needs of the government so that the need of reforming the exploitative land relations between the cultivators and the landlords did not receive the attention it deserved. Consideration of the welfare and security of the cultivators influenced these policies and programs only to the extent necessary to check depopulation[18].

The system of land assignment to military personnel was crucial to the expansion of the Gorkha kingdom from a few hundred square miles to an area spanning over ninety thousand square miles. It was the land that set the limit on the military expansion. As Stiller aptly puts it, "as a result of this practice the double dichotomy was set up; the limit of the army was the land: the limit of the land was the army".[19] Describing the importance of land-military nexus in Bahadur Shah's military conquest in the west, he writes:

> Continuing Gorkhali conquests brought large areas of the *tarai* under Gorkha control, valuable land that Bahadur Shah could dispense as *Jagirs* to the hill men who saw fit to join the Gorkhali fighting machine. This was a reward beyond the dreams of the land-hungry hill man, and the promises of it guaranteed the Gorkhali fighting machine a constant stream of recruits. The fuel was there. The fighting machine was there. The opposition confronting it was negligible. It was a combination practically guaranteeing success.[20]

Besides military *Jagirs*, there were at least five other demands made on new land acquisitions.[21] In keeping with Prithvi Narayan's policy, some land had to be provisioned for the widows and children of those who were killed in the war. Second, some territory was also assigned as *Birta* land to an increasing number of those showing exemplary valour in the fields of battle. Third, land was also assigned as *Birta* to those who facilitated the conquest by defecting to the Gorkhali rulers. Fourth, land was assigned as *Guthis* for the maintenance and services of the temples in recognition to the divine blessing for the military victories. Last, with each military success, the lifestyle of the courts became progressively extravagant and starkly contrasted the austerity prescribed by Prithvi Narayan. These new luxuries would have to be financed by land assignments and the appropriation of new territories to meet these demands did not leave enough land to be assigned as military *Jagir*. Therefore, the hunger for territorial expansion remained perennially unsatisfied, and manifested itself in the ambitious thrusts the Nepali military machine was making both eastward and westward. The government also required financial resources to procure arms, ammunitions and supplies as well as to finance the salary and emoluments of the military and administrative personnel. Land tax was an important and convenient source of public revenue. Other sources included the customs, the mint and the exports of forest products, particularly timber. As the *Birtawals* and the *Jagirdars* owning vast chunks of agricultural land were exempted from paying taxes, the tax burden fell squarely on the peasantry and other non-privileged classes. This caused considerable suffering to the peasants. An author summarizes the prevailing situation in the following words:

> The demands of the enlarged state apparatus—the army that was required for the conquest of new territory and the annexation of insubordinate vassals; and the bureaucracy needed for the collection of tax and tribute and for the administration of the new territories—meant that there was undoubtedly increasing pressure from the centre to increase the level of exploitation of direct producers and to increase the levies on traders which not only affected the peasantry and the agricultural production but also the local manufacturing, mining and trade. [22]

The objective of maximizing the revenue from land led the government to adopt the *Ijara* system of tax collection under which the task of revenue collection was entrusted to contractors (*Ijaradars*) who were often the highest bidders in most parts of the *tarai*. These contractors paid stipulated revenue amount to the government and appropriated for themselves any additional amount they could extract from the sources and territories assigned to them. Despite the excesses committed by these contractors, much to the suffering of the peasantry, this system continued to remain in practice. Occasionally, the state reverted to the *Amanat* system, when it was not politically administratively expedient to appoint *Ijaradars*. Under this system, revenue was collected and accounts rendered to the government on the basis of actual collection by officials and functionaries appointed for the purpose.[23]

Since the ownership of large portions of land was concentrated among a few *Birtawals* and *Jagirdars*, peasants were left with smaller holdings. In the absence of alternative income sources, and because income from smallholdings were not sufficient for their subsistence, it was natural for small landholders to seek cultivation of *Birta* and *Jagir* lands. But the high demand for work on such land strengthened the bargaining position of the landlords, helping push up the rents payable by the cultivators. The cultivators in general paid a stipulated amount of produce to the landlords, irrespective of the periodic variations in the land productions caused by weather and other conditions. In case of a crop failure, the cultivator was forced to borrow at high interest rates to meet his rental obligations. In such cases, more often than not, the peasants failed to repay the loans as they seldom could produce the required surplus from the land with which to pay such loans. The failure to pay loans gave rise to the *Bandha* (bonded labour) system under which the debtors remained the property of the creditors and were used for any types of labour services required by the creditors. The bondsmen could technically free themselves from the bondage upon servicing the debts. Since this was not possible under normal circumstances, bondsmen usually ended up remaining the properties of the landlords for their entire lives and after their deaths the bondsmanship was transferred to their subsequent generations.

Tenurial security was absent, and there was no restriction on the power of the *Jagirdars* to evict their tenants, unless otherwise protected. This power enabled them to extract higher rents which the new tenants would be readily prepared to offer if the incumbents did not agree. In particular, as *Jagir* land was temporary in nature and could be withdrawn by the state at any time, the *Jagirdars* tried to maximize the returns for themselves during the period the land belonged to them. Furthermore, the *Jagirdars* were generally absentee landlords as in most cases their civilian and military responsibilities required them to be assigned elsewhere. The job of managing their *Jagir* land fell on their relatives or agents who enjoyed the prerogative of not only exacting fifty per cent of the land produce and other levies from the peasants, but also exercised minor judicial functions—a practice which was subject to routine abuses at the expense of the poor peasants. The peasantry was thus divorced from the direct government administration twice: at the level of *Jagirdar* and then at the level of his agent.

The state attached high importance to the reclamation of wasteland to increase revenue both in the hills and in the *tarai.* One important consequence of the *Jagir* and *Birta* land assignment of the new territories was the reclamation and development of waste land. In view of the low density of population in the country, immigration was encouraged from India. In the *tarai*, land reclamation on a large scale was successfully undertaken through a mutually rewarding contract arrangement with individual entrepreneurs. Contracts were granted to local landlords, revenue functionaries and senior government officials under an agreement which required them to pay stipulated revenue to the state. This revenue was subject to annual increments throughout the prescribed period. In consideration of this payment, the contractors were permitted to collect taxes and other revenue from the settlers on the reclaimed land. This method of land reclamation proved particularly successful in the eastern *tarai*.[24]

The reclamation and development of new land did not contribute much to state revenue as the benefits accrued largely to individuals. Nor did it have any direct impact on the lives of the peasantry who had to surrender a minimum of half of their crop yield to the *Jagirdars* and *Birtawals*. However, it did contribute to the overall land development, increased food production, and enhanced land value.

THE *JHARA* SYSTEM

The expanding size of the nation and the unchecked growth of military activity required an increasing use of labour services for such tasks like the transportation of arms, ammunitions, food and other military supplies, and the maintenance and repair of trails, roads, bridges, canals and forts. The state resorted to *Jhara* system (compulsory forced labour) for this purpose and mobilized an army of labourers who were paid no wages. The entire male adult population, with the exception of members of the nobility and high officials, were required to tender their services. The *Jhara* labour played an important role to process salt-peter for gun powder, supply fuel-woods and make grinding stones for gunpowder factories. The system was utilized for carrying building materials, loads of royal guests, mail supplies and for the construction of public works. The authority to use of this service was not limited to the state. It was liberally utilized to fulfill the needs, whims and caprices of the courts. They were used for activities ranging from carrying imported goods and fresh mangoes from the *tarai* to hunting snakes and crocodiles to extract ingredients for special incense; capturing wild elephants and to supplying fodder to the royal elephants.[25] The misery to which the peasantry was subjected on account of this system was worsened by abuses of the system by government officials and other influential persons. The deleterious effect of this system and other exploitative practices on the economy has been summarized in the following passage:

> Along with the insecure and inequitable land tenure system prevalent during this period, forced labour and slavery constituted the major factors, which inhibited the growth of a stable and prosperous agrarian society. Moreover, this system ensured that the economy remained stagnant even during a period of intensive military activity. Prospects of the expansion of economic activity and the accelerated flow of money incomes, which generally accompany such activity, were belied by the obligation of the

> people without wages not only while providing porterage services but also while processing forest and mineral products for supply to munitions factories and other military establishments. It is true, of course, that territorial expansion would hardly have been possible without sacrifices on the part of the people. But the upper class of the society underwent no such sacrifices. In any case, the adverse effect of these systems on the national economy as a whole is a fact which territorial expansion in itself may explain, but hardly deny.[26]

Most of the burden of the war was borne by the peasantry. They had to work hard to produce enough surplus to feed the army, procure arms and ammunition to the soldiers and meet normal government expenditure. On the other hand, for the military elite, war was a prized enterprise which offered them an opportunity to acquire new land for their contribution and sacrifices in the war.

In the meantime, the population of Nepal had been growing slowly but significantly since the days of national unification in the mid eighteenth century. Population increased in response to the deliberate policy of the government to encourage immigration to augment the labour supply for land reclamation, and due to change in farming practices with the introduction of new crops, particularly maize in the 18th century. Livestock production was replaced by cereal cultivation as the core agricultural activity. Pastoralism and the simple shifting cultivation had, similarly, given way to more organized farming and stable settlement. The growth of population, on the other hand, led to a rise in agricultural output and consequently state revenue. The major effect of this in the *tarai* was the rise in agricultural surplus.

> In the case of Nepal, it seems highly probable that the introduction of new crops during the 18th and 19th centuries, the demands of the newly emergent Nepalese state for increased revenue, its policies of immigration and settlement, all contributed to a significant growth in the population of Nepal; on the other hand there can be no doubt that population growth in turn made possible and, equally necessary, further developments in agricultural production—increasing the area under cultivation, intensifying production methods, and making possible the generation of larger surpluses from agriculture.[27]

ADMINISTRATIVE PRACTICE

It is interesting to note that despite the enormous value of the nobility in civilian and military positions—*Mukhtiyar, Chautaria, Kajis, Sardars, Subbas, Jagirdars, Birtawals* and other functionaries—in the unification days and afterwards, the class did not grow and develop as a powerful bloc capable of asserting independent power. The authority derived by the nobility and feudal families was by virtue of their official status and position, and the assignment and use of *Birta* and *Jagir* lands granted to them by the state, which was not permanent, and hence of no long-term value. Making comparison with their status with the European feudal lords, Shaha writes:

> Unlike the European lord in medieval times, who had taken advantages of the breakdown of the central authority in asserting their independent authority based on the ownership of land, the feudal retainers of all categories in Nepal enjoyed their right to hold land at the pleasure and discretion of the ruler at the center. As a result, there were constant changes not only in the ownership of land but also in the composition of the nobility. This actually hindered the growth in Nepal of a powerful feudal class strong enough to challenge the absolute authority of the King, the sort of class that did develop in European countries, notably in England and Germany.[28]

The official position of the nobles and the *Birta* and *Jagir* land assignments could be revoked by the state through a uniquely indigenous Nepali practice in those days called *Pajani.* Under this system, the state would annually review and call into question the performance of every government official from the highest noble to the lowest ranked soldier. This review led to either the renewal of their services or to the termination if they did not measure up to the demands of jobs. The occasion was also used to relieve the services of the soldiers who were not required during the peace time or when the state could not afford to meet their costs. Such soldiers, called *Dhakres,* would be brought back on the payroll as and when required for the services of the nation. This system enabled the state to keep a reserve army without paying their regular salary, and by dangling the hope of recalling them when needed, also ensured their loyalty.

The *Pajani* practice which was designed to place the right man on the right job for effective administration and governance, by its very nature, implied that the authority be used with extreme fairness, justice, and impartiality. The *Pajani* system was also used to remove disloyal elements from official positions and land assignment. This system effectively insured that the nobility remained loyal and committed to the interest of the state and the Crown. The system was also subject to rampant abuse at the hands of incompetent and selfish rulers as often exhibited by false accusations, imprisonment, dispossession, and even execution of prominent members of the court. Such incidents have happened at various crucial moments in Nepal's history when the court was rife with factionalism, conspiracies and intrigues.

Particularly after the death of the strongman Prithvi Narayan, Nepal's court politics became faction-ridden under the reign of minors, regents, and weak rulers. Internal struggle for power, conspiracy and jealousy led to the imprisonment and death of even a person of the stature of Bahadur Shah under whose regency the Nepali state had emerged as a major power of the sub-continent. He became the victim of *Pajani* at the hands of his nephew King Rana Bahadur Shah. Bhimsen Thapa, another leader who provided unwavering leadership as *Mukhtiar* in the most demanding and turbulent period of Nepal's history met with a similar fate under extremely humiliating conditions during the reign of Rajendra Bikram Shah, the fifth King of the Shah dynasty.

Another impediment for the emergence of a strong feudal class was the traditional rivalry among the leading families, particularly the Thapas, Pandes and Basnets who competed and indulged in intrigues and plots against each other to gain the confidence of the court and assume power. By exploiting the *Pajani* system, the clan in power almost inevitably rescinded the privileges enjoyed by the other families including the dispossession of their titles. These three families remained in power for most of the period of Shah rule until the emergence of the Rana autocracy.

The rapid expansion of the Nepali state gave rise to the question: How effectively can the House of the Gorkha administrate a much larger kingdom extensive not just in its size but also in its diversity? Pragmatism dictated the Court not to disturb the existing local administrative structures and practices of the newly conquered territories. Local administrators were asked to give consideration to local conditions and adapt accordingly. As many of these new territories were very far from the central authority and communication was difficult, the *Sardars* and *Subbas* in charge of the administration were given wide-ranging discretionary authority so that the local conditions were fully taken into account while administering the central instructions. Even in the case of major law promulgated by the Centre for the whole kingdom, latitude was given to local customs, practices and conditions. Decentralization was the principal component of the Gorkhali government structure and allowed local authorities a high degree of flexibility to adapt to the local conditions. By tempering their rules to the needs of time and place, they enabled the local people to identify more easily with the new rulers, than would have been the case if the Government were conceived in terms of a more distant seat of authority.[29]

PRICE OF UNRESTRAINED MILITARISM

Initially the Nepali state had followed Prithvi Narayan's policy of isolationism and friendly relations with China and Britain. But in its drive for further territorial expansion, it invaded Sikkim in 1787, and in subsequent years made incursions into Tibet, a vassal state of China. The latter adventure proved costly for Nepal. From 1790 onwards, it began a major campaign of expansion westwards. The success was swift and absolute. The unrestrained military expansion towards the West effectively controlling all Himalayan trade routes successfully thwarted possibilities of British trade with Tibet. The British policy of conciliation towards Nepal did not pay off in opening up the Himalayan trade which had been their commercial interest for long. This had hardened the British attitude towards Nepal. The formidable military might created by the Gorkhali state and their growing ambition was of serious concern to the British. The prospect of this power making an alliance with the Marathas and Sikhs of the Indian states against the British was also looming in the horizon. Overtures for the same were being made by Bhimsen Thapa. All this brought Nepal into a collision course with the British. The East India Company was secretly probing and studying Nepal's military secrets and preparing for war. Every possible move was made to prevent the proposed alliance from being a reality.

Eventually, when the British laid claim to stretches of land in the *tarai* that Nepal had been occupying for a while—particularly in Rautahat and Butwal—the Nepal-British War of 1814-1816 started. Nepal achieved initial success in Nalapani, Jyathak and Jitpur in which the British suffered heavy casualties, but the subsequent reverses with the fall of Kumaon, Almora, Maloan and Jyathak weakened the Nepali position considerably and prompted the British to impose a treaty on their terms. The Treaty forced Nepal to cede all territory west of Mahakali and east of Mechi, and the *tarai* land. The Nepali government refused to accept the terms of the Treaty, particularly on the provision regarding the surrender of all the low lands of *tarai* from the Kali to Tista. The loss of *tarai* territory in the South would have been a major blow to Nepal which the Company had wanted to deliberately inflict to reduce the military potential of the Gorkhas. The British knew that most of the army officers depended on the land grant in the *tarai* for their maintenance.

The failure to ratify the Treaty negotiated by Pandit Gaja Raj Mishra on behalf of the Nepali government within the stipulated time led the British to start the second phase of the war by attacking Makwanpur.

Sensing the possible danger from the advancing British troops under the command of Ochterlony, the Nepalese side ratified the Treaty. As a concession to the Nepali side in the end, Nepal was permitted to retain the possession of the *tarai* land in the east. The British did not regret this concession because they knew that a friendly Nepal could be "a buffer between the arrogance of China and as yet an unsettled state of India", and that the Indian soldiers of the East India Company would not be able to hold their own against the Nepalese mountaineers.[30] The Sugauli Treaty reduced the size of the kingdom by about 40,000 square kilometres depriving the proud expansionary state of about one third of its territory mainly in the west and the south. This effectively halted the Gorkhali expansion by confining them to the hills east of the Mahakali river. The country paid dearly for unrestrained expansionary drive without consolidating power in the already acquired territories.

The end of hostilities led to increased trade with British India. Although the inward-oriented economic policy with emphasis on domestic self-reliance initiated by King Prithvi Narayan Shah had already been discontinued with the signing of a commercial treaty in 1792 with the East India Company, trade relations between the Company and Nepal hadn't quite taken off. The end of war now gave impetus to trade between the two countries. The addiction of imported luxury goods on the part of the upper classes of Nepalese society had already started for some time and created a natural demand for higher imports.

The treaty of 1816 brought an end to Nepal's expansion efforts and hostilities with the British ceased. The Government could have used this opportunity to reduce the size of the army and lower the financial burden on the people. Similarly, the peacetime was an opportune moment for the state to channel its efforts and energy towards the welfare of the people, economic development and progress. But this was not to be. The size of the army was kept intact. This was conditioned perhaps by Prime Minister Bhimsen Thapa's fear of creating any discontent among the army. But the cost of the army was too heavy for the poor Nepalese peasantry to bear at peacetime. A Nepalese historian has depicted the agony and sufferings of the village peasantry during the post-war period in the following words:

> He (Bhimsen Thapa) had only to see that the cost of the army was far too heavy for the people to bear. And this he must have seen. When the column of figures were being adjusted and a search was being made to find ways to meet the military payroll, it must have occurred to him or not, however, it is clear that the cry of village Nepal did not penetrate to the point where he realized that something must indeed be done to answer it.[31]

The writer further portrays the cost of war borne by the Nepalese peasantry both in the war front and afterwards in the following words:

> The Nepalese veteran returning from Makwanpur (the place where the last battle was fought with the East India Company which led to the treaty of Sugauli in 1816) to his native home and hearth had to estimate and pay the cost of war. In his case the cost of war was high. The trail that had led to Makwanpur had been long and expensive. Honest toil could pay some of this during the years of his lifetime. But the wounds to the economy lay deep, and long after generation that had fought the British at Makwanpur had left his life behind him, the people of Nepal would have to pay the price of their national unity.[32]

The poor peasantry had no choice but to silently bear the burden which was itself the consequence of a complex interplay of exploitative and inequitable fiscal, judicial and administrative practices of the medieval society. The high burden of *Kut*, the tenurial insecurity, the unpaid forced labour, the bondage system and the administrative and judicial abuses of the *Zamindars, Birtawals, Ijaradas* and the government officials made the life of a poor peasant difficult and miserable. Throughout the period after the war and until the rise of Jang Bahadur in 1846, the government was solely preoccupied with the maintenance of the status quo and the security of the territorial integrity of the nation against outside threats. The drive for expansion also precluded the possibility of an emotional national integration of the diverse regions with numerous cultural, ethnic, religious and language backgrounds. Shah writes:

> The Government's function mainly consisted in collecting fixed revenue and mobilizing additional resources to meet the growing expenditure of administration and military operations. Even the concept of the country as a single customs area was not immediately realized in practice, as transit duties were levied on river and highway traffic, persons and goods, as in the days before the conquest. Territorial expansion under the Shah dynasty of Nepal merely created skeleton form of the basic political framework for eventual national integration. Mere subjugation of different regions inhabited by polyglot ethnic groups, with diverse religious and cultural backgrounds, could not possibly have imbued the entire population all at once with a sense of communal harmony and belonging together. Territorial expansion under the Shah Kings, however, has given the country a single name and a strong central government.[33]

SUMMING UP

Under Prithvi Narayan and his immediate successors, the ruling nobility was single-mindedly preoccupied with expansionary pursuit through military conquests. In the intermittent peacetime, they were engaged in court politics, intrigues and perennial manuvres to wrest power for themselves. They devoted very little time and resources for the welfare of the people and showed little interest to undertake administrative reforms, socio-economic development and other nation building activities. The internecine battle between hostile contenders of political power, which was often soaked in blood and violence, characterized the political process. None of the *Mukhtiyars* or regents between 1769 and 1846 died a natural death; their lives ended abruptly either at the hands of their assassins or by their own hand.[34] The economic policies which had evolved around the national priority of militarism and territorial expansion continued even after the end of war in 1816. The poor peasantry who bore the ultimate cost of war during expansion, continued to carry the burden of maintaining a huge military and the administrative superstructure. In addition to meeting their obligation to the state, poor peasants were subject to other exploitative practices from the landowners.

Prithvi Narayan's policy of autarky and self reliance fostered partly by deep suspicion towards the British power was slowly loosening up. The pressures of internal politics, geopolitical considerations, the British mercantilist policy, and increasing addiction of the nobility to imported goods contributed to bringing about this change. What began with the Treaty of 1792 was shrewdly followed up by the British in 1801 when—capitalizing on the split between the King and his Court—they were able to force a treaty of trade and alliance, which among others, provided for the stationing of the British Residency in Kathmandu. This formalized the entry of British influence into the unstable Nepali politics; an influence that was to have a profound impact over the Nepali political economy in the next one and a half century.

NOTES

1. M.C. Regmi, *A Study in Nepali Economic History 1768-1846*, New Delhi: Manjusri Publishing House, 1971, pp. 19–20.
2. The narrative is based on the records left by Wang Hiuen-tse about the year 657 A.D, See Perceval Landon, *History of Nepal*, Delhi: Adarsa Enterprises, 2001, p. 257.
3. Narottam Prashad Baskota, *Indo-Nepal Trade and Economic Relations*, Delhi: B.R. Publishing Corporation, 1981, p. 90.
4. Rishikesh Shaha, *Modern Nepal* 1769–1955 Vol. 1, New Delhi: Manohar Publishers, 1996, pp. 29–32.

5. D.R. Regmi, *Modern Nepal*. Calcutta: Firma K.L. Mukhopadhyaya, 1961, pp. 143–44.
6. Ibid.
7. Perceval Landon, *History of Nepal*, Vol 1 pp. 66–67, 2001, Delhi: Adarsa Enterprises.
8. Bhuban Lall Joshi and Leo Rose, *Democratic Innovations in Nepal: A Case Study of Political Acculturation*, Berkeley: University of California Press, 1966, p. 15.
9. See Shaha (1996). Chapter 2.
10. A. P. Coleman, *A Special Corps: The Beginning of Gorkha Service with the British*, Durham: Pentland Press, 1999, pp. 10–11.
11. Ibid, p. 12.
12. Shaha (1996), Chapter 5.
13. See Prithvi Narayan Shah's *Dibyopadesh.*
14. For details *see* Ludwig F. Stiller, *The Rise of the House of Gorkha*. Human Resource Development Research Centre, 1995, p. 216.
15. Ibid, p. 216.
16. Stiller ibid. pp. 242–243, Quoted from Kirkpatrick's *Account of Nepal*. The prevailing salary of a soldier was estimated at Rs. 76 a year. Calculating the salaries of the commissioned and non-commissioned officers, and the cost of equipment, arms and ammunitions required for the troops, he estimated that every thousand soldiers would represent a drain of four–five lakh rupees a year.
17. Regmi (1971), p. 37.
18. Ibid, p. 55.
19. Stiller, op. cit., p. 239.
20. Ibid, p. 154.
21. *See* Stiller op. cit. pp. 244–46.
22. David Seddon, *Nepal: A State of Poverty,* New Delhi: Vikas Publishing House, 1987, p. 14.
23. *See* Regmi (1971): Chapter VII.
24. Ibid, pp. 144–46.
25. Details in ibid, Chapter VI.
26. Ibid, p. 123.
27. Seddon (1987), p. 5.
28. Shaha, (1996), pp. 207–208.
29. Stiller, op. cit. pp. 217–25.
30. Landon (2001) op. cit., p. 84.
31. Ludwig Stiller, *The Silent Cry*, Kathmandu: Sahayogi Prakashan, 1976, p. 312.
32. Ibid 57.
33. Shaha (1996). pp. 208–209.
34. Joshi and Rose, p. 25.

Chapter Two

The Rana Shogunate

The reign of Rajendra Bikram Shah was marked by political instability, court intrigues and conspiracies. The strongman Bhimsen Thapa, who had provided uninterrupted leadership for almost thirty years, was removed from the scene in an extremely humiliating and cruel manner. Rajendra Bikram himself was a weak, wavering and suspicious king torn between the influences of his two queens with their politically exclusive agenda. The senior Queen Samrajyalaxmi, with her pro British policy, was frantically trying to coerce the king into placing her son Surendra, the Crown Prince, to the throne. The junior Queen, Laxmi Devi was more hawkish towards the British and nursed the ambition to replace Surendra by her own son Ranendra as the crown prince. Amidst the fluid court politics of the period following Samrajyalaxmi's death, the king used his *Hukum* (ultimate order) to delegate power to Laxmi Devi in January 1843.

A massive Court Massacre known as the *Kot Parba* in 1846 is a major landmark in Nepal's history as it ushered an era of Rana oligarchy which would last for more than a century. This gruesome spectacle of human carnage was precipitated by the mysterious murder of Laxmi Devi's paramour, Gagan Singh. The queen, in a rage to find the culprit, summoned all high-ranking civil and military officers to an emergency State Council in the *Kot* (courtyard). The assembly immediately broke into a sword battle after a vigorous exchange of allegations and counter-allegations. Several prominent generals, nobles, and army officers, including Prime Minister Fatte Jang Shah were killed in the melee. The few survivors included Jang Bahadur, a military strongman, six of his brothers and their men who had come fully prepared for any eventuality. The exact loss of lives in this butchery is unknown. The names of fifty-five high officials and notables have been recorded as killed, but the actual number is believed to be many times more.

This event catapulted Jang Bahadur Rana to Nepal's political centre stage. Through his military prowess and shrewd manipulation of turbulent politics of the time, Jang Bahadur was not only able to wrest absolute power by making himself the Prime Minister and the Commander-in-Chief, but also start an era of hereditary prime ministers for more than a century. This effectively reduced the kings to the status of figureheads. He confiscated the property of all high officials and nobles who were killed or had fled. He banished their family members from the country and decreed that their return would be regarded as capital offence. Through the use of the *Pajani* system, he removed from the offices of responsibility all those whom he did not trust, and rewarded others who helped him in the Massacre. The most prominent beneficiaries were naturally his brothers and family members. The Queen was reduced to the status of a nominal regent. Soon afterwards, the Queen became the victim of her own ambition and conspiracy—she was stripped of her title and eventually banished. Summing up the total consolidation of power by the new ruler after the Massacre, a British Residency staff in Nepal at that time wrote:

> From the time Jang Bahadur has been the undisputed ruler of the country. The Old king is the prisoner in the palace. The present King is kept under the strictest surveillance and not allowed to exercise any power whatever. The heir apparent is also kept in a state of obscurity, being never permitted to take part in any public business or even to appear in the Darbars, to which the British resident is invited. In fact, one may live for years in Nepal without either seeing or hearing of the king.[1]

INCREASED TIES WITH THE BRITISH

After the swift consolidation of his position at home, Jang Bahadur turned his attention towards improving relations with British India. Convinced of the wisdom of friendship with the British, in May 1848, he offered to the Government of India six regiments of Nepali troops under his personal command, should the war between the British and the Sikhs break out again. The British politely declined the offer but with the proviso that, should the need arise, they would ask for his help. In 1850, he paid a historic visit to Great Britain and France.

> Friendship with Britain, or rather with the British power in India, henceforth became the cornerstone of Nepal's foreign policy, while Nepal at the same time persisted in continuing its traditional policy of isolation and exclusion of foreigners and of maintaining minimal contact with them at the official level only. Jang Bahadur's visit to Europe set a pattern for this

> policy, which was rigidly and conscientiously followed by Jang Bahadur, and his successors for a century with real success in achieving the desired objective. This objective of course had been the maintenance of the independence and territorial integrity of Nepal in the face of the fierce wind that was blowing strongly across the entire region and had brought nearly the entire Indian subcontinent under foreign domination.[2]

Jang Bahadur went into war with Tibet in 1854 and 1855 for some territorial and commercial reasons. The war ended with the signing of a treaty in March 1856. This treaty regulated the commercial relations between the two countries for almost a century and provided for: a trade fair every spring in Kuti and Kerung where Tibetans could come and exchange tea and salt for the Nepalese merchandise, a Nepali agent in Lhasa and an annual tribute of ten thousand rupees by Tibetan government to Nepal. The treaty also stipulated that sons born out of the marriages between Nepalis and Tibetans would be entitled to Nepali citizenship while the daughters would become Tibetans.

Jang Bahadur offered Nepali troops to the Governor General of India to help quell the Sipoy Mutiny in 1857. After the fall of Lucknow at the hands of the rebels, Jang himself left Kathmandu commanding 9,000 troops. A total sum of Rs.230,615 was involved in the deployment and training of the Nepali troops and an additional Rs.450,000 as gratuities *in lieu* of pension and compensation was paid as cash gifts to the troops involved in the operation. In recognition to these services, in 1860, the British restored parts of the *tarai*—extending from Karnali in the west to the British territory of Gorakhpur in the east—which were surrendered in 1816.[3] In his drive to deepen ties with the British, Jang Bahadur invited the Prince of Wales and King Edward VII during the latter's visit to India in 1876 for a hunting expedition in the *tarai.* As many as 300 elephants were marshalled for the occasion. Jang Bahadur's descendants invited King George for similar expeditions in 1911.

British Commercial Interest

Notwithstanding Jang Bahadur's own policy of limiting commercial relations with British India and reviving trans-Himalayan trade, political circumstances presented the British an opportunity to broach their long-standing trade proposal with Nepal. The prospect of using Nepal as a transit route for Indo-Tibetan trade and to consolidate trade relations with Central Asia had always been high on the British agenda. From the time of Warren Hastings, the British had already spent considerable time and energy in the pursuit of the trans-Himalayan trade as evidenced by the Turner, Bogle, Kirkpatrick and Knox missions.[4]

British Resident Brian Hodgson (1833–1843)[5]strongly took up the question of trans-Himalayan trade with the Governor General in the 1830s. Referring to the conclusions of the last mission, he highlighted the advantages Nepal possessed over Sikkim and western hills from the point of view of demand and supply. The natural produce of this region including that of Nepal was held in high esteem in Europe. Goods demanded by Europe, at that time, were sourced from various Indian cities like Calcutta, Dacca, Mirzapur, Gazipur and Benaras. Hence, they saw an extensive and flourishing trade prospect in this region.[6] Nepal's advantages were also based on the fact that Nepal possessed easier routes, and extensive commercial networks that the Newar traders in Nepal had established with both Tibetan and Indian traders. According to Hodgson, there was a deeper political motive beneath the commercial veneer of the British trade proposal. The British wanted to bind Nepalis to the Company by changing their material lives and increasing their dependence on imported Indian goods. Furthermore, Hodgson's aim was to "convert Nepal from an interposing obstacle into the common mart where the merchants from Hindostan might interchange their commodities with the traders from inner Asia".[7]

> ...it was thought by the British that the opening of Tibet, Bhutan, Sikkim, and Nepal would provide scope not only for an increased flow of trade but also for investment of British capital in tea gardens, orchards, woolen mills, saw mills, and similar industries. But Nepal's traditional apprehension about motives of foreign traders proved to be an insurmountable obstacle to the growth of free trade from British India. Jang Bahadur's extreme opposition to commercial intercourse with the British Government was also motivated by his desire to monopolize lucrative trade with India[8].

More than the Tibetan trade itself, the allure of Chinese and Central Asian markets was what excited the British. There were two routes for Chinese trade at that time: the Peking–St. Petersburg route on the extreme north and the Peking-India route *via* Kathmandu. Despite the long transit route, high customs duty charged by the Russians (20–25 per cent) and a lot of other obstacles, Chinese trade with Russia via St. Petersburg was flourishing. Compared to this, China's trade across the Himalayas offered many advantages including shorter distance, easier routes, better climatic conditions and low customs of 8 per cent imposed by Nepal.[9] In order to provide further incentives to the Chinese and to make a leap forward in Central Asian trade, the East India Company even made a major proposal to extend the Darjeeling Himalayan railway by 82 miles up to Arun Valley of eastern Nepal in 1889.[10] But in keeping with the policy of caution and suspicion in relation to the British overtures, Nepal politely turned down the proposal.

It is significant that although Jang Bahadur wanted to have amicable relations with the British, it was only from a distance since he was always suspicious of their territorial motives. He even refused to improve the road leading to Kathmandu because he did not want to facilitate the entry of the East India Company's troops into his country with ease and confidence.[11]

Despite the refusal from the Nepali side to enter into any formal trade agreement with the Company, through time, Nepal's trade started to increase with India. The most important export products from Nepal were rice and timber which accounted for two-thirds of the total exports to India in the latter part of the 19th century. The huge tracts of *tarai* adjoining the Indian territory was not only where most trade trafficking activities were transacted but also contained some of the most valuable forests in Nepal. The three major river systems of Nepal, together with many other smaller ones were used in transporting timber, grain and spices. During the 1870s, the East India Company extended the Indian railway system to convenient points of the Nepali border to facilitate trade with Nepal. Extensions of railway lines up to Farbeshgunj in Purnia district, Pertappur in Bhagalpur district and up to Sitamadi from Mujaffarpur were completed by 1890 and facilitated trade with eastern Nepal. Connections with Raxual and Tulsipur were completed respectively in 1897 and 1905 to capture the timber and grain trade in the central and western Nepal. The expansion of railway construction in India was accompanied by hugely increased revenue to Nepali state from timber sales.

These new railway lines significantly altered the traditional trade passages and accelerated trade growth. Consequently, the total volume of trade with India rose to Rs.33 million in 1891 from a level of Rs. 3 million in 1831.[12] This figure almost doubled by 1911–12. The expanding trade with India was accompanied by a strong trade surplus in favour of Nepal—the value of exports was double that of imports towards the end of 19th century. This surplus was produced at a time when the Nepali migration to India had increased and reached a level of one million in 1900 and an additional 30,000 by 1911. An indication of the potential opportunity provided by favourable trade position is that, by using the balance of trade surplus to purchase textile mill machinery during these years, the Nepalis could have employed all those who moved to India during the period 1900–11[13].

Nepal's increasing trade with India was, however, accompanied by declining volume of trade with Tibet. Trade with India had now become more important than with Tibet.This was, indeed, a complete reversal of the traditional trade pattern. The already declining trans-Himalayan trade ultimately came to an end with the opening of the Gangtok route to Tibet in 1902 as the entrepot role of trans-Himalayan trade shifted from Kathmandu to Gangtok. Consequently, a large number of Newari commercial families shifted their operations to Kalimpong where they were able to enjoy special custom exemption privileges.[14]

Gorkha Recruitment and War Assistance

Another significant development in 1885 deepened Nepal's economic ties with the British India. The Rana Prime Minister Bir Shamsher formally met the long-standing British interest in recruiting Nepali manpower for their fighting force. British India was granted permission for unrestricted recruitment of Nepali youth in the Gorkha regiment being raised in the Indian army. The British had an eye on the martial tribes of Nepal whose gallantry and fame they held in high esteem. Impressed by the military prowess of the Gorkha highlanders in 1814–16 war, the idea of inducting the Nepali troops in the Indian army was first suggested by General Ochterlony.[15] In fact, at the conclusion of the first phase of the war in 1815, General Ochterlony recruited 4,700 men of Nepali army in the west who had surrendered after the war. This was in accordance with the Clause 5 of the Convention signed between Ochterlony and Kaji Amar Singh Thapa on 15 May 1915. Of the 4,700 soldiers who were enlisted in the Bengal army of British service, two-thirds were the Kumaonis and Garhwalis, and the rest were Gorkhalis.[16] The suggestion for formal enlistment of the Nepali youth in the British service was followed up also by Sir Edward Paget, the Commander-in-Chief in India,in 1825. The British Resident, Gardner (1816–1829) had favoured an arrangement with the Nepal government for the service of a portion of their troops.[17]

Brian Hodgson, who succeeded Gardner as Resident, had made a deep study on the Kingdom of Nepal, its population, military tribes, roads and wildlife. In a paper entitled Origin and Classification of Military Tribes in Nepal presented at the Asiatic Society of Calcutta on 9 January 1833, he had identified the *Khas, Magars* and *Gurungs* as the military classes of Nepal and spoken highly of their character, love of enterprise, freedom from caste prejudices, military habits and amenability to discipline. He also proposed to absorb them in the Indian army. He had estimated the total number of *Dhakres* (relieved soldiers) at about 30,000 and pointed out that their services could be obtained by the British without any insuperable obstacle.[18]

The Rana rulers seem to have anticipated the inevitability of the outbreak of war in Europe after the assassination of the heir of the Austrian throne. The view was expressed by Prime Minister Chandra Shamsher more than once during the month of July 1914 to the British Resident. On the 3rd of August, before the news of war reached Kathmandu, Chandra Shamsher had written a letter to the Resident expressing his fear, and offered—through him to the Viceroy, and through the Viceroy to the King Emperor—the services of the military resources of Nepal "however little that may be" as a symbol of "devotion and friendship" to His Majesty's person and Empire. The British Government immediately accepted the offer with great appreciation and gratitude. Initially, a request was made for a loan of six thousand troops for general service within the borders of India. The assistance of troops was accompanied by gratuitous offer to the Government of India, the whole stock of Lee Enfield rifles, which the state possessed at that time. In June 1915, a gift of thirty-one machine guns was sent. These men replaced a large number of British and other troops who were deployed in various theaters of war. With further reinforcements and additions, a total of 16,544 of Nepal's finest soldiers were freely loaned to the British at the most critical moment in history.[19] By taking the risk of depriving the country of its entire fighting force to support the British in the war, the Rana rulers had shown a gesture of supreme sacrifice. A British writer described the qualities of the Nepali troops as follows:

> They are very good shots, expert with the bayonet, most excellent hill fighters, and in fact, regular first-line troops. They are extraordinarily well behaved and disciplined—crime being conspicuous by its absence—very pleasant to deal with, and like all Gurkhas, the greater the hardships to be suffered the more cheerful they become.[20]

In addition to the 16,544 soldiers sent from Nepal in 1914, 26,000 Gurkha soldiers already existed as part of the regular Indian army. There were also a large number of Nepalis in non-combat contingents. It is estimated that those who left the country for various military purposes numbered more than 200,000. Nepal's countryside was stripped of the youth population. Only women, old, boys and crippled remained at home. Chandra Shamsher quartered the whole country and put in place intensive drafting and training programmes. The Rana rulers also recalled and mobilized men of Gorkha regiments in the Indian army holidaying at home in Nepal. Nepal lost more men in the war in proportion to country's population—which was about five million at that time—than any other nation that participated in the First Great War. The massive exodus of working age men depleted the labour force and adversely affected the hill economy. But the Ranas were not perturbed.

Alongside personnel support, Nepal also contributed in cash and other in-kind donations. In September 1914, Nepal offered the British a sum of Rs. 300,000 out of which, Rs. 250,000 came from the Prime Minister's private purse. Further contribution of Rs. 300,000 was made on the first of January in 1916 and 1917 through the Viceroy for any purpose connected with the war. In the following year, yet another Rs. 200,000 was presented in honour of the silver jubilee of the King and the Queen's marriage. Yet, cash represented only a small part of the gesture. Over 500,000 mounds of cardamom, 84,700 mounds of tea, a large quantity of army blankets, and 200,000 broad-gauge sleepers contributed to the Indian railway system free of royalty were part of this generosity. Furthermore, Nepal also loaned 125 lakhs of British and Nepali silver coins at a moment when the war scare had "driven most Indian homes to bury specie beneath their hearthstones".[21]

> British rule in India had never received before so deep a compliment as that which is implied by the willing and unprejudiced help given to it from outside its own dominions by a friendly people, who not only had every right to retain their soldiers and their funds for their own possible need, but deliberately and without hesitation threw themselves on the side of the English at a time when half Asia was secretly convinced that victory was a foregone conclusion for Germany.[22]

The British reciprocated Nepal's contribution in the War by an annual and unconditional gift of one million rupees in perpetuity. Nepal's wish for additional territory was, however, not granted. Not just during the Great War, Nepal sent a contingent of two thousand troops to Waziristan to the aid of the British when war broke out between British India and Afghanistan in May 1919. A new Anglo-Nepal Treaty was signed in 1923, which recognized "each other's independence, both internal and external". The treaty also made provisions enabling Nepal to import goods from overseas for its own direct use through India without any payment of duty. Perversely, the treaty made it easy for the Rana family to import duty-free goods from overseas in the name of the government and sell them in the market at a profit. Chandra Shamsher, in fact, got one of his favoured traders to set up a shop called Bhadrakali House to sell imported goods and merchandise.[23]

During the war and afterwards, Nepal's hill economy suffered acute shortage of manpower even for normal agricultural activities. Most Nepalis who participated in various duties in the war did not return home even after their decommissioning; they settled down in India because of brighter employment prospects and better living conditions.

Their interaction with the outside world made them increasingly aware of the injustices at home and sowed the seeds of discontent against the regime in Nepal. Prudently, Chandra Shamsher put a ban on the recruitment of youth from Kathmandu valley and neighbouring districts for the British army.

With the Rana regime at helm, Nepal extended similar gestures of assistance to the British Government during the Second Great War as well. Prime Minister Juddha Shamsher, who had made a tentative offer of assistance even before the outbreak of the war, reiterated his commitment to support after the war started. A contingent of 8,000 troops was dispatched for garrison duties in India. As the war progressed, a Nepali contingent was mobilized for active duties as well. The peacetime strength of twenty battalions in India was doubled. The total number of recruitments from Nepal in the course of the war was estimated at about 160,000. Nepal also agreed to permit the use of Gurkha Indian army for overseas duties. Consequently, the Gurkhas were fighting shoulder to shoulder with their British counterparts on various battlefronts throughout the world, showing exemplary valour, dedication and skills. The war-time British Prime Minister Winston Churchill paid handsome tribute to the Maharaja and the Gorkha troops for their heroic contribution in bringing about the downfall of the Axis Power. After the war, the Nepali contingents were allowed to bring back modern standard equipment worth Rs. 330,000. The British, in recognition to the services rendered by Nepal, increased their annual gift to Nepal from one million to two million rupees, and in keeping with Nepal's wish they agreed to capitalize fifty per cent of the increased annual gift to assisting development programmes of the country. The actual amount was subsequently fixed at 2.5 million rupees.

FAMILY ENRICHMENT AND METHODS

The Rana period represents a distinct phase in the Nepali history; it was a period marked by unprecedented personal enrichment of the ruling family. All successive Rana Prime Ministers pursued the process of vigorous self-aggrandizement because due to complex succession rules—which generally went from brother to brother as opposed to by primogeniture—they normally did not benefit form the previous accumulations. The enrichment process was enacted in several ways.

Land Grant System

First, they lavishly exploited the traditional land grant system for their selfish interest. In contrast to the past pattern of favouring the nobility through land grants, the Ranas used this system largely to enrich themselves. Jang Bahadur seized the opportunity of his accession to power for confiscating the *Birta* land from most of those who were killed in the course of the infamous *Kot Parba.* This set a precedent for the confiscation of properties of fallen rulers by the victors and was practised quite frequently during this period in Nepal's history. It happened, for example, when Bir Shamsher assumed power by assassinating Prime Minister Ranoddip Singh. The accumulation of the rent-free *Birta* land in the hands of the ruling family continued until the end of the Rana rule. The *Birta* land grants were made in the name of the crown. But the royal seal was used at the discretion of the Rana rulers. Regmi estimates that by 1950, three leading Rana families owned a total of 227,105 acres representing 42.5 per cent of the total cultivated *Birta* land in the *tarai,* including the entire district of Bardia in the western *tarai.*[24]

It was the tenants who ultimately cultivated the *Birta* land, but there were no laws to protect their interest with regard to the size of rent and the security of their tenancy. Attempts were made in 1906 for the first time to control rents and ensure tenancy rights on *Birta* land. The rent on *Birta* land was fixed up to the level of taxation prevailing on adjoining holdings of *Raikar* land. Eviction of tenancy was permitted only if the tenants vacated the land voluntarily or defaulted on the payment of rents. But these measures suffered at the implementation level in the absence of effective implementation mechanism at the villages. The problem was further complicated by the sub-infeudation process in the ownership and the use of land. Legislation regulated the relations between the Birta owner and his tenants. The actual cultivators were, however, at the mercy of the intermediaries who were in the nature of contractors, often the highest bidders. This inevitably enhanced the burden on the cultivators, particularly in a situation where rents were unregulated by law. [25]

The importance of the *Jagir* land diminished significantly during the Rana period. In his desire for centralizing the administrative authority of the country, Jang Bahadur started a process of reducing the ambit of the *Jagir* system. This task was facilitated by the killings and banishment of many high-ranking members of the nobility who owned extensive plots of *Jagir* land which were subsequently confiscated following the *Kot Parba*. The diminution of the *Jagir* land helped raise the state revenue. This was much to the delight of the rulers, as the entire revenue surplus ultimately ended up in the private coffers of the rulers. The dismantling process of the *Jagir* land got further impetus during the time of Prime Minister Chandra Shamsher who reorganized the land revenue collection system in the hilly regions and in Kathmandu valley by setting up *Mal Addas*. These *Addas* were manned by cash salaried employees in place of *Jagirdars* as revenue collection agents. In 1910, he also replaced the *Jagir* assignments of certain categories of government employees by monthly cash salaries.[26] However, the award of extensive plots of land as *Jagir* and *Birta* to selected members of the Rana family and their cronies continued.

Jhara/Rakam and Lavish Palaces

The Rana period also witnessed a major transformation in the use of *Jhara* and *Rakam* labour. The cessation of expansion efforts and the modernization of the Nepali army had dramatically reduced the need for unpaid labour for the services of the nation. But this did not result in the dispensation of this practice. The compulsory forced labour was now increasingly utilized for the personal requirements of the ruling elite, particularly in the construction of palaces. In some cases, *Rakams* were converted into cash payments to increase the state revenue. In other cases, *Rakam* labour was used for porterage services in tours and hunting expeditions of the rulers, transporting timber and other building materials for the construction of palaces, and a host of other services of personal nature. The working conditions of such labour were generally hard and oppressive—particularly when they had to carry heavy loads or walk long distances without receiving any food or wages. Sometimes they had to discharge multiple obligations for more than one government department and for personal purposes. Regmi, for example, highlights the plight of the inhabitants of Nakhu in Lalitpur who "were required to supply not only a monthly load of fuel wood to a particular military official, but also charcoal at the bungalow belonging to the British Residency at Kakani".[27]

One conspicuous aspect of the Rana period was the construction of the most lavish palaces. Built with European imitations along the lines of neo-classical and Greco-Roman architecture, most of these palaces served as personal residences of the Rana families. Some famous ones built by Bir Shamsher were the *Seto Durbar* and the *Lal Durbar*. The *Seto Durbar* was modelled on the Belvedere Palace of Calcutta. The main hall of *Seto Durbar*, called *Thulo Baithak* was famous for its crystal from ceilings down to the bars of the balcony railings. It displayed chandeliers, life-size mirrors, and Bohemian glassware imported from London, Rome and Venice along with valuable paintings. The baroque ceiling rested on eight crystal pillars, 22 feet tall and 12 feet in circumference. Its floor was paved with Italian marble slabs and was covered from wall to wall with beautiful and costly Persian and Belgian rugs.

The most prominent and the largest among all palaces built during these times was the *Singh Durbar.* Fashioned after the chateau of Versailles and used as the residential building for the Rana Prime Ministers, it was built by Chandra Shamsher. As almost the entire palace was gutted by fire in 1973, only the front portion of this palace remains in its original form at present. The palace was a vast structure with seven interconnected courtyards carrying four-storeyed buildings, boasting over a thousand rooms. Set in 50 hectares of manicured lawns and elegant gardens, its splendid compound contained numerous gardens, a deer park, a polo ground, tennis-courts, neo-Grecian statutory, streams, fountains and vast verdure with finely spaced trees. It had its own theatre and gallery which now serves as the parliamentary building. The palace had a magnificent façade of entrance with three well-proportioned archways, between which rose double Corinthian columns.[28]

This mammoth structure, considered the largest in South Asia, was constructed at the cost of only Rs. 360 thousand, largely due to the free and cheap labour available under the *Jhara* and *Rakam* practices. Forty-one such palatial mansions—large, white and each designed along similar Victorian and Greco-Roman models—that dotted various parts of the 200 square kilometres of Kathmandu valley and towered over poor and small hamlets in which the ordinary people of Kathmandu lived were built largely with *Jhara* and *Rakam* labour.

> In those days, as even now to an extent, Kathmandu presented a striking picture of contrast between extreme poverty and vast wealth. On the one side there stood clustered together red and yellow mud hovels in the congested section of the city, which with its dirty, narrow and winding lanes was largely reminiscent of the ghettos of some of the European cities of the medieval times. In contrast to this were the vast and glittering palaces of the Ranas in the Greco-Roman style, with balustrades pillared columns, standing amidst spacious grounds enclosed by high compound walls. Public buildings such as courts, hospitals and colleges suffered in comparison with the private residences of the Ranas and their favourites. The pattern of contrast was fairly widespread and, generally speaking, was true of the country as a whole, though its effects in Kathmandu might have been heightened.[29]

Revenue Surplus in Personal Coffers

Large and increasing revenue surplus created by maximizing the state revenue and minimizing public expenditure presented what was perhaps the most lucrative source of enrichment. Nepal's total government revenue around the year 1837 was about four to five million rupees. The sale of timber and customs duty were the main sources of revenue. All revenue surpluses after meeting the government expenditure were appropriated by Prime Minister. In their drive for revenue maximization, no potential revenue source was left untouched. State monopoly was established over the trade of oil, tobacco, sugar grain of all kinds, cotton, salt, clarified butter (ghee), and other necessities of daily life. All of Jang Bahadur's brothers, close relatives and senior civil and military officials, were engaged in this monopolistic trade. Favoured merchants were awarded monopoly rights in return for huge share of profits to the Prime Minister. Marts that were set up on the Indo–Nepal border were given to his close kin and confidants. Jang Bahadur also brought about changes in the land revenue collection system in the *tarai* by assigning selected *Jimdars* at the village level along side the *Chaudharies* at the divisional level. They were encouraged to reclaim virgin lands for cultivation by using unpaid forced labour. This policy led to an increase in the reclamation of land and the state revenue.[30]

The desire to maximize revenue led Prime Minister Chandra Shamsher to introduce the *Bazar Adda* system (auctioning the customs to the highest bidder) in collecting customs and contract system in timber export—the two principal sources of the state revenue. The treaty of 1923 concluded with the British, which paved the way for unrestricted entry of British goods, was also motivated by the desire for increasing state revenue.

The remittances brought back by the Nepalis serving in the British army were increasing. Even by conservative estimates, the remittances from the 200,000 soldiers who participated in the First Great War and from those who remained abroad for seven years, were around Rs. 250 million.[31] The massive injection of purchasing power in the form of these private transfers created disruption in the simple rural life which was largely based on the principle of self-sufficiency. Indigenously produced household goods, agricultural tools and implements, utensils and other consumer goods were displaced by cheaper machine-made substitutes. The imitation of foreign life style and consumption practices destroyed the fabric of traditional life. Inflation made life miserable and led many to dispose of their property. The rulers once again missed not only the opportunity to utilize the war income for the country's economic development, but in their unbridled pursuit of raising state revenue for purely selfish interest, destroyed domestic crafts, skills and industries. For British India, which had been suffering from limited domestic demand for low quality commodities produced by factory methods since 1900, the presence of a captive Nepali market capable of absorbing over 1 per cent of total Indian manufactured exports and over 5 per cent in such products as cotton textiles, and pharmaceutical products was far from insignificant.[32]

The unprecedented rise in the state revenue was, however, accompanied by minimal state expenditure. Public expenditure was confined to national defence, internal security, and the dispensation of justice with minimum administration. Some of the earliest development activities undertaken in the 1920s during the time of Chandra Shamsher—such as the 500 kw power plant in Pharping, the construction of 14-mile Matatirtha–Dhursing Ropeway, the Bhimphedi–Amalekganj Road and the 19-mile Amaekhgunj–Raxaul Railway—were financed by utilizing the cash grant awarded by the British in return for the military assistance rendered in the First Great War. The entire revenue surplus, which occurred after meeting this minimal expenditure, was appropriated by the ruling family. This, coupled with the continuous flow of income from the vast size of *Birta* land brought about a phenomenal rise in the fortunes of the Rana family. An indication of the fortune amassed by the Ranas is given by the fact that Prime Minister Chandra Shamsher alone appropriated roughly 300 million during his thirty years of rule; an amount equivalent to one-third of the total state revenue during the period.[33] The Rana rulers used the massive fortune to lead an opulent life with imported luxuries, building large bungalows and palaces, creating and sustaining a large body of servants and retainers, making investment in stocks and bank deposits and buying properties in other metropolitan centres.

REFORMS AND DEVELOPMENT

During Jang Bahadur's rule some administrative institutions were created to run the government. *Moth Tahabil* was created for administering all revenue, and *Kathmahal* for forest administration. *Saraf Khana* was started for the exchange of Nepali rupees with East India Company rupees. *Kitab Khana* was established as the registrar office of all civil and military employees. *Mulki Khana* was set up as the government treasury. *Toshakhana* continued as disbursement office. *Munsikhana* had already been initiated as the foreign office by Bhimshen Thapa, and Prithvi Narayan had established the *Kumari Chowk* as audit and accounts office.

Upon his return from Europe, Jang introduced some reforms in the country's administration and the penal system. Impressed by the rule of law system in Europe, he introduced legal code called the *Mulki Ain* in 1854. The *Ain Khana* and *Kausal* were established to codify the existing laws and draft new ones. He also outlawed capital punishment except in selected cases. For carrying out general administration, he established a *Mulki Adda* as the central secretariat. *Jangi Adda* was established to administer the army on modern lines based on a detailed manual.

Jang Bahadur also introduced some reforms in land administration and settlement. His policy of granting tax exemption on reclaimed land for ten years resulted in reclamation of large areas of *tarai* land. Under Chandra Shamsher, the practices of *Sati* (self immolation by the widow upon husband's death) and slavery were abolished. Tri Chandra College was established in 1918, and until 1951, remained the sole educational centre for under-graduate studies in Nepal. *Gorkha Bhasa Prakasini Samiti* was set up in 1913 for publishing books in Nepali. During Juddha Shamsher's time, the judicial function at the district level was separated from the executive by dispossessing the *Badahakims* (district commissioners) of their judicial power. Appeals courts were set up at four centres in the *tarai* (*Goswara*), four in the hills (*Gaunda*), and two in Kathmandu valley (Appeal). Some hospitals, including the Bir Hospital of Kathmandu, a tuberculosis centre, Nepal's first newspaper, a few public and private schools were also established. Bir Shamsher also initiated a piped drinking water project for Kathmandu and Bhaktapur.

As discussed above, a few development projects were completed in the 1920s under Chandra Shamsher by using the annual cash gift from the British government. A more serious desire for economic development started to dawn during the reign of Prime Minister Juddha Shamsher (1932–45). He was motivated by a desire to present a progressive and developmental image at a time when the internal resentment against the repressive rule was increasing. The *Udyog Parishad* (Industrial Development Board) was established in 1935. In the following year, a Company Act was promulgated and a number of industries were started with state encouragement. These industries included the Biratnagar Jute Mill, Plywood and Bobbin Factory, Mining Exploration Co., Juddha Match Factory (Birgunj) as well as a few soap, oil and furniture industries. The Nepal Bank Ltd. was set up in 1936 as the first commercial bank. These industries prospered under the stimulus of the scarce conditions of the Second Great War. In 1934, a Bombay-based National Mining Syndicate and Trading Company was given license to work on the cobalt mines in Palpa, Sindhupalchowk, Kavre

Palanchowk and other eastern districts. German experts were brought in to conduct geomagnetic survey of the country. Pension system was introduced for the civil and military employees of the Government. For the first time in Nepal's history, currency notes were brought into circulation.

Telecommunication systems were extended to Dhankuta in the east and Bhairahawa in the west. Automatic telephone system was introduced in Kathmandu valley largely for the benefit of the Rana family members. Cottage industry centres were established in Kathmandu, Baglung, Palpa, Banepa and Bhojpur. Attempts were made to promote domestic production of cotton and salt. Four students were sent to Japan for technical education for the first time in 1938. Machinery was imported to manufacture ammunition. An additional hydropower plant was set up in Sundarijal to generate 750 kw of power. An agriculture research farm was set up in Parwanipur. Some other offices set up with developmental objectives during that period included the Forest Department, the Agriculture Board, and the Bureau of Mines. Foreign advisers were invited to assist in the development of forestry and mining sectors. Juddha Shamser also expressed his desire to get British assistance for Nepal's economic development in 1941.[34] Irrigation canals were developed in Bilhul of Saptari, Manusmara in Rautahat, Sirsiya in Birgunj, and Sifale Bas in Syanja. New irrigation schemes were constructed in Pharping, Lele, and twelve other villages in Kathmandu valley. Improved seeds were brought and distributed to farmers in the Valley.[35]

In the early 1940s, a blueprint of Nepal's 15-year development plan with an outlay of Rs.100 crore was prepared with the blessings of the Prime Minister. As part of the preparatory exercise for this plan, an industrial survey was undertaken to determine the country's potential for industrial development. A sample survey conducted in East No. 1 in this connection brought to light the highly exploitative rural money lending practices. As a follow-up to the recommendations of this survey, a land mortgage bank and a cooperative society were set up in Banepa on a pilot basis. The former was aimed at rural lending at favorable interest to retrieve the land mortgaged to the usurious moneylenders. The latter was to supply agricultural inputs and industrial raw materials and buy back the industrial products produced in the village.[36]

During the premiership of Padma Shamsher, some liberal and innovative ideas were introduced to meet the emerging threat to the Rana rule. Padma had led the first contingent of the Nepali troops to India in support of the British in the Second Great War and was fully aware of the strong force of liberal ideas blowing across Asia. Upon his installation to the high office in 1945, he declared himself to be the "servant of the nation". This was quite unlike the pattern set by his proud predecessors. Immediately, he also announced the policy statement of his Government emphasizing the development of primary education, hydroelectricity, ropeway, railway and road systems, and promising an increment to civil and military salaries. He also announced his decision to bring about constitutional reforms, hold elections for municipalities and district boards, introduce annual budgets, promote female education, and appoint consuls at places in India and Burma to protect the interests of the Nepalis there. He dispatched some of the younger Ranas to study the educational and industrial systems in India and involved them in the policy making of his administration. Concurrently, he was also trying to make contacts with the leaders of the Indian National Congress and the Nepali Congress. Padma's bold and reformist initiatives fetched him favourable opinion from both inside and outside the country. During this time, a US mission visited Nepal and a Treaty of Friendship and Commerce was signed. Municipal election was held in June 1947. Indian constitutional experts led by Sri Prakash Gupta were brought in, and a draft constitution was prepared. But the pressures from the powerful conservative elements in the family did not allow the draft to reach its final phase in the original form.

The Constitution eventually announced in January 26, 1948 had some modern features including the council of ministers, a bicameral legislature, a high court, and municipal and village bodies for local self government. But it retained the hereditary rights of the Ranas and their special privileges despite suggestions to the contrary from the constitutional advisers and liberal elements within the Rana family. Padma himself would have been amenable to this position, but was not bold enough to face strong conservative elements in the family and wanted to avoid a situation where he would be blamed for putting the future interests of the family in jeopardy. Padma did not remain in office to implement the political reforms envisaged in the Constitution, and was succeeded by an arch conservative Mohan Shamsher. During his rule, Mohan brought about more repressive laws to quell political dissent. Municipal authority was curtailed, private education discouraged, and the process of political liberalization was effectively reversed.

The subject of economic development had become fashionable and dear to the Rana rulers in their last days. Even the conservative Mohan Shamsher (1945-51) revived the idea of development planning after becoming Prime Minister; he formed the *Arthik Yojana Samiti* (Economic Planning Board) and inaugurated its first meeting. The moving spirit being this newfound love was his progressive son Bijaya Shamsher who had also drafted the earlier 15-year plan during the time of Juddha Shamsher. However, such was the atmosphere of suspicion and fear under the autocratic regime that nobody could gauge the Prime Minister's mind regarding the financial resources required to operationalize the proposed development plan. Nor could anybody venture to raise this question without incurring grave personal risk. The revenue and expenditure of the state was a closely guarded secret.

Attention was given to the development of hydropower. A power-cum-irrigation project with a potential of generating 22,000 KW of electricity was identified at Kali Gandaki near Gainda Kot. A British consultancy firm had studied its feasibility and prepared a detailed technical report. The project was approved at the cost of Rs.18 million to be completed in three years. However, the Prime Minister reversed the decision soon afterwards. Apparently, he was led into false belief by the then Indian Ambassador C.P.N. Singh that India would soon meet Nepal's power requirement at one-third of the price envisaged under the project.[37] Some other development initiatives proposed in the latter half of the 1940s by the Rana regime included the development of Chitawan Valley for agricultural production, the construction of Kathmandu-Hetauda Road, the setting up of a cement plant at Bhainse, and the construction of airfields at Kathmandu, Pokhara, Bhairahawa, Simra and Biratnagar.

Several factors may explain the sudden enthusiasm for economic development shown by the authoritarian regime during their last days. First, the internal opposition to their autocratic rule was increasing. The enlightened youth educated in India—inspired by the Indian struggle for independence under Mahatma Gandhi and influenced by the liberal ideas sweeping throughout the world in the aftermath of the Second Great War—were organizing themselves to overthrow the autocratic regime. The Rana family itself was a divided house and some Ranas, who were denied the position in their succession roll, had revolted and joined forces with the Nepali Congress. The soldiers who had participated in the Second Great War were exposed to modern influences and enterprise and wanted to excel in peacetime activities in their own country, but conditions at home thwarted their ambitions. Second, there was mounting pressure from some progressive elements within the Rana family for some economic and political reforms to avoid their immediate downfall.

Third, with India's independence the British could no longer provide the protective umbrella to their regime. Fourth, the last Rana Prime Minister had considerably benefited from the vast accumulation of his father Chandra Shamsher and, therefore, was not so much interested in amassing a fortune as in prolonging his rule. Last, the cosmetic nature of some of these reform initiatives indicated that they were largely for demonstrative purpose intended for internal and external consumption. That they would not bring about any fundamental change in the monopolistic control of the Rana family in social, economic, administrative and political life of the country was a forgone conclusion.

END OF THE RANA REGIME

Mohan Shamsher tried to expand international relations to escape diplomatic isolation after the end of British rule in India. The Rana rulers had not anticipated the end of British rule in India so early, and were confident of continued British support for their survival. Mohan established diplomatic relations with the United States, France, Belgium, the Netherlands and Brazil. India-based ambassadors of the United States and France were concurrently accredited to Nepal. An application was made for membership to the United Nations. Attempts were made to cultivate friendship with the Congress government of independent India. Nepali troops were offered for garrison duties in India during the Hyderabad and Kashmir crisis in mid-1948. Mohan Shamsher paid a visit to India and signed a Treaty of Peace and Friendship. The Treaty, among others, provided that neither government would tolerate any threat to the security of the other by a foreign aggressor. To deal with any such threat, the two governments would consult with each other and devise effective counter-measures.[38] The treaty also promised national treatment in its territory to the national of others in regard to industrial and economic development, and in grants of concessions and contracts. Reciprocity in matters of residence, ownership of property, participation in trade and commerce for each other's nationals was provided for. Similarly, the Treaty of Trade and Commerce was also signed. This treaty guaranteed full and unrestricted transit rights for all goods and manufactures through Indian territories, but it also obliged Nepal to impose the same amount of levy as India on both imports and exports from third countries.

The dispatch of Nepali troops to India, and the signing of the two treaties on Indian terms and in the form drafted by them were parts of the appeasement policy intended to secure the political support for the oligarchy's survival. The Ranas wanted to prevent Indian support to the anti-Rana movement in Nepal by mollifying them against any pressure for political reforms. The last-minute initiatives for economic development were intended to reverse the tide of growing opposition to their rule. Despite these desperate attempts, the conservative and anti-reform attitude towards political reforms only hastened the end of the Rana oligarchy. The new rulers thought, rather naively, that the people yearning for freedom and participation in the political process would be contented with a few development initiatives. Even the expansion of diplomatic relations and appeasement to the new Indian rulers did not help the Ranas ensure their grasp on power. Prime Minister Nehru advised Mohan Shamsher to keep abreast of the march of time.[39]

During their rule, the Ranas held effective control over the country's politics, administration and economy. In furthering their own interest, they were able administrators. Rivals within the family were controlled by the threat of virtual banishment to remote provinces in the guise of governorships. To control potential dissent among non-Ranas and junior Ranas, the *Chakari* system was developed and formalized. *Chakari* system required the concerned nobles to formally and publicly attend the Rana courts at some specified hours each day in order for them to remain in close proximity of the Ranas. This effectively controlled the movement and activities of the potential troublemakers and conspirators. Furthermore, the practice of night-time curfew rendered impossible night-time visits and activities.[40]

Despite all attempts to keep the country in virtual isolation from modern influences and the march of time by the despotic and autocratic Rana administration, the anti-Rana movement had started from the mid 1930s. It started out with the publication and dissemination of anti-Rana political literature in India and the establishment of a school and civil rights committee inside the country to raise political consciousness. A group of dissatisfied youth formed an underground political organization called the Nepal Praja Parishad to overthrow the Ranas. Their activities were dealt with mercilessly. Four of the dissenters were executed; others were served life sentences. This brutal suppression could not contain the rising opposition. Discontent was fast spreading. Nepali political exiles and those domiciled in India formed the All India Nepali National Congress and All-India Gorkha Congress in 1946. The two organizations merged into one under the banner of Nepali National Congress on 24–25 January 1947 with the declared objective to establish democracy in Nepal under a constitutional monarch through non-violent movement. This party started political demonstrations inside Nepal. A labour strike was called in Biratnagar. In April 1947, the party announced the launching of the Civil Disobedience Movement. A large number of political activists, including the leader B.P. Koirala were detained in various parts of the country. Koirala was released only after an intervention by Mahatma Gandhi. Around the same time, some enlightened youth in Kathmandu formed a new political party named Nepal Praja Panchayat to press for political reforms.

National Congress decided to launch non-violent movement for political rights. B.P. Koirala was arrested once again in May 1, 1947 and in jail, he went on a fast unto death demanding better prison conditions and political freedom. Another political party was formed under the name of Democratic Congress with the support of dissatisfied Ranas led by Suvarna Shamsher and Mahavir Shamsher. Its objective was to establish a democratic government in Nepal under constitutional monarchy. To consolidate the struggle for democracy in Nepal, the National Congress and Democratic Congress were merged to form Nepali Congress in April 1950. A Nepali Congress conference in Bairgania of Bihar decided to launch armed struggle inside Nepal. King Tribhuvan, meanwhile, had established contacts with anti-Rana political forces, particularly the Nepali Congress. On 6th November, he, together with other family members left Narayanhiti palace pretending to be on a hunting trip, and sought asylum at the Indian embassy in Kathmandu. He was subsequently flown to New Delhi. The only member of the family left in the palace was the King's three year-old second grand son Gyanendra. The Rana regime hastily declared Gyanendra as the new king.

Events started moving fast. Nepali Congress had procured and mobilized arms and ammunitions from various sources, particularly from the socialist government in Burma. Armed Nepali Congress volunteers under the banner of *Mukti Sena* made a surprise attack in Birgunj on November 11, 1950. After capturing the *Badahakim*, they moved to other adjoining districts. This was followed by attacks in Biratnagar, Bhairahawa, Udayapur and other places. The armed garrison of Palpa under Rudra Shamsher defected to Nepali Congress. Subsequently Syangja was also occupied. Spontaneous demonstrations against the regime were becoming daily events in Kathmandu. In the face of the deteriorating situation and breakdown of law and order, India hammered out a formula for the future political set-up of Nepal. Through persuasion and coercion, consensus was secured from both sides. Direct talk was held between the Rana representatives and Nepali Congress under the guidance of the king. New Delhi acted as a midwife to give birth of a democratic set-up in Nepal. The agreement known as the Delhi Compromise was concluded on February 7, 1951. Under the compromise, a 10-man cabinet was to be formed immediately with equal representation from the Ranas and the Nepali Congress. King

Tribhuvan, his family members and prominent leaders of the Nepali Congress made a triumphant return to Kathmandu on 15 February. This marked the end of the 104-year old autocratic rule.

SUMMING UP

The Rana period offered unprecedented stability for over a century. Initially it proved to be a welcome change from a period which was marked by court intrigues and conspiracies under an extremely weak monarch. Convinced of the overwhelming might of the British Empire, the Ranas extended hands of friendship and courted their support from the very beginning, which got further cultivated and strengthened in subsequent years. Among other things, Jang Bahadur's assistance during the Sipoy Mutiny, the permission for Gorkha recruitment in the Indian army, the personnel and material assistance extended by Nepal during the two Great Wars and the increased trade relations with the British consolidated the relations between the two countries. The relation was not without benefit to Nepal from a national and economic perspective. Nepal's assistance during the Sipoy Mutiny was reciprocated by the return of western *tarai* lost in the Sugauli Treaty. Furthermore, the Treaty of 1923 recognized Nepal as an independent country. Nepal's contribution to the British war efforts in the two Great Wars fetched huge cash flow to the country. The government revenue increased. For the Ranas, the increased relations with the British served as a protective umbrella to their family rule.

While shielding the country from modern influences, the Ranas used the period of their reign for their family enrichment through a variety of ways. All national resources were exploited to promote self interest and personal wealth of the family. The distinction between the state treasury and the personal coffers of the rulers was non existent. The constantly increasing revenue surplus was appropriated privately after meeting bare expenses of the skeletal state administration. No serious effort was made to mobilize and channel the unprecedented cash inflow towards creating development assets and capital investment. Instead, the injection of cash in the rural economy only led to import of cheap machine made consumer goods inflicting setbacks on local crafts and cottage industries. The neighbouring Indian states viewed the development of railway network in the last quarter of the nineteenth century as a new foundation for economic progress. But that did not change the attitude of the Rana rulers towards modern development. They continued to discourage education and external travels and were determined to keep the country in extreme backwardness and ignorance. Traditional feudal practices dominated production relations in agriculture.

The Rana political system was undisguised military despotism with absolute total control over all aspects of public life. Any internal voice of dissent—from family rivals or popular revolt, was ruthlessly suppressed. But the country could not remain immune from the influence of liberal and progressive ideas and the winds of change that were blowing around the world, and particularly in India. The last-minute developmental efforts and constitutional reform attempts by the Rana rulers proved too late and too little. The protective umbrella of the British came to an end with India's independence. Ultimately the regime bowed down before the rising tide of internal opposition that culminated into a nationwide armed uprising with overt and covert support from the newly independent India.

NOTES

1. Quoted in Perceval Landon, *History of Nepal Vol.I*, 2001, p. 132 from Dr. Wright, a British Resident Surgeon.
2. Rishikesh Shah, *Modern Nepal*, Vol. 1 Delhi: Manohar, 1996, p. 242.
3. Ibid pp. 251–253.
4. References made in the last chapter.
5. Hodgson was also the officiating Resident during 1829–1831.
6. K.L Pradhan, *Brian Hodgson at the Kathmandu Residency*, Delhi: Spectrum Publications, 2001, p. 44.
7. Ibid and Landon, Vol., p. 98.
8. Shaha, op. cit., p. 259
9. K.L.Pradhan, op.cit pp. 26–30.
10. Jahar Sen, *Indo-Nepal Trade in the Ninteenth Century*, Calcutta: Firma KLM, 1977, pp. 127–132.
11. B.D. Sanwal, *Nepal and the East India Company*, Bombay: Asia Publishing House, 1965, p. 295.
12. Sen op.cit., p. 33
13. Blaike, Cameron and Seddon, *Nepal in Crisis*, Oxford: Clarendon Press, 1980, p. 37
14. Joshi and Rose, *Democratic Innovations in Nepal*, Berkeley: University of California Press, 1966, p. 16.
15. General Ochterlony was the commander of the British forces in the 1814–16 Nepal-British war.
16. Two Nasiri batallions and a Sirmoor battalion composed of the Gorkhas and other hill troops were raised in the British service. *See*. A.P. Coleman, *A Special Corps: The Beginning of the Gorkha Service with the British.*

Durham: The Pentland Press. 1999, Part III, Chapter 8, and Appendix F.

17. Landon, op.cit. Vol. I pp. 96-98.
18. Pradhan (2001), p. 31–35.
19. Perceval Landon, *History of Nepal vol. 2* Delhi: Adarsa Enterprises, 2001, pp 138–40.
20. Quoted op. cit., p. 141.
21. Ibid, p. 144.
22. Ibid.
23. Shaha, *Modern Nepal* vol. 2. New Delhi: Manohar, 1996, p. 56
24. M.C. Regmi, *Land Tenure and Taxation in Nepal,* Ratna Pustak Bhandar, Kathmandu, 1978, p. 274.
25. Ibid, p. 322
26. Ibid, p. 494.
27. Ibid, p. 517.
28. Shaha, (1996) vol. 2, p. 19. Also, Pravakar, Pashupati and Gautam Rana, *The Ranas in Nepal,* Geneva: NAEF, 2002.
29. Shaha, (1996) vol 2, p. 242.
30. Risikesh Shaha, *Essays in the Practice of Government in Nepal,* 1982, New Delhi: Manohar, p. 88.
31. Sardar Bhim Bahadur Pandey, *Tyas Bakhat KO Nepal,* Kathmandu: CNAS Tribhuvan University. 1982, p. 187.
32. Blaike et.al. (2001), p. 36.
33. D.R. Regmi, *A Century of Family Autocracy in Nepal.* Benaras: Nepali National Congress, p. 197.
34. For details, Pandey, op. cit, pp. 395–408.
35. Shaha, (1996). pp. 151–153.
36. Pandey, op.cit.
37. The Indian Ambassador told Prime Minister Mohan Shamsher that India was developing a massive hydro project on the Indian side, which would produce electricity at 2 rupees per unit compared to 6 rupees per unit proposed in the Kaligandaki project, which would be made available to Nepal also. Mohan Shamsher believed this version, and the project was abandoned. *See,* Pandey (2045 B.S), *Thyas Bakhatko Nepal* vol. 4, pp. 132–134.
38. This portion did not appear in the main part of the Treaty, but was in the form of attached exchange of letter on the same day. Shaha, (1996), vol. 2., p. 198.
39. Explaining his policy towards Nepal, Nehru told the Indian Parliament on 17 March 1950 that in the Nepali context it is desirable to pay attention to the forces which are moving in the world, the democratic forces and forces of freedom, and put themselves in line with them.
40. Dor Bahadur Bista, *Fatalism and Development,* Orient Longman. 1993, p. 102.

Chapter Three

The 1950s: Towards Modernization

Upon his return to Kathmandu, King Tribhuvan made a historic announcement. According to his announcement, the country would, henceforth, be governed under a democratic constitution prepared by a constituent assembly elected on the basis of universal adult franchise. An interim cabinet was formed by the king in accordance with the Delhi Agreement with Mohan Shamsher reappointed to the position of Prime Minister. An interim constitution was also brought into effect on 11 April 1951 to provide the framework for the country's governance until the new constitution could be prepared by the constituent assembly. This put an end to the Rana Prime Ministers' rule by preemptory command as laid down in the 1846 *Lal Panja*, the Red Seal document with the king's palm print, and also in the 1948 Constitution of Nepal under Padma Shamsher.

INSTABILITY AND CONFUSION

Contrary to the traditional practice of rule by fiat, the new arrangement ushered in a modern constitutional concept of the King-in-Council power sharing arrangement between the king and ministers as the representatives of the people. The Interim Act also accepted the principle of separation of power. It provided for independent judiciary and other institutions like the Public Service Commission, the Election Commission, the Auditor General and the office of the Comptroller General as safeguards. The principal task of the Interim Government, as defined by the Act, was to create conditions suitable for holding election for the constituent assembly as early as possible.

The new Rana–Congress power sharing arrangement was not a smooth affair in view of mutual distrust and suspicion. The two sides came from different backgrounds, and represented different constituencies. The king naturally sympathized with the Congress. The ruminants of the Rana regime gave birth to a new political organization called the *Vir Gorkha Dal* to overthrow the new government. They started holding demonstrations against the government, and even attacked the residence of B.P. Koirala, the Home Minister and leader of the NC faction in the coalition. In the tussle between the two factions, India started playing the role of a mediator, thus enhancing its role in Nepal's internal affairs. The king announced a 35-member Advisory Council comprising mainly Nepali Congress representatives and independents without consulting the Prime Minister. In the midst of continuing crisis, the death of a student following the police firing on a demonstration precipitated a new development. Prime Minister Mohan Shamsher issued a public statement regretting the incidence with indirect insinuation on the Home Ministry. B.P. Koirala took it as a violation of the principal of collective responsibility and resigned. In his resignation letter, he bitterly attacked the unnatural coalition and demanded a homogenous Cabinet. His position was supported by other Congress members of the Cabinet who tendered collective resignation. Finding no other choice, the resignation of the Rana bloc of ministers followed soon.

The king was now free to set up a new government without the Ranas. Despite the overwhelming support for B.P. Koirala as the head of the new Government from the Congress Party, King Tribhuvan favoured M.P. Koirala who had the Indian support as the next Prime Minister. Thus, a new Nepali Congress government, with M.P. Koirala as its first commoner Prime Minister was announced on 16 November 1951. Triggered by the unnatural way in which the new Prime Minister was appointed, the government suffered from internal dissension. Three prominent ministers, including Ganesh Man Singh, Suvarna Shamsher and Surya Prashad Upadhaya resigned, blaming the Prime Minister for the failure to implement the Party's socio-economic and political programme. The crisis was further precipitated by the civil servants' strike. Ultimately, the Prime Minister was forced to resign. Contrary to all expectations, the king did not invite the Nepali Congress to form the next government, but instead, decided to act on his own as Prime Minister, assisted by six Councillors.

The Interim Government Act was amended to provide the legal basis for the consolidation of the king's power. This effectively restored the king to the position of a traditional monarch with all sovereign power vested in him. Meanwhile, internal squabbles within the Nepali Congress ultimately led to its split, with M.P. Koirala forming a new party called Nepal Praja Parishad with the help of a splinter group. The king recognized this party, and reappointed M.P. Koirala to the position of the Prime Minister on 18 February, 1954. Koirala's cabinet was later on expanded to include representatives from smaller parties in an attempt to give it a 'national' character. The biggest party, the Nepali Congress, refused to join the cabinet.

Nepali Congress launched the *Satyagraha* (Civil Disobedience Movement) in January 1955 demanding, among other things, protection of civil rights, early elections, restoration of peace and security, and price control. Already suffering from internal dissension, the government resigned. Meanwhile, King Tribhuvan died on 14 March 1955, and was succeeded by his son, King Mahendra. While still holding negotiations with political parties for a multi-party cabinet over which he would preside, Mahendra made a surprise announcement on 14 April 1955 of a Council of Royal Advisers under his direct leadership. This experiment did not succeed. On 27 January 1956, Praja Parishad leader Tanka Prashad Acharya was chosen as the next Prime Minister. He was subsequently succeeded by Dr. K.I. Singh in July 1957. The Government lasted for less than four months, and was followed again by the king's direct rule.

In the immediate post-Rana period, the lack of unity and fragmentation among and within political parties considerably strengthened the role of the king, who, in turn, started to manipulate the situation in his favour. King Tribhuvan had himself become increasingly dependent on India and sought their advice on important matters. This was costing his personal image.[1] India's influence in Nepal's politics remained dominant up to 1955, as the king and the political parties who came to power felt obligated to India for their support.[2] The election for the constituent assembly could have helped in building up political institutions and forced political forces to go to the people to build up organizations. However, this agenda was relegated to the background because of internal bickering and preoccupation with short-term political gains. Furthermore, the new King Mahendra did not have the same commitment towards democratic institutions and the constituent assembly as his father who had staked his own life and crown for the sake of democracy in Nepal. The shrewd and ambitious king was looking for a larger political role for himself. He was making direct contacts with the people, and dispatching tour commissions to sense public opinion. The promised election continued to be postponed.

Under these changed circumstances, a new United Democratic Front was formed under the leadership of Nepali Congress with National

Congress and *Praja Parishad.* The Front opposed the king's handling of political matters and blamed him for harbouring autocratic ambitions. The Front also launched a *Satyagraha* in December demanding recognition to the principle of people's sovereignty and an early election. Ultimately, the king did announce the date for new elections, but it was election to the Parliament and not the constituent assembly. In view of the risk of losing even this opportunity to seek the people's mandate, pragmatism dictated Nepali Congress and other parties and prompted them to accept the election for the Parliament as a step forward towards the institutionalization of democracy. In March 1958, the king formed a Constitution Drafting Committee and in May, he formed an election government under the chairmanship of Suvarna Shamsher Rana. The Constitution, which was promulgated just a week before the elections, recognized the king as the source of sovereignty. Although it had all the trappings of multi-party parliamentary democracy, it left many ambiguities and loopholes for the king to play a political role.

DEVELOPMENT SCENARIO

When the first government of the post-Rana period took over, the economic base of the country was extremely rudimentary and poor. The economic infrastructure of the country comprised 1.4 megawatts of power-supply, one airfield, 51 miles of narrow-gauge railways, 100 post offices, and a little more than 300 telephone lines. There was only 1 college, 11 secondary schools and 200 primary schools. About 50 doctors and 649 hospital beds represented the modern health system. The total area under irrigation system was about 50,000 hectares and the use of chemical fertilizer was unknown. The annual budgeting system was non-existent. The only financial institution in the country was the Nepal Bank Ltd., a commercial bank; and the national currency circulated only in Kathmandu Valley and some parts of the hill region. The Indian currency remained the medium of transaction in the economically important *tarai* region.

The country's mineral resources were largely unknown. Large parts of the country were under subsistence agriculture and feudal order prevailed in land relations. The country was rich in forest and water resources, which, together with its land resources could have provided a strong foundation for modernization. The industrial base of the country was represented by two jute mills, a sugar factory, two match factories, plywood and bobbin factory, a textile mill and a few food processing mills. These industries were established under the stimulus of the scarce conditions created by the World War II and existed in the border towns of Biratnagar and Birgunj.

The overthrow of the century-old family autocracy had unleashed a flood of rising expectations from the people. The Directive Principles of the State Policy, as enshrined in the Interim Government Act itself laid down an ambitious goal for the state. It introduced the concept of welfare state to ensure economic, political and social justice to the people and guaranteed all political rights and freedoms. However, the country was very poor in internal resources and the physical infrastructure was extremely limited. With such low endowments of physical and human capital, it was difficult for the state to start any meaningful development programme in a way that could have made an immediate impact on the lives of the masses. The civil administration brought up and trained under the Rana autocracy was hopelessly out of tune with the new demands and requirements.

Moreover, the national scene was increasingly dominated by intense power struggle amid the need for building up institutions for a viable democratic polity. As summed up by D.R. Regmi, a prominent politician of the national scene in 1952:

> We are not so much concerned with economic issues as much as with the question of laying a foundation of the democratic institutions. All schemes of economic development can wait for the duration of the interim administration.... American Point Four or Colombo Plan grants will be ineffective for a long time to come for similar reasons. [3]

Even in this state of confusion and instability, the impact of democracy in unleashing the creative energy of the people which was stifled by the repressive and oppressive Rana regime for more than a century was enormous. The pent-up feelings of the people found their creative expressions in the fields of art, literature, and culture. After years of non descript existence, the Nepalis began to rediscover their identity. Joshi and Rose write:

> The Nepali intellectuals—the Western educated, the literati, the pamphleteers, the newspaper editors, the public orators, and the politicians—were all engaged in feverish political activities. And Kathmandu, the traditional home of these elites, became both the political and cultural Mecca of Nepal.
>
> The release of these creative energies saw its various manifestations in the phenomenal expansion of educational opportunities in the form of new schools and colleges, adult schools, professional schools, and libraries all over the country, mostly on private initiative. The people also exhibited enormous desire for education for themselves and for their children: and girls in unprecedented numbers enrolled in schools and

colleges, in most cases defying existing social traditions and restrictions.[4]

A number of economic measures were undertaken during the period. These measures signaled a policy shift towards the creation of a modern administration, new political economy, and heralded the end of the exploitative feudal order.

New State Policy

The first Rana-Congress coalition government promulgated as state policy a number socio-economic reforms aimed at breaking the feudal practices which had become an integral part of the political structure for centuries. These included the abolition of a number of institutional features like: the *Jhara* system, monetary extractions in the form of mandatory gifts and presents, free state allowances to the members of Rana family and their favourites, and land grants to favourite officials. The Rana monopoly over high positions in the government and the army was also brought to an end. The most significant development was, however, the acceptance of the principle of abolition of the holdings of *Birta* lands. As the first step towards this process, the transfer of *Birta* land above 25 *ropanis* by sale or mortgage was prohibited. The government issued a notification requiring all government and government-supported schools to admit students of 'untouchable' castes.[5]

In September 1955, a 13-point programme defining the government policy on the questions of tenancy rights, land rents and the interest rates was announced. This policy statement stipulated that the landlords could not demand more than 50 per cent of the produce as rent and the annual rate of interest was fixed at 10 per cent. Tenancy rights were automatically granted to those who cultivated the lands for two consecutive years and paid the rent regularly. These reforms were, however, merely statements of policy and did not have adequate legal backing.[6] The Tenancy Rights Act was adopted only in 1957 but its implementation was questionable.

New reforms were also started in the civil service with technical assistance from India. Attempts were made to reorganize the civil administration along modern lines of ministries and departments. An examination system was introduced to recruit civil servants. However, radical change in the composition and character of civil service was not immediately possible in view of the lack of educated and trained manpower and the need for continuity of the old regime's civil servants for practical considerations. Singha Durbar, the massive building which served as the official residence of the Rana Prime Ministers, was itself converted into the Government Secretariat housing all ministries and departments.

The Annual Budget System

Another significant economic reform was the inauguration of the annual budgetary system. In February 1952, Finance Minister Suvarna Shamsher Rana announced a comprehensive statement of the government's financial position with all its assets and liabilities left over from the Rana regime. The balance remaining from the Rana government in the forms of gold, silver, coins and foreign currency was estimated at Rs. 80 million.[7] A budget of Rs. 52.5 million was presented, of which Rs. 22 million represented the deficit to be covered partly from the reserves. The balance of the reserve was earmarked in the forms of Currency Reserve Fund, Exchange Stabilization Fund, and a Budget Equalization Fund. Some of the revenue mobilization measures proposed by the budget were ambitious. For instance, the budget proposed to float public bonds, change the tax collection methods and introduce income tax. However, income tax was not introduced until 1959 and the public bonds were floated only in 1961. The government announced a policy of mixed economy for the country, assuring full scope for private enterprise without allowing the exploitation of any individual or class. In budgetary allocation, priority was given to the construction of roads and airports, postal improvements and radio development, and the promotion of health and education facilities. The government also committed itself to the establishment of a central bank.

Foreign Assistance

The 1950s witnessed the beginning of foreign assistance to Nepal. The United States had signed a Point Four Agreement on 23 January 1951 when the Rana regime was in its last days. The motivation for the first US technical mission that started its work in 1952 was the desire to prevent the spread of communist influence—both internal and external—in Nepal. They were particularly conscious of the fact that the impoverished peasantry of Nepal could have provided a fertile habitat for communism.[8] The first development project in Nepal with American aid was the establishment of a Village Development Training Centre under which community development workers were trained by US instructors. Other fields of US assistance were: agriculture, health, mining, education, malaria eradication, and the ambitious Rapti Valley Project.

Indian economic assistance started in 1953 with the construction of the Gauchar airport and the Kathmandu–Raxaul road. Both of these were valuable additions to Nepal's meagre infrastructure at the time. The Indian Aid mission was set up in 1954 to coordinate the Indian assistance in Nepal. Somewhat similar to the US interest, the Indian assistance also appears to have been motivated by the desire to keep Nepal outside the influence of the Communist China—both politically and strategically. The Indians considered the Himalayas as their defence frontiers vis-a-vis China. It was perhaps for this reason that they helped reorganize and modernize the Nepali army. Further assistance was provided in the form of hospital equipment to improve existing medical facilities in Nepal. On September 8, 1954, India announced a grant of $1.2 million for irrigation and drinking water projects in Nepal.[9] Assistance was also provided in the field of manpower training at Indian universities. The most controversial Indian assistance in the 1950s was the Multipurpose Kosi River project concluded in 1954 under the four-party Government headed by Prime Minister M.P. Koirala. The project envisioned the construction of a barrage, headworks, flood banks and canals in the Nepali territory to provide flood control and irrigation facilities largely to India. The major criticism against the project was that Nepal had surrendered extra-territorial rights to India at the project sites for an indefinite period without receiving adequate compensation or benefits in terms of irrigation and power.

The United Nations, Ford Foundation, People's Republic of China, the Soviet Union and Switzerland were some other sources that started assisting Nepal in the 1950s. The UN provided technical assistance in the fields of malaria eradication, dairy development, nurses training and geological surveys. The Ford Foundation provided assistance in the development of cottage industries such as woodcarving and other domestic handicrafts, and in the establishment of a domestic science school. Swiss assistance started in 1955 with the establishment of a series of dairy and cheese plants, the central dairy being set up in Kathmandu in 1956. The Chinese offered an assistance of $12.6 million ($ 4.2 million in cash and $ 8.4 million in commodities) for the first time in Nepal. This was followed by an Indian assistance of $ 21 million for the First Plan. The Soviet Union announced an assistance of $100,000 plus equipment along with necessary technical assistance to build a 50-bed hospital. It also offered scholarships for Nepali students.[10]

Development Planning

Another landmark achievement of the 1950s was the initiation of development planning. A draft outline of the country's First Five Year Plan was announced by King Mahendra on 10 October 1955 with the estimated outlay of Rs. 21 crore. A 9-member Central Planning Commission was also formed to finalize the Plan.[11] The draft outline was apparently prepared in a hurry for presentation to the Colombo Plan meeting in Singapore scheduled to be held after a week. This represented the first official commitment to the philosophy of planned economic development, which had become a catchword for many Asian countries just liberated from the yoke of colonial rule.

The final version of the First Five Year Plan was presented in September 1956. The plan itself—prepared with advisory assistance from the United Nations—reflected the widespread ideological orientation and contemporary rhetoric prevailing at the national scene. The Plan was committed to establishing a welfare state by increasing production, employment and living standard of the people with emphasis on just and equitable distribution of income and wealth. The total outlay of the Plan was Rs. 33 crore and 71 per cent of this was proposed to be mobilized from the external sources. Of the total outlay, 34.5 per cent was earmarked for transport and communications.[12]

The Plan was formulated without sufficient statistics and proper assessment of the country's resources and it was, as Mihaly put it, "a catalogue of wants and desires". [13] The Plan laid the foundation for future planning process in Nepal and it correctly reflected the development needs and priorities of the country. More importantly, this Plan made the nation more aware of the preconditions required for a development plan. It was realized that a plan formulated without detailed knowledge of actual conditions and the development potential of various sectors was of limited usefulness.[14] The biggest problem for this Plan, however, was the absence of real political commitment to put it into implementation. Again, in the words of Mihaly:

> Little notice was taken of it until well into 1957. Even when the Plan was supposedly being acted upon by 1958, decisions on expenditure were usually made without reference to it but were rather the product of what Himsworth calls momentary enthusiasms of the various ministries which competed with each other to come up with the most attractive projects—on paper. The plan never played the role marked for it, namely to give a sense of direction and coherence to a multi-faceted development effort. [15]

As soon as he came to power in mid-1957, Prime Minister Dr. K.I. Singh discarded the Plan. He announced his own Two-Year Plan which proposed the development of several all-weather roads, about 100 suspension bridges, eight hydro-electric power stations, irrigation dams, paper mills and a cement factory.[16] This plan was discarded immediately after Dr. Singh's dismissal, and the Five Year Plan was revived. A Planning Commission Act was passed in December 1957 and under it, a National Planning Commission subsequently established under the chairmanship of Prince Himalaya Bir Bikram Shah.

Currency Unification

Another important set of measures enacted during the period was in the field of the country's monetary system. After the political change of 1951, the excess of public expenditure over revenue resulted in the expansion of currency circulation. The increase in money supply coupled with the increased imports from India led to depreciation of the Nepali rupee (NR) vis-a-vis Indian rupee (IR). Nepali rupee hit its lowest when the value of IR 100 rose to NR. 185 in July 1955.[17] Another monetary problem was the circulation of two currencies. The Indian currency was in circulation not only in the entire *tarai* region but also in many hilly regions. Public revenue and expenditure were maintained in both Nepali and Indian currencies. The government initiated a number of measures to stabilize the exchange rate and bring about currency unification. Hoping to prop up the depreciating national currency, the government announced in 1954 to supply Indian currency at the official rate of 150 NR for 100 IR to bona-fide traders to import essential goods. Imports of luxury goods were curbed. The Currency Exchange Regulation Act of 1954 was announced to put a check on speculative activities. The Act provided for elaborate licensing requirements and investigative systems in foreign exchange dealings. But all these steps failed to stabilize the exchange rate as the market price of Indian rupee always exceeded the official rate.[18]

Meanwhile, the Nepal Rastra Bank (NRB) was established in 1956 under the Nepal Rastra Bank Act of 1955. The NRB was entrusted with all central banking functions including the issue of paper currency, monetary and exchange regulation, mobilization of capital and stimulating economic growth. NRB was immediately preoccupied with the tasks of halting the deterioration of the value of NR vis-a-vis IR. A temporary success was achieved in arresting the deteriorating value under specific circumstances in 1957. However, the exchange stability could not be achieved fully until 1960 when a significant portion of the Chinese cash grant ($ 4.2 million equivalent of IR) afforded NRB the reserves to keep the NR from sliding.[19]

Stabilization, however, was only a temporary solution as the problem of volatility in exchange rates would resurface as long as the dual-currency system was maintained. In 1956, NRB initiated a program to gradually eliminate the use of dual currency in Nepal. On 16 April 1956, the government announced that all payments such as land taxes, custom duties and other dues except contractual payments such as royalties, would be collected by the government in NR at the rate of 128 for IR 100. This was a bold measure but hinged upon an unrealistic exchange rate; it defied economic logic and could be rationalized only on nationalistic grounds. The situation was quickly exploited by the landlords who made huge profits by paying land taxes in NR and receiving rents from tenants in IR, as had been the traditional practice. In July 1956, the government announced a supplementary measure, which required, *inter alia*, payment of 25 per cent of the salary and emoluments of the government employees of the *tarai* in NR.[20] In 1957, the Expansion of Nepalese Currency Circulation Act was adopted with the objective of securing a nation-wide circulation of NR on a gradual basis. Under this Act—initially implemented in a few selected districts—all payments including wages, rent and interests were to be accepted in NR even in the traditionally IR areas. This measure was applicable even for those transactions which were made previously in IR.

THE FIRST ELECTED GOVERNMENT

Contrary to all expectations, the Nepali Congress secured a majority in the general elections to the House of Representatives in May 1959 catapulting the Congress leader B.P. Koirala to power. The assertive victory of the Nepali Congress brought welcome relief after a period which was profusely marred by confusion and political opportunism. The Nepali Congress was weeded to the ideology of democratic socialism propounded by B.P. Koirala and adopted at the party convention of January 1956 in Birgunj. The election manifesto on which the party fought and won the election articulated an approach that looked beyond the immediate frustrations arising from a climate of short-term political gains and expediency of practical politics that marked the politics of the time. According to Joshi and Rose:

> In the context of unenlightened practicality and unethical expediency, B.P.Koirala's future-oriented vision of a socialistic utopia was a sorely needed corrective. Even more credible is the fact that eight years out of political office seemed not to tarnish his idealistic zeal, and in fact had probably intensified his dedication to a socialistic ideology.[21]

The socialist programme in the context of the country's economy in those days focused mainly on the problem of the feudal land relations, concentration of land holdings, and exploitation of the tillers. B.P's emphasis was on the abolition of the feudal order and creation of a new industrial society. Not being dogmatic, he believed in defining the ideology based on the Nepali conditions. He would not accept socialism at the expense of individual freedom. Among other things, the Nepali Congress election manifesto promised to bring about the following changes:

(*i*) A radical change in the land tenure system and ownership through redistribution of land to tenants and landless labourers which involved the abolition of *Birta* land and the ceiling on land holding.
(*ii*) Abolition of *Rajya* system (the semi-autonomous small principalities in the western hills).
(*iii*) Nationalization of forests.
(*iv*) A scientific reform of the currency system to put an end to the dual currency practice and bring about exchange stability.
(*v*) Promotion of cooperative farming.
(*vi*) Rapid industrialization.

The main objectives behind the government's policy of creating a socialistic system was further articulated by the Finance Minister Suvarna Shamsher in the first budget speech in August 1959. They were: increase national income, bring about fundamental changes in agriculture, provide adequate social welfare to the people, solve the problem of unemployment, reduce income inequalities and redistribute wealth.[22]

Development Programmes

The immediate priorities for the government after coming to power was to expedite the implementation of development projects and formulate a new Plan. It did not abandon the First Five Year Plan started in 1956, but endeavoured to bolster its implementation with suitable modifications to its programme and targets. Although the plan had a total outlay of Rs. 330 million, only Rs.60 million had been spent in the first three years.

With the objective of meeting the expenditure target of the First Five Year Plan, the new government gave a massive boost to development expenditure. It proposed an outlay of Rs. 140 million in its first annual budget out of which Rs. 79 million was actually spent. The second budget proposed a spending purse of Rs. 250 million. To expedite the development activities the new government repealed the Planning Commission Act of 1957 on the very first day after taking over its office on 27 May 1959. A committee of two senior cabinet ministers was formed to coordinate the implementation of development projects. In the following week, a Planning Board was established under the chairmanship of Suvarna Shamsher. In his capacity as both the Finance and the Planning/Development Minister, he was expected to provide necessary leadership and coordination in planning and execution of projects. This enhanced the implementation capacity considerably. Projects started moving faster and with fewer jurisdictional squabbles.[23] The enhanced absorptive capacity of the government was evident from the increased development expenditure of Rs. 78.9 million in 1959/60 from a level of Rs. 32.7 million in 1958/59.

In order to improve the technical capacity of the Planning Board, negotiations were held with the Ford Foundation for the services of a team of experts who could advise the Planning Minister in an impartial and objective manner. Mr. Ladjinsky, a planning expert of international renown was proposed to lead the team of advisers. The agreement with the Ford Foundation was approved on 26 February 1960, and the first adviser to be fielded was William O. Thwealt, a Tax and Fiscal Economist.[24] The formulation of the Second Plan was underway; the first indication of this came in the second budget speech of the Finance Minister on 6 July 1960, when he indicated that the Plan would be submitted in about six months. The Prime Minister had spoken about the Second Plan earlier at a press conference on 26 June. The total outlay of the Plan was reported to be Rs.1, 960 million out of which nearly 450 million was earmarked to the agricultural sector and 1,510 million in the non-agricultural sector. The order of priorities was: industrial projects, road building, and agricultural production. The plan was expected to generate 500,000 new jobs and increase the national income by 30 per cent. [25]

The new government's confidence in formulating an ambitious plan was largely attributed to its success in mobilizing external assistance. Within a very short time in office, it had negotiated a large amount of assistance from external sources. The United States promised a $15 million grant in rupees during King Mahendra's state visit there in April 1960. This was to be utilized over a period of two years. The UN Special Fund had approved US$ 1 million to conduct a survey for hydropower development in the Karnali basin. In January 1960, during B.P.Koirala's visit, India pledged a development assistance of 160 million Indian rupees and agreed to revise the controversial 1950 Indo-Nepal Treaty of Trade and Commerce. Furthermore, India and Nepal signed five more project agreements covering the development of an engineering school, an industrial estate and for projects in horticulture, veterinary services and forestry. In October 1960, India also agreed to assist Nepal in the establishment of a national archive. All these projects were to be implemented under the Second Five Year Plan.

Resources were also successfully mobilized from the socialist countries. China approved a grant US $ 21 million. It also agreed to investigate the feasibility of establishing three specific projects: a cement factory, a paper mill, and a tannery-shoe factory. The Chinese had started surveys for the same in 1960. The paper and the cement projects were dropped in 1963, because they were no longer able to acquire the needed machinery from Eastern Europe. Just before the Nepali Congress took office, an agreement had been signed with the Soviet Union on 29 April 1959. This agreement on economic and technical assistance, stipulated the construction of a 1200 KW hydroelectric power project at Panauti, a sugar and a cigarette factory, and a survey for an East-West Highway. Following B.P's visit to Israel, a three-member Israeli team was fielded in November 1960 to investigate possible areas of cooperation in water and irrigation development, river training, and resettlement. Resources were also being mobilized from other sources including Switzerland, Great Britain, Australia, New Zealand and the United Nations.

Confronted with rising expectations of the people kindled after the first general election, the government realized that it had to attend to the basic needs of the villages in terms of education, health services, transportation and communications if it were to retain their confidence and trust. A separate ministry was created to handle the demands for rural development progammes from the people and their elected representatives throughout the country. The local institutions during this period, being part and parcel of the welfare and development activities of the new government, further expanded and assumed a new context and tone.[26]

Inspired by the desire to increase the visibility of its action, the government launched a programme to set up 2200 primary schools at various parts of the country. The idea was to ensure at least one primary school in each of the polling centers. Out of this, 1600 schools were actually established in one single year. In addition to the provision of primary education, these schools would provide additional benefit of facilitating public activities, such as serving as election booths. District Development Officers (DDOs) were appointed for all districts to expedite the implementation of development programmes at the local level. These officers were given direct control over the administration of short-term development projects, and since their position was semi-official, they were not constrained by the normal red tape and other bureaucratic hassles. District Development Boards were established with necessary decision-making authority. They were empowered to authorize the execution of development works up to the budget of

Rs.30,000. Another programme was launched to set up 109 hospitals and dispensaries in 1960/61 in accordance with the government decision to set up at least one dispensary in each electoral constituency. Village development centres were installed to distribute, among others, improved seeds to the villagers as well as to grant subsidized loans to rural entrepreneurs.

Fiscal Innovations and Exchange Stability

Alongside mobilizing external assistance, the government was also mindful of the need to enhance domestic revenue collection in order to give continuity to the development projects that had been initiated. Hence, to increase the mobilization of internal resources, the government widened the economy's tax base. A number of new taxes including the tax on income, urban property, foreign investment, trade profits, *Birta* land, water taps and radio receivers were introduced. The tax rates were, however, moderate and their revenue contributions negligible. They were estimated to have brought in only Rs. 2.5 million as additional revenue. As part of the resource mobilization scheme, government bonds were introduced for the first time in Nepal's fiscal history. The second budget presented by the Congress government proposed to float such bonds up to the value of Rs. 20 million at 5.5 per cent interest rate. The maturity of these proposed bonds would be five years.[27]

One notable achievement of the NC government was its success in bringing about exchange rate stability. The exchange rate volatility that marked the 1950s came to an end in April 1960 when the new official exchange rate was announced after giving careful consideration to past experiences. This rate continued successfully until the middle of 1966 when it had to be revised following the devaluation of Indian Currency in relation to other currencies. The Foreign Exchange Control Act enacted in July 1960 prohibited foreign exchange dealings in markets except by authorized dealers of the central bank. Extensive terms and conditions were specified to the authorized dealers and they were also required to comply with the directives of the central bank. They were under obligation to record all their transactions in a specified manner so that they could be inspected by the central bank and the government whenever it considered necessary.[28]

The Treaty of Trade and Transit 1960

The trade treaty with India signed by Mohan Samsher during the last days of Rana rule had practically bound Nepal's foreign trade with that of India. Some provisions of the treaty were so restrictive that they might be considered an affront to Nepal's status as a sovereign nation. For example, under the treaty, Nepal could not have trade relations with any other country without India's express consent. Since Nepal did not have its own foreign exchange account and any foreign exchange earnings made by Nepal through third country trade would go to the Reserve Bank of India, Nepali merchants had to apply for import licences and foreign exchange to Indian authorities.

The Congress government successfully negotiated the 1960 Trade Treaty with India convincing the latter to remove the unreasonable features of the 1950 treaty. Although some provisions of the new treaty were not still fully aligned to Nepali commercial interests, this treaty was widely acclaimed as one of the most significant achievements of the Congress government.[29] The treaty provided for mutual duty-free and license-free access to respective markets of either country for the goods originating in either country for the consumption in the territory of the other. Nepal's disadvantages particularly due to lack of access to ports and relatively low level of economic development was taken into consideration. India even made a unilateral commitment to open up its market for Nepali commodities free of duties and quantitative restrictions. On the other hand, Nepal was allowed to levy revenue and protective duties or impose quantitative restrictions.[30] Under the earlier treaty signed by Mohan Shamsher, Nepal was obliged to impose the tariff on imports and exports at the same rate as India. By subjecting Nepal's trade interest to Indian jurisdiction, this provision had hampered Nepal's expansion of trade with the outside world.

The new treaty also recognized Nepal's right to maintain its own foreign exchange account and pursue an independent trade policy. Another important feature of the treaty was that Nepal got transit rights from India to conduct trade relations with third countries without making any distinction with regard to the flag of vessels, the places of origin, departure, entry, exit, destination and ownership. The transit traffic was exempted from all customs, transit or any other duties.

The Gandak Project

The most controversial decision of the elected government was the signing of the Gandak Project Agreement. The project had been agreed in principle long before the Congress came into power but none of the prior governments had mustered enough courage to sign it in view of the potential political risk. Furthermore, the earlier postponement was also due to the fact that the Nepal side was trying to extract as much benefit as possible in terms of power supply and irrigation benefits from the project. The project was a multi-purpose hydroelectric dam, which would irrigate 3.7 million acres of land and generate 20 megawatts of power. It would be completed in a period of ten years with an estimated cost of 500 million Indian rupees. Under the signed agreement, Nepal would obtain irrigation water for 150,000 acres of land free of cost which was considerably higher than the figure of 50,000 acres offered earlier in 1957. Nepal would also receive 10 megawatts of power. The rest of the benefits would go to India who also bore all the capital cost of the venture.

The controversial aspect of the project was the construction of a barrage and one of the two power houses in Nepali territory. This was interpreted by the government critics as a 'sell out' of national sovereignty and rights and also 'bartering away' of Nepal's future to India. The government, however, defended the agreement arguing that India would have constructed the dam in its own territory if Nepal had not given the permission. This would have deprived Nepal of the benefits that were made available under the agreement. Under the circumstances, the only sensible thing Nepal could do was to extract maximum benefits from the project in terms of irrigation and the power supply, which it did.

PROGRESSIVE AGENDA, OPPOSITION AND TAKEOVER

The representatives of the Nepali Congress had pressed for the abolition of the *Birta* system in the Rana–Congress coalition government in 1951. Consequently the *Birta* abolition had been accepted in principle. It had not been, however, translated into a legislation by subsequent governments. The onus of overthrowing this deeply rooted land tenure system ultimately fell on the Congress government The Party had received an overwhelming electoral mandate to abolish the old feudal order. The bill for the abolition of the *Birta* system was approved by the House of Representatives within four months of the Party's coming to power and the bill became law on 7 October 1959. This measure converted all *Birta* land into the *Raikar*, and the registered tenants into owners. In May 1960, the NC Government announced the abolition of the *Rajya* Courts and integrated their functions to the existing regional courts. The prevailing *Rajya* practices allowed the feudal hereditary rulers in a few principalities in western Nepal a semi-autonomous status in matters of dispensation of justice and maintenance of law and order. Some other measures undertaken by the first elected Government included the nationalization of the forests previously under private ownership, and the reorganization of the administration along scientific lines.

Predictably, these bold progressive measures met with stiff resistance from the groups that had a vested interest in the old order. Strong conservative elements pervaded every aspect of Nepali life, and the structure of Nepali polity itself was deplorably antiquated.[31] It was also becoming increasingly obvious that B.P. Koirala's charismatic image and his progressive and liberal ideas were making the ambitious monarch uneasy. Despite having been elected unanimously as the leader of the victorious Congress Party, B.P. Koirala's appointment as Prime Minister itself had been delayed by three weeks. The king was looking for an appropriate opportunity to strike and reclaim power. Some of the prominent political leaders who were defeated in the general election opposed the government, and sided with the king. As Mihaly writes:

> With minor exceptions, the political opposition had made no attempt to emulate the grand success of the Nepali Congress in building a nation-wide organization. This lack of support in the country, combined with the fact that virtually all the oppositions represented the interests of the small segment of Nepalese society, ensured that the opposition politicians would concentrate their energy on palace intrigue—their only avenue to power.[32]

The king and the Prime Minister were often confrontational and looked to be headed on a collision course. The tension and even combative posturing between the two sides can be sensed from some of the speeches made by the king and the Prime Minister at that time. In less than a year of the elected government, during the royal tour in Banke-Bardia, the king warned on 30 January 1960:

> ... Let all the Nepali people watch their steps in their journey ahead so that I may not be constrained to initiate other actions in discharge of my duties and responsibilities...I too have certain duties to my country, and these are: to maintain the sovereignty of the country; national integrity; improve relations with other countries and initiate actions oriented to public good. Should I feel let or hindrance along the path of my performance of these duties, I would not hesitate to take whatever step that may be necessary and whatever cost...let there be no misunderstanding on this score.[33]

Koirala, on the other hand, complained at the Nepali Congress party convention in Birgunj in May 1960 that the constitution had not given adequate power to the elected government. He had earlier asserted in a Nepalgunj public meeting that he derived his authority from the mandate of the electorate. Several organizations sprung up overnight to oppose the progressive measures of the government. One such organization was the *Jana Hit Sangha* (Union of Public Welfare) formed in April

1960 with the avowed aim of fighting the government's taxation and land reform policies. This organization became active in inciting general strikes in the three cities of Kathmandu valley demanding the repealment of the new economic measures.[34] A royalist-religious party named *Karmavir Mahamandal* led by Yogi Narahari Nath started inciting innocent people of the Gorkha region to oppose the *Birta*-liquidation scheme. This created problems in enforcing law and order in Gorkha.

The government strongly defended its radical measures arguing that they were necessary to usher in a modern era in the country. The Prime Minister felt that the disturbances and opposition were inevitable in a period of transition when new values are replacing the old ones. Evidences support the theory that the Palace itself instigated some of these protests against the Koirala government. The Gorkha incidents instigated by Yogi Narahari Nath were alleged to have links with the palace.[35] In response to a petition to the Royal Palace by the *Jan Hit Sangh* against the government's taxation and land reform measures, the Palace secretariat wrote:

> If you think that the Government you have chosen for your own welfare has acted detrimental to the welfare of the country or the countrymen, at that time every Nepali has the right to oppose the government.... His Majesty will also act for the protection and welfare of the nationality, country and the people.[36]

The statement was interpreted as the virtual incitement to the *Jana Hit Sangh* to continue the agitation, basically with the implicit objective of toppling the Nepali Congress government and reinstating the direct-rule of the King.[37] Koirala remained undeterred. Responding to the demonstration by the *Jana Hit Sangha*, Koirala declared in a public meeting on 11 December 1960:

> .... People who have been suppressed for centuries are awake. History has now taken a different turn and the country is passing through a revolution. Election manifestoes, posters, blood and fire alone do not make revolution. The country is moving towards a new situation and a new wave of awareness is pervasive...Outdated values are being replaced by new ones...some reactionaries are attempting to forestall the earth shaking changes.
>
> The economy of the country has so far depended on land alone. Now we have to discover alternative sources of employment for the establishment of a new industrial and socialist order. The product from the land is not sufficient to bring economic development. The abolition of the *Birta* system and the levying of taxes are very important aspects of our programme.

> Those who wear clean clothes, live in palatial buildings, depend on the earnings of others are opposing the taxes because the system in which they are living is coming to an end. Air, water, sunshine and land belong to those who consume them. It is the tillers who must own the land.
>
> .... The country is not the same it was before. A new order has come in. You have chosen this government and it is up to you now to share the responsibilities. If some persons suffer in the process of change, this is natural. Without sacrificing personal interest we cannot build the country from the resources obtained from land alone. How can we expect friendly countries to provide us assistance out of the funds raised from their taxpayers, if we ourselves remain idle? ... I want to remind the feudal elements that they should not be confused by writings on the forehead as far as land ownership is concerned[38].

King Mahendra dissolved the NC government four days after the above speech, and 18 months after it had assumed power. The Prime Minister, together with his cabinet members, party leaders and many rank and file members were arrested and imprisoned to facilitate the way for the king's direct leadership. Parliamentary democracy—a dispensation that provided: a competitive arena for different political ideologies, a government accountable to the people, and the hope for a better future for the majority of Nepalis yearning to break out of the shackles of a feudal history—was brought to an abrupt end. Joshi and Rose draw a historical parallel between Mahendra's action and that of King Rajendra Bikram Shah in 1836, when another outstanding figure had met with similar fate:

> Fundamentally, the December coup represented an authoritarian resolution of the basic conflict between two antithetical by-products of 1950 revolution. Historically, the nearest, parallel to King Mahendra's action was the arrest of Prime Minister Bhimshen Thapa in 1936 by King Rajendra on specious charges, later recanted by the King himself, of disloyalty to the royal family. Those were the days of conspiratorial politics, and vicissitudes in political fortunes were sometimes expressed through poisonings, hired assassins, bloody massacres, and dark dungeons. In 1960 the participants were different, and the political methods and vocabulary were modern, but the basic spirit and idiom of Nepali Court politics remain unchanged.[39]

The experiment with the decade-long democracy came to an end. While the parties wasted initial years by forming unstable coalitions and jockeying for power, the king played a series of deft hands manipulating the situation to create a wider space for his own political role. The first general election of 1959 brought the Nepali Congress to power with a charismatic leader with a clear vision for the country's future at its helm. The elected government under an enlightened leadership started radical reforms to bring about socio-economic transformation in a traditionally agrarian society. They articulated a clear strategy to redress some of the age-old social inequities and economic injustices prevalent in Nepali society and went about implementing them. But the ambitious monarch, with the army under his control, was getting increasingly uncomfortable with the personal popularity of the Prime Minister. He had sweeping authority in a constitution written under his own directive to dismiss the government. But the toiling masses, for whose welfare and emancipation the Government had made efforts, were too ignorant and not conscious enough politically to resist and revolt against the king's retrogressive action. Consequently an era of authoritarian rule that was to last for another three decades was ushered.

NOTES

1. The British Ambassador in his annual political report for 1952 wrote, "much of the popularity he had gained as a champion of people's rights had been affected by his subservience to India". Quoted from Shaha (1996), vol.2.p. 282.
2. Shaha, ibid, p. 320.
3. Eugene Bramer Mihaly, *Foreign Aid and Politics in Nepal,* 2002, p. 29, Kathmandu: Himal Books., quoted from D.R. Regmi, *Whither Nepal* (1952), Kathamndu.
4. Joshi and Rose, p. 172.
5. Joshi and Rose, *Democratic Innovations in Nepal,* Berkeley: University of California Press., 1966, p. 160.
6. Ibid, p. 232
7. *Nepal Gazette*, 3 February 1952.
8. Mihaly op. cit. pp. 31–33.
9. Ibid : 48.
10. Ibid, Chapter VIII.
11. Naresh Man Singh, *Nepal's First Five Year Plan,* Kathmandu: Nepal Council of Asian Relations and World Affairs, 1957, p. 23.
12. The shares of other sectors were agriculture 21 per cent, irrigation and power 15.2 per cent, industry and mining 7.6 per cent, social services 13.3 per cent, survey and statistics 4.2 per cent and the Rapti Valley Project 4.2 per cent.
13. Mihaly op. cit., p. 78.
14. B.B.Thapa, *Planning For Development in Nepal: A Perspective for 1965-80,* California: Claremont Graduate School, 1967, p. 115.
15. Mihaly, p. 78.
16. Joshi and Rose, p. 234.
17. Shrestha, *The Economy of Nepal,* 1981, p. 175.
18. Ibid, p. 178.
19. Through massive sales of the Indian rupees for the Nepalese rupees, the

Government succeeded in lowering the exchange rate from NR.152 in 1956 to 138 in 1957 for IR 100.But the rate shot back to NR 159 in 1958. Ibid, pp. 175–178.

20. Shrestha, p. 182.
21. Joshi and Rose, p. 307.
22. Ibid, p. 348.
23. Ludwig Stiller and Ram Prakash Yadav, *Planning For People,* Kathmandu: Sahayogi Prakashan., 1979, p. 88.
24. Ibid: 189.
25. Joshi and Rose, p. 350.
26. Hem Narayan Agrawal, *The Administrative System of Nepal,* New Delhi: Vikas Publishing House, 1976, p. 248.
27. Joshi and Rose, p. 349.
28. Shrestha (1981), p. 179.
29. Joshi and Rose, pp. 352–353.
30. Narottam Baskota, *Nepal India Trade and Economic Relations*, Delhi: B.R. Publishing House, 1981, p. 37.
31. Mihaly, op.cit. p. 121.
32. Ibid.
33. Nath, p. 200.
34. Joshi and Rose, p. 338.
35. It was alleged that the Yogi had received Rs. 25,000 from the Palace for the purpose. See, Sanu Bhai Dangol, *Palace In Nepalese Politics*, Kathmandu: Ratna Pustak Bhandar, 1999, p. 80.
36. Ibid, pp. 83–84.
37. Joshi and Rose, p. 383.
38. Translated from B.P's speech.
39. Joshi and Rose, p. 396.

Chapter Four

Panchayat, Politics and Economy

The royal takeover of 1960 was an imminent outcome of a system that, according to some political analysts, suffered from the dichotomy between an elected Prime Minister with popular mandate, and the monarch with sweeping power. It was a royal coup staged for rewriting history that put the monarchy at the centre stage of Nepali politics.[1] Political parties were outlawed and all prominent political figures, including the Prime Minister were put behind bars. Civil liberties were curtailed and press freedom muzzled. In order to place close allies in key positions and to purge those whose loyalty was suspect, massive reorganization of administrative machinery was announced.

In dismissing the Koirala government and dissolving both Houses of Parliament and assuming emergency powers, King Mahendra gave a litany of 'sins' committed by the democratic government. The allegations included—abuse of power, failure to maintain law and order, inefficiency, bribery and corruption, lack of mutual trust among ministers, failure to properly utilize foreign aid, poor planning based on crude theories and failure to achieve development targets. The king's action was defended to preserve the "country's unity, national integrity and sovereignty". The king declared that the country was in imminent danger and the nation's future was threatened. None of the charges were, however, substantiated. Nor was there any explanation as to why the whole parliamentary constitution and the accompanying political process had to be sacrificed, even if the allegations against the short-lived government in power were true.

THE 'CLIMATE AND SOIL' THEORY

King Mahendra, through an "exercise of the sovereign powers and prerogatives inherent in us (him)" promulgated a new constitution on 19 December 1962, introducing the party-less *Panchayat* polity. The direct and active leadership of the king was thus formalized. Parliamentary democracy was publicly disavowed as being 'unsuitable and alien' to the Nepali conditions. The new political system was, in the words of its proponents, suited to the "climate and soil" of the country and was consistent with the nation's tradition, culture and genius. Democracy had to be built gradually, layer by layer from the bottom upwards, it was claimed. The new political system imbibed in it some features of the constitutions of Burma, Pakistan, Yugoslavia, Indonesia, and the UAR.[2] All executive, legislative and judicial power was vested in the king, who exercised it through various organs established in the constitution. The king himself assumed the role of the Chairman of the Council of Ministers. It was in early 1963 that the king relinquished this position to handpicked Tulsi Giri.

The king invoked the monarch's traditional authority to justify the legitimacy of his action. The regime turned to the 1500-year old form of polity for philosophical justification and sought to cast the monarchy in its traditional mould.[3] The new system was considered a refurbished form of traditional polity but based on popular participation Although *panchayat* was a traditional practice of village level dispute settlement by the village elders through direct participation of the community, it was never elevated to a level of national governance. In the words of a political observer:

> In support to his climate and soil theory, King Mahendra refurbished the *Panchayats* on the model of traditional polity that basically derived its authority from the spirit of reverence for hierarchy based on caste and age in a caste ingrained society. King Mahendra's *Panchayat* was in practice a means of exploiting, under the garb of 'tutelary democracy', the age-old Nepali tradition of unquestioned obedience to autocratic authority of any kind. Even so, King Mahendra took great care to avoid the impression that his *Panchayat* system had, in practice and theory, discarded the basic tenet that power belongs to the people. He professed faith in the concept of popular sovereignty by emphasizing in public the principle of decentralization. He did not, however, make it clear whether or not decentralization implied in actual practice any gradual diminution of his royal powers and prerogatives.[4]

The new regime needed an ideology to justify and mobilize support for the takeover. King Mahendra used nationalism loaded with anti-Indian overtones as this ideology. It was also convenient since most political activists not in jail were living in India as exiles, and launching armed raids in border towns. Hence, the principal defence of the direct

Photograph 1: Supreme Leader Ganesh Man Singh addressing the historic NC convention on 5 January 1990

Photograph 2: A scene of the 1990 People's Movement

rule was to safeguard "national independence and territorial integrity under all circumstances and free the nation from unhealthy influence of anti-national elements". The rebels fighting for a multi-party system were branded 'anti-national elements'. To further arouse nationalistic sentiments, the cult of nationalism was pushed in all propaganda channels and fed to the people through mediums such as radio broadcasts, news bulletins, pamphlets and newspapers. In addition to territorial integrity and monarchical authority, the concept of nationalism was subsequently extended to span language and dress.

The regime also exploited the religious sentiments inside and outside the country, particularly India, where the Nepali monarch is venerated as the only *Hindu* king in the globe. The orthodox religious *Hindus* were apprehensive of the secular and socialist tilt of the Koirala government. The new Panchayat constitution declared Nepal an "independent, indivisible, and sovereign monarchical *Hindu* state". It was different from the 1959 Constitution, which only called Nepal as a country with a *Hindu* king.

Traditional conservatives, religious forces, feudal lords, bureaucrats, the army, and the police represented the main support pillars of the *Panchayat* system. The king also relied on the support of the landowning class and the commercial interest groups who were opposed to the progressive land policy and the taxation proposal of the Congress government. The most important source of the king's support and power, however, was the army. King Mahendra, in his capacity as the Supreme Commander-in-Chief, carefully and consistently ensured the loyalty of the army through direct exercise of authority and control over matters of appointments and control of officer corps. Some tactics pursued by the king to consolidate his political authority and weaken the base of the outlawed political parties included: consolidation of state apparatus under firm control, direct contact with the masses, repression and fragmentation of opposition forces led by political parties, mobilization of communist forces for countering the Nepali Congress activities, and the stationing of Royal Nepal Army along the Indian borders.[5]

Despite its professed emphasis on popular sovereignty and local participation, the *Panchayat* system was a centralized political system opposed to political pluralism and dispersion of power. The existence of the requisite paraphernalia of a modern state including the legislature, judiciary, civil service, and the public service commission notwithstanding, all political and executive powers were concentrated with the monarch. The Palace secretariat acted as the nerve centre of all administrative and political authority. Particularly under King

Birendra, the palace secretaries were empowered to supervise the functions of even ministers and their respective ministries. The ministers and government secretaries were often made to clarify even the most trivial matters before the Palace secretariat. The government practically became an agent to carry out and execute the commands of Palace secretaries than the wishes of the people.[6]

The Secretariat was formally armed with institutions like *Jaanch Bujh Kendra* (the Enquiry and Inspection Centre) commanding jurisdiction over all state institutions, and dictating policies and instructions to the government. The *Kendra* was established initially to look into development issues and prepare reports. Later on, it assumed the role of the investigative arm of the palace; it could investigate and analyze issues relating to anything and anyone, from developmental issues and administrative questions to charges of corruption and personal pleas for royal justice.

ADVANTAGES TO THE REGIME

The post-1960 regime enjoyed a number of comparative advantages over previous governments in pushing forward the economic development agenda for the country. The period was marked by a long period of political stability—devoid not only of power takeovers, coup d'etats, and insurgencies, but also of inter-party squabbling and parliamentary horse-trading. Almost all political leaders and actors in the opposition were either imprisoned or in exile. Whoever remained in politics had unquestioned loyalty to the king's new polity. Therefore, domestic and foreign investors were not exposed to the dangers of life and property typical in countries prone to political instability. As the Prime Minister and cabinet were accountable only to the Crown for their performance, they did not have to worry about the public criticisms and needlessly succumb to economically untenable populist demands. They now had the opportunity to concentrate on, and single-mindedly pursue the country's development and growth agenda.

Following a number of reform measures debated and introduced since 1951, a strong public opinion had also been created among the intelligentsia and the political elite of the country in favour of reforming the country's land relations and social order. The country was psychologically more prepared to absorb major socio-economic reforms. Moreover, since political dissent was now muzzled and any opposition to progressive reforms would have meant a direct confrontation with the royal regime, the conservative elements offered less resistance.

In addition, a number of economic and political institutions, already established during the decade of 1950s, could now play meaningful roles in the process of the country's modernization. These included the Nepal Rastra Bank, Nepal Industrial Development Corporation, the National Planning Commission, the Supreme Court, the Public Service Commission, the Royal Nepal Airlines Corporation, and the District Development Boards. The system of annual budgets and medium-term development planning had also been already introduced.

Understandably, there was an initial setback to the civil administration after the Royal takeover. A good number of able and dedicated civil servants became the victims of the Royal purge. As Mihaly pointed out:

> ... the new situation presented formidable administrative problems to the mission... In the chaos and suspicion that followed in the wake of the take-over, a significant number of most skilled and highly-trained officials (especially American- trained) were dismissed. The leading men in agriculture and planning, to name just two vital fields, were banished from the civil service. The purge went far down the line. By the time the new government was constituted, the coup had wrecked havoc in the administration. The delicate fabric of elementary administrative competency which had been painstakingly created by time and experience and with foreign assistance, mainly American, was ripped to shreds.[7]

However, this setback was temporary. The period following the 1950 revolution including the brief period of elected government witnessed the slow but definite building-up of civil service institutions and the administration system geared towards the developmental needs of the country. A reformed, and considerably strengthened bureaucracy had been built up. The following paragraph sums up the achievements in democratizing the administrative system of Nepal during 1951–60:

> The Nepalese administration did respond to the new situational compulsions and imperative of socio-economic planning. The administrative reforms during 1951–60 in the midst of political instability and ministerial changes, set up new structures and discarded many old ones at the central level more than at district level...new dimensions of developmental administration were added to the district and local administration after the revolution. The chasm between the rulers and the ruled, which existed till 1950–51, was bridged during 1951–60 by appointing commoners as prime ministers and other ministers and associating people with the process of government at the different levels in various capacities.[8]

Departing radically from the predominantly administrative role of a feudal mould under the Ranas, the bureaucracy had gradually expanded both in number and quality to assume its new developmental role. The total number of civil servants had increased from 18,853 in 1952–53 to 31,104 in 1958–59. It expanded further during the 1959–61 period.[9] The increased size of the civil service was accompanied by training in new jobs and skills to keep abreast of the emerging developmental needs. During a period of 8 years between 1954 and 1961 alone, 12 permanent training institutes were established to develop lower and middle level skills. A total of 6,351 persons were trained in these institutes. In addition, 2,163 persons were sent abroad for higher education and advanced training on scholarships supported under bilateral and multilateral schemes. The fields covered included general education, agriculture, forestry, engineering, health, administration, industry and mining.[10]

Achievements had been made in the fifties in creating some socio-economic infra-structure for the country. As of 1961, the total number of primary schools had risen to over 4,000 and the enrollment to 200,000. There were more than 500 secondary schools and 32 colleges. The Tribhuvan University, which remained the only university offering modern education for a long period, was established during this period. The literacy rate was 9 per cent in 1961. A total of 6,800 villages covering 22.5 per cent of the population were brought under village development programmes. A total of 790 kilometres of road, which included the Kathmandu–Raxaul highway, was constructed during the First Plan period. The ropeway between Kathmandu and Hetauda was nearing completion. Three industrial districts and twenty-one cottage industries centres were established representing some spadework to promote new industries. The total number of industrial firms registered up to 1961 stood at 459. Some progress had also been made in the fields of telecommunications, postal services, power supply, irrigation facilities and health services (Table 4.3).

The country did not suffer from any shortage of resources for economic development in relation to its absorptive capacity. A large number of donors, representing both the Western and Eastern blocks, had initiated their operations in Nepal in the 1950s and the flow of resources from them remained by and large unaffected by the royal take-over. The take-over created initial setback in the USAID programme. This led to the temporary curtailment of activities, and realignment of programmes. But subsequently, USAID deepened its commitment to the new regime. This was based on the US perception that the alternative scenario of not providing economic assistance to the Royal government could be worse and the new government's economic priorities were along the lines of the American programme.[11]

India had openly expressed its displeasure at the royal takeover through Jawaharlal Nehru's famous "reversal of democratic process" statement. But even Indians reconciled themselves with the new situation. India went ahead with business as usual as far as the development assistance was concerned. A series of agreements were signed with India in 1962 broadening the scope of Indian assistance to cover such fields as forestry, mineral development, local development, maternity care, irrigation and drinking water supplies. And for many years to follow, India remained the single largest donor to Nepal. Assistance from other bilateral donors also continued to expand. From the 1970s, international development banks such as the World Bank and Asian Development Bank emerged as major sources of assistance.

PLANS AND PRIORITIES

Due to the confusion following the political change, the Second Plan started only in July 1962—one full year after the completion of the First Plan. The plan-gap period was "devoted more to correction action including collecting statistical data and other information and the preparation of Second Plan."[12] A total of Rs. 86 million had been spent as development expenditure in that year. Unlike the First Plan, which was a five year plan, the Second Plan took the form of a three-year plan. It was preparatory in nature and intended to establish "the pre-requisites for the introduction and smooth execution at some future date of a more comprehensive Plan". Four other development plans were executed since the completion of the Second Plan. The Seventh Plan was in the last year of execution in 1990 when the *Panchayat* era came to an end. The planned and actual expenditure by sectors under the various plans are summarized in Table 4.1.

Broadly speaking and in general, Nepali plans have met their expenditure targets. The Second Plan met the expenditure target by 92 per cent. The actual expenditure under the Third Plan was 96 per cent of the target. Under the Fourth and the Fifth Plans, the actual expenditures exceeded the targets by 16 and 44 per cent respectively. It was only in the Sixth Plan that the investment shortfall to the extent of 28 per cent was recorded. This was at constant price. The expenditure in current prices had actually exceeded the target. Despite this apparent success in meeting the expenditure targets, almost all development plans in Nepal were characterized by significant gaps between financial targets and achievements in physical terms.

Let us now review some of the objectives and priorities of the development plans during the three decades of planning under the *Panchayat* era.

Increase in National Production

All developments plan emphasized the increase in national production as one of their principal objectives. The Second Plan stressed the objective of providing for the needs of a growing population. The Third Plan was a part of the Perspective Plan that aimed at doubling the national income in fifteen years. This target was considered feasible "on the basis of the experience of other developing nations".[13] The income growth target set for the Third Plan was 19 per cent, which, assuming an annual population growth of 2 per cent would generate a 9 per cent increase in the per capita income over the Plan period. The Fourth Plan added a 'public welfare' dimension to the government strategy in attaining the production maximization goal of the plan. The Plan identified 'low productivity' as the root cause of poverty[14] and proposed a target of four per cent GDP growth per annum. The Sixth Plan also stressed "the maximization of output objective" with a proviso that output should conform to the basic needs of common people. The emphasis on higher growth rate in production was reiterated in the objectives of Sixth and Seventh Plans as well. Under all plans, agriculture was slated to play the lead role in attaining the objectives. Similarly, emphasis was also placed on industrial growth with a focus on consumer goods and construction materials, conservation and utilization of forest resources, and the exploitation of hydro potential.

Expansion of Productive Employment

Although the language and the extent of emphasis might have differed from one plan to another, employment growth was a theme common to all of these plans. The Second Plan stressed the need for creating employment opportunities, particularly in the non-agricultural sector, through labour intensive projects. The Fourth Plan underscored effective utilization of manpower resources and population control and the diversification national economy to transfer surplus manpower on a large scale from agriculture to non-agricultural sectors. The Fifth Plan considered "maximum utilization of manpower" in the actual process of production to raise the purchasing power as one of its twin basic objectives. The Sixth and the Seventh Plans also reiterated the "increase in productive employment opportunities" as one of their

TABLE 4.1

Planned Outlay and Actual Public Expenditure under Various Plans

(Rs. in million)

Plans	Expenditure	Agriculture, Irrig. & Forestry	Industry and Mining*	Transport & Communication	Social Service	Others	Total
2nd	Planned	117	152	235	103	63	670
	Actual	98	109	224	97	88	616
	(A) as % of (P)	83.8	71.7	95.3	94.2	139.7	91.9
3rd	Planned	377	125	875	293	70	1740
	Actual	349	83	806	228	178	1644
	(A) as % of (P)	92.6	66.4	92.1	77.8	254.3	94.5
4th	Planned	663	470	1050	352	35	2570
	Actual	642	449	1236	600	56	2983
	(A) as % of (P)	96.8	95.5	117.7	170.5	106.0	116.1
5th	Planned+	1840	1380	1433	1517	—	6170
	Actual	2350	1679	2381	2461	—	8871
	(A) as % of (P)	127.7	121.7	166.2	162.2	—	143.8
6th	Planned	6600	5600	4230	5160	160	21750
	Actual	4353	3380	3009	4437	404	15583
	(A) as % of (P)	65.9	60.4	71.1	86.0	252.5	71.6
7th	Planned	8876	7547	5132	7330	115	29000
	Actual	11487	2673	13539	12057	3580	43336
	(A) as % of (P)	129.4	35.4	263.8	164.5	311.3	149.43

* Includes electricity also since the Fourth Plan.

Note: Plan figures are not strictly comparable. Up to the Third Plan, the figures are at current market prices and figures thereafter at the constant prices of the base year of corresponding Plans.

Sources: HMG, Various Plan Documents, NPC and the *Economic Surveys*, MOF, HMG/N.

planning goals. Accelerating agricultural growth, adopting labour intensive industrial development policy, and giving priority to agro and allied, industrial and cottage industry products for export promotion were some of their priorities.

Social Justice and Meeting Basic Needs

Earlier plans up to the Fourth Plan had consistently stressed social justice as an important development objective. Equitable distribution of the national produce and income were considered important as the establishment of a "progressive welfare state" and "an exploitation-free society" were among the buzzwords of the 1960s and early 1970s. These priorities were reflected adequately in the development plans. Accordingly, some of the most progressive social measures under the *Panchayat* system were initiated during these years. The land reform legislation was enacted in 1964 to redistribute land and improve the conditions of the peasantry. *The Mulki Ain* (Civil Code) was amended during this period with the express objective of eliminating individual distinctions based on caste and religious considerations.

From the Fifth Plan onwards, there was a subtle shift in Nepal's development policy paradigm. From administering "social justice" to foster an "exploitation-free society", the priorities shifted to meeting the "minimum-felt needs" and "minimum basic needs" of the people. The Sixth Plan identified food, fuel wood, drinking water, health and sanitation facilities, primary, vocational and adult education and minimum transport facilities (mule trails, suspension and wooden bridges) as the basic minimum needs and proposed to channel investment to provide for these needs. Adding clothing as another basic need of the people, the Seventh Plan gave continuity to this approach. These "basic needs" objectives were envisioned to be met through prioritized development of agriculture, forestry and soil conservation, water resources, industries, tourism and population control.

Basis for Sustained Long-term Growth

The creation of physical infrastructure to provide the foundation for sustained economic growth was the main priority until the Fourth Plan. This was felt necessary because the country utterly lacked modern physical infrastructure. The desire for faster economic growth in the face of the imperative of developing its infrastructural pre-requisites created a dilemma for the Nepali planners. For example, agricultural development was accorded the highest priority in the Third Plan, but when it came to public sector investment the largest share (50.3 per cent) was channelled to transportation, communications and power.

Agriculture and village development sector received only 21.7 per cent. This share rose to 33 per cent in the Fourth Plan but the transport and communications sectors continued to receive the largest share. The Fourth Plan attempted to reconcile this difficult trade off between focusing on income generation at present, on the one hand, and laying down the necessary groundwork for income growth in the future on the other. It said, "while selecting projects and programmes for investment, effort has been made to strike a balance between the two objectives: to increase per capita income by immediate increase in production and to build necessary base for long-term growth".[15] It was only since the Fifth Plan that the share of public investment in infrastructure started to decline and the higher priority to productive sectors in resource allocation was firmly established. The budgeted spending on infrastructure development declined to 28 per cent in the Fifth Plan, while agriculture received 30 per cent. This trend accelerated under Sixth and Seventh Plans.

Economic Stability

Earlier development plans, particularly the Second and the Third, were acutely concerned with the adverse effects exchange volatility and rising prices would have on the cost calculations of proposed projects and programmes. Policy makers placed a great deal of emphasis particularly on stabilizing the prices of construction materials and daily necessities. The Fourth Plan viewed "economic stability" in a slightly broader sense. It was not just the stability of prices and exchange rates, it also recognized that erratic and frequent changes in economic policies adversely affected the planning process. When low growth rate and macroeconomic imbalances threatened to push Nepal into serious economic crisis in the mid-eighties, the government requested for a Standby Arrangement Loan from the International Monetary Fund to stabilize the economy. Further economic reforms and adjustments were also facilitated by the Structural Adjustment Credit from the World Bank from 1987 onwards. The previously conservative economic and fiscal policy was abandoned in favour of relatively liberal and expansionary economic policy. A 15 per cent devaluation in the exchange rate to correct for external imbalances, structural reforms to liberalize the import regime, the introduction of duty drawback and bonded warehouse schemes, and the liberalization of industrial licensing were among the measures implemented under this programme. These measures were expected to relieve constraints on long-term economic growth.

Balanced Regional Development

The need for regional approach in planning based on the resource availability and development potential of specific regions was highlighted as one of the development policies in the Third Plan. But a systematic regional development policy based on the concept of growth centers was introduced only in the Fourth Plan. A series of North–South growth axes linking the three ecological regions of the country were identified and development programmes in the axes were proposed. The Plan said the juxtaposition of a wide range of resources (the *tarai*, the hills and mountains) within a common development corridor would permit economic viability, and generate greater inter-regional circulation of goods, services and people. Comprehensive development programmes along the four growth axes, namely, Koshi (Biratnagar to Hedangma), Gandaki (Bhairawaha to Jomsom), Karnali (Nepalganj to Jumla) and Kathmandu (Birgunj to Dhunche/Barabise) were planned. The country was subsequently divided into four Development Regions with designated centres for development activities. Later on, the Far-Western Region was subdivided into Mid-Western and Far-Western, bringing the total number to five. The Fifth Plan made the regional approach its integral part and emphasized on specialization of various ecological zones, based on their comparative advantages. The North-South road link in each axis was expected to act as catalyst. The livestock production in the northern region, horticulture in the hills, and food grains and other crops in the *tarai* was regarded as the most rational approach of leveraging maximum benefit out of the country's eco-agricultural endowments. It was expected that the set of growth poles along the arterial link would induce further growth in terms of agricultural transportation, location of industries, trade activities and social services.[16]

However, this landmark concept in the Nepali planning history seemed de-emphasized in the Sixth Plan in favour of target-oriented and specific area development strategies such as the Small Area Development Programme, Integrated Rural Development, and Small Farmers Development Programme. This new approach reflected the influence of donor community and the international institutions such as the World Bank and FAO. The Fifth Plan had allocated investment by development regions—73 per cent of the Plan outlay was classified by development regions in various sectors. The remaining 27 per cent was left for projects of national importance or those which did not lend themselves to classification by region. No systematic evaluation was made regarding the actual investment by region. In its brief remark, the Sixth Plan said that in the first two years of the Fifth Plan, only 6.2 per cent of the development expenditure against the target of 16.5 per cent was expended in the Far-Western Region.

SLOGANS AND THEMES

There was no dearth of catchy themes and slogans under the Panchayat system. In the early years of the regime, land reform programmes were introduced with provisions such as: fixation of land ceiling, guarantee of tenancy rights, the compulsory savings scheme, and fixation of maximum interest on agricultural loans. But the actual implementation of the programme in a feudal society and by a government supported by traditional landed class was far short of being satisfactory. The primary constraints were the absence of accurate land measurements and numerous other built-in loop holes. Big landlords were successfully able to transfer large tracts of land either under 'industrial use' (to benefit from the liberal ceiling provision for land under industrial use) or hide them in the name of their relatives and confidants. The actual surplus land available for redistribution was too little, and qualitatively too poor, to be of any use and interest even to the landless. Furthermore, there was widespread misuse and misappropriation of the compulsory savings deposits by its managers and officials.

The East–West Highway was another high-profile development scheme proposed with internal resources. This was a crucial project as the country lacked basic road to link one part of the country with another, forcing people to use the Indian territory even for purely internal travels. However, the project proved to be a non-starter until generous bilateral and multilateral assistance started flowing. Even three decades after its initiation, the remote Far-Western region had not been fully connected in 1990. Moreover, the immediate as well as long-term effects of a project of such magnitude were not taken into full consideration in the design and alignments of the highway. Consequently, the *tarai* region had to bear the brunt of numerous natural as well as man-made disasters like floods and droughts due to excessive migration and unplanned and haphazard human settlements that came at the heels of this project. The regions of *Churia* and the *Charkose Jhadi*, once acclaimed as the treasure house of forest resources, bore a big brunt of this degradation. The rehabilitation of the environment in view of the magnitude of degradation that has occurred has become a momentous task for the country.[17]

In the same vein, the Go-Back-to-the-Village National Campaign

(GBVNC) was launched with a view to promote the village-oriented philosophy of the *Panchayat* regime. Every individual, including political functionaries, was required to contribute a certain number of days of labour annually towards the creation of rural infrastructure. A massive amount of manpower was mobilized in building much-needed rural roads and other social capital. But, in the absence of proper planning, design and back-up support, these social assets proved to be ill-conceived temporary projects which could not be sustained for long-term use. Notwithstanding some of these weaknesses, what was more unfortunate was that a movement that had the potential of becoming a genuinely people oriented development campaign degenerated into a mechanism for evaluating Panchayat workers for elective posts.

A New National Education Plan was also launched in 1972 to link education with the emerging human resource needs and priorities of the nation and to maintain a balance between the skills demanded and supplied in the labour market. However, it turned out to be an attempt to control education and produce manpower loyal to the *Panchayat* regime. The scheme proved to be a national disaster. Educational institutions managed and run with genuine community efforts were nationalized, and brought under government management and budget. The secular decline in the quality of education was accompanied by the skyrocketing of government expenditure on schools. Local participation and private initiative in education came to a virtual halt. The experience was too costly and disastrous for the nation to bear for too long and therefore had to be abandoned in most respects.

Achieving a living standard comparable to the Asian norm was another slogan forwarded by the regime in one of the royal addresses to the nation. There was no such thing as an Asian norm in view of the income diversity among Asian countries. The idea of a "norm" itself being a dynamic concept, even if there were one, the slogan evoked predominantly critical reactions from the intelligentsia. The theme was ultimately given up in favour of a more benign and humane 'Basic Needs' approach. The Basic Needs programme, which became the principal slogan and priority of the Seventh Plan, proposed to fulfill the basic minimum needs of the people including food grains, clothing, shelter, health, education, and public security. The approach emphasized supply side interventions paying little or no attention to the income side demand creation. Ambitious targets—unthinkable in historical perspective—further set the performance bar high for this programme. In the analysis of an economist:

> The Basic Needs Programme, though politically motivated, was at least helpful to realize the role of income pattern in alleviating poverty.... One of the main strategies of the Basic Needs Program was to raise the share of poor people in total disposable income from 12.5 per cent in 1984/5 to 23.0 per cent in 2000 A.D. No detail programs, however, were developed to translate the desired objectives into action—a traditional procedure of the Nepalese planning system. On the contrary.... emphasis was given to develop "administrative organization and other system to create needed infrastructural facilities" to increase the share of the poor people in total national income in the eighth and ninth plan periods.
>
> The income policy of Basic Needs Program raised more questions than it has tried to answer.... The per capita income of absolute poor by 2000 A D., if the Basic Needs Program is to be implemented in the form as it was originally designed, will be Rs.2, 212, about 12 per cent lower than average per capita income of 1984\85.... As a result, the disparity in income in absolute term between the absolute poor and others will increase further by Rs. 3,240 in the fifteen-year period between 1985 and 2000 A.D. Thus, the basic needs program has a definite and clear bias against the poor, though it was initiated to help the poor.[18]

The Panchayat regime also professed other catchy slogans, such as, the goal of an "exploitation-free society", "class coordination" and decentralization. It was probably to counter the Marxist theory of class struggle gaining currency in many developing countries including Nepal, that the *Panchayat* ideologues invented the theory of "class coordination". Various class organizations representing peasants, labour, women, youth, and ex-servicemen were formed and given seats in the *Rastriya Panchayat,* the national legislature. These class organizations, however, were not based on real grassroots demand and articulating and fighting for genuine class interests of the constituencies they represented were the least of the leader's concerns. They were rather sponsored by the political establishment to promote loyal leadership masquerading as class representatives.

Decentralization of administration was promised in the very preamble of the 1962 constitution. A four-tier *Panchayat* political structure was created, with some 4,500 odd Village *Panchayats* at the base level, 75 District *Panchayats*, and 14 Zonal *Panchayats*, with the *Rastriya Panchayat* at the apex. Subsequently, Zonal *Panchayats* were removed. However, the positions of Zonal Commissioners remained. Their main responsibility was to deal with political opposition in their respective Zones. The posts of *Bada Hakims* were replaced by Chief District Officers who, as functionaries of the central government, also acted as member-secretary of the District *Panchayats*. They wielded substantial powers at the local level and exercised administrative control over elected functionaries. What was centralization in effect was termed decentralization of authority for the purpose of public consumption? In fact, the Constitution itself ensured centralization of authority in the Crown with the exception of some trivial and non-essential subjects.[19]

DEVELOPMENT PERFORMANCE

Growth and General Performance

Basic data on economic growth since 1964/65 has been presented in Table 4.2. The Nepali economy grew at an annual rate of 12.4 per cent at current prices during the 26-year period since 1964/65. When adjusted for inflation, the annual growth comes to 3.9 per cent. The performance was, however, not uniform over time. The annual growth rate in GDP in the latter half of the sixties was only 2.6 per cent against the population growth rate of 2.1 per cent resulting in only a marginal increase in per capita GDP from Rs. 2192 in 1964/65 to Rs. 2205 in 1970/71 at 1984/85 prices over the period of five years. The annual growth rate rose to 4 per cent in the 1970s against the population growth rate of 2.1 per cent, resulting a net rise in per capita GDP which reached Rs. 2523 per annum in 1980/81.

TABLE 4.2
Trends of GDP and Per Capita GDP in Nepal (1964/65–1990/91)

Year	*GDP at Current Prices (Rs million)*	*GDP at Constant Prices (Rs million)*	*Per Capita GDP (in Rs.)*
1964/65	5602	22381	2192
1970/71	8938	25493	2205
1980/81	27307	37895	2523
1990/91	116127	59768	3232
Growth rate %			
1965 to 1971	9.79	2.64	0.12
1971–1981	11.82	4.04	1.36
1981–1991	15.58	4.66	2.51
Overall Growth Rate			
(1965 to 1991) in %	12.37	3.85	1.50

Note: GDP figures for constant prices series are at 1984/85 prices. The conversion into 1984/85 series has been made by using GDP deflators.

Source: CBS Publications and Economic Surveys for different years, Ministry of Finance, HMG/N.

In the following decade, annual growth rate increased to 4.7 per cent resulting in the growth of per capita GDP by an average annual rate of 2.51 per cent. The World Bank's estimate is that the annual growth of real per capita GDP was 0.8 per cent during the seventies, while it rose to an average of 2.2 per cent in the eighties.[20] The following paragraphs, giving an assessment of the economic performance of two decades since 1965, have been reproduced from its recent report :

> ...between 1965 and 1985, the first two decades for which data are available, per capita economic growth was stagnant at round 0.6% more or less mirroring the economic growth the economic growth rate of India but with the additional burden of Nepal's rising population growth rate and without the fruits of the Green revolution that India enjoyed. With a significantly appreciated real effective exchange rate in the first half of the 1980s, economic growth was heavily concentrated in the non-tradable activities, mainly in construction and restaurants and hotels. Further suppressed interest rates and overvalued exchange rates led to capital-intensive production and employment growth was too slow to match the growth of people entering the labor force.
>
> Private sector investment rates were low during this period (at 9 per cent of GDP) and the economy remained closed and undiversified with agriculture accounting for close to 60 per cent of GDP and more than 90 per cent of employment at the end of this period—the mid 1980s. Infrastructure was very limited: the end of the decade. As recently as in 1985, 78 per cent of the working age population of above 15 years had no schooling compared to 61% and 63% in India and Bangladesh respectively. Finally excessive Government expenditures and burgeoning deficits pushed Nepal into a fiscal and external crisis in the early 1980s.[21]

The economic performance can be regarded as low, high, satisfactory, or unsatisfactory only with reference to an assumed norm or in relation to the performance of other countries under similar conditions and situations. The *Panchayat* era took some significant strides in infrastructural development and the provision of social services, compared to the situation prevailing under the Rana regime and in the 1950s. This, however, should be judged against the near total absence of developmental base in the country in the early 1950s. General concerns for such critical issues like economic development and performance, the dismantling of feudal production relations, the mobilization of development assistance and the planning process—all started in the 1950s. The process matured and picked up momentum in the sixties and the seventies.

Achievements made in the fields of transportation, communication and social services since 1961 appear impressive while compared to those achieved during a century of family autocracy. But, taking the Rana era as the basis of comparing economic performance is meaningless. Even the fifties is not the appropriate decade for comparison, as this period—of transition from family autocracy to democracy—was also characterized by extreme confusion and political instability with frequent changes in government and jockeying for power. Moreover, much of the efforts in this period were devoted towards creating institutional and administrative base for economic development.

Historically, the *Panchayat* era enjoyed a distinct advantage for undertaking economic development activities for reasons already explained. It is also worth recalling that the principal justification for the royal takeover was economic. In a radio broadcast to the nation on January 5, 1961, King Mahendra himself castigated the dissolved NC Government for poor development planning and outlook. He said:

> There was no overall planning outlook, no regard shown to existing conditions, necessary resources, technical personnel and practicability, nor were schemes properly formulated. Individual and uncoordinated projects were taken up in haste. The result was that targets could not be achieved and our limited resources were wasted. Aid received from friendly countries could not be properly utilized, as the ministries could not make the administrative machinery meet the requirements of the Plan. The present Government (the council of ministers he had appointed under his own chairmanship) will bear these defects in mind and prepare a new plan that will be practicable.[22]

In the same speech, he had justified the ban on political parties on the ground that they would create obstacles in the task of creating a favourable climate for national reconstruction. He also said that it was his wish to achieve economic development in ten or twenty years what other countries have taken centuries or so. The Fifteen Year Perspective Plan formulated by the *Panchayat* regime, of which the Third Plan was a part, had set a target of doubling the national income in fifteen years.

Table 4.3 presents some comparable data in order to assess and compare the physical progress made in various sectors in periods before and after 1961. Surprisingly, the annual growth of physical progress was much less in almost every socio-economic category in the *Panchayat* era since 1961 in comparison to the previous period. One explanation for the better record in the decade of 1950s was that starting from near zero bases at the beginning of the decade the tempo of physical growth would appear high in the beginning and then gradually taper off. This is evident in the slackened growth since 1961 in fields ranging from primary education to road building to industrial production.

The economic performance can also be evaluated in relation to other developing countries. There were, of course, both high performers and low performers in the development scene in the postwar era. Countries and territories like South Korea, Hongkong, Taiwan, Singapore, and lately Thailand have been the star performers with an average growth rate averaging more than 7 per cent per annum during the last 3–4 decades. Performances of other countries have been less dramatic. The average growth of the countries classified as low-income economies by the World Bank was 4.9 per cent in 1965–80 and 6.1 per cent in 1980–90. The rates come down to 2.4 and 2.6 per cents respectively, if China and India are excluded from this group.

Evidently international comparisons are difficult particularly when they ignore differences between countries in economic structure, resource endowments and socio-economic characteristics and peculiarities. As Nepal is part of the South Asian region and a member of the SAARC community and most of the initial conditions and resource endowments were similar to those of other countries of this region, a comparison in the regional context may be appropriate and relevant.

Data on the growth performance of the South Asian countries is presented in Table 4.4. South Asian economies seem to have grown at an average rate of 3.3 per cent in 1965–80 and 5.3 per cent in 1980–90. During 1980–90, Bhutan seems to have recorded most impressive growth rate of 7.5 per cent, followed by Pakistan (6.3 per cent), India (5.3 per cent), Bangladesh (4.3 per cent), and Sri Lanka (4.0 per cent). Though slightly better than that of Bangladesh, Nepal's record is one of the poorest.

Comparison of Nepal's growth performance with that of India, Pakistan and Sri Lanka may not always be fair. These countries, compared to Nepal, had far more favourable initial conditions in terms of socio-economic infrastructure developed under the colonial rule. Nepal, on the other hand, started meaningful development only in the mid-fifties and with very low levels of human and capital endowments.

Despite this distinct disadvantage, Nepal had a few other opportunities not available to neighbours. Being a small and independent country, Nepal was favoured and supported with generous flow of development assistance by both the western and eastern power blocks as well as by both northern and southern neighbours. Under the *Panchayat* regime, the country enjoyed a long spell of political stability; it did not have to deal with political opposition within the country and aggression from abroad. The country performed skillful diplomacy with both power blocks, and between New Delhi and Beijing. These

TABLE 4.3
Major Physical Achievements (1951–1961–1991)

Sector	Unit	1951	1961	1991	Annual Growth Rate (%)	
					1952-61	1962-91
Agriculture						
Food grain+	In '000 MT	NA	3145	5597	—	1.02
Cash crop++	In '000 MT	NA	184	1221	—	1.06
Irrigation* +	Area in '000 ha.	62	127	3383	15.42	11.98
Industry and Power						
Processed jute*	'000 mt	13	15	18	2.55	0.63
Sugar*	MT	NA	1836	44548	—	11.62
Cigarettes*	In million sticks	NA	250	6691		12.00
Matches*	'000 boxes	120	306	1091	20.59	4.48
Electricity*	MW	1.400	9.826	231.873	21.51	11.52
Transport and Communication						
Roads*	Km	390	790	7401	15.16	1.08
Airfields	No	1	12	43	20.21	1.04
Post offices	No	100	413	2231	15.24	1.06
Telephones lines*	No	300	1420	65298	36.47	14.11
Social services						
Primary schools	No	200	4000	18681	34.93	5.46
Primary school enrolment	No in '000	9	200	3693	36.36	10.58
Secondary schools	No	224	532	2081	9.04	4.82
Colleges	No	1	32	197	41.42	6.47
Hospital beds*	No	649	1019	4798	9.44	5.49

\+ Includes only paddy, maize, wheat and millet.
++ Includes sugar cane, oil seeds, tobacco and jute.
* The base year data pertain to 1956 instead of 1951. The growth rate has been calculated accordingly. + Represents additional irrigational facilities.
@ Campuses

Sources: HMG, The Draft Five Year Plan, The Three Year Plan, The Third Plan and the Economic Surveys, HMG/N.

TABLE 4.4
Growth Performances of South Asian Countries (1965–1990)

(Average Annual Growth Rate in %)

	GDP Growth		*Per Capita GNP*	*Per Capita GNP in US$*
	1965–80	*1980–90*	*1965–90*	*1991*
Bangladesh	1.7	4.3	0.7	210
Bhutan	NA	7.5	NA	190
Nepal	1.9	4.6	0.5	170
India	3.6	5.3	1.9	350
Pakistan	5.2	6.3	2.5	380
Sri Lanka	4.0	4.0	2.9	470
Average	3.3	5.3	1.7	295

Source: The World Bank, The World Development Report, 1987 and 1992.

conditions were certainly ideal compared to other South Asian countries. Due to its vast size and socio-economic diversity, India had a formidable problem of developmental management. Additionally, it faced four major military confrontations during this period, three of which were with Pakistan. Wars with India accompanied by political instability and frequent changes between civilian and military rules in Pakistan were no less obstructive to smooth economic development. Sri Lanka's situation was much better, but the ethnic violence that started from 1981 had devastating economic consequences for the economy. Nepal faced none of these problems.

Per capita income remained generally static in Nepal. Its annual growth rate during 1965–90 period was half a per cent. The growth performance improved considerably in the eighties. A comparative review of the growth in the per capita income of South Asian countries during the period 1965–90 shows that Nepal recorded the lowest annual growth rate of 0.5 per cent, compared to Sri Lanka's 2.9 per cent, Pakistan's 2.5 per cent, India's 1.9 per cent and Bangladesh's 0.7 per cent. In 1990, Nepal's per capita income was US $170, the lowest in the Region. Nepal's per capita income was crucially affected by the country's evolving demographics. As it is, low growth of per capita income is the consequence of both inadequate macroeconomic growth process and high population growth. In the case of Nepal during this period, modest gains made by the economy in terms of economic growth was offset by the rate of growth of population.

Structure of Production

The structure of production tends to change as the process of economic development evolves and deepens; the contribution of non-agricultural sectors in total production typically increases. Economic growth is accompanied by a progressive decline in the share of agriculture with a corresponding rise in the share of manufacturing and services sector. This change in the sectoral composition of production is symptomatic of the changes in production technology, income elasticity of demand for products and input combination that accompany the process of economic growth. Income elasticity of agricultural products is low. On the other hand, the demand for goods and services produced by the non-agriculture sector tends to increase with economic growth and rising incomes. Consequently, there is not only a decline in the share of agriculture in the national production but also a shift in the labour force from agriculture to other sectors. The growth in labour productivity in agriculture will accompany these changes as a result of more efficient and productive uses of labour supported by technological improvements. Therefore, it is generally observed that the increase in agricultural productivity is accompanied by an increase in industrial production. Agricultural modernization and industrial development reinforce each other. A modernizing agriculture supports industrialization by providing its surplus labour, market for industrial products, agricultural raw materials, wage goods for industrial labour and by acting as a source of investible funds.

Data regarding the structure of production since 1964/65 set forth in Table 4.5 indicate that the production structure in Nepal and other South Asian countries has been changing in line with the historically observed pattern. The change is, however, very slow.

The share of agricultural production went down from 65 per cent to 51 per cent with corresponding growth in the share of non-agricultural sector between 1965 and 1990. A word of caution, however, is necessary here. Sectoral comparisons on the basis of time series data could meaningfully reflect the situation only if the relative prices prevailing at the latter years correspond to the base year ratios. While we have no sectoral data on prices for the whole period, available data since 1964/65 indicate that agriculture prices have lagged behind other prices. The decline in the agricultural share in the national production would, therefore, require a more cautious interpretation, which to some extent probably reflects the price changes.

There had been a sharp decline in the share of agriculture between 1965–91 in varying degrees among SAARC countries. For instance, in the case of India, the share of agriculture sector declined from 44

TABLE 4.5
Sectoral Distribution of GDP of South Asian Countries (1965–1990)

(In %.)

	*Agriculture**		*Industry***		*Services****		*Total*
	1965	*1990*	*1965*	*1990*	*1965*	*1990*	
Bangladesh	53	38	11	15	36	47	100
Bhutan	NA	44	NA	27	NA	29	100
Nepal	65	51	15	16	19	33	100
India	44	31	22	29	34	40	100
Pakistan	40	26	20	25	40	49	100
Sri Lanka	28	26	21	26	51	48	100

* Includes forestry and fishing.

** Includes mining, manufacturing, construction, electricity, water and gas.

*** Includes other sectors- transport and communications, finance and real estate sector, community and social sector.

Sources: The World Bank, *World Development Report*, 1987 and 1992. Figures for the year 1964/65 relating to Nepal were taken from the *Progress Report of the Third Plan*, Appendix. These are only crude estimates. Figures for 1990 are from the revised series.

per cent in 1965 to 31 per cent in 1990, and in Pakistan from 40 per cent to 26 per cent. These declines are more conspicuous when compared to other countries. Sri Lanka witnessed a marginal decline of two per cent from its already low share of 28 per cent in 1965. In the case of Nepal, the fall in the share of agriculture sector from 1965 level was by 14 percentage points. Still, Nepal's reliance on agriculture for national production remained the highest, reflecting the most traditional production structure among the South Asian countries. The occupational structure of Nepal's working population did not undergo major changes until 1980. The share of agricultural employment was as high as 90 per cent until then. However, the ratio declined in the eighties to reach 81 per cent in 1990.

There have also been some variations in the shares of other sectors, particularly those of manufacturing, finance and business, personnel/commercial services and others/unstated in the production structure. It is difficult to say how far the variations seen in their relative shares were due to redefinitions of various sectors and other methodological reasons. It is hard to believe that the share of industrial production in Nepal's GDP grew only by 1 per cent between 1965 and 1990. Notwithstanding this question, which may affect a few percentage points on either side, the data brings out some important aspects of the nature of production structure in Nepal—the most traditional in South Asia.

The lack of progress towards structural transformation of the economy can largely be attributed to the poor performance of agriculture itself. Industrial development on a scale that can substantially change the existing structural imbalance is fundamentally dependent upon the level of real income at which a sufficient demand for industrial products could be forthcoming. The rate of industrial development in a predominantly agricultural country like Nepal depends essentially upon the rate of increase in the average productivity per man and per acre. The relationship is in fact interdependent. The rate of increase in the agricultural labour productivity would depend on the rate at which the surplus labour is transferred from agriculture to non-agricultural sectors which in turn depends on the non-agricultural sector's capacity to create new jobs.

Poverty and Inequality

As discussed earlier, the *Panchayat* Plans had consistently harped on such themes as the creation of a progressive welfare state, an exploitation-free society and the fulfilment of all basic needs of the people. The latter approach was conceived as an attack on two facets of deprivation, namely, physical deprivation due to inadequate means of subsistence including food, shelter, and clothing, and associated deprivation of essential services like safe drinking water, education, transportation and health facilities. Absence of reliable data makes the task of measuring the progress on these fronts during the *Panchayat* period difficult. However, indirect evidence based on per capita income distribution, consumption expenditure and income pattern indicated that poverty was rampant and widespread in Nepal. Although some improvements were seen in social indicators relating to health and educational services as indicated in Table 4.6, attainments remained well short of South Asian averages. With reference to basic educational indicators, however, Nepal's record was better than that of Bangladesh and Pakistan.

The standard of living of the people of a country is ultimately determined by the interrelated pattern of income and consumption. Consumption is part of income, be it cash or kind, available for current expenditure. It is usually what's left after setting aside part of the income for future consumption (savings) or used in capital expenditure. On the other hand, consumption also includes that amount of goods and services obtained through credit or in lieu of the services rendered. The Employment, Consumption and Income Distribution survey

TABLE 4.6
Social Indicators of South Asian Countries
(1965–1988)

Indicators	*Year*	*Nepal*	*Bangladesh*	*India*	*Pak*	*Sri Lanka*	*Average*
Life Expectancy at Birth	1965	41	45	45	46	64	48.2
	1989	52	52	59	56	71	58
Infant Mortality per 100 Births	1965	171	144	150	149	63	135.4
	1985	124	106	95	106	20	90.2
Total Fertility Rate	1965	6.0	6.8	6.2	7.0	4.9	6.18
	1989	5.7	5.9	4.1	6.6	2.5	4.96
Daily Calories	1965	1887	1984	2103	1797	2164	1987
	1988	2078	1925	2184	2200	2319	2141.2
Primary School Enrolment (%)	1965	20	49	74	40	93	55.2
	1988	86	59	99	40	107	87.2
Female Primary Enrolment (%)	1965	4	31	57	20	86	39.6
	1988	57	49	83	28	105	64.4
Secondary School Enrolment in (%)	1965	5	13	27	12	35	18.4
	1988	30	18	41	19	71	35.8

Source: The World Bank, (1991) *World Development Report, 1991.*

conducted by the National Planning Commission in 1977 represents a pioneering exercise on this subject. Defining the poverty line for the country as a whole based on the minimum subsistence level of expenditure per capita at 2 rupees per day for rural areas, and 1.7 rupees for urban areas at 1976-77 prices, the survey concluded that 37.33 per cent of the rural and 27.58 per cent of the urban households fell below the poverty line. At the national level, the figure was 35.50 per cent.

Disaggregated data by development regions showed that the incidence of poverty was the highest in the Far-Western and Mid-Western regions, under both income and consumption criteria. In the absence of comparable data, the change in the poverty level since then is highly debatable. But considering the marginal increase in the per capita income due to sluggish economic growth and the absence of redistributive measures or special anti-poverty packages, there does not seem to have been much of a dent in the country's poverty situation. On the other hand, a cross-country study of seven countries in South Asia conducted by the ILO observed:

> In Bangladesh, Nepal and Bihar, poverty has risen or remained unchanged at extremely high levels and this has been accompanied by declining real wages, rising landlessness and reduced employment opportunities. In all cases, rising demographic pressure has been identified as a strong causal factor responsible for the persistent poverty and this has not been counteracted either by rising productivity of land or structural reforms. Agricultural output per capita has fallen continuously in Nepal and has no tendency to increase in Bihar and Bangladesh.[23]

Another ILO study of South Asian countries in 1980 concluded that even during the period of rapid economic growth, there was no indication of improved share of lower decile groups in aggregate and income and consumption.

> Those studies, which contain the relevant data, show that the shares of the lower decile groups in the aggregate income and consumption have been declining even during periods of relatively rapid agricultural growth. There are significant differences from country to country as regards the proportion of population that has been adversely affected, but in each country for which data exist, a substantial proportion of the lowest income groups appears to have experienced a decline in their share of real income over time.[24]

According to the ILO, the rice equivalent of wage rate in 1976/77 was 1.3 and 1.9 kilograms of rice in the hills and the *tarai* respectively, against the figure of 2.5 kilograms in Bangladesh. Available agricultural statistics put the overall per capita consumption of all cereals at 129 and 286 kilograms in the hills and the *tarai* respectively. Based on these statistics, ILO concluded that the incidence of third degree malnutrition was as high as 15 per cent in Nepal as compared to 2 to 5 per cent in the sample of 59 other developing countries.[25]

Analysis of the data provided by the Nepal Rastra Bank Household Survey of 1973/74 and the 1977 NPC survey also indicated that the Nepali households had inadequate clothing and housing. The NPC survey showed that an average household in Nepal spent Rs. 547 per annum in clothing and footwear. The figure was Rs. 941 and Rs. 527 for urban and rural areas respectively. The ILO converted this figure into in kind per capita and came up with 17 metres of cloth, adequate by the requirement standards of neighbouring South Asian countries, but inadequate for the temperate climate of the hills and mountains where the majority of Nepalis lived. The cold climate necessitates a greater variety and higher quality of clothing, which is more expensive as well. On the question of housing, both the studies indicated that although Nepali households did not suffer from the problem of extreme homelessness as in other South Asian countries, the real problem was in relation to the shelter quality and sanitary conditions. The NPC survey showed that only 6 per cent of the households had access to piped water, and another 8 per cent had tube well facility. Toilet facility was available to only 6 per cent of the households, while electricity was a luxury enjoyed by only 1 per cent. Another study based on some fieldwork in western Nepal observed:

> The vast majority of households interviewed lived under conditions of great material deprivation, no matter whether viewed from the perspective of nutrition, clothing or shelter... . Most households possessed no stock of food grain or cash to purchase food grain for the next meal...we feel confident in concluding that frequent statements of days in this period without food for any member of these households were true and reveal the seriousness of their difficulties. In such circumstances the activity of the household is dominated by the search for food on days when no work is available. It was in this context of a daily yet chronic shortage of the basic necessities of life with a fundamental insecurity that our interviewed households acted[26].

The incidence of poverty is associated with both the low-income level of the people and a high degree of inequality in its distribution. According to the NPC survey of 1977, 44 per cent of Nepal's households had income less than one-half of the average income level. On the other hand, 4 per cent of the households earned income higher than Rs. 44,000 annually. One can also gauge the concentration of income at the national level by the fact that the top 10 per cent of the households controlled over 47 per cent of income flow, whereas the poorest 44 per cent received only 10 per cent. The study concluded that Nepal's income structure had a few at the top and the masses at the bottom. The GINI coefficient for the entire country was 0.59.

The ILO study on rural income distribution showed that the poorest 40 per cent shared 13.9 per cent of income in the hills and 10.7 per cent in the *tarai* indicating higher income concentration at the top in the *tarai*. The gini coefficients were 0.43 and 0.51 respectively for the hills and *tarai*.[27] This distribution of income compared unfavourably with other South Asian countries. The poorest 40 per cent received 18 per cent of the national income in Bangladesh, 16 per cent in India, 17.5 per cent in Pakistan, and 15.1 per cent in Sri Lanka, as compared to less than 10 per cent in Nepal. On the other hand, the richest 20 per cent claimed 44.5 per cent in Bangladesh, 52 per cent in India, 45.5 per cent in Pakistan, and 52 per cent in Sri Lanka, as compared to some 60 per cent in Nepal.[28] Nepal compared unfavourably with its neighbours even in relation to rural income.

In a predominantly agricultural economy like that of Nepal, structure of land ownership is the fundamental basis of inequality. Since land is the major source of income in rural areas, differences in landownership translate directly into differences in income distribution. The structure of ownership is, therefore, a major contributory cause of rural poverty.[29] One of the objectives of the Land Reform Act of 1964 was to reduce the extreme disparity in land holdings through the imposition of ceilings on land ownership. Excess land was to be acquired and distributed to landless farmers. However, as we noted earlier, the impact of the reform on the land distribution was negligible. An evaluation of the impact of the Land Reform in 1973 showed that only 9,136 landlords were affected by the Act with 50,580 hectares acquired as excess land. Out of this 34,705 hectares were allocated to some 10,522 households.[30]

> The disparity between holdings continued to remain substantial even after the reform. The survey found that the average size of holdings of the sample landlord-households was 18.33 hectares while the average size of holdings of the sample households of (i) owner-cum-tenant and (ii) tenant-cultivator was 1.64 hectares and 1.74 hectares respectively.[31]

A sample survey undertaken by the study found out that the concentration of land holding had in fact worsened in 1971. In 1961, 10 per cent of the cultivated area was shared by 46 per cent of the households and ten years later, the same 10 per cent was shared by 63 per cent! The gini coefficient of land holding rose from 0.566 in 1961 to 0.687 in 1971.

> The change in the distribution of landholdings towards greater concentration in favour of the larger farms does not appear very surprising because of the forces (e.g. demographic pressure, indebtedness and usurious money lending, mortgaging of land acute poverty leading to distress sale etc.) working towards the marginalization of the poor farmers seem to have been in operation in rural Nepal.[32]

Acute poverty forced the rural poor to mortgage their land to borrow from moneylenders to meet their consumption and other requirements eventually leading to distress sale. The demographic pressure and the law of inheritance which cause fragmentation of holdings further squeezed a land base which was already too narrow to support the needs of the majority. So together, the demographic pressure combined with the dispossession following indebtedness to the local landlords, forced a large number of rural households to join the ranks of agricultural labourers and/or marginal landholders who had to rely solely on agricultural labour to support consumption expenditure. Estimates based on fragmentary pieces of information showed that the paddy equivalent of money wages fell by about 30 per cent during the period 1967/68 and 1976/77.[33]

The analysis of data from another source, namely, the agriculture census does not indicate an increased disparity. But it clearly shows that the distribution pattern did not improve between 1961/62 and 1981/82. Nearly 49 per cent of the land holdings had the size of 3 hectares and above in 1961/62. The distribution pattern remained more or less the same in 1981/82. The total land area comprising above the size of 3-hectare holding came down to 27 per cent only in 1991/92. The concentration index came down to 0.52 in 1991/92 from 0.64 in 1961/62 (Table 4.7). However, it must be noted that the data on land holdings here pertain to operational units and not ownership holdings. On the other hand, the sample survey data on the evaluation of land reform mentioned above relate to household ownership holdings.

The above evidence indicates a trend towards immiserization of the rural population in the decade of seventies. The reduction in the land base of the lower strata of population created a steady decline in their asset holdings. Stagnation in the economy and absence of alternative sources of employment in non-agricultural sector pushed down real rural wages. But, the price dynamics in a country with low interest on capital, under-valued foreign exchange and state policy supporting economic activities for short-term gains, encouraged private investment in capital-intensive ventures with urban biases. This limited the employment creating potential of the available capital. A relatively better macro performance in the decade of 1980s, particularly the

TABLE 4.7

Distribution of Land Area by Size of Holdings in %
(1961/62–1991/92)

S.No.	Size of holdings	1961/62		1981/82		1991/92	
	Holdings	*Holdings*	*Area*	*Holdings*	*Area*	*Holdings*	*Area*
1.	a. <0.5 ha	56.3	11.8	50.4	6.6	43.1	11.3
	b. 0.5 - 1.0 ha	18.8	12.2	16.3	10.8	26.3	19.2
	c. 1 - 3 ha	17.1	27.1	24.5	35.3	25.8	43.0
	d. 3 - 5 ha	4.2	14.8	5.4	18.5	3.3	12.6
	e. 5 - 10 - ha	2.6	16.4	2.7	15.8	1.2	8.1
	f. > 10 ha	1.0	17.7	0.7	13.0	0.3	5.8
	Total	100.0	100.0	100.0	100.0	100.0	100.0
2.	Concentration index	—	0.64	—	0.65	—	0.52

Source: NSCA Nepal 1991/92, *Analysis of Results*, CBS, NPCS, Kathmandu, June 1994, Table 2.5, p. 16.

second half, brought about improvements on the situation somewhat. The economy started growing faster and there was also some diversification. The share of agriculture in GDP dropped and there was an attendant shift in employment structure. However, these improvements were grossly inadequate to cure the economic malaise the country suffered from.

POLITICAL DEVELOPMENTS

The *Panchayat* regime failed to justify its development rationale. Its economic and social welfare goals did not materialize. At the same time, the direct rule of the king was not without resistance from the very beginning. The Nepali Congress workers who were in exile in India—absconding potential imprisonment and prosecution under the new regime—started armed insurgency in various parts of the country under the guidance of Suvarna Shamsher Rana. Suvarna, who was in India at the time of the Royal takeover, was elected the party's acting president after B.P's imprisonment. The insurgency continued through the latter half of 1961 and the spring of the following year. With well calculated overtures and increased friendship with Communist China, the king successfully convinced the Indians to withdraw their tacit support to the insurgency. The resistance movement was formally terminated under pressure from the Government of India.

Opposition to the *Panchayat* regime continued at the popular level, especially among the youth, students, and academia. The aura and authority of the king's leadership was not sufficient to ensure unquestioned submission to the dictates of an authoritarian regime. In the absence of political parties, the student unions affiliated predominantly with the Nepali Congress and Communists became the hotbed of political activities opposing the regime. The presence of pro-monarch students was practically nil in colleges and the University.

The Constitution was amended in 1967, stressing the party-less character, and the principle of decentralization in administration. The designation of the Chairman of the Council of Ministers had changed into the Prime Minister, who could be appointed by the king "after ascertaining the wishes of the members of the *Rastriya Panchayat* members if he so wished". Ministers were individually and collectively answerable to the King. The Prime Minister could be removed by a vote of no confidence in the *Rastriya Panchayat* by a simple majority.

When B.P. Koirala and his colleagues were released from prison in 1968, a new wave of political activities took over the nation. B.P vowed to work for the attainment of democratic aspirations of the people. Subsequently, he went into exile in India, and started engineering a violent movement inside the country for the restoration of multi-party democracy. Contradictions within the *Panchayat* started to emerge as prominent *Panchas* like Surya Bahadur Thapa and others were imprisoned when they started demanding reforms. Practically all stalwarts of the *Panchayat* including Tulsi Giri, Biswabandhu Thapa, Rishikesh Shaha and Surya Bahadur Thapa were meted out prison sentences, at one time or the other, for taking position which did not conform to official line or for reasons of personality clashes.

King Birendra's ascendancy to the throne in 1972 did not make much difference to Nepal's internal politics. With political power firmly consolidated by his father, the new monarch, however, showed active interest in the supervision of development activities by making annual visits to various parts of the country. The fragility and vulnerability of an autocratic system under the growing pressure from internal forces coupled with the system's inherent contradictions and the wind of change blowing across Asia and other countries were compelling the monarch to initiate reforms. In the election for four seats to the *Rastriya Panchayat* from among the graduates, which provided an opportunity for direct voting by all the graduate population of the country, candidates with avowedly anti-*Panchayat* platform were elected.[34] This showed how unpopular the system had become.

Bangladesh acquired independence from India in 1971. B.P., who was based in India at the time, had actively campaigned for the independence of Bangladesh by mobilizing national and international opinion. He had supported the freedom struggle by supplying arms and ammunitions he had collected for the violent movement inside Nepal. Insurgency-related incidents launched by Nepali Congress started taking place in various parts of the country. The Naxalite activities intensified in Jhapa district of Eastern Nepal. Many prominent landlords were killed by radical communists in their campaign to exterminate 'class enemies'. The *Panchayat* Constitution was amended for the second time in 1975 further expanding the monarchial authority. It abolished the Graduate Constituency election to the *Rastriya Panchayat*. The GBVNC was elevated to the constitutional status with the task of evaluating *Panchayat* workers and screen candidates for the *Panchayat* election.

The political direction started to take a different course after the mid-seventies. Sikkim was annexed to become the twenty-second state of India. After Indira Gandhi clamped the state of emergency, B.P's relation with the Government of India worsened. Against the backdrop of these events, B.P. took a historic decision to return to Nepal, with the slogan of national reconciliation. Nepal's special tribunal had passed seven death sentences against him for instigating various 'subversive activities'. He was imprisoned immediately. But his mere presence inside the country had given a new lease of life to opposition politics in Nepal.

The American President Jimmy Carter's emphasis on human rights, and the election of Janata Party in India with a massive mandate after the emergency created a new atmosphere in favour of democracy and human rights. The overthrow of the Shaha of Iran and the killing of two Nepalis, Capt. Yagya Bahadur Thapa and Bhim Narayan Shrestha, on charge of taking up arms against the state, were other landmark events that charged the atmosphere in Kathmandu. In the meantime, the execution of Bhutto by the military regime in Pakistan, gave an excuse to the restive student community in Kathmandu to take out a protest demonstration that resulted in clashes with the police. A series of violent demonstrations against the regime followed in various parts of the country with numerous academic and political demands. This compelled the king to make a historic proclamation to hold a National Referendum to let the people choose between a reformed *Panchayat* system and a multi-party system. In what was believed to be a widely rigged referendum, the outcome went in favour of the Panchayat by a narrow margin.

The Constitution was amended after the referendum result. It incorporated a few features of the Parliamentary system as window-dressing. Election on the basis of adult franchise was introduced for the first time for 80 per cent of the members to the *Rastriya Panchayat*. The remaining 20 per cent were to be nominated by the king. The Prime Minister would now be chosen at the recommendation of the *Rastriya Panchayat* members and would require at least 60 per cent support. The amendment also created an all-powerful *Panchayat* Policy, Enquiry, and Investigation Committee (PPEIC) accountable only to the king. It was vested with power to take action against anybody who, in its opinion, acted against the Constitution or befitting to his/her position. Its action could not be questioned in any court of law. The PPEIC was the reincarnation of the earlier GBVNC to act as the direct instrument of the king's will and power. It was entrusted with the task of correctly interpreting the *Panchayat* ideology, training, indoctrinating and evaluating the *Panchayat* workers, and enforcing political discipline. It had all the paraphernalia of a full-dress political party.[35] The Constitution also authorized the king to rule with the help of nominated Prime Minister under special circumstances.

The two general elections held under the amended constitution brought out new contradictions in the system. The members to the *Rastriya Panchayat* were elected on individual basis with personalized campaigns. But there were also many among them who believed in multi-party politics. And then there existed PPEIC with the mandate of enforcing political discipline and subscription to the party-less *Panchayat* ideology. In this situation, the members were torn between the multi-party mooring of the enlightened public and their own professed commitment to the non-party ideology. They had to pledge allegiance to the principles and policies formulated under the active leadership of the Crown. The floor of the *Rastriya Panchayat* itself was divided into personal camps of Surya Bahadur Thapa and Lokendra Bahadur Chand. Rather than defined policies and principles, the members were guided by personal and selfish interest in offering their loyalty to either of these camps. In the absence of discipline inherent in organized political parties, loyalty to a particular personality kept on changing with self-interest and short-term expediency that resulted in unstable alliances. The legislature under the reformed *Panchayat* could not graduate from its earlier status of a rubber-stamp body endorsing the royal wishes and the king continued to be directly involved in the country's administration.

DEMISE OF THE *PANCHAYAT* ERA

Demanding the lifting of the ban on political parties, the outlawed Nepali Congress launched a *Satyagraha* in Kathmandu and other towns of the country in May 1985. Party workers numbering more than 6000, together with its top leaders were imprisoned. But the explosion of bombs at different parts of the country including the *Rastriya Panchayat* secretariat in *Singha Durbar*, western and southern gates of the Royal Palace, and the Annapurna Hotel, compelled the Nepali Congress to call off its *Satyagraha*, for fear of providing an alibi for greater authoritarian rule. The bombings were organized with the avowed aim of toppling monarchy by the outlawed *Janawadi Morcha* of Ram Raja Prashad Singh.

The developments around the globe towards the end of 1980s were once again fast changing in favour of democracy and human rights. Gorvachev's rise to power in the Soviet Union, the collapse of communist regimes in Eastern Europe were symptomatic of deeper changes sweeping across the world and had an impact on Nepal as well. After the two parties failed to agree on the terms of renewal of the

Trade and Transit Treaty, India imposed a trade embargo on Nepal effective from April 1988. The preferential trade arrangements between the two countries gave way to the *most favoured nation (MFN)* arrangement and helped compound Nepal's economic difficulties. India also closed down 19 of the 21 trade and transit routes through India previously used by Nepal. The Indian action was triggered by Nepal's decision to procure arms from China and have them delivered directly through overland route without consulting India, as required under the bilateral treaty. This development embittered the relationship between the two countries which reached a new low in the late 1980s.

Meanwhile, the Nepali Congress—at the party convention held on 5 January 1990—took a historic decision to launch a country-wide peaceful and non-violent movement for the restoration of multiparty democracy. The movement was planned to start from 18 February 1990, a day which is celebrated as the National Democracy and King Tribhuvan Memorial Day. The convention was addressed, among others, by prominent Indian leaders including Chandrasekhar, who expressed solidarity with the people of Nepal and their fight for the cause of democracy and human rights. On 18 February, what kicked off as a demonstration of about 10,000 slogan-shouting Congress youth, was soon joined by leftist forces and snowballed into a spontaneous nation-wide People's Movement.

Spontaneous processions and demonstrations chanting various slogans became a daily occurrence in all major cities. This was met by police firings, *lathi*-charges, and other atrocities, resulting in numerous deaths of innocent citizens. Arrests of protesters and killings only added fuel to the deepening crisis. The movement was joined by trade unions, writers, artists, teachers, lawyers, civil servants, doctors and nurses, and practically by every section of the society. Civil servants started "pen-down" strikes; appeals for night-time blackouts by protesters received overwhelming response, and imposition of curfews became a routine affair. Support to the democratic movement started pouring in from the international community as well. Leading US senators and Congressmen including Edward Kennedy, Patrick Moynihan, and Claiborne Pell wrote to the King in support of the Movement. Foreign governments and the donor institutions such as the former West Germany, Switzerland and the United States started adding their voice in favour of democracy and human rights. The government's inability to control the news seeping out to foreign media, particularly the BBC, Voice Of America and other Indian outlets helped the movement gain further momentum.

The king made a last-minute attempt to save the regime by

Photograph3: Another scene of the 1990 People's Movement

appointing Lokendra Bahadur Chand as Prime Minister, promising constitutional reforms and constituting a commission to investigate the incidents. The move turned out to be counterproductive as it only provoked the masses. There was general strike in Kathmandu Valley and life in the capital city came to a standstill. An angry mass of 200,000 slogan-chanting Nepalis gathered at Tundikhel and started marching towards the royal palace. On their way, they attacked the late King Mahendra's statue located about 250 metres from the palace gates. The security forces retaliated with brutal force killing several protesters. Although, "shoot at sight" orders were imposed, violence erupted in many parts of the town. Desperate to restore order, the state imposed round the clock curfews. The transport system, both surface and air, came to a complete halt. All these developments led the monarch to open dialogue with the political leaders. Ultimately he bowed down to the minimum demands for an interim government, and a multi-party polity with constitutional monarch. The king offered the Prime Ministership of the interim set-up to Ganesh Man Singh, the Supreme Leader of the Nepali Congress and Commander of the People's Movement. Singh declined the offer on ground of ill health, and at his recommendation, Krishna Prasad Bhattarai was sworn in as the Prime Minister on 19 April 1990.

The *Panchayat* polity's rationale rested on claims to three foundations, namely, nationalism, economic development, and the indigenous character based on tradition and religion. The concept of nationalism was based on the shallow concept of one language, one dress, one crown and one country. This definition was too narrow to incorporate the diverse cultures, ethnicities, languages and religions prevalent in the country, and too restrictive to adequately address the diverse demands and aspirations of the citizens in a globalised and interdependent world. The painful reality of the country's vulnerability and external dependence became apparent in the wake of the Indian trade embargo. The rhetoric of nationalism touted throughout the three decades of *Panchayat* rang hollow when the embargo literally brought the country down on its knees. Anti-Indianism was the main component of the country's nationalistic ideology in the early 1960s. But the royal government had signed a secret agreement with India in 1965 designating India as the sole supplier of arms to Nepal. Nepal was obligated to consult with India in case it wanted to procure such materials from other sources and/or transport such materials through Indian territory. King Birendra had also declared Nepal a Zone of Peace in 1975 as a means of maintaining, among others, a policy of equidistance between India and China. Despite strong support received from more than 100 countries around the world, including the United States, the failure to receive India's endorsement rendered the whole exercise inoperative. These realities exposed the country's external limitations.

The king's direct leadership promised better development performance and improved living conditions for the people as political parties were considered obstacles to the achievement of these economic goals. But the three decades of 'partyless democracy' with suppression of all 'incompatible' political voices could not deliver what other countries under democracy delivered during the period. The economic performance was doubtful compared even to the pre-*Panchayat* decade. So in essence, the regime confiscated the political and civil rights of its citizens and in return, was unable to bring about any meaningful advancement to their economic lives. Near stagnation of per capita income during the *Panchayat* period reflected the fact that there was no perceptible change in the living standard of majority of the people. Majority of the population were bereft of the basic minimum conditions of human life. Disparity of income and wealth was increasing. The structure of production, the technology in use, the linkages between the agriculture and industrial sectors, were all glaring evidences of the negligible economic transformation that had taken place in the three decades.

The arguments of 'soil and climate theory', divine rights, and indigenous conditions, could not stand the demands and imperatives of the emerging realities of the modern world. The tidal waves of liberal ideas, human rights and democracy were dismantling much stronger citadels of authoritarian regimes backed ideologically and militarily by international alliances. When the right time came, the *Panchayat* edifice crumbled like the house of cards. Even the aura and glamour of the king's leadership, which was not subject to any question or scrutiny, could not save the system. This very fact brought unprecedented controversy to the monarchy, holding him responsible for all the shortcomings and failures of the system. Even the concept of a *Hindu* kingdom in a country with 80 per cent *Hindu* population came under question, as the intelligentsia of various religious backgrounds including *Hindus*, started questioning the need for calling the country a *Hindu* state. Furthermore, the grand experiment started by king Mahendra collapsed under the weight of its own internal contradictions arising from its inherently autocratic character with democratic pretensions.

NOTES

1. Lok Raj Baral, 'The Unclear Roadmap: Parties and the Parliamentary Practice', in Baral (ed) *Political Parties and Parliament*, Delhi: Adroit Publishers, 2004.
2. Tribhuvan Nath, *The Nepalese Dilemma*, New Delhi: Sterling Printers, 1975, p. 213.
3. Prayag Raj Sharma, 'Values in the Doldrums: Does the West Meet the East in Nepal?', paper presented at a seminar Political Development and Social Change in Nepal, 7–11 December, 1986, Kathmandu.
4. Rishikesh Shaha, *Politics in Nepal 1980–1991,* Delhi: Manohar, 1993, p. 10.
5. See, Sanu Bhai Dangol, *The Palace in Nepalese Politics*, Kathmandu: Ratna Pustak Bhandar, 1999, p. 96.
6. Dangol, ibid, p. 46.
7. Mihaly, (2002), p. 139.
8. Hem Narayan Aggrawal, *The Administrative System of Nepal*, New Delhi: Vikas Publications, 1976, pp. 344–45.
9. One estimate of the size of bureaucracy in 1963 was 27,589 regular personnel of which 1274 were the gazetted officials (477 technical personnel), 11,214 non-gazetted (3,334 technical) and 15,100 peons. Added to this were the personnel under the developmental budget which numbered 9,061 in 1964 of which 3 142 were administrative and 5,919 were technical personnel. See M.K. Shrestha, *A Handbook of Public Administration in Nepal*, Kathmandu, 1965, pp. 80–81.
10. The largest number (1401) was sent to India, followed by USA (225), UK (162), USSR (61) and other countries NPC (1963), *The Three Year Plan* pp. 134–137.
11. Mihaly (2002), p. 142.
12. Y.P. Pant, *Economic Development of Nepal*, Allahabad: Kitab Mahal, 1982, p. 3.
13. National Planning Commission, *The Third Plan*, 1965, p. 14.
14. NPC, *The Fourth Plan*, 1972, p. 2.
15. Ibid.
16. Ibid, Appendix III
17. NPC, *The Eighth Plan*, 1992.
18. Raghab Dhoj Pant, *Nepal: Towards a New Development Policy*, Tokyo: Institute of Developing Economies, 1991.
19. Tribhuvan Nath (1975), op.cit., p. 130.
20. World Bank (2004), p. 2.
21. Ibid.
22. Tribhuvan Nath, op. cit., p. 78-80 quoted from *The Commoner*, Kathmandu, 5 Jan.1951.
23. Azizur Rehman Khan and Eddy Lee (Eds) *Poverty and Rural Asia*, p. 14 Bangkok: ILO ARTEP, 1984, p. 14.
24. ILO, *Poverty and Landlessness in Rural Asia*, Geneva, 1980, p. 9

25. Islam et. al., *Employment and Development in Nepal*, Bangkok: ILO ARTEP. 1982, p. 3.
26. Blaike, Cameron and Seddon (1979), op.cit., p. 57.
27. ILO, *Nepal Rural Household Study,* p. 19 ARTEP, 1976, p. 19.
28. ILO, *Poverty and Landlessness in Rural Asia,1980,* p. 20.
29. Ghai and Raman, *Rural Poverty and Small Farmers Development Programme in Nepal,* ILO, 1979.
30. M.A. Zaman, *Evaluation of Land Reform in Nepal,* Kathmandu: HMG, 1973, p. 287.
31. Ibid., p. 33.
32. Rizwanul Islam, 'Poverty and Income Distribution in Rural Nepal' in *Poverty in Rural Asia,* Bangkok: ILO, 1985, p. 181.
33. Ibid. pp. 178–179.
34. The most prominent case was that of Ram Raja Prashad Singh, who stood as a candidate in the 1971 election openly questioning the constitutional validity of the royal action of 1960. Along with a number of other candidates with anti-Panchayat credentials, Singh secured comfortable victory. He was subsequently imprisoned and convicted of sedition in an in-camera trial by a special tribunal.
35. Rishikesh Shaha (1993), p. 145.

PART II
DEMOCRACY AND DEVELOPMENT

Chapter Five

Plans and Reforms

INTERIM GOVERNMENT AND NEW CONSTITUTION

The successful conclusion of the People's Movement brought an end to the party-less polity under the king's leadership. An interim government took over power on 19 April under the Prime Ministership of the veteran Nepali Congress leader and its president, Krishna Prasad Bhattarai. The new Cabinet was composed of representatives from the Nepali Congress, the Left Front, two royal nominees and two independents. The new government set itself for the following three tasks in order of priority:

- *(a)* Restoration of status quo ante to 1 April 1988 with respect to the trade and transit facilities with India.
- *(b)* Drafting and promulgating a constitution that guarantees the rule of law, fundamental rights, multiparty parliamentary democracy, constitutional monarchy and an independent judiciary.
- *(c)* Holding general elections no later than mid-May 1991.

The new Prime Minister lost no time in mending fences with India which had imposed a trade embargo on Nepal for nearly two years. Within two months of the installation of the new government, Bhattarai paid an official visit to India and successfully broke the trade impasse between the two countries by mutual agreement. Immediate measures were taken to restore the status quo ante to April 1988. The two countries also agreed to usher in a new era of cooperation in the areas of human resources development, trans-boundary rivers, and the environment for mutual benefits. The government constituted a Constitution Recommendation Commission under the chairmanship of Justice Bishwo Nath Upadhyaya on 29 May 1989. The Commission presented a draft constitution to King Birendra in September 1990. But the new draft released by the royal palace on 21 October was different from the draft prepared by the Commission. This provoked hostile reactions from the public and the media. The issue was ultimately settled in a compromise. Some features of the palace draft were incorporated by the cabinet in the final version submitted to the king and the constitutional crisis was averted. The top brass of the military made a last minute plea to the Prime Minister that the nation's sovereignty should reside with the king and not with the people as proposed in the constitution. The Prime Minister, however, did not yield.

The king promulgated the new agreed draft as the Constitution of the Kingdom of Nepal, 1990. While announcing the Constitution, the king said he promulgated the Constitution by exercising the 'constitutional and royal powers and prerogatives inherent in him'. The Preamble, however, recognized that the Constitution was in response to the desires expressed by the people through the People's Movement. Its Article 3 clearly mentioned that the sovereignty of Nepal shall be exercised in accordance with the provisions made in the Constitution. The Constitution recognized certain features described in its Preamble as basic and not amenable to change or amendment. These are: sovereignty based on the people, multiparty parliamentary democracy, guarantee of human rights, and constitutional monarchy. All other provisions of the Constitution could be amended through two-third votes in the parliament.

The constitution incorporated all the basic features of parliamentary democracy. The king was accepted as a Constitutional monarch to act on the advice and consent of the Council of Ministers, except for some prerogatives which were to be exercised exclusively by him or at his discretion. These powers were largely of ceremonial nature and related to palace affairs, its administration, royal privilages and succession. The Constitution declared Nepal as a multiethnic, multilingual, democratic, independent, sovereign, and Hindu Monarchial Kingdom. Commenting on the Constitution, Shaha wrote:

> The Constitution of 1990, on the whole, represents a milestone in the evolution of a constitutional order in Nepal. The actual experience of the Nepali people with the Constitution will largely depend on how it is worked in practice. It is yet to be seen whether the king and the political parties who have so far assumed the responsibility for promulgating the Constitution will cooperate with one another in implementing it with care and integrity. The King will still have an important role to play in effecting a smooth transition from unlimited monarchy to limited or constitutional monarchy suited to the needs of intrinsically democratic modernization.[1]

The new government also completed its third task of holding the general election for the 205-member House of Representatives. Elections were held as scheduled on 12 May 1991 with the Nepali Congress returning as the majority party with 110 seats. They were followed by Nepal Communist Party (UML) with 69 seats, United People's Front 9 seats, Nepal Sadvabana Party 6 seats, National Democratic Party (Chand) 3 seats, Nepal Peasant and Workers Party 2 seats, Nepal Communist Party (Democratic) 2 seats, and National Democratic Party (Thapa) 1 seat. It may be noted here that the United People's Front was, later on, split into two factions. One faction remained a constitutional party and the other one went underground to start an armed Maoist movement under the name Nepal Communist Party (Maoists). The other conspicuous outcome of the election was the virtual annihilation of the party of former Panchas who had fought as two parties under the leaderships of Surya Bahadur Thapa and Lokendra Bahadur Chand. Their combined tally was a meagre 4 seats. The election, by all accounts, was conducted in a fair manner. The incumbent Prime Minister Krishna Prasad Bhattarai himself lost the election from Constituency One of Kathmandu district.

BUDGET, PLAN AND PHILOSOPHY

The First Budget

The Nepali Congress government under Girija Prasad Koirala quickly swung into action and announced its policies and programmes. Initially, the Prime Minister himself assumed the responsibility of the Finance Minister. This author, together with Mahesh Acharya from Morang, had the privilege of serving as economic advisers in preparing the first budget which had to be quickly presented in the new parliament. Subsequently, Mahesh Acharya was appointed Minister of State of Finance and presented the budget to the joint session of the two legislative houses of democratic Nepal. The total size of the budget was Rs. 26.64 billion of which Rs. 9.75 was allocated for regular expenditure and the rest Rs. 16.89 billion for development expenditure. Committing itself to reduce the budgetary deficit to 1.8 per cent of GDP, the budget proposed to raise the revenue mobilization by 17.4 per cent. The budget projected GDP growth of 4.6 per cent for the year. The principal aspects of the new policy and programmes announced by the government as part of the royal address to the Joint House and the budget were:

— Commitment to social justice in favour of the under-privileged, poor and destitute population who had been deprived of the benefits from development.

— Emphasis on development of rural areas and backward regions with increased budgetary allocation to such areas as primary health, education, drinking water, rural roads, irrigation and environment conservation. Free education up to Class 5. Subsidy on biogas. Allocation of 70 per cent of the development budget to rural areas.

— Increased national production with emphasis on equitable distribution and productive employment opportunities. Subsidized credit on small loans up to Rs. 10,000 under various pro-poor schemes.

— Emphasis on macroeconomic stabilization and price control. Increased revenue and improved revenue administration.

— Review of ongoing development projects in line with new national priorities. Control in unproductive expenditure. Setting up of a Pay Commission to review the salary and service conditions of civil servants.

— Emphasis on market oriented investment friendly policies in economic activities. Privatization of sick and commercial public sector enterprises.

The Eighth Plan and Planning Philosophy

Similarly, a new National Planning Commission was constituted in August 1991.[2] The Commission set itself to the tasks of developmental policy review in various sectors to reformulate policies and feed into the preparation of the Eighth Plan. A draft Approach Paper of the Plan was completed within three months and submitted to the newly constituted National Development Council. The following two paragraphs of the Approach Paper reflect the dilemma and optimism of the new administration at that time:

> The approach of the plan represents a unique set of characteristics which are shaped by two major countervailing elements. On the positive side, there is the nascent optimism and genuine enthusiasm of the general public. On the negative side, there are the stark and daunting realities of a dilapidated economy left behind by the Panchayat regime.
>
> The present challenge to planning is to reconcile the burgeoning demands of a rapidly growing population and its rising expectations with the meager financial and natural resources available within the economy. The challenge is further accentuated by the erosion and deterioration of the natural resource base and the degradation of the natural environment. The situation is characteristically one which

> demands high political discipline, severe austerity and hard economic sacrifices. However, there is also a great optimism amongst the general public at large. This represents the basic energy with which the process of modernization of the economy can be initiated.[3]

The Plan proposed a total gross investment of Rs. 166 billion of which Rs. 106 was from the private sector and Rs. 60 billion from the public sector. The three objectives of the Eighth Plan were: higher sustainable economic growth, alleviation of poverty and reduction of regional disparities. The total development outlay was Rs. 112.3 billion, as compared to Rs. 71.4 billion of the Seventh Plan.

The full fledged Eighth Plan document was published in July 1992. The total investment was raised to Rs. 170 billion, including Rs. 109 billion from the private sector and Rs. 61 billion from the public. The incremental capital output ratio was planned to be brought down from 4.5 to 4.3. In view of the importance of raising investment efficiency to achieve better returns, the preamble of this document stressed the need for curtailing development costs and enhancing the returns from development efforts. The total government outlay was Rs. 113.5 billion, the largest share of which was allocated to social services (31.5%), followed by agriculture, irrigation and forestry (25.7%), electricity (20.9%), transport and communications (17.7%), industry and mining (2.0%) and trade and tourism (1.3%). Compared to the Seventh Plan, there had been a marked increase in the share of social services, transport and communications and electricity, but a sharp decline in industry in line with the new priorities. The increase in power investment was particularly on account of the huge investment proposed for Arun III hydroelectric project. The decline in the share of the industrial sector corresponded to the government policy of rolling back public investments in the industrial sector to create a greater role for the private sector.

The Eighth Plan recognized the importance of macroeconomic stability for higher growth and for bolstering competitive strength. The expansionary economic policy pursued in the past had left the economy unstable with excess liquidity, trade imbalance and high inflation. The emphasis was therefore placed on enhanced domestic mobilization, rational allocation and better management of public resources. The Eighth Plan proposed to raise internal savings from 9 to 12 per cent of GDP, reduce deficit financing from 1.7 per cent to 1 per cent of GDP and cut down current account deficit from 10 per cent to 8 per cent of GDP. The International Monetary Fund's ESAF (Extended Structural Arrangement Facility) in 1992 was helpful to ensure internal fiscal discipline in line with these targets.

The most important philosophical and paradigmic shift after democracy as outlined in numerous policy documents was the greater emphasis placed on the role of the private sector, market forces, and investment friendly policies. Some critics questioned this policy as a contradiction to the philosophy of democratic socialism espoused by the Nepali Congress. The new government did not abandon this ideology and its objective, but redefined it in the context of Nepal's own experience and the realities of the contemporary world. The liberal policy was aimed not just at the private sector in the narrow sense but at creating an environment conducive to unleashing and tapping the initiative and creative energy of all sections of the society including the non-government organizations, local authorities and grassroots organizations. The Eighth Plan said:

> As Nepali Congress is committed to democratic socialism, the development concepts will be guided by this ideology and the principal objective of the economic policy will be the amelioration of the standard of living of the deprived citizens through economic processes. Socialism as conceived by Nepali Congress, is not orthodox socialism where the state dictates but the one by virtue of which the state in a supporting role will bring about social and economic justice through increase in production, creation of employment and special programmes directed towards the upliftment of the socially and economically deprived poor people who are left out of the mainstream of development.
>
> It is evident from the changes occurring in the socialist countries that the traditional state directed socialism is no longer suited to the existing global economic scenario. Therefore, the state directed and state controlled economic systems pursued for the last thirty years will be gradually phased out and policy will be adopted to carry out development through free market-oriented liberal economic systems. In this perspective, the goals and perspective, the goals and objectives defined in the Eighth Plan will be considered as indicative and as guidelines, the fulfillment of which requires the participation and support of all sections of the nation together with the capabilities of the state.[4]

It had no illusion about the efficacy of the traditional trickle-down approach in ensuring proper distribution of developmental benefits to those in the lower rungs of the economic ladder. In fact, the Plan observed: "the experience of several developing countries has demonstrated the fallacy of the concept that a high economic growth rate automatically benefits the people".[5] As far as the government investment was concerned, the new priority was on building development infrastructure. Activities like extension of roads and irrigation, education, health and drinking water in rural and backward areas, and institutional and technical improvements in agricultural systems and employment opportunities for the rural population were high on the government's spending agenda.

The planning philosophy was reflected in the procedural structures and its methodology of implementation. Acknowledging that "development planning is not merely a mechanical function of capital and technology but it is also a political process of mobilizing and organizing people commensurate with the desired goals"[6], the Plan committed itself to the philosophy of decentralization. The Eighth Plan promised to delegate sufficient authority to local bodies in matters of selection, formulation and implementation of projects and in the distribution of benefits. Simplifying the process of budgetary allocation and distribution, and empowering the local bodies with financial authority with respect to approval of tenders in development projects were some proposed strategies.

The Plan promised to dismantle the highly regulated economic regime of the past. Discretionary economic authority in the hands of a meddlesome state had created distortions in the industrial and trading activities limiting private investment to the trading business and some low value added industries aiming to make some quick money by exporting to the highly protected Indian market. The role of the public sector would now be one of a catalyst and promoter of private sector investments. The state would roll back and limit itself to a few areas where private participation is not desirable or unattractive. To quote the Plan:

> The principal role of the Government will be to develop physical infrastructure necessary for economic development, such as roads and communications, to bring the people so far left out of the mainstream of development, by providing basic social services such as health care, education and drinking water to rural areas, to protect the environment and to create the conditions conducive to the growth of the private sector. Although the government will have a primary role in the development of physical infra structure and social sector such as education, health care and drinking water essential to long-term national development, the participation of the private sector too, will be welcomed... The government will initiate a process of disengagement and disinvestments from a number of areas that may be managed more efficiently by the private sector without jeopardizing social interest. In accordance with this policy, government-owned enterprises and corporations will be gradually privatized.[7]

The new policy also had a fresh approach towards the non-governmental sector which had been forced to function under the tight jurisdictional control and under the direction of the Social Service Coordination Council chaired by Queen Aishworya herself. NGOs were offered a wider space in recognition of their effectiveness "in terms of cost, flexibility, motivation and initiative" and their proven experience "in working in close association with rural people and suitability to the tasks of rural development and poverty alleviation". To raise the effectiveness of this sector, the Plan committed itself to simplifying administrative processes, removing delays in decision making from the government side, and further liberalizing and clarifying the policy. International NGOs were also encouraged to be involved in areas of their comparative advantages and expertise while keeping in view local demands and regional requirements.

WAVE OF REFORMS

Trade, Industry and Tourism

A strong departure was made from the previous policy of external trade control through tariff walls, quantitative restrictions and import licenses. The practice of foreign exchange auction for the import of raw materials was terminated. All imports except those in the negative list were put under an Open Generalized Licensing (OGL) system. The products in the negative list started with 31 products in February 1992, came down to 12 in July 1992, 6 in March 1993, and to complete elimination by July 1993. It was a bold move for two reasons. First, it meant the loss of substantial auction revenue to the government. Secondly, with current account convertibility, imports of consumer goods were also made free from quantitative restrictions.[8]

Rationalization of tariff structure proceeded concurrently. Peak tariff rates came down from 255 per cent in 1991 to 110 per cent in 1994. To simplify the tariff structure, the large number of existing slabs was brought down to 6 with the Finance Act of 1994/5. The largest number of import items were placed under 20 to 30 per cent slabs. Only a few items, such as luxury motor vehicles, were placed under 110 per cent slab. Additional duties imposed on third country imports were also eliminated.

Export procedures were simplified with facilities for duty drawback, bonded warehouse, and simpler documentation requirements. To free imports from the control of the central bank, the practice of fixing import cash margin rate by the central bank was abolished. This was left to the discretion of commercial banks themselves. The new arrangement required the importers only to deposit two per cent of the LC (letter of credit) amount at the central bank. The deposit requirement was subsequently raised to 10 per cent.[9] Exports were now exempt from all duties except for the 0.5 per cent fees imposed for monitoring purposes. With the introduction of the value-added tax since 1998, taxes levied on the import of goods and services used in the production of exportable goods are refunded to the exporters. The main objective of these reforms was to remove anti-export bias arising from high tariffs and excessive procedural requirements.

A new industrial policy was devised and codified in the Industrial Enterprise Act introduced in 1992. This heralded significant reforms in the industrial sector in order to promote new investment in line with the liberal policy. The most important feature of the Act was the abolition of the licensing practice to start all industries except those related to defense and with the potential to cause adverse impacts on public health and environment. All businesses were now required only to register themselves at the newly established office of the Company Registrar. This was not a licensing requirement but a simple registration for legal recognition to the enterprise. The new arrangement dealt a serious blow to those who were profiteering from the sheltered market for certain goods by restricting new entry through influence in the license system. This also eliminated an important source of bureaucratic corruption inherent in the discretionary power of issuing licenses.

Another landmark was the enactment of Foreign Investment and Technology Act, 1992. The Act allowed foreign investment up to 100 per cent in industries with a fixed investment of a minimum of 20 million rupees. The Act defined the terms and conditions for repatriation of profits and proceeds from the sale of investment assets. It also provided guarantees against nationalization. The hydropower sector was now open for foreign investment. The One Window system was announced to provide all government related services including taxation, utilities, and foreign exchange to domestic and foreign investors under a single institution. The Act was further amended in 1996 paving way for foreign investment in all areas—including the services sector—except those in the negative list which comprised cottage industries, arms and radioactive substances, land transactions, and personal services.

The national air policy was already announced in 1992 to allow private airlines in the domestic and external sectors. It permitted Nepali nationals to register, possess and operate private aircrafts. This policy made an immediate impact on domestic travel and tourism. A number of private airlines and helicopter services were established and started operating services to various parts of the country including remote places. This helped ease serious bottlenecks in the aviation sector. The policy also allowed private airlines to operate in external sectors and licenses were issued. But private operation in the external sector started much later.

A large number of virgin mountain peaks were opened for expedition. The Upper Mustang Valley, hitherto forbidden for foreign nationals, was opened for tourism for a fee defined by clear regulatory guidelines. To free the aviation sector from bureaucratic hurdles and red tape, the Civil Aviation Department was converted into a Civil Aviation Authority in 1996. The Authority was given mandate to monitor the operation and quality control of domestic and international air services, air communications, air transportation and air navigation. It was also entrusted with the power of issuing and revoking flying certificates. Later, the Ninth Plan further promoted the concepts of eco and medical tourism, convention tourism, festival tourism, village tourism, holiday tourism and sports tourism. Particular emphasis was placed on the preservation of environment, heritage monuments and diverse cultures and ethnicity.

Foreign Exchange Regime

A dual foreign exchange rate was in practice until the early nineties. This arrangement required all foreign exchange earnings in the country to be surrendered to the central bank at the officially fixed rate, which was generally lower than the prevailing market rate. This created distortions such as under invoicing of exports and the over invoicing of imports by importers who had to apply for foreign exchange at the official rate. Exports were discouraged and precious foreign exchange was siphoned off illegally to foreign banks. In March 1992, the new government made the Nepali currency partially convertible (to the extent of 65 per cent) in current account. This meant that the exporters were now allowed to retain 65 per cent of their foreign exchange earnings to be converted at the market rate. Only 35 per cent of the earnings were to be surrendered at the official rate. The ratio of convertible portion was subsequently raised to 75 per cent in July 1992, and full convertibility in current accounts was announced in February 1993. All foreign exchange earners were now allowed to retain their whole earnings in convertible current accounts. This brought an end to the dual exchange rate system.

Similarly, another important decision was taken with regard to the use of convertible currency for Indian imports. Traditionally, all imports from India were paid in Indian currency and the Nepali importers had the benefit of unlimited convertibility to Indian currency from the local banks. The shortfall of Indian currency arising from the deficit in the balance of payments was met through the purchase of Indian currency from the Reserve Bank of India with dollars. Instead of continuing this practice, Nepal, in agreement with India, introduced the practice of foreign exchange payment on some selected items directly to the Indian exporters. The total value of these products was calculated to approximate the annual BOP deficit with India covered by hard currency payment. The advantage of the hard currency payment arrangement was the supply of cheaper and better export quality products from Indian exporters. The number of such products which was limited initially stood at 60 at the end of 2004. The total value of foreign exchange payment on Indian products in the fiscal year 2003/04 was 15.26 billion rupees.

A number of other allied reforms constituted the liberalization package of the early 1990s. Commercial banks were allowed to hold their balances abroad. Since 1994, Nepalese nationals were allowed to maintain foreign exchange accounts of their earnings in local banks. Those maintaining foreign exchange accounts abroad were allowed to transfer their accounts inside the country within a defined period. Industrial firms engaged in export trade were permitted to borrow in convertible currency for import of raw materials from June 1993. From 29 July 1998 onwards, exporters were permitted pre-shipment and post-shipment loans in convertible currency from local banks at an interest rate not exceeding 7.5 per cent. If required by the commercial banks, the Nepal Rastra Bank offered refinance facilities for this purpose at an interest rate of 5.5 per cent. The whole purpose of this arrangement was to make export credit cheaper. The previous practice imposed significant transaction costs on exporters as they had to borrow in local currency at high interest, and additionally, bear the costs due to buying and selling rate differential in foreign exchange transaction.

Banking and Capital Market

The liberal entry policy for commercial banks started in 1991 resulted in the opening of several private banks with foreign collaborations. But these banks had low capital base and were headquartered in Kathmandu. To overcome this unhealthy development, the Nepal Rastra Bank raised the minimum capital requirement for a new bank to Rs. 50 crore. The capital base was further raised to a minimum of Rs. 100 crore. The existing banks were also required to raise their capital base to this level within five years. The reform measures were further extended to capital markets, insurance, finance and leasing activities. The new policy brought about not only increased competition and efficiency in the banking sector, but also expanded, deepened and diversified the banking and financial sector.

Call money market was established to facilitate inter-bank transactions. Apart from commercial banks, this also benefited the overall monetary system as the inter-bank rate used in the large volume of their transactions is indicative of the money market conditions.[10] The deregulation of interest rate from August 1989 brought down the deposit rate without commensurate reduction in the lending rate. Against this background, the Nepal Rastra Bank issued a moral suasion in 1993 to limit the spread to six per cent. In 1998, the NRB directed commercial banks to maintain the weighted interest spread to below 5 per cent level. Statutory liquidity ratio was also withdrawn in July 1993 to facilitate a larger credit flow to the private sector.

With the view of introducing private sector culture and strategic alliance, some portions of the shares of the government-owned Nepal Bank Ltd. (NBL) and the Rastriya Banijya Bank (RBB) were offloaded. The regulatory norms for commercial banks were standardized with respect to loan classification, provisioning requirements, liquidity norms (1996), capital adequacy (1991), the discounting in the treasury bills (1996), together with the definitions of core capital and supplementary capital (1996).[11]

The most recent phase of the financial sector reforms was launched with the financial support from the World Bank, IMF, ADB and the DFID. The main purpose of this reform was to strengthen the supervisory and regulatory capacity of the NRB, and build a strong banking and non-banking sector. It also proposed to improve the legal and judicial aspects of the financial system, improve auditing and accounting standards and promote financial discipline. A number of legislations including a new NRB Act (2002), a Debt Recovery Act (2002), and Deposit Taking Institutions Ordinance were enacted. A core component of this reform programme included the restructuring and reforms of the two government-owned ailing commercial banks accounting for about 60 per cent of the total depositors' money. Services of expatriate management teams have been procured to execute the restructuring and proposed reforms in these banks.

In the nineties, the government also explored the feasibility of developing Nepal as a centre for international financial services. The purpose of such a centre was to encourage international financial institutions–banks, finance and insurance companies, mutual funds and investment banking–to physically locate within the country to conduct financial services outside the host country. A study showed that Nepal's excellent time-zone location, good air access, modern communications, low cost and business friendly environment made it an ideal location for such a hub.[12] If the plan materialized, the country would reap the benefit of increased revenue, creation of modern skills and jobs, increased investment and growth in tourism. As a first step towards this, a International Financial Centre Act was passed in 1996. This was designed as an enabling legislation and established the principles for future legislation and the administrative framework for the centre. Further studies done by reputed international authorities suggested additional legislative framework for substantive legal standards and regulations and enforcement mechanism to ensure their compliance.[13] However, further work on this was stalled after the Nepal Rastra Bank accorded a higher priority to strengthening its internal regulatory and supervisory capacity under the new wave of financial sector reform with external assistance.

Capital market reforms started with the enactment of the Security Exchange Act in 1992 which, among other things, provided for a regulatory body and the stock exchange. The trading floor of the Nepal Stock Exchange started its trading activities from 13 January 1993 in both the secondary and primary issues. Commenting on the pace of reforms introduced in the initial years of the democratic government under Nepali Congress, an US Aid expert observed:

> Wide ranging structural reforms were carried out by the Nepali Congress Government that encompassed, among others, the financial, trade, legal, and industrial sectors. From privatization of public enterprises to tax reform, from elimination of the Statutory Liquidity Ratio to current account convertibility, from the introduction of a new Finance Company Act to the establishment of trading floor at the Nepal Stock Exchange, the changes were sweeping.[14]

Taxation and Tariff

The prevailing system of taxation suffered from a number of deficiencies. There were ambiguities in tax objectives. The system had low elasticity and a narrow tax base. The administration wielded wide discretionary power which inevitably led to frequent complaints of arbitrariness. Many reforms were pursued to remedy these maladies. The focus was on simplicity, both in concept and structure.[15] The Eighth Amendment to the Income Tax Act introduced a self-assessment scheme by the taxpayers which was subsequently revised to address the criticism from the business community.

As preparatory measures towards the introduction of Value Added Tax, a two-tier sales tax scheme was adopted in 1992/93 at the manufacturer and dealer/distributor level for nine selected items. The scope of this two-tier system was further extended in the following year. A task force was subsequently formed in September 1993 to complete further preparatory works for the introduction of VAT. The technical support for this was received from the Harvard Institute of

International Development with USAID assistance. The VAT legislation was drafted in 1994 and enacted in 1995. Development of operation manuals, and various educational and awareness campaigns were completed in 1996 and 1997. Amid much controversy and criticism, the VAT was formally introduced on 16 November, 1997 replacing sales, hotel, and contract and entertainment taxes. The VAT law stipulated consumption-type VAT using the credit method, based on a "destination principle" down to the retail level. It was levied at a single rate of 10 per cent, with zero-rating of exports. Exemptions were provided to a few items such as unprocessed food, livestock, and medicines. The threshold was fixed at an annual turnover of 2 million rupees. Exporters were entitled to immediate refund, while other taxpayers were allowed to carry forward excess credit, and could claim a refund if not adjusted within the following six months.[16]

Reforms were introduced in the excise, customs and income taxes as well. The number of excisable items fell from 38 in 1991/92 to 6 in 1994/95. Similarly, the sales tax slabs were reduced from 5 to 2, and the rates fixed at 10 per cent and 20 per cent. The old excise law was replaced by a new one in 2002 under which excise duty could be levied on both domestic and imported products and services. Excise duty was levied at specific rates on all items, other than vehicles which were subject to ad valorem rates. The excise administration based on a physical control system was replaced by self-removal system, except in liquor and cigarettes. Custom duties were rationalized, bringing down the rates as well as the number of slabs. Only six slabs (5, 10, 15, 25, 40, and 80 per cent) remained. Basic and additional duties were combined. With the introduction of VAT and accession to the World Trade Organization (WTO), customs valuation system was switched from the administratively fixed value to the transaction value.

Reforms in taxation led to the reduction of the corporate as well as personal income tax rates. After the reform, only two rates each for personal and corporate tax remained. Personal income tax consisted of two slabs—15 per cent and 25 per cent. The corporate tax rate was 25 per cent, except for banks and other financial institutions that were charged 30 per cent. Before the reforms in 1991, the highest personal income rate was 50 per cent, and the corporate tax rate was 40 per cent.

The most important legislative action on taxation was, however, the Income Tax Act of 2002. This Act brought all income tax related tax provisions under a single legislation. Elimination of earlier exemptions and tax holidays broadened the income tax base. Additionally, it encouraged self-assessment, offered a liberal deduction system, a longer period of carrying losses forward or backward, and a pooled system of depreciation. It provided for deduction of all expenses incurred in the earning process. All earnings, within and outside the country, were brought under the taxable income. Reforms were also introduced in strengthening tax administration. All inland tax offices were brought under Inland Revenue Department. The VAT and Income Tax departments were amalgamated to ensure better coordination and improve the quality of service and compliance at lower transaction costs. The VAT revenue offices were fully computerized, and computerization was introduced in income tax offices as well. All prominent customs offices were brought under the Automated Systems for Customs Data (ASYCUDA).

Reforms in the revenue system, particularly the introduction of VAT and the new Income Tax Act, were not without problems. VAT was greeted by controversies, harsh criticisms and angry street protests from a section of the business community.[17] The new Income Tax Act was also severely criticized for its 'archaic and unintelligible language', irrelevance of some of its new provisions to the Nepali conditions, and its complexity. The political instability and uncertainty characterized by the frequent changes in government during the period of its implementation exacerbated the situation. However, the reforms survived and the VAT has come to stay as the foundation of Nepal's revenue system. Some problems and weaknesses, however, remain. Implementation of VAT is inherently difficult in the Nepali environment where, as a noted tax expert observed:

> The tax awareness is minimal, the practice of maintaining tax accounts is negligible or improper, smuggling and under valuation is rampant, and tax leakages take place with negotiations between the tax payer and the tax administration, it was not easy to implement VAT and the political instability only aggravated the situation and made it more complex. Since those who opposed VAT took advantage of this situation it proved even more difficult.
>
> Despite these hurdles, VAT implementation is becoming more effective. The statistics related to the expansion of the VAT net and revenue collection are positive and this proves that the tax has been established in our country.[18]

The share of VAT in the total revenue shows an increasing trend. VAT collection amounted to around 3 per cent of GDP in 2000/01 compared to its predecessor's (the sales tax) share of 2.6 per cent in 1996/97. The VAT, however, replaced entertainment, hotel and contract which yielded separate revenue before. Therefore, from the point of view of revenue generation, there was only a marginal increase. The growth, however, must be seen in the context of only 10 per cent rate of VAT as against 15 sales tax rate applied before. At the same time, in the absence of tax credit and other refund systems, there was double and even multiple taxation prior to the introduction of VAT. The system to be fully effective requires further reforms in the customs and taxation system, which still suffer from various practical problems and anomalies. Experience from other countries also shows that the revenue impact of VAT will be low in initial years.[19] The lower VAT rate initially was intended to ensure wider compliance and to make the system broad-based. Despite initial hiccups and reservations, the reformed taxation system has been established now and further refinements and reforms based on experience are always possible.

Energy, Hydro Power and Environment

It was felt that the progression towards market-oriented economy would have impact on the profile of energy consumption and energy investment in different ways and this would, in turn, permeate into the performance of the non-energy sectors and the overall macroeconomy. Therefore, the National Planning Commission commissioned a Perspective Energy Plan (PEP) which was completed in 1995 to provide a twenty-five year perspective on the implications of alternative economic strategies. The PEP was meant to offer a comprehensive understanding of implementable strategies for energy development, propose a framework for energy planning linked with economic performance, and establish an integrated sustainable economic and energy planning process. The study estimated various economic growth scenarios with corresponding implications on energy planning. It projected a decreasing availability of fuel-wood and increasing reliance on other biomass fuels, making it necessary to promote new and renewable energy resources. Import of petroleum fuel was deemed necessary to sustain the demand from urban consumers and modern sectors of the economy. The PEP considered the mandatory introduction of efficient energy technologies inevitable. It designed detailed strategies to ensure growth in the volume of fuelwood as well as the supply of new and renewable energy. The study projected the share of indigenous electricity in total energy demand to reach 13 per cent by 2017/18 from a level of 6 per cent. The reduction in the supply price of electricity was considered a must to achieve this. The study also suggested a diversified strategy for energy financing schemes including private and public-private partnerships.

Significant developments took place in the hydropower sector. The need for exploiting the immensely untapped hydro potential of the country required a review of existing policy and laws related specifically to hydropower sector and to water resources in general. The government sought expert advice from Norway and United States to help in formulating new policies. Hydropower Development Policy was announced in 1992 and was followed by the enactment of the Water Resources Act and the Electricity Act the same year. The Water Resources Act defined the priorities for water use in the order of– drinking water and domestic use, irrigation and agricultural uses, hydroelectricity, industrial use, navigation, recreational use and others. Legal arrangements were made with regard to the determination of the water use and the prevention of environmental and other hazards to keep the water from pollution. The Electricity Act exempted hydropower development up to one megawatt capacity from licensing requirement and income tax. It allowed up to 100 per cent private investment in hydropower and power supply with or without reliance on the NEA transmission and distribution networks. An income tax exemption for ten years was provided for investment in hydropower generation and distribution above one megawatt. Other regulations were related to royalty, power sale to the national grid, import and export of electricity, tariff rate and Electricity Tariff Fixation Commission, and security arrangements. The Act also promised guarantee against any nationalization of private investment.

Important activities were started in the field of environment protection. Environment Impact Assessment (EIA) was institutionalized for all major development projects, and mitigation measures were made an integral part of the project. A high-powered Environment Protection Council was established under the Chairmanship of the Prime Minister. The National Planning Commission acted as the secretariat for this Council. One of the first decisions by this Council was the introduction of vehicular emission standards to control air pollution. For the first time, standards for diesel vehicles was fixed at 65 Hartritz Smoke Unit (HSU), and for petrol vehicles 3% carbon monoxide by volume. The first vehicle to have been subjected to the emission test was that of Prime Minister Koirala's himself. Green stickers certifying acceptable emission level was introduced, and vehicles without these stickers were barred from entering Singha Darbar, and subsequently Kathmandu valley. At the initiative of the National Planning Commission, a SAFA Tempo Project was started with USAID support. The idea was to introduce electric vehicles in Kathmandu valley to replace the polluting three wheelers (called Vikram tempos locally) that ran on diesel. This author remembers his test ride of the first prototype SAFA tempo around the Singha Durbar compound. One can see these tempos plying some routes in the city even now.

The World Environment Day of 5 June 1993 was observed in an unconventional way. Without the normal fanfare that characterizes such occasions, we identified about 45 heritage protection sites needing immediate restoration with costs ranging from 20,000 to 50,000 rupees. An invitation to the private sector and individual sponsors to renovate these sites was met with overwhelming response. Similarly, all recyclable wastes—internationally categorized green, amber or red waste—were banned from entering the country. The disposal of solid waste of solid waste emerging as a major environmental issue of Kathmandu Valley. Several sites were studied to serve as landfill. Upon completion of the Environment Impact Assessment (EIA), Okharpouwa of Nuwakot district was selected as the landfill site for the valley waste.

After the establishment of a separate Ministry of Population and Environment, all functions relating to environmental coordination was transferred from the NPC to this ministry. Important measures such as The Environment Protection Act and Environment Protection Regulations have been enacted since then. The subject of environment and population were made compulsory in primary education. A modern liquid waste treatment plant was developed in the Pashupati area to treat the sewage being directly discharged to the Bagmati River. Protected areas were extended in Langtang, Annapurna and Kanchanjanga national parks taking the total protected area to approximately 20 per cent of the country's territory.

Agriculture Perspective Plan

The graduation of agriculture from the level of subsistence to commercial is widely considered to be the prerequisite or the necessary condition for the country's economic prosperity and poverty reduction. Agriculture is the only sector with the potential to absorb a large portion of the 250,000 strong labour force that enters the job market every year. Without accelerated growth in agricultural income, the development possibility of industrial and other non-agricultural sectors too will be limited. High farm income, because of strong multipliers in the rural areas, generates jobs and income for industrial goods and other services. The bulk of non-agriculture employment in Nepal is linked with agriculture, either through production or consumption activities.

Recognizing this reality, John Mellor, an internationally known agricultural economist, was invited by the National Planning Commission with the support of the Asian Development Bank. He was asked to assist in the development of a long term vision plan for agriculture-led economic growth in Nepal. Two years of work completed by a team of experts from APROSC under his guidance culminated into what is known as the Nepal Agricultural Perspective Plan (APP) in June 1995. The implementation of this APP was expected to increase agricultural growth by additional two percentage points. Combined with an estimated 0.5 per cent decline in population growth, this would expand the per capita annual agricultural growth six-fold, from the prevailing 0.5 to 3 per cent. The report stated:

> Such expansion would provide jobs for the poor, particularly poor women, and thereby greatly reduce the number of rural people in poverty, whose lot has been gradually deteriorating over the past few decades. It would allow Nepal to withdraw its most fragile land resources from arable agriculture and return them to environmentally sound forestry and other suitable and natural uses. And it would diffuse the pattern of urbanization away from Kathmandu and its immense environmental problems towards other areas. The kind of disbursed pattern of urbanization has proved extremely successful in countries where vigorous agricultural growth has led to economic transformation[20].

The principal strategy proposed to bring about the technology-based green revolution in agriculture was the adoption of a large concentrated investment in selected priority inputs in a coordinated manner. The input package of priority inputs comprised of well controlled year-round irrigation, a grid of agricultural roads, rural electrification, fertilizer, the technological know-how and extension services. Separate strategies were devised for the *tarai* and the hills. High value commodities including livestock (particularly milk), citrus, vegetables and vegetable seeds, apples, apiculture and sericulture were the focus products for intensive hill agriculture. Basic food, livestock, vegetables and fruits (mango and banana) represented the priorities for *tarai* agriculture. The Plan envisioned a significant role for women in implementing the APP strategy as they would be the principal beneficiaries of increased income flows at the household level. Their anticipated role was limited not just to the provision of labour inputs but also active participation and entrepreneurship. A detailed mechanism for implementing and monitoring the APP—both at the national and local level—was also devised. The total investment requirement for all the programmes within the 21-year duration of the Plan came up to US $1.74 billion at 1988 prices. For the first five years (1995/6 to 1999/2000), the estimated investment for the APP was Rs. 4,201 million per annum. This translated to roughly a fifty per cent increment on the existing level of investment in agriculture. The total investment breakdowns for various inputs were: irrigation 56%, roads 20%, fertilizer 13%, research and extension 9% and institutional strengthening 2%.

THE POVERTY FOCUS: NINTH AND TENTH PLANS

The Eighth Plan had stated the poverty alleviation as one of its three principal objectives. The Ninth Plan, which was prepared as part of the Twenty Year Perspective Plan, defined the poverty alleviation as its only objective. Goals and targets were set accordingly. The Perspective Plan targeted to bring down the proportion of Nepali population below the poverty line from the level of 42 per cent in 1995 to 10 per cent by the year 2016/17. This was to be achieved through strategies aimed at generating broad-based economic growth and reducing population growth. Priority areas of emphasis were: employment generation, higher productivity and production, food security, agriculture development, rural public works, electrification, human resource development, people's empowerment and decentralization. It also proposed that the growth rate of six per cent for the Ninth Plan be eventually raised to 8.3 per cent in the Twelfth Plan—effectively taking the twenty-year growth average to 7.2 per cent.

The Ninth Plan established short and long term targets and development indicators in each sector based on its potential contribution to alleviate poverty. The total estimated capital investment in the Plan was Rs.373 billion (248 from the private sector and 125 from the public sector). The expected incremental capital output ratio was 4.1. The total planned outlay was Rs.129.56 billion. The Plan targeted to reduce the poverty level from 42 per cent of the population to 32 per cent. Several indicators of human poverty such as illiteracy, infant mortality rate, maternal mortality rate, average life expectancy at birth were identified, and the targets set accordingly. The three pronged strategy postulated to attain the Plan goals was comprised of:[21]

(a) Achieving a high, sustained and broad-based economic growth rate (a minimum of six per cent annually) through liberal and market-oriented policies.
(b) Developing social and rural infrastructure.
(c) Introducing targeted programmes to those communities and areas not mainstreamed in the development process.

The Plan also sought to bring down the unemployment rate to 4 per cent and underemployment to 35 per cent by the end of the Plan period.

The annual target for the agricultural growth was 4 per cent with the APP forming the centrepiece of the strategy.

The Tenth Plan was prepared amidst escalating Maoist insurgency. By the end of 2001, the Maoist war had intensified and its widened coverage affected a large part of the countryside, posing serious challenges to the implementation of development plans. In fact, the execution of the Ninth Plan itself was seriously hampered by the Maoist violence.

> The Tenth Plan's campaign against poverty is being launched against the backdrop of a fragile economy. After a decade of fairly robust growth, Nepal's real GDP growth became negative (–0.6%) in 2001/02 for the first time in nineteen years. In part, this has been due to: a) the global recession and the after-effects of September 11 (2001) events. (b) More importantly, the present turmoil has been an even bigger destabilizing factor, through increased insecurity, destruction of physical assets/infra structure, *bandhs* (strikes) and loss of working hours and loss of business confidence, among others. Together, these developments had adversely affected activity levels in virtually every sector of the economy—industry, trade, construction, tourism, exports, services etc. —as well as savings and investment levels and overall economic growth. In particular the effects of the disorder on the government budget have been disastrous, (due to slowing revenues and a sharp rise in security-related expenditures) at a time when substantially more (domestic and external) resources are needed to vigorously implement the development/poverty reduction agenda.[22]

The Tenth Plan also declared a remarkable and sustainable reduction in the poverty level of Nepal as its sole objective. To achieve this objective, the Plan formulated a strategy around "four pillars" of poverty reduction:

(a) *Broad-based economic growth*: A four per cent growth in agriculture would lead to wide distributional benefits to all income groups and triggering private sector-led growth in non-agricultural sectors.

(b) *Social sector development*: This was required to reduce human poverty and improve the quality of life in rural areas. Of all the dimensions of human development, education, health, rural drinking water and sanitation were particularly emphasized. For effective delivery of services in these areas, the roles of local governments, INGOs, NGOs, and CBOs were particularly stressed.

(c) *Social inclusion and targeted programmes*: To address the gender, ethnicity and caste-related disparities, the Plan proposed to mainstream this social agenda. Special attention was given to ensuring the access to state-provided benefits and services for women and deprived communities. Targeted anti-poverty schemes were planned under the umbrella of Poverty Alleviation Fund. These targeted schemes would employ a multi-dimensional/integrated area development approach for the construction of rural infrastructure supported by appropriate skills training, credit and technical support activities. The target groups' access to resources, skills and opportunities for income and employment opportunities would be simultaneously increased. These targeted activities were also expected to increase the employment opportunities. The government would also explore the possibility of providing assistance to enable the landless poor to acquire land through subsidized bank loan or cash grant.

(d) Governance reforms: A broad spectrum of actions was proposed under this heading. These included improving civil service efficiency, controlling corruption and leakages, making service delivery more effective, increasing accountability through beneficiary/community participation, and decentralization. A civil service reform programme was proposed to right-size the government and reduce the growth of administrative overhead costs.

The Plan's macroeconomic framework envisaged two scenarios. The Normal Case scenario, which assumed a speedy restoration of peace, would produce 6.2 per cent annual growth with the investment of Rs.610 billion (of which 72 per cent would come from the private sector and the rest from the public sector). The development outlay of the government under this scenario was Rs. 234 billion. The Low Case scenario, in case of delayed restoration of peace, estimated a 4.3 per cent growth rate with an investment of Rs. 457 billion, of which the public sector would contribute 129 billion rupees.

Poverty alleviation and creation of employment opportunities were not only the priority objectives of the development plans, but also the recurring themes in the slogans forwarded by all governments formed by various parties and coalitions. These objectives duly permeated every budget speech and numerous special programmes. For example, the government formed and led by the Nepali Congress launched such programmes as the *Grameen Swabalamban Karyakram* (Village Self Reliance Schemes), *Bisheswor* With the Poor, *Gaun Gaun Maa Bikas, Ghar Gharmaa Rojgaar* (Development in Each Village and Employment for Every Home), *Gaun Ko Adhikar Gaun Lai* (Power to the Village). The UML government launched such programes as *Aafno Goan Afaile Banaoun* (Build Your Own Village), and *Nau Sa* (Nine themes started with the Nepali alphabet S). The principal components of all these programmes were rural development, employment creation, poverty reduction, and empowering local bodies. A separate policy was launched to encourage foreign employment. Private manpower companies were encouraged to explore external labour markets. The budget speech for 1998/99 proposed to treat foreign employment promotion as part of the government's employment policy. Passport policy was liberalized and emphasis was placed in expanding training schemes for gainful and productive employment. An Employment Promotion Commission was set up to coordinate the numerous training schemes implemented under various ministries to avoid duplication of resources and efforts, and ensure the relevance of the imparted training to the market conditions. Private and non-government sectors were encouraged to establish training centres and poly-techniques for skills training in response to market demands.

MORE REFORMS

National Accounts

Nepal started the systematic national accounts system since the fiscal year 1964/56. The estimates were first revised in 1974/75 and the methodology developed for that estimate continued for another two decades. Meanwhile, major changes were taking place in the social and economic structure of the country. No attempt was made to develop suitable methodology to capture the effects of these changes in the macroeconomic aggregates. For example, no systematic attempt was made to capture the contribution of new economic activities such as NGO activities, private hospitals and nursing homes, consultancy services, photography, informal sector, tourism and communications-related services to the national accounts.

Even where activities such as private schools, trade and services were included in the estimates, reliable, comprehensive and updated data was lacking. In sectors such as construction and business, significant changes had taken place over time specifically in the production techniques and their respective cost structures. But the estimation technique was not revised and updated to reflect these changes. Furthermore, agriculture related data in the national accounts was simply not reliable. The new cadastral survey data clearly showed that the cropped area was higher than those estimated in the national accounts. The newly estimated district-wise data based on the cadastral survey and the results from the Land Resources Mapping Project showed sudden jumps as high as 144 per cent in some districts in a single year. This was due to the incorporation of new data without retroactive adjustments. Lastly, the constant price data of the national accounts was prepared only in two broad categories, agriculture and non-agriculture and was clearly insufficient.

Some of these inadequacies were noted by the National Planning Commission while formulating the Eighth Plan itself. Therefore, preparatory works to remove these anomalies started in 1992 with the help of a number of experts and technical teams. Detailed systematic surveys were carried out for 25 different activities.[23] Comprehensive review and analyses of existing and new data were done and appropriate adjustments made to ensure the quality and consistency of the collection methods. Various surveys and census carried out by the Central Bureau of Statistics, the Nepal Rastra Bank and the Ministry of Agriculture were used extensively in this process. The exercise resulted in the development of a more reliable and comprehensive disaggregated national accounts data, with a new base year of 1984/85.

The new national accounts series revealed that GDP for the year 1993/94 was 196.97 billion rupees or equivalently, 16 per cent higher than estimated by the previous series! Upward adjustments were made similarly in the estimates for all the years since 1984/85. The revised data showed significant structural changes in the GDP. The share of agriculture declined from 49 per cent to 42 per cent and there was a corresponding increase in the non-agricultural sector. Expectedly, variations were found in the sectoral as well as overall growth rates in previous years. Like many other things, this exercise was also not without controversy. Issues as sensitive as the estimation of a nation's GDP naturally assumed some political overtones. This author, who as the Deputy Chairman of the NPC had initiated this exercise, had to face personal criticism for "deliberately inflating the data". In view of the controversy generated, a team of experts was invited from the IMF for a thorough review of the exercise. The IMF mission—after a careful review—validated the methodology and techniques used in the revision and the new series were accepted.[25]

Refinement of the national accounts data is a continuous and a dynamic process that needs to keep pace with the changes taking place in the economy. A one-time effort would naturally be insufficient. This was the first major attempt to make Nepal's national accounts more accurate and reliable. Further work was required with respect to other aspects such as consumption, capital formation, investment and savings related statistics. I doubt if any further exercise has been done in this area since then. I still have a feeling there could be underestimation in our national accounts even now.

Administration Reforms

The first elected government constituted the Administrative Reform Commission to identify the deficiencies in the prevailing administrative structure and systems, and make suggestions to make them more efficient, cost effective and responsive to the changing requirements. The task also included suggestions specific to the public enterprises. The Commission was headed by Kula Shekhar Sharma, a retired civil servant of high repute. The Commission report, which was submitted in April 1992, still remains a major reference point for administrative reforms in Nepal. The major weaknesses identified in the Nepali administration were low motivation, overstretching and extension of the government making its vast operation unwieldy and expensive, and unnecessary growth of bureaucratic structure and civil servants. The excessive layers of decision-making process and paper work, lack of clear accountability system, and inadequate decision-making authority at the field level were other constraints.

The report recommended the government to limit its functions to national policy making, infrastructure creation and the provision of security, public health and environment, and other basic services. The Commission also recommended that the government reduce the number of government ministries from 21 to 18, restructure government departments, and increase delegation of administrative and budgetary decision making authority to departmental and district levels. It further recommended that the ministries confine their role to policy making, monitoring, and evaluation.

Other recommendations were concerned with the decentralization of authority to local bodies, privatization of government enterprises, working procedures in the government system, financial regulations, corruption control, and human resource development training for government employees. The most prominent recommendation was to reduce the size of civil service posts by 25 per cent, from 102,744 to 77,000. The report also suggested a timeframe and an associated monitoring mechanism for the implementation of the reform measures recommended. The government promptly accepted the report and committed itself to implementing the recommendations in phases. A monitoring mechanism for the implementation was also put in place.[24]

Although all the recommendations of the report were not fully implemented, the major impact of this report was that the ballooning trend of the civil service witnessed in earlier years was checked. Consequently, the size of the civil service was virtually frozen at around 85,000 since the early 1990s. Voluntary retirement schemes with attractive incentive packages was implemented in 2000/01and 2001/02 under which approximately 2500 government employees sought early retirement. The vacated posts were frozen or cancelled. To address the problem of frequent transfer of civil servants with every new cabinet, the Civil Service Act was amended prohibiting the transfer of any government servant without completing a mandatory two-year in one job. Civil servants were spared of the humiliation of being sent to the obnoxious reserve pool for more than thirty days. New performance criteria were instituted for promotion, and a fixed ratio of mid level positions was made open for free competition to allow lateral entry.

A new phase of administrative reforms was initiated with the financial support from the Asian Development Bank in 2003. The programme started with the objective of making the civil service efficient, accountable and transparent and proposed actions on various fronts. The first was in the field of instituting a merit-based and transparent system of recruitment, transfers and promotions. Second, a long-term pay policy together with appropriate decompression of the pay scales was proposed. The reform measures were also accompanied by efforts to reduce the size of the civil service, increase the representation of women and deprived groups, promote training and career development opportunities, and strengthen the accountability framework within the civil service.

Decentralization

The process of decentralization involves the transfer of authority and responsibility to local bodies from the stage of identification of projects and plans to their effective operation and management. Despite the recognition of the importance of decentralization in the *Panchayat* days, its actual implementation suffered due to a variety of reasons. There was a highly centralized administrative structure and decisions were imposed on the lower levels. The demarcation of the responsibility and authority delegated to the local bodies was ambiguous. The political mobilization of the masses that dovetailed the advent of democracy provided the right environmental setting for the task of real decentralization. The lack of sustainable local ownership, and the high cost of development interventions inherent to the top–down and bureaucracy-led development approach was quickly recognized by the government.

Laws were enacted in 1991 to specify the organizations, functions and authorities at the village, municipal, and district levels. The previous Village and District *Panchayats* were renamed Village Development Committees (VDCs) and District Development Committees (DDCs) to emphasize the developmental nature of their functions. Town Panchayats became municipalities. These bodies were given the responsibility of formulating and passing annual programmes for their respective areas. The government employees belonging to line ministries in these bodies were made accountable to the elected representatives at the local levels. A legal basis was provided to make use of the "users committee" comprising stakeholders of the local community to implement local level projects. Simple operation manuals were prepared for these user committees. Central level grants and revenue collected from local taxes were the sources of income for these local bodies.

The resource base of the VDCs got a significant boost from the fiscal year 1995/96 when a policy of providing a uniform grant of Rs. 500,000 was announced. From 1996/97 onwards, the local bodies, VDCs and municipalities were allowed to retain all land revenue collected from their respective areas. Decentralization was the recurrent cross-cutting theme of all plans and policy documents of governments in the post-Panchayat period. The landmark development was the passing of the Local Self Governance Act (LSGA) in 1999. This Act guaranteed the devolution of fiscal authority, and transfer of management and operation of basic service delivery functions with respect to schools, health posts, postal services, rural roads, agriculture and small irrigation projects to the local bodies.

Institutional arrangements for a separate local service cadres under the institutional umbrella of Local Service Commission was also proposed. The Tenth Plan intends to transfer 25,000 primary schools, all sub-health posts and agricultural extension services to VDCs under the premise that the local bodies are better placed and better able to perform these tasks effectively. Future emphasis should be on building up technical, administrative and managerial capabilities of the local bodies through the provision of adequate manpower, training and equipment. A separate Local Bodies Finance Commission to suggest specific fiscal devolution measures and a Decentralization Implementation and Monitoring Committee were set up to oversee the execution of decentralization programme in an effective way. Implementation progress on this front, however, has been hampered in the absence of elected local bodies after 2002.

Responding to widespread concern on the increasing urbanization in the country, coverage of municipal areas has been expanded. According to the LSGA, the government could declare any area populated by more than 20,000 people (10,000 in case of hills and mountainous areas) and having access to electricity, road, drinking water and communications as municipal. The total number of municipalities at the end of 2004 stood at 57 with the total urban population of 3.14 million representing 14 per cent of the country's total population. The law has empowered municipalities with wide-ranging functions in public utilities, social services and urban-related activities such as street lighting, public parks, sanitation, garbage collection, and public constructions. Sources such as land tax, urban property tax, entertainment tax, rent tax, professional tax, vehicle tax, and various forms of fees and user charges form the revenue base of municipalities and local bodies.

Privatization and Public Enterprise Reforms

The history of public enterprises in Nepal can be traced back to the establishment of Nepal Bank Ltd. in 1934. Some more enterprises were set up by the state in the 1950s, but most of them came into being in the sixties and seventies during the Panchayat period. They covered a wide range of fields, including finance, industry, transportation, trade, telecommunications, water supply, culture, and entertainment. Their function varied from filling the gap in the absence of private ventures providing such services to revenue generation and public well being through the supply of goods and services at favourable prices. But the main reason for the proliferation of public enterprises was the government to government assistance from friendly countries and institutions in industrial, trade and other infrastructural sectors, which required separate institutions for handling and operation.

When the first elected Nepali Congress government took office in 1991, the total capital invested in public enterprises (PEs) was Rs. 6,303 million in equity and Rs. 5,584 million in loans. The enterprises whose accounts were audited up to the fiscal year 1989/90 showed a loss of Rs. 240 million. This further increased to Rs. 1,870 million in 1990/91. The average capacity utilization in this sector was 52 per cent.[26] Evidently, the enterprises which were expected to generate capital surplus for public investment in the economy were themselves running inefficiently. They were incurring heavy financial loss, absorbing disproportionate shares of domestic credit, and posing significant budgetary and economic burden. Attempts were made to sell some PEs during the Panchayat period but without much success.[27] The new government was concerned about the costs of maintaining these enterprises. In 1992, the gross transfer to PEs was more than the expenditure on health and education combined while the net transfers were more than the total foreign grants to the country.[28]

To deal with inefficiencies in these enterprises, the new government announced the privatization policy in the very first budget speech. This policy was further elaborated in the Eighth Plan. Justifying the policy, the Plan said the PEs produced negligible returns on the huge capital and credit investment. In fact, some of them had to be kept alive through hefty government subsidy. Excessive regulations, overstaffing, and poor management reduced their operational flexibility and competitiveness. Government resources were required for more urgent social programmes than in subsidizing poorly-run enterprises. The Plan also described the criteria for selecting PEs and the methods of privatization. A separate policy was prepared concurrently to improve the management of the enterprises that would continue to remain in the government sector. In 1992, the Privatization Act passed by the parliament elaborated on the modalities, process and institutional mechanism of privatization.

The privatization process codified in the Act was very elaborate as it detailed out the process starting from the initial evaluation of the concerned enterprise, preparation of a detailed information kit with project evaluation, terms and conditions of sale, and the invitation of public bids. Each stage was required to be approved by the High Level Privatization Committee chaired by the Finance Minister, and participated by the respective line minister, secretaries of the concerned ministries and the Labour Ministry, Members of Parliament representing the Parliamentary Finance Committee, ruling and opposition parties, and the chairman of the FNCCI. The Cabinet decision was also necessary at the initial and final stages of the privatization decision. To ensure full transparency, press releases at various stages were also required.

The government started the privatization programme in early 1990s, by privatizing three PEs in the first phase, and seven in the second phase. Others were either privatized or liquidated in subsequent phases. By the end of 2003, privatization or liquidation was completed for 24 enterprises. Various modalities were adopted depending on the nature of the enterprise to be privatized. These included the public sale of business and assets, asset sale, share sale, liquidation, contracting out the management, leasing of assets, and dissolution. All enterprises that were sold except one, went to Nepali nationals.[29] It was also made mandatory for the privatized enterprises to sell 25 per cent of their share to the general public and five per cent share to the employees at a 25 per cent discount on a deferred payment schedule.

By the end of the fiscal year 2002/03, 38 enterprises were still in the government sector. The total investment in these enterprises amounted to Rs. 85,809 million –32,076 million in equity and 53,733 million in loan. The total loss from these undertakings in the year 2002/03 had reached Rs. 4,867 million. The dividend paid by some of the profit making enterprises added up to a paltry 645 million rupees. Losses were rampant in all types of enterprises—manufacturing, trading, and services, financial and social.[30]

With respect to PEs remaining in the public sector, steps were taken to improve operational efficiency. Introducing flexible pricing policy, terminating the practice of guaranteed commercial credit, trimming down the excessive staff, and the freezing of new recruitments were some of the measures taken. Performance contract system was introduced to run a few enterprises like the Udaypur Cement, Hetauda Cement, *Karmachari Sanchaya Kosh*, Agriculture Development Bank and Janak Education Materials Centre. The performance would be evaluated on the basis of such indicators like capacity utilization, turnover, and return on investment, labour productivity and net profit.

Some public corporations were creating long-term liabilities beyond the institution's financial capacity. Inevitably, the burden of these contingent liabilities would ultimately would fall on the government's shoulders. Such enterprises were instructed to make mandatory allocation of necessary funds each year for such schemes as pension and gratuity. Enterprises were required to seek prior approval from the Ministry of Finance before making any decision regarding the creation of new posts, increases in salary, allowances and other fringe benefits, which would add to the financial liabilities of the enterprises. This contradicted the need for operational flexibility to the commercial enterprises. But such an imposition had become imperative under the prevailing scenario where decisions were being taken more on political and trade union pressures than on business considerations. The chief executive officers of the concerned enterprises were held accountable if any such decision was made without following the due process. The Ministry of Finance also made provision to penalize the CEOs of those enterprises that did not have the audited accounts for the last two years.[31]

Monitoring and Evaluation System

One well-known problem of Nepal's development is that programmes suffer at the implementation level. Delayed decisions or lack of them often cause cost and time overruns and projects do not meet the intended objectives and targets. Systematic monitoring and evaluation system were non-existent in many development ministries and departments. Proper interactions between the ministries/departments and project management in order to take timely corrective actions on the obstacles and problems faced at implementation were lacking. The only mechanism for feedback in the existing system was the submission of trimesterly progress reports to the superior level. To overcome this problem, a new monitoring and evaluation system was put in place in 1992.

Under the new system, a National Development Action Committee was formed under the Prime Minister with the Finance Minister, concerned Ministers, Deputy Chairman of the National Planning Commission, concerned Members and the Chief Secretary as members. The primary function of the Committee was to ensure inter-ministerial coordination and address the problems requiring highest level of attention. The Committee would meet once in every four months to monitor the implementation of nationally important projects and those that required the attention of more than one ministry. The Central Evaluation and Monitoring Division of the NPC acted as the focal point for this interaction. A separate monitoring and evaluation division was put in place in every department and ministry. A ministry level Development Action Committee was formed in each ministry under the chairmanship of the respective minister to meet every trimester to monitor, take stock of, and evaluate project performances and take necessary corrective actions. Result and output oriented performance indicators together with detailed guidelines were prepared and put in action for regular reporting. To increase the efficiency and motivation of employees, a system of performance based reward, punishment and career development was proposed.

Public Expenditure Management

With the proliferation of development projects and the attendant increase in public expenditure, the increasing size of the government was causing serious concerns. The number of development projects was increasing under popular pressure without adequate budgetary provision. The problem, if not corrected in time and brought within the manageable proportion, was threatening future macroeconomic sustainability. Therefore, the Public Expenditure Review Commission was constituted in August 2000 with the task of reviewing government expenditure, prioritizing them, recommending the termination of low priority regular and development expenditure heads, and suggesting improvements in financial regulations. The Commission completed the report in six months and made far reaching recommendations to rationalize public expenditure to bring it to a sustainable level.

The report recommended the outright termination and merger of a number of government departments and offices, decentralization and delegation of authorities from higher level functionaries, ministries and departments to lower levels, changes in civil service regulations to promote accountability, and also developed criteria for selecting development projects. The report further recommended a ceiling on the regular expenditure at 70 per cent of the public revenue. For this, a cap was proposed on the internal security and defence expenditure at 7 per cent each of the national revenue. The 700 or so projects and programmes included in the annual budget were found unmanageable. Only the properly studied programmes and projects with adequate financial backing and those at the advanced stage of implementation were recommended for continuation while others were either recommended for termination or amalgamation with similar projects. For example, a good number of road projects from the heavy transportation portfolio were recommended for further techno-economic review.

The Commission proposed the elimination of a large number of posts, particularly at the lower levels. Reductions were proposed particularly in the Ministries of Health, Information and Communications, Agriculture and Cooperatives, and Forest and Soil Conservation. In order to reduce the long-term liability of the state, most of the low-ranking jobs were proposed to be filled up through 'service contracts' than through permanent recruitments. Zero base budgeting was recommended for a number of public organizations. A 'performance-based appropriation system'—under which budget would be approved based on physical and financial performance—was recommended for high priority development projects. Other recommendations were related to: improvement in the accounting system to reduce *Beruju* (irregularities) and hiring of temporary staff; privatization and reforms in public corporations; and, the review of the Development Board Act under which the government could set up publicly funded bodies.

The government lost no time in implementing some of the recommendations immediately while committing to execute others gradually. The budget for the year 2000/01 which this author had the honour of presenting before the Parliament declared that a few central, regional and district-level offices had been removed, merged and restructured. A large number of government offices were either closed or amalgamated immediately. Some ineffective committees and commissions were dissolved. Breaking from past practice, no new development project other than those with guaranteed source of financing was added in the portfolio. Instead, the total number of projects was brought down significantly.

To assure required level of financing to projects of national priority, a system of multi-year allocation based on implementation schedule and projected expenditure was introduced. Many ongoing construction projects suffered from the uncertainty of funds for project continuation and completion. They were, therefore, compelled to go through all the procurement and contracting process each year based on the annual budgetary appropriation. This not only delayed project implementation, but also led to tremendous wastage of time and resources in procedural formalities. To overcome this problem, the government now permitted a single contract system covering a three year period with the approval of the National Planning Commission.[32]

This idea of improved expenditure management further matured and led to the introduction of the Medium-Term Expenditure Framework (MTEF) from the fiscal year 2002/03. The objective of this tool was to align the annual budgets with Plan priorities and to act as a bridge between the five-year plans and the annual budget cycles in order to effectively shield or ring-fence resources to key priority programmes. Under this framework, projects under development ministries are prioritized under various categories based on sectoral objective and strategies, and projects with high priorities are fully assured of funds. For others, funds would be provided depending on the availability of resources at hand and based on monitorable outcomes. Targets were established in the context of the Tenth Plan's objective, and made monitorable with reference to their contribution to poverty eradication, economic growth, literacy, agricultural production, and health improvement goals.

The budget also made an attempt at addressing the long standing problem of mounting long term liabilities of the government and public corporations because of the un-funded pension system. It proposed to deduct a portion of the remuneration from all new entrants in the pensionable posts in civil, police, military and teaching services, and, together with matching contribution from the government, deposit the proceeds in the pension fund. The objective was to make the pension system self-sustaining. The minimum service period for voluntary retirement of those serving in the army, police and armed police was fixed at twenty years and the minimum age was fixed at 45 years.

Foreign Aid Policy

The role of foreign aid has been a matter of much debate and controversy in Nepal. While its contribution in the overall development of the country has generally been accepted, questions are often raised about its effectiveness in leading the country towards sustainable growth. Concerns have been expressed from both the donors and recipient sides. The donors blame the state for weak governance and institutions, corruption, lack of ownership and motivation. The other side blames the donors for 'donor imposed' priorities and values, excessive use of technical assistance, and the high cost of projects.

This author had an interesting experience about a donor-proposed project immediately upon assuming his responsibility in the NPC in the early 1990s. The case in point was a Primary Health and Population Project proposed with World Bank assistance of more than 70 million US dollars. The project staff mission had visited Nepal for at least half a dozen times and the project development was at the last stage. Armed with the popular mandate to the Nepali Congress from the recently held general election which, among others, promised to avoid loans for social sector programmes as much as possible, this author found the loan project too big for the country. Furthermore, we knew that there were other multilateral and bilateral donors specialized and interested in the field willing to provide grant money for various components proposed in the project. This author proposed scaling down the project size, and substituting some project components with grant money. The Bank staff found the proposal difficult to accept, as the project had already cleared various stages of preparation. We also dug our heels and refused to accept the project in the form proposed. Ultimately, a compromise was mooted under which the government itself would convene a pledging conference for the project with interested donors. If grant money were pledged, that would substitute the loan. The Bank loan would be used only to meet the shortfall not covered by the grant. After the pledging conference, a large part of this project was funded by grants from multilateral and bilateral sources. The proposed Bank loan was brought down to about 20 million US dollars.

In view of the concerns expressed from both sides—donors and the recipient—the budget speech for 2000/01 proposed to formulate a foreign aid policy for the country. The draft policy document was presented at the Nepal Development Forum in January 2002, and its final version announced subsequently. The document defined the overarching goal of foreign aid as poverty reduction through fostering growth and supporting critical social infrastructure needs. The policy emphasized convergence and compatibility of external assistance with national goals and priorities, stressing particularly the need for the donors and the government to work as partners in order to increase the transparency, effectiveness and efficiency of aid. Regarding the sectors and sub-sectors for aid priorities, the Policy said:

> In broad terms, these include infrastructure development (energy, transport, tourism, science and technology), agriculture, irrigation and forestry including the environment, human resource and social development, education, health, population, and to specific activities focusing on poverty alleviation, employment promotion, and development of backward regions. With these broad sectors and issues, emphasis will be placed on areas such as rural infrastructure development including rural electrification and rural roads and transport, minor irrigation and agricultural extension and crop diversification, and basic and technical education, public health, access to drinking water and addressing the population problem. Foreign aid will be utilized in these sectors and sub sectors to improve primarily the outlook of economic growth and poverty reduction as well as capacity building.[33]

The document proposed a very cautious policy even towards concessional loans, giving preference to grant assistance so as to help keep the long-term debt burden of the country within sustainable levels. The preferred field for such loans is infrastructure development where rates of returns are likely to be higher. The policy also promised to avoid loans for technical assistance activities such as training and consultancies. Another important aspect of the policy—frequently stressed but little implemented at operational level—is the emphasis on the ownership and leadership of the government in externally-assisted projects. The role of the donors should be minimal and they should be limited strictly to being facilitators and supporters. Measures proposed to operationalize this included the use of national stakeholders in project preparation and implementation, avoiding the establishment of parallel and separate institutions to run projects, and the recognition of government mechanism for expenditure reporting and accountability. Some other elements of the strategy addressed issues on the development of sector-wide approaches and strategies to address specific sector and sub-sector requirements, need to improve financial transparency and accountability, strengthening aid coordination, joint programming approach and the continuous donor-recipient dialogue and interaction.

CONCLUSION

The reform measures described above relate mainly to economic development. A separate treatment will be necessary to cover other fields of governance, including the formation and strengthening the democratic institutions such as the legislative bodies, judiciary and other constitutional organs, and reforms in the social sector. Similarly, no attempt has been made here to review the efforts made in expanding and diversifying Nepal's international relations and the economic thrust given in our international and diplomatic arena.

One conspicuous aspect of the reforms was in the direction of reducing the stranglehold of government control and regulations over economic activities. A liberal and democratic polity introduced after the People's Movement was now accompanied by a liberal economic and social policy. It recognized the fact that nation building requires a coalition and creative partnership among the state, private sector, and the civil society with the state assuming the leadership role by putting in place an appropriate development framework. The 1990s saw a gradual dismantling of the command and control policy of the previous era. The state role in business was reduced effectively creating more space for the private sector. The social sector was made open to non-government and community based organizations whose access, flexibility and creative energy deemed them better capable of providing services efficiently. A new environment was created to encourage the application of creativity and entrepreneurship of the private and other non-government sectors and domestic and foreign private investment was encouraged in practically all areas of the economy.

The state's role became more pronounced in creating an enabling environment for private sector players. More importantly, its role became much wider in extending education and health facilities, providing basic services in rural areas, launching anti-poverty programmes, protecting the environment, and decentralizing authority to the local levels. The role of the government shrank from production and other economic fields, but expanded in social, infrastructural and other sectors. This was accompanied by an effort to make the public administration leaner and more efficient. The expanding trend of public administration not only came to a halt, but it shrank from a level of more than 100,000 posts to around 85,000 at present. On the other hand, the size of education and health personnel and administration underwent rapid growth with a 50 per cent increase in the share of social sector investment. Higher priority was accorded to increasing the access to state resources and opportunities for neglected and marginalized sections of the population. Backward regions and rural areas were explicitly targeted. And sustainable use of natural resources and devolution of administrative and fiscal authority to the local level were encouraged to the extent possible.

High priority was also given to maintaining macroeconomic stability and reducing budget deficit by greater mobilization of internal resources and improved expenditure management. Attempts were made to control and optimize public expenditure and streamline long-term liabilities to ensure sustainability in government finance. The revenue system underwent modern reforms and policy initiatives to modernize and diversify agriculture, reform administration, and reduce the effectiveness as well as transaction cost of foreign aid were put in place. Particularly from the second half of the 1990s, a focused attention was given to the problem of poverty as reflected in the Ninth and Tenth Plans. Both of these Plans identified poverty alleviation as their sole objective. The Tenth Plan accorded special emphasis on the social inclusion agenda, targeting specifically the deprived and marginalized social groups and communities—the women, *Dalits*, and indigenous minorities. The overall impact of these policies on the economy will be discussed in the next chapter.

NOTES

1. Rishikesh Shaha, *Politics in Nepal 1980–91*, New Delhi: Manohar, 1993, pp. 242–243.
2. The new Comission comprised of Dr. Ram Sharan Mahat as Deputy Chairman, Dr. Ram Prakash Yadav, Dr. Binayak Bhadra, Prithvi Raj Ligal, Dr. Bal Gopal Vaidya and Sri Krishna Upadhyaya as members.
3. National Planning Commission , *The Eighth Plan: Draft Approach Paper*, 1991, p. 1.
4. National Planning Commission, *The Eighth Plan*, 1992, p. 85.
5. Ibid.
6. Ibid p. 86.
7. Ibid, p. 89.
8. Praveen M. Dixit, 'Economic Reform in Nepal: A Cursory Assessment', paper presented at seminar organized by Centre for Economic Development and Administration, 8 March 1995, ibid, p.3. The author was Director of USAID project IRIS-Nepal.
9. For this and more, see NEFAS/FINNIDA, *Development Challenges for Nepal,* Madan Dahal, Keshav Acharya, and Dev Raj Dahal (ed.) Chapter III, 1999.
10. Ibid, p.67.
11. Nepal Rastra Bank, 'Financial Sector Reform' paper presented to the Nepal Development Forum 2004.
12. Collins and Associates, *A Financial Future For Nepal: Creating an International Financial Services Center,* Boston: Collins and Associates, 1995.
13. Prof. Howell E. Jackson and William W. Park, *An International Financial Services Center in Nepal: The Legal Foundation,* 1998. A report to submitted to Nepal Rastra Bank through Collins and Associates, Boston, Massachusetts, USA.
14. Dixit op. cit.

15. Ibid.
16. Rup Khadka, *Tax Reform in Nepal: A Unique Experience* (unpublished mimeograph).
17. A section of the business community forced the market to shut down for several days holding protest rallies and burning the effigy of this author who was the Finance Minister at that time.
18. Rup Khadka, 'Value Added Tax: The Concept, International Experience and Its Application in Nepal' in Rup Khadka (ed) *Value Added Tax: Four Years of Implementation,* Katmandu, 2001, p. 141.
19. Arthur Mann , *Nepal: A Feasibility Study for the Establishment of a Semi-autonomous Revenue Authority, 2004* (unpublished report).
20. Agriculture Projects Services Centre and John Mellor Associates, *The Agriculture Perspective Plan* (Final Report), June 1995, p. 3.
21. National Planning Commission, *The Tenth Plan (2002/03–2006/7) Summary*, 2003, pp. 8–9.
22. Ibid p. 2.
23. Ram Sharan Mahat's press statement on the revision of National Accounts on June 24, 1994.
24. Impressed by quality of work by the Nepalese experts, the IMF recruited Manik Lall Shrestha, one of the principal experts involved in the exercise , to work in similar job in other countries.
25. The mechanism was headed by a former Finance Secretary Gorakshya Bahadur Nuchhee Pradhan.
26. NPC (1992), op. cit. p.690.
27. Ibid.
28. Dixit, ibid p.7.
29. This was the Bansbari Leather and Shoe where an experienced Indian party made the highest offer. The factory was shifted to Chanauta of Kapilbastu district. The land occupied by the factory was not sold and remained with the Government. The land was ultimately used for the Ganga Lal Heart Centre.
30. See, HMG Ministry of Finance, *Targets and Performance of Public Enterprises (FY 2002/2003–2004/05), 2004.*
31. See *Budget Speech 2001/02.*
32. Ibid.
33. Ministry of Finance, *Foreign Aid Policy*, 2002, p. 19.

Chapter Six

Performance and Delivery (I)

Before reviewing the development performance in the post-Panchayat democratic era, it would be pertinent to summarize the key political developments during this period. This discussion will offer a meaningful backdrop against which the performance of the institutional and policy reforms initiated should be judged.

EMERGING POLITICAL SCENARIO

The First Parliament

Amidst popular euphoria and elevated expectations that came at the heels of democracy, the elected government assumed office with an agenda for reforms and economic upliftment of the country and its people. But things were not smooth and easy on the political front. This period was characterized by significant political turbulence and it is noteworthy that not a single government completed its five-year term. The struggle for power among and within parties motivated in general by short-term expediencies became more frequent. This struggle and bickering for political power did not allow the governments to fully devote themselves to economic and social agenda. Furthermore, the Maoist conflict that began in 1996 started taking heavy toll on the country's economic development and growth prospects.

The only period marked by relative political stability was the first three and a half years of the Nepali Congress government. Relative is the key word here since even this period was not free from intra-party feuds and power struggle, particularly between an assertive Prime Minister and the powerful party organization. On the one hand there was an elected Prime Minister—bestowed with constitutional powers patterned on the Westminster model and answerable to the parliament that elected him—trying to assert and expand his authority by appointing the cabinet members and other functionaries of his choice. On the other hand, there was the Nepali Congress party and its Supreme Leader Ganesh Man Singh—who had not only led the historic democratic movement of the country but also declined the opportunity to become the Prime Minister upon the movement's success. Singh considered it a matter of his right to have a say in the governance and party matters. The initial years of the new regime were dominated by the intra-party power struggle between these two stalwarts over various issues. K.P. Bhattarai, the party president tried to act as a balancing force but his inner loyalty was to the latter. The intra-party feud led the anti-Koirala faction to push Bhattarai's candidature in a parliamentary by-election from Kathmandu Constituency One in February 1994, where he was defeated.[1] This defeat amid charges of alleged intra-party sabotage deepened further bitterness in the party, which had previously revolved around such issues like vital political appointments[2] and cabinet reshuffles.

In the meantime, the opposition parties, particularly the Nepal Communist Party (UML) were doing everything possible to make life difficult and miserable for the new government from the very beginning. They adopted aggressive and extremist tactics including boycotts of parliamentary sessions, physical obstruction to the House proceedings, street agitation and violence, and nation-wide shut-downs causing loss of life and property. The UML proclaimed a policy of opposing the government with the slogan of *Sadan-Dekhi-Sadak-Samma* (from-parliament-to-street). The opposition stalled the proceedings of the parliament for two weeks in the very first session of the House over the issue of civil servants' agitation for a pay hike. The Speaker of the House of Representatives, Daman Nath Dhungana postulated a controversial theory that further emboldened the aggressive posturing of the opposition. He declared the House belonged to the opposition while the government belonged to the treasury. The Dasdhunga incident involving the death of the UML leader Madan Bhandari in May 1993, and the Tanakpur Agreement, which the government had signed with India during Koirala's official visit, were two issues whipped up by the opposition with extremist methods.[3]

The power struggle within the NC climaxed when 36 anti-Koirala members from the treasury bench of the House of Representatives abstained from the crucial voting on the Vote of Thanks to the Royal Address on the government's annual Policy and Programmes in July 1994. The government was defeated on the vote. The Prime Minister swiftly dissolved the House and declared mid-term elections for a fresh mandate in November 1994. Opposition parties, including the rebel faction within the NC, attempted to revive the House through a court battle but failed. The following election proved to be NC's undoing. The winning prospects of the Nepali Congress—already marred by internecine battles within the party—suffered further blows from widespread intra-party sabotage. The election produced a hung parliament with the UML emerging as the largest single party with 92 seats. NC was relegated to second place with 79 seats.

Turbulent Years

As the leader of the largest party in the House of Representatives, Mana Mohan Adhikary formed the minority government. Sher Bahadur Deuba became the new leader of the opposition after G.P. Koirala declined to offer himself for the leadership post of the NC parliamentary party. The new UML government had a different approach on the economy. Policies for sweeping market reforms, macroeconomic stability, privatization and liberalization of foreign investment initiated by the previous regime were not to UML's liking. Ignoring the limitations of a minority government, they presented a budget which promised a review of past policies, stressed the promotion of 'national capital' and brought about a host of populist budgetary proposals. One prominent feature of their programme was the distribution of annual grant of Rs. 300,000 to all VDCs, which was subsequently raised to Rs. 500,000 to be spent at the latter's discretion. The number of projects in the government portfolio multiplied. Limited resources were dispersed widely over poorly conceived and funded schemes. The stance taken by the new government on the reform process initiated in the past created significant uncertainty and a threat of reversal of major policies. The outraged opposition parties including the Nepali Congress, Rastriya Prajatantra Party and Nepal Sadvabana Party reacted to the UML's impatience and haste to expand the party's power base by tendering a vote of no confidence against the UML government. The Prime Minister dissolved the House and declared mid-term elections to avoid the voting. The issue was deliberated in the Supreme Court which reversed the Prime Minister's decision and restored the House. The UML government was defeated in the vote of no confidence.

A coalition of three parties led by NC formed the subsequent government in September 1995. Deuba became Prime Minister of this coalition that included the RPP and Nepal Sadvabana Party (NSP). The Deuba government lasted for two years. It was during this time that the Maoists started their violent insurgency in February 1996. In the fast-changing political scenario, with numerous permutations and combinations between and within political forces, the Deuba government was succeeded by another coalition under the leadership of Lokendra Bahadur Chand of the RPP. This coalition was joined by the UML and NSP. Chand was soon replaced by Surya Bahadur Thapa of RPP with the support of Nepali Congress in October 1997. Even this government did not last long, and G.P. Koirala became the new Prime Minister, with the help of the Nepal Communist Party (ML), the breakaway faction of the UML led by Bamdev Gautam. The coalition of convenience between the NC and ML started to crumble very soon. The UML became the new coalition partner of the NC government led by Koirala.

It was during the second parliament that the country witnessed shifting coalitions, frequent motions of no-confidence, intra-party factional splits and alliances, and the use of money and other unsavoury methods to win parliamentary votes. There were five Prime Ministers during this period. Open horse-trading and defections became part of the parliamentary behavior. The role of minor parties and independents became crucial in determining the fate of governments. Such a parliamentary equation had a direct bearing upon governance. It not only brought political instability, but also created many unhealthy practices and brought about erosion of values among parliamentarians.[4]

The third parliamentary election in May 1999 catapulted the Nepali Congress back to power. This time Koirala proposed K.P. Bhattarai as the new leader of the NC parliamentary party and consequently for the Prime Minister's job. However, the intra-party power struggle soon resulted in Bhattarai's forced resignation in March 2000. Koirala was elected the new leader of the parliamentary party. The escalating Maoist violence, militant opposition from the opposition parties and the internal party feud marred his tenure. The infamous Royal Massacre which involved the killings of King Birendra, all of his family members and closest kin also happened during this time.

The gruesome carnage inside the heavily protected family room of the Narayanhiti Palace shocked the nation. The monarchy's image as a sturdy pillar of the nation's stability and unity received a serious jolt. The *Shangri-La* appearance of the country which was being eroded by the Maoist violence dented further. The country was engulfed in unprecedented outpourings of grief and uncertainty. All types of conspiracy theories started making rounds in the country. The unimaginable and sleazy things which frequently happened in the Palace came to light. This naturally provoked demands for transparency in the palace affairs and review of the constitutional provisions which

Photograph 4: NC leaders after averting an internal crisis

Photograph 5: A scene of the parliamentary session

kept the palace administration outside the purview of parliamentary control. The Maoists shrewdly tried to cash in on the precarious situation by declaring that the 'traditional monarchy' was dead and a 'new republic' was born. This was the most trying time for the nation and the Koirala government. The transition, however, was smooth. Amidst grief and uncertainty, His Highness Gyanendra was enthroned as the new monarch.

One important parliamentary highlight of this period was the prolonged stalling of the House proceedings affected through physical force by the UML. Fifty-seven scheduled House sessions in 2001 were obstructed, rendering the entire winter session of the parliament futile. The opposition was demanding the Prime Minister's resignation over the alleged Lauda Deal by Royal Nepal Airlines Corporation (RNAC). This was happening at a time when the CIAAA was already investigating the matter. Evidently the purpose was to influence the CIAAA investigation. Koirala resigned in July 2001 over his differences with the king and the Royal Nepal Army; his order to mobilize the RNA against the armed Maoist insurgents after the Holleri massacre was not fully carried out.

This was the most trying time for the nation and the Koirala government. His Royal Highness Gyanendra was enthroned as the new monarch. One important parliamentary highlight of this period was the prolonged stalling of the House proceedings affected through physical force by the UML. Fifty-seven scheduled House sessions in 2001 were obstructed rendering the entire winter session of the parliament futile. The opposition was demanding the Prime Minister's resignation over the alleged Lauda Deal by Royal Nepal Airlines Corporation (RNAC). This was happening at a time when the Commission on Investigation Against Abuse of Authority (CIAAA) was already investigating the matter. Evidently the purpose was to influence the CIAAA investigation. Koirala resigned in July 2001 over his differences with the King and the Royal Nepal Army; his order to mobilize the RNA against the armed Maoist insurgents after the Holleri massacre was not fully carried out.

Deuba become Prime Minister for the second time. Even before the new Prime Minister had taken the oath of office, a 'cease fire' was negotiated through secret talks with the Maoists. The peace talk started. After two rounds of dialogue, the Maoists walked out of the peace talks and attacked the army barrack in Dang in November 2001, provoking the government to declare a state of emergency and mobilize the RNA to deal with the insurgency. This decision received parliamentary endorsement in February 2002. When Deuba registered a motion in parliament to extend the emergency period beyond the initial six months in May 2002, a new political situation had evolved. Other political parties were no longer in the mood to support the resolution. Nepali Congress directed the Prime Minister to withdraw the 'extension motion' from the parliament. In the NC parliamentary party meeting, the Prime Minister promised to consider the party instruction in the Cabinet meeting the following morning. But he caught every body off-guard by dissolving the House of Representatives overnight calling for fresh elections.

The king's instant acceptance of the recommendation was announced at midnight. The decision was odd and rather divorced from the reality on the ground. How could general elections be held when even the local elections had been postponed on account of the deteriorating security situation? This author, who was Finance Minister in the government, together with Education Minister Amod Upadhyaya and State Minister for Women and Social Welfare Rajendra Kharel, resigned from the cabinet immediately, protesting the Prime Minister's action. We did not foresee the election taking place in the near future and believed that Deuba's move had put the future of democracy in jeopardy. His move was also an affront to the principal of collective responsibility as he had not consulted with any of his cabinet colleagues before taking such a drastic action.[5]

The NC suspended Deuba from primary membership for six years. Deuba convened a 'General Assembly' of party members loyal to him and the congregation declared Deuba the 'Party President' of Nepali Congress. This splinter group was subsequently given the name Nepali Congress (Democratic). A last-minute attempt by a group of party members including this author to prevent the formal split did not succeed.[6] Following the House dissolution, the Nepali Congress, together with the Jan Morcha, filed a case in the Supreme Court to restore the House. The Court, in a controversial decision, upheld the Prime Minister's prerogative to dissolve the House to call fresh elections. The Court also asserted that the election could be held even in the state of emergency. But, as widely expected, the election could not take place. The Prime Minister recommended a postponement of the election date by about a year to the king. The political development took a new turn when the king, on 4 October 2002 responded by sacking Deuba and taking over the executive power citing the latter's 'incompetence' in holding the promised election. Since then, major parts of the constitution including the executive and the legislature remain suspended. The king started to rule through hand-picked nominees.

PLAN PERFORMANCE

The summary of the post-1990 political scenario described above shows that except for the first three and half years, the period was marked by frequent changes in governments, political instability and violence. Even in the din of instability and increasing violence, development activities and policy reforms continued with some hiccups and occasional interruptions. As the available indicators and statistics will show, the delivery and performance was far from disappointing under the new order until 2002.

The macroeconomic performance of the Eighth Plan (1992–97)was good. The Plan had set a target of achieving an average annual economic growth of 5.1 per cent, 4.8 per cent at factor cost. The actual growth was 5.1 per cent, and 4.9 at factor cost, thus marginally exceeding the target. Based on the estimated population growth of 2.3 per cent, the per capita income increased by an annual 2.8 per cent. The principal contributor to this performance was the non-agricultural sector, which grew at an average of 6.3 per cent, against the target of 6.1 per cent. Performance in this sector was particularly attributable to the economic reform measures. The agricultural sector fell a little short of the expectation, with an annual 3 per cent against the estimated 3.7 per cent.

Although some crops like millet, barely and pulse did quite well, surpassing their respective targets the target of adding 400,000 metric tonnes of food grain each year did not materialize mainly due to the failure to increase productivity in principal crops like paddy. Cash crops such as tea and sugarcane met targets and satisfactory performances were recorded in horticulture. The performance in agriculture was affected by the adverse weather conditions that caused floods and landslides and large-scale devastation throughout the country, most notably in 1992/93 and 1994/95. The estimated supply of agricultural inputs such as chemical fertilizers, improved seeds, and credit also fell short of their targets.

Reviewing the component-wise performance on the non-agricultural side, the response to liberal industrial policy resulted in an industrial growth of 6.8 per cent. Although substantial, this was far short of the 10.9 per cent targeted. Quite a few new investment ventures came up in the early years, but the momentum could not be sustained due to political developments after 1994. Furthermore, the power shortage resulting in frequent load shedding took its own toll on industrial activity. These factors also contributed partially in the non-fulfilment of targets in trade, power, hotel/restaurants and public works. However, the shortfall in these sectors was more than offset by the robust growth recorded in transport and communications, banking and financial sector, and social sectors where the performance exceeded targets by overwhelming margins.

Another positive development was the structural change in the economy. Agriculture's contribution in the GDP came down from 45 per cent to 41 per cent during the Plan period, with a corresponding increase in the share of the non-agricultural sector.

During the period, gross fixed capital formation reached Rs. 188.9 billion rupees at 1991/92 prices. Total investment rose from 21 per cent to 25 per cent of GDP. National savings rose from 13 per cent to 15 per cent of GDP accounting for 59 per cent of the total investment. The actual development expenditure at constant price reached Rs. 87.1 billion, which was only 76.7 per cent of the planned outlay. Internal sources contributed 43.4 per cent of the development expenditure and the rest, 56.5 per cent, was met from external sources. Of the internal sources, revenue surplus and internal loans accounted for 26.4 per cent and 17.6 per cent respectively.[7]

The National Urban Consumers Price Index increased by an annual average of 8.3 per cent, less than the 9 per cent that was estimated. Expected export growth of 19 per cent did not materialize and an average increase of 24.6 per cent in imports thus resulted in high trade deficit. But the deficit was more than offset by services and transfer incomes. The surplus in capital accounts resulting from foreign grants, loans as well as new investments led to a rise in foreign exchange reserves to 48 billion rupees at the end of the plan from a prior level of Rs. 23 billion.

The macroeconomic performance of the Ninth Plan (1997–2002), however, was less than satisfactory.[8] The overall GDP growth averaged only 3.6 per cent against the target of 6 per cent. As the population was growing at the rate of 2.25 per cent, the growth in annual per capita income was estimated at a modest 1.3 per cent. The performance of agriculture improved slightly; agricultural sector grew by 3.3 per cent compared to the 3 per cent growth achieved during the Eighth Plan. However, serious shortfalls occurred in the non-agriculture sector, which grew at an average of 3.9 per cent against the target of 7.3 per cent. The most conspicuous slowdown was witnessed in the industrial sector, which grew at an average of 2 per cent against the target of 9.1 per cent. The performance of the economy up to the fourth year of the Plan was reasonable. But several factors—including the fluctuations in weather conditions, deteriorating law and order situation on account of an intensifying conflict and the consequent disruptions in the supply of key inputs negatively impacted the economy. Furthermore, the deteriorating external environment following the September 11 incident in the United States, and the subsequent war against terror in Afghanistan also took its toll. Explaining the factors, which affected growth performance of the Ninth Plan, the Tenth Plan document says:

> The annual average growth rate of 4.6 per cent marked the first four years of ninth plan heralding a set of positive achievements in several sectors. Unfortunately they could not be sustained in many sectors up to the fifth year. The GDP growth in the fifth year was negative by –0.5 per cent due to internal and external adverse situations, which brought home unhealthy stress on poverty alleviation and employment generation.
>
> Due to the lack of increased investment in agriculture, the expected rate could not be achieved as designed by the Plan. The other factors were the weakness on implementation side of Agriculture Perspective Plan (APP), loss of agricultural production during the first and last year of the Plan due to adverse monsoon, low level of investment and production in non-agricultural sector caused by worsening law and order situation, considerable damage inflicted upon development infrastructure. Recession in the export and tourism on the final year of the Plan due to pervading depression in the international scenario affected the achievement of the Plan. The growth rate of all sectors except the social sector, therefore, got setback, as compared to targets on this Plan period. Important economic indicators such as industries and commerce, hotel and restaurant witnessed low progress. The growth rate of several sub-sectors of them diminished to negative on the last year of the Plan.[9]

The actual capital investment in the Ninth Plan was Rs.310.4 billion against the target of 372.7 billion at the constant price of 1996/97. The public sector contributed 37 per cent to this investment. The national investment ratio in the Plan period was 24.4 per cent of the GDP, and the savings ratio 16.1 per cent. The actual government expenditure was Rs. 129.1 billion or 32 per cent short of the target of Rs. 189.6 billion. The level of external financing in development expenditure was roughly about the same as the Eighth Plan at 56 per cent. Of the internal sources, the share of revenue surplus slipped to 17.6 per cent and the rest, 26 per cent of the development expenditure was financed by internal loans including cash balances.[10]

The average annual price rise (consumer price index) was maintained at 4.7 per cent. On the trade front, the first four years of the plan witnessed rapid growth in the export trade from a level of 8 per cent of GDP to 14 per cent in 2000/01. This was followed by a sharp deceleration in the fifth year largely because of the quantitative restrictions imposed on a number of Nepali exports in the new Trade

Road Network

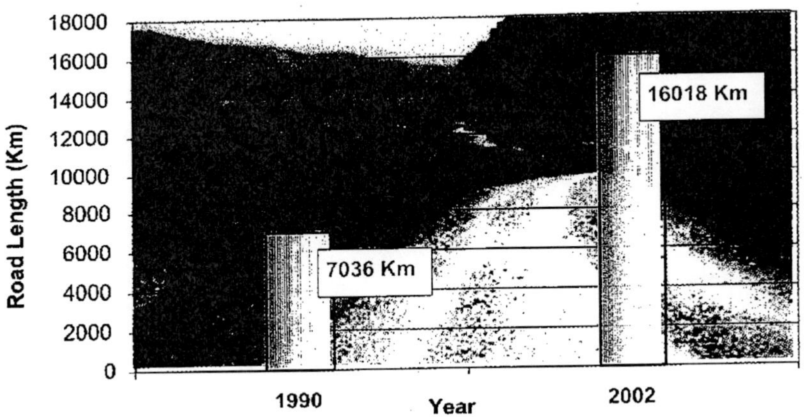

Source: Economic Surveys, HMG

Population with Access to Electricity

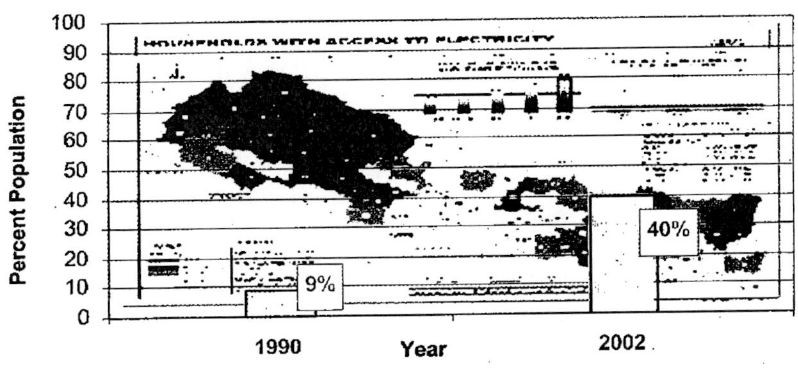

Note: Electricity generation increased from 232 MW in 1990 to 550 MW in 2002

Source: Population Census and others

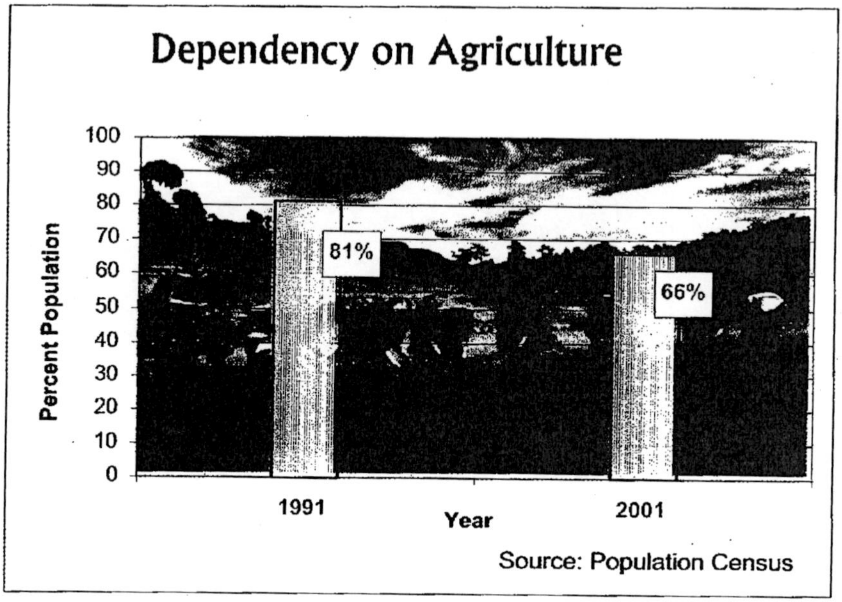
Dependency on Agriculture
100
90
80
70
60
50
40
30
20
10
0
Percent Population
81%
66%
1991
2001
Year
Source: Population Census

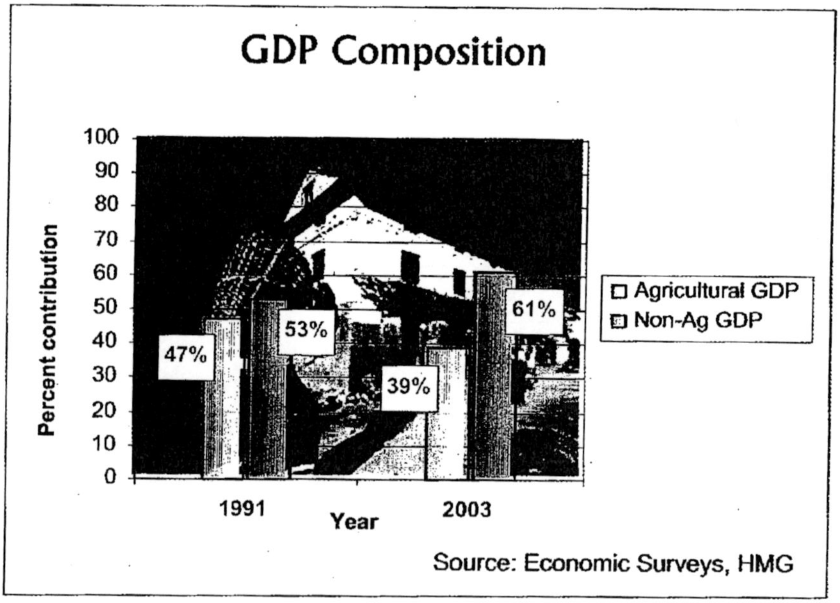
GDP Composition
100
90
80
70
60
50
40
30
20
10
0
Percent contribution
47%
53%
39%
61%
Agricultural GDP
Non-Ag GDP
1991
2003
Year
Source: Economic Surveys, HMG

Literacy

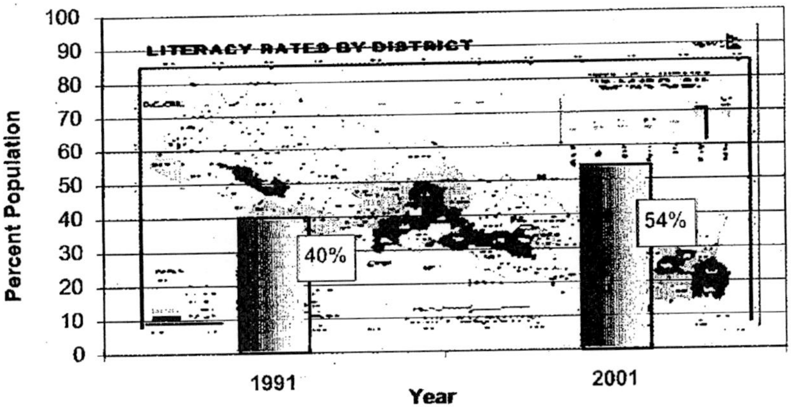

Source: Population Census

Population with Access to Improved Drinking Water

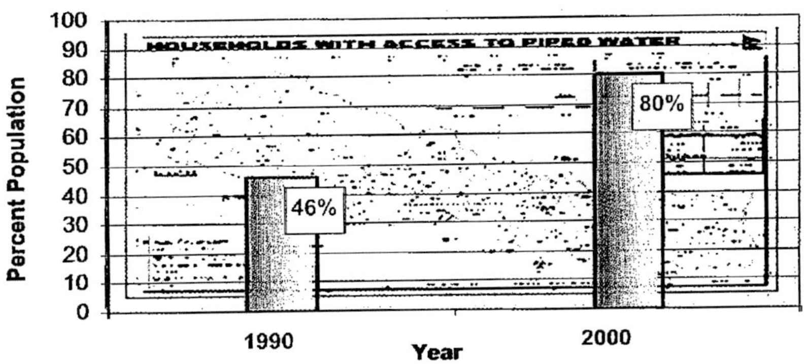

Source: The World Bank

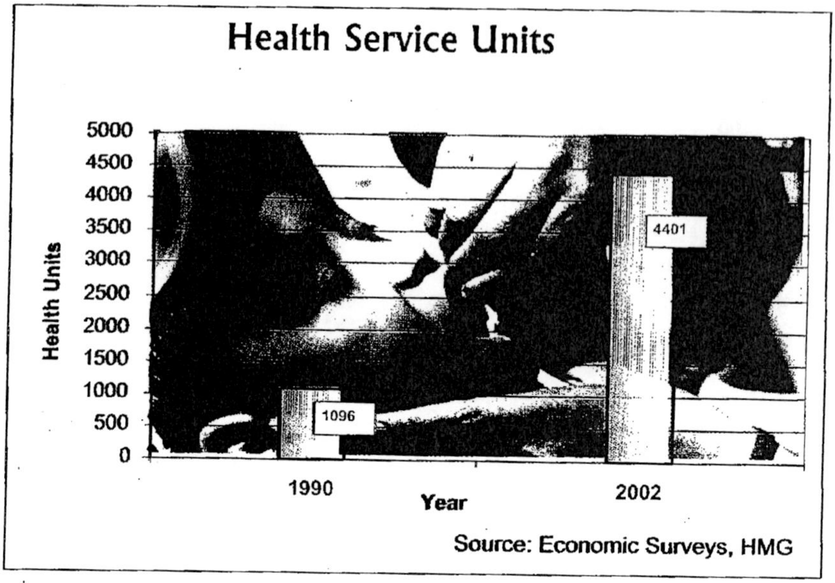
Health Service Units
Health Units
5000
4500
4000
3500
3000
2500
2000
1500
1000
500
0
1096
4401
1990
2002
Year
Source: Economic Surveys, HMG

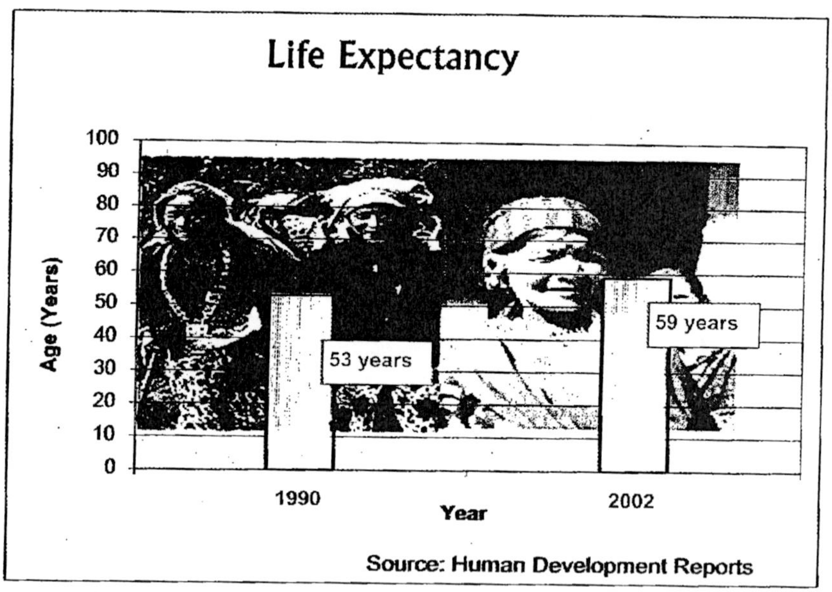
Life Expectancy
Age (Years)
100
90
80
70
60
50
40
30
20
10
0
53 years
59 years
1990
2002
Year
Source: Human Development Reports

and Transit Treaty with India in 2002. Similarly, imports also declined towards the latter end of the Ninth Plan period reflecting a slowdown of economic activity. Meanwhile, increasing migration of Nepali workers abroad resulted in the sharp rise in remittances. All these factors impacted to reduce the current accounts deficit from a level of 9 per cent of GDP in 1996/97 to around 7 per cent in 2001/02. The total gross foreign exchange holdings rose from US $850 million in 1996/97 to US $1.7 billion at the end of the Plan period. This was, at the time, equivalent to 13 months of imports of goods and services.

MACRO-ECONOMY AND STRUCTURAL SHIFT

The growth performance in the decade of 1990s averaged 4.7 per cent, and in fact, 4.8 per cent if the growth rate of 2001 is also taken into account. The reform measures introduced in the early nineties as described in the preceding chapter were rewarded by robust growth in practically all sectors. The performances in the non-agricultural sectors were particularly pronounced. This, to some extent, reflects the fact that most of the reforms were targeted specifically towards these sectors.

As the data presented in Table 6.1 amply illustrates, significant improvements were recorded in all macro and fiscal indicators over the decade of the 1990s. This contributed to an overall improvement in the country's economic structure. Overall investment ratio increased from an average 20 per cent in the eighties to about 23 per cent in the nineties. The public investment to GDP ratio declined slightly from 7.7 per cent in the eighties to 7 per cent in the nineties while private investment increased from 10.8 per cent to 13.7 per cent during the same period. Gross domestic savings rose from 10.5 per cent to 12.8 per cent of GDP. It reached 15 per cent in 2001, and subsequently declined to 11 per cent in 2003. Revenue collection progressed from an average of 8.5 per cent of GDP to 9.8 per cent. Further improvements have been recorded in subsequent years and in 2003 revenue collection had reached a level of 12.4 per cent of GDP. The remarkable improvement in revenue collection over the years despite the adverse security climate prevailing in the country can be attributed to a series of tax reform efforts initiated in the previous decade. Some of these included broadening the tax base, lowering tariffs, simplifying the collection procedures of income tax and strengthening the revenue administration.

Another important indicator of fiscal health is the containment of fiscal deficits. Large fiscal deficits are the symptoms of macroeconomic

TABLE 6.1
Economic Performance Indicators in Various Periods

	1971-1980	1981-1990	1991-2000	2001	2003	2002	2004 est
1. **Growth (%)**							
Real GDP Per capita Income	0.8	2.2	2.4	3.1	-2.8	0.7	1.4
Real GDP	2.8	4.5	4.7	5.5	-0.6	3.0	3.7
Population	2.1	2.3	2.4	2.3	2.3	2.3	23.0
2. **Investment and Savings (% of GDP)**							
Investment (Including Stocks)	16.3	19.9	23.3	24.1	25.6	26.9	27.2
Public Fixed Investments	3.9	7.7	7.0	7.6	7.6	6.9	7.2
Private Fixed Investments	9.2	10.8	1.7	11.4	11.7	12.3	12.8
Gross Domestic Savings	9.0	10.5	12.8	15.0	12.0	11.4	11.3
3. **Fiscal Indicators (% of GDP)**							
Revenue	6.5	8.5	9.8	11.4	9.3	12.4	12.2
Expenditure	11.0	17.6	16.5	17.5	17.6	16.1	17.4
Deficit	2.2	6.5	5.3	6.1	8.3	3.7	5.2
O/w Domestic Financing	1.1	2.8	1.5	2.7	4.8	0.9	0.9
Public Debt	—	—	64.4	63.8	69.7	66.6	64.0
Public Savings	—	—	—	0.2	0.2	0.8	0.1
4. **External Sector (% of GDP)**							
Export to GDP	11.4	11.7	21.0	24.1	19.3	16.9	15.7
Import to GDP	16.1	21.1	32.2	35.6	30.6	31.5	31.8
5. **Money and Credit (% of GDP)**							
M2	16.2	27.2	37.5	52.2	53.0	54.2	56.1
Domestic Credit (Net)	9.6	24.9	32.6	44.7	47.4	49.4	51.1
Domestic Credit to Private Sector (net)	6.1	11.3	21.4	33.2	33.6	35.9	
6. **Prices and Interest rates(%)**							
Inflation	7.5	10.6	9.3	2.2	2.9	4.5	5.3
Lending Rates	13.5	15.6	12.4	7.7	—	—	—

Source: Adapted from the World Bank Report (2004), *Nepal Development Policy Review*, p. 2.

Photograph 6: The Finance Minister with the Prime Minister and Cabinet Ministers towards the parliament building on the Budget Day

Photograph 7: Budget presentation for the fiscal year 2001/02 at the parliament

TABLE 6.2

Structure of GDP in % (1991–2003)

	1990/91	*2002/2003*
Agriculture	46.5	38.9
Industry	**19.4**	**22.5**
Manufacturing	7.5	9.4
Electricity, Gas and Water	1.4	1.9
Construction	10.5	11.4
Services	**34.2**	**38.3**
Trade, Restaurants and Hotels	10.7	10.3
Transport, Communication And Storage	5.7	7.7
Financial and Real Sector	9.5	10.2
Community and Social Services	8.3	10.2

Source: Based on data published in *Economic Survey* Reports.

mismanagement. The fiscal deficit showed a rising trend throughout the 1980s. The average deficit during the decade was 6.5 per cent of the GDP, but it had reached as high as 8.7 per cent in 1991/92. Similarly, the internal borrowing had reached more than 2 per cent of the GDP. Strenuous efforts were made to bring the deficit down to a more manageable level of around 5 per cent and as evident from the data, these measures were successful. The average fiscal deficit in the nineties was only 5.3 per cent. The deficit level subsequently rose in the following two years, but declined to 3.7 per cent in 2003 and 5.2 per cent in 2004.

Data also shows that the economy has undergone plausible structural change away from the traditional production pattern. As seen from Table 6.2, the share of agriculture declined from 46.5 per cent in 1990/91 to 38.9 per cent in 2002/03, while the shares of industry and services increased from 19.4 to 22.5 per cent and 44.2 to 38.3 per cent respectively. In particular, there has been noticeable growth in such sectors as manufacturing, construction, transport communications, finance and social sectors. The shift in the pattern of national production away from agriculture—whose performance hinges critically on the vagaries of monsoon—will reduce the volatility in income.

The static occupational structure of the Nepali economy which started undergoing some transformation in the eighties got further momentum in the nineties. The proportion of population depending on agriculture—which had declined to 81 per cent in 1991 from a level of 91 per cent in 1981—further declined to 65.7 per cent in 2001. The shares of industry and services sectors made significant gains, from 2.7 and 16.1 to 13.4 and 20.9 percentage points respectively.

This is an important shift in the employment structure in the country. Even more interesting is the ratio of female population getting engaged in industrial sector, particularly manufacturing. The female population engaged in manufacturing increased from 1% in 1971 to 10% in 2001.[11] Another important development is the growth of the country's urban population, an indication of the territorial response to the changing economic structure of the economy. The total urban population which was 1.696 million in 1990 increased to 3.228 million in 2001, a 90 per cent growth in a decade[12]. This shift reflects the changing division of labour, technology-based production of goods and services, and high level of spatial and economic interactions.

TABLE 6.3

Distribution of Economically Active Population by Industry (1971–2001)

	1971	*1981*	*1991*	*2001*
Agriculture	94.4	91.2	81.2	65.7
Industry	1.2	0.5	2.7	13.4
Service	4.4	8.3	16.1	20.9

Note: Based on tables of Usually Economically Active Population—a classification that was introduced in 2001 Census, as distinct from 'current' economic activity. Agriculture also includes forestry and fishing, industry includes mining & quarrying, manufacturing, electricity, gas and water and construction, while service includes all other activities.

Source: D.P. Shrestha, *Population Monograph of Nepal, Vol. I.* CBS/HMG. 2003, p. 354.

Another conspicuous aspect of the changing economic structure is the expanded role of the private sector. The participation and contribution of the private sector in the national production increased both in magnitude and variety of activities. Published data is not easily amenable to the analysis of private sector in the generation of national income. However, available data from the Economic Survey reports on the gross capital formation indicate the substantially increased role of the private sector. The share of private sector in the gross capital formation increased from 53 per cent in 1989 to 64 per cent in 2003/04.

Similarly, the share of private sector in the total domestic credit rose significantly. The domestic credit scene was strongly dominated by the government and the public enterprises sector until 1990. Together, they accounted for 61 per cent of the total domestic credit while the private sector share was limited to the remaining 39 per cent.

This scenario was almost reversed over a period of thirteen years. In 2003, the share of private sector in total domestic credit rose to 66 per cent, while that of the public sector slipped to 34 per cent.[13] The claims on the private sector from banking was even higher at 73 per cent in 2003.[14] Figures in Table 6.1 also show that the private sector, which accounted for about one-third of the total domestic credit in the eighties, claimed about two-third in the nineties. It accounted for about three-fourth of the total domestic credit in 2001 to 2003.

CHANGING POVERTY PROFILE

The term "poverty alleviation" has been widely used in contemporary development discourse and is a subject of much public policy debate. When this author met Clare Short, the then powerful British Development Assistance Minister, at the sidelines of the Labour Party Convention at Blackpool in October 2000, the lady showed her disenchantment with Nepal's development performance on the issues of poverty and corruption. When I started talking of our Government's commitment on poverty alleviation, she responded, "the words poverty alleviation give wrong connotation, let us talk about poverty eradication". I recall this experience here to indicate not only the seriousness with which the international community views the issue of poverty, but also the genuine humanitarian concern implicit in what they try to do about it. It was during Short's time, for example, that British ODA received a big boost and a separate Ministry was created to work specifically in the area of international development.

Earlier Studies

Even before one gets into any discussion on the poverty profile or the poverty trends of a country, it is important that a reasonable and hopefully, a widely accepted definition of poverty be established. Indeed, although the arts and science of poverty diagnostics has become considerably advanced, the definition of poverty itself remains one of the most vigorously debated subjects in the literature. In Nepal, the first poverty survey was conducted by the National Planning Commission in 1976/77. The nationwide surveys conducted since 1977 used different data sets and methodologies to collect data on income and consumption. Differences in the methodology naturally produce different types of results, which cannot be compared across time and often lead to debate and controversies.

The 1977 NPC survey defined the poverty line for the country as a whole based on minimum subsistence level of expenditure and income per capita. The minimum subsistence level of expenditure was arrived at by costing the nutritionally minimum balanced diet in terms of the daily calorie requirement of 2256 per person as determined by the FAO and the Nepal Food Research Laboratory, and other items of daily consumption such as clothing, footwear, education and medicines. Based on 1976/77 prices, the average subsistence level of expenditure was calculated at 2 rupees for rural areas and 1.7 rupee for urban areas. According to this criteria, 33.24 per cent of the households (35.53 in the rural areas and 23.49 in the urban areas) were estimated under the poverty line. Similarly, based on the income criteria of 2 rupees per capita daily, the study found 35.50 per cent of the households (37.33 rural and 27.58 urban) to be below the poverty line. The relatively higher proportion of households below the poverty line under the income criteria compared to the consumption criteria probably indicated that a small portion of the households consumed more than their current income through borrowings, past savings or free gifts.

Other important works conducted to measure the living conditions of Nepali households were the 1984/85 Multi-Purpose Household Budget Survey (MPHBS) by the Nepal Rastra Bank and the 1995/96 Nepal Living Standards Survey (NLSS) by the Central Bureau of Statistics (CBS). The Rastra Bank survey calculated Rs.5.95 for the hills/mountains and Rs. 4.94 for the *tarai* as the basic income need per capita per day at the prevailing price. Based on this survey, the incidence of poverty was estimated at 42.5 per cent of the total population. A World Bank mission in 1989 used US$ 150 per capita per annum as the poverty benchmark for the sake of international comparability. Based on this definition, the updated and adjusted NRB survey data indicated the poverty level to be as high as 71 per cent of the population.[15]

The estimates of poverty obtained on the basis of these earlier surveys cannot be directly compared with the figures derived from the latter day surveys.[16] Poverty figures vary depending on the survey data used and the definitions applied. Despite shortcomings related to comparability, some broad observations can be derived but only after minutely analyzing the two data sets and making appropriate adjustments.

NLSS I

The Nepal Living Standard Survey of 1995/96 (NLSS I) is one of the most recent studies based on the standard model of living standard measurement survey developed by the World Bank. It was a multi-purpose household survey conducted by the Central Bureau of Statistics to create the baseline data against which future poverty trends could be measured and the impact of anti-poverty programmes assessed. Using 4,404 rupees per capita per annum as the minimum consumption expenditure considered sufficient to provide basic calorie intake (2124 kcals of a given consumption basket) and other non-food expenses, the survey classified 42 per cent of the total population as poor, i.e., below the poverty line.[17] This national figure, however, does not reveal the sharp disparities across regions and socio-ethnic groups.

Unsurprisingly, rural poverty was found much deeper than urban poverty. The incidence of poverty in urban areas was 23 per cent compared to 44 per cent in rural areas. Particularly in the Kathmandu valley, a vast majority of the population fell in the upper quintiles of the national consumption distribution. Poverty incidence in other urban areas was slightly higher. By national standards of measurement, poverty level in the Kathmandu valley was only 4 per cent compared to 34 per cent in other urban areas. Disaggregated data showed that the poverty incidence was highest in the mountains (56 per cent), compared to *tarai* (42 per cent) and *hills* (41 per cent). Similar disparities were found across ethnic and gender lines. The people belonging to occupational castes known as *Dalits* (*Kami, Sarki, Damain,* etc.) and minority ethnic groups were worse off in terms of social and economic indicators.

After careful analysis followed by appropriate statistical adjustments to the various surveys of the past in order to introduce consistency across time, the World Bank report in May 1999 made some broad observations about the poverty trends in Nepal until 1995/96:[18]

1. There is no evidence of a decline in poverty as a whole between 1976 and 1996/97.
2. There is also no evidence of a decline in poverty in Nepal as a whole between 1984/85 and 1995/96.
3. However there is some evidence of a decline in poverty in rural areas between 1991/92 and 1905/96.

One explanation, which is also consistent with the data, is that there has been some progress since 1991/92 in rural areas. But this has clearly not been enough to compensate for the deterioration that took place in the previous fifteen years.

NLSS II

As noted above, in the past no two surveys have used identical methodology in a manner and to the extent to which they could be comparable. But, for the first time in Nepal, uniform methodology developed by the World Bank and the same data set were used in NLSS I and NLSS II, in order to enable a realistic measurement of the changes in poverty profile over the period. The NLSS II in 2003/04 used a two-stage stratified sampling scheme to select a nationally representative sample. It conducted panel surveys in 972 of the 1160 households it interviewed in 1995/96 and a cross-country survey with 3912 new households. While the full analysis of the survey results are still awaited, some of its principal findings indicate significant reduction in poverty, and improved living conditions of the people.

Using the poverty line income definition of NLSS I with price adjustments to reflect the inter-temporal differences in the cost of living, the new survey comes up with poverty line consumption definition for various geographical regions. The overall change in price level between 1995/96 and 2003/04 was 47.8 per cent–41.3 for food and 61.8 for non-food items, with some regional variations. The definition of the poverty line for NLSS II is a consumption expenditure of Rs. 620 per month (Rs. 7,440 per annum) per capita at the national level with regional variations. The survey has concluded that the incidence of poverty in Nepal has declined dramatically by 11 percentages points over the course of eight years, from 42 per cent in 1995/96 to 31 per cent in 2003/04. While poverty in urban areas has more than halved from 26 per cent to 10 per cent, poverty in rural areas has also declined appreciably from 43 per cent to 35 per cent, at one percentage point per year. As the figures in Table 6.4 indicate, poverty had declined appreciably across all development regions and ecological belts. At 27 per cent, the Central and Western regions continue to have poverty levels below the national average, while the mid-western and far-western regions with 45 and 41 percentage points respectively continue to remain way above the national level. In terms of ecological belts, the *tarai* has the lowest poverty level with 27 per cent, compared to 33 per cent in the mountains and 35 per cent in the hills. The poverty level of Kathmandu valley has declined from 4 per cent to 3 per cent, and those of other urban areas 32 per cent to 13 per cent.

Some other important conclusions of the study with respect to changes in poverty, income and employment situation are as follows:[19]

1. *Consumption Expenditure and Income*: The overall real per capita expenditure increased by 42 per cent over the period of eight years or an equivalent annual growth of 4.52 per cent. The annual rise in per capita expenditure in urban areas was 4.46 per cent, compared to 3.01 in rural areas. Variation existed within regions and the increase in per capita

TABLE 6.4
Poverty Measurement by Geographic Regions (1995–96 and 2003–04)

	1995–96	*2003–04*	*Change in %*
Urban*	21.6	9.6	-56
Rural	43.3	34.6	-20
Total	41.8	30.8	-26
Development Regions			
Eastern	38.9	29.3	-25
Central	32.5	27.1	-17
Western	38.6	27.1	-30
Mid-western	59.9	44.8	-25
Far-western	63.9	41.0	-36
Ecological belts			
Mountain	57.0	32.6	-43
Hill	40.7	34.5	-15
Tarai	40.3	27.6	-32
Nepal	41.8	30.8	-26

* The decline in poverty level of Kathmandu was from 4.3 per cent to 3.3 per cent while that of other urban areas from 31.6 per cent to 13.0 per cent.

Source: The World Bank and the Central Bureau of Statistics, *Poverty Level in Nepal between 1995–96 and 2003/04*, April 9, 2005. (Work in Progress. Internal Document).

expenditure was higher (5.36 per cent) in other urban areas than in Kathmandu (3.64 per cent). Within the rural region, the improvement in rural western *tarai* was the highest (4.73 per cent), followed by rural eastern *tarai*, rural western hills and rural eastern hills. The improvement in real per capita income is even better than the progress in consumption expenditure. The real per capita income increased at the rate of 4.75 per cent annually over the period –4.79 per cent in urban areas and 3.60 per cent rural areas. Like in other categories, variations between regions existed in income as well. Real agricultural wages increased in all ecological belts and regions. The rise in real agricultural wages of rural Nepalis compared favourably with the neighbouring Indian states of rural UP, Bihar and Bengal.

2. *Consumption and Income Disparities*: Although all income groups have benefited from the increased consumption and income levels, the households in the upper quintiles have benefited more indicating a widening disparity in both

TABLE 6.5

Changes in Real Per Capita Consumption Expenditure (1995/96–2003/04)

	1995/96	*2003/04*	*Change in %*	*Annual Change*
Kathmandu	1675	2320	33	3.64
Other Urban	942	1432	52	5.38
Rural Western Hill	496	647	30	3.38
Rural Eastern Hill	621	651	5	0.58
Rural Western *Tarai*	515	746	45	4.73
Rural Eastern *Tarai*	586	769	31	3.44
Urban	1210	1715	42	4.46
Rural	558	707	27	3.01
Lowest Quintile	241	293	21	2.45
2	362	431	19	2.21
3	474	593	25	2.83
4	640	854	33	3.66
Highest Quintile	1290	2112	64	6.35
Total	603	858	42	4.52

Source: CBS & the World Bank (2004), *Measuring Poverty in Nepal: Results from NLSS-I & II.*

TABLE 6.6

Changes in Real Per Capita Income (1995/96–2003/04)

	1995/96	*2003/04*	*Change in %*	*Annual Change*
Kathmandu	1500	1825	22	2.49
Other Urban	815	1394	71	6.93
Rural Western Hill	490	777	59	5.94
Rural Eastern Hill	527	656	42	2.77
Rural Western *Tarai*	576	779	35	3.85
Rural Eastern *Tarai*	636	764	20	2.32
Urban	1063	1545	45	4.79
Rural	560	743	33	3.60
Lowest Quintile	294	353	20	2.34
2	412	519	26	2.93
3	514	654	27	3.04
4	628	886	41	4.41
Highest Quintile	1137	1904	67	6.66
Total	594	862	45	4.75

Source: CBS & The World Bank (2004), *Measuring Poverty in Nepal: Results from NLSS-I & II.*

consumption and income pattern. The households at the highest quintile improved their consumption level by 6.35 per cent annually in real terms, while the households at the three low quintiles improved their consumption levels at less than 3 per cent per annum. Similar pattern is observed with respect to the increase in the real per capita income. Data on the consumption pattern in nominal terms show that in 2003/04, the bottom 20 per cent of the population accounted for a mere 6 per cent of the total consumption, while the richest 20 per cent of the population a whopping 53 per cent.

3. *Employment and Wages*: The ratio of people classified as employed increased from 67 per cent to 74 per cent, while the share of unemployed has decreased slightly and the group classified as inactive has declined by 6 percentage points. The percentage share of agriculture wage employment decreased from 53 per cent to 37 per cent, while that of non-agricultural income increased by 16 per cent. Among non-agriculture industries, concentration of wage earners remains in manufacturing, construction and personal services. The modality of wage payment has shifted more in favour of piece rate, contract or longer term basis from the daily payment practice. The average nominal wage rate increased by 87 per cent in agriculture and 80 per cent in non-agriculture.
4. *Income Composition and Remittances*: The share of farm income has gone down from 61 per cent to 48 per cent over the period under review, while that of non-farm income increased from 22 per cent to 28 per cent. The share of other sources including remittances increased from 16 per cent to 25 per cent. The proportion of households receiving remittances has increased from 23 per cent to 32 per cent, and the average transfer earnings per household more than doubled in nominal terms—from Rs. 15,160 in 1995/96 to 34,698 in 2003/04. Another important change witnessed is the source of remittance. The share of remittance from within Nepal and India accounted for 75 per cent of transfer income eight years ago. Now the share of other countries including the Gulf region has increased to more than 50 per cent.
5. *Housing and Household Durables*: Ninety two per cent of the households own their dwelling units This represents a 2 per cent decline from 1995/96. The proportion of renters increased from 2 to 5 per cent. The average size of dwelling declined from 604 to 531 square feet. There have, however,

been significant improvements in the ownership of household durables such as radio/cassette players, bicycles, furniture and jewelry across regions and in all quintiles of households.

6. *Literacy and Health*: Overall adult literacy rate has increased by 12 percentage points, the increase being slightly higher for females. The proportion of population aged 15 years and above that ever attended school increased from 34 per cent to 46 per cent. Similarly, the incidence of fully immunized children increased from 36 per cent to 59 per cent. The number of children ever born per 15–49 year old woman decreased from 2.6 to 2.4, while total fertility rate declined from 5.1 to 3.6 during the same period.
7. *Subjective Poverty*: Self-reported welfare has improved across all types of consumption. During this period, percentage of households reporting "less than adequate" consumption has declined by 21 per cent in food, 23 per cent in housing, 22 per cent in clothing, 31 per cent in health care, and 24 per cent in schooling. Percentage of households reporting inadequate income declined by only 6 per cent.

Other findings from NSSL II regarding the improvement in the quality of life in terms of educational, health, literacy and access to other economic services are even more positive and encouraging. The contributing factors to this remarkable improvement in living standards—the progress made in various sectors including agriculture, infrastructure development, remittances—have been elaborated in the relevant chapters and sections. Increase in agricultural and remittance income accompanied by lower than expected population growth is one of the most compelling reasons for this decline in poverty. Rapid expansion of road network by about 9000 km. in the last decade contributed to the development and commercialization of agriculture through facilitated access to agricultural inputs and market network. Modernization of agriculture is strongly correlated with road access as this encourages production of off-season vegetables, horticulture and livestock products. Commercialization of agriculture is reflected in the increased exports of agricultural products. Expansion of micro-financing to poor families have helped in the growth of micro enterprises and raised the income of the lowest strata of population. All these have contributed to the growth in real agricultural wages. The significant improvements seen in the rural income and consumption pattern is corroborated also by the Rural Household Consumption Survey of 2001. Positive changes were witnessed in all agro-climatic belts and regions, although the regional rankings did not change.[20]

NATIONAL DEBT

The governments of the post-*Panchayat* era have often been blamed by some for leading the country to a external debt trap through reckless borrowing. They allege that while the country has recorded relatively better economic progress in the post *Panchayat* period, it has been at the cost of unbearable debt burden on the Nepali citizens. The national debt increased from a level of Rs. 80 billion in 1991 to 304 billion rupees in 2003. It is alleged the country will soon go bankrupt under the weight of unsustainable debt burden. Let us review the factual situation.

That the foreign debt stock has increased almost four-fold during the period is evident from data and cannot be denied. As the country's investment requirements far exceed the internal savings and the revenue base, tapping into external savings, in the form of loans or grants, is inevitable. The savings-investment gap is manifested in current accounts deficit which was around 3 per cent of GDP in 2003. Compared to other South Asian countries, this is very high.[21] Unlike in the old days when external funding came mainly as grant aid from bilateral sources, loan is the principal form of official development assistance (ODA) in the contemporary world. This explains the changing profile of external assistance in Nepal. The emergence of the multilateral banking institutions like the World Bank and the Asian Development Bank as the principal funding sources and the concurrent reduction in bilateral assistance after the end of the Cold War have brought about this shift.

But there is no truth in the allegation of excessive borrowing in the last decade. The reason behind the apparently sharp growth in external debt was due to the sharp depreciation of Nepali rupee vis-a-vis the international reserve currencies against which the borrowings were made. For example, one US dollar was equivalent to 74.75 rupees in 2003 as against 42.70 rupees in 1991. In dollar terms, the total outstanding external debt rose from US $1.39 billion in 1991 to approximately US $2.98 billion in 2003, an increase of 114 per cent. During the same period the GDP in dollar terms increased by 117 per cent. In other words, the rising external debt level is keeping pace with the growth in national income.

The sustainability of debt burden is related to a number of economic variables including the country's national income, growth rate, export figures including earnings from goods and services including remittances, and the internal revenue generation. The total national debt as percentage of GDP in 1991 was 66.8 per cent of which domestic and external debts accounted respectively for 17.3 and 49.5 per cent. The relative size of this debt has remained generally constant since 1991 with minor variations in some years (Table 6.6). Incidentally, the total national debt as percentage of GDP in 2003 was also 66.8, of which 18 per cent was domestic debt and the remaining 48.8 per cent was external debt. This clearly shows that Nepal's debt stock in relation to the size of the economy has not undergone significant change. An assessment of Nepal's debt sustainability by IMF prepared in the context of Poverty Reduction Growth Facility 2004 (PRGF) forecasts a decline in Nepal public-debt-to-GDP ratio to around 50 per cent by 2007/08.[22]

Two ratios—the present value of debt service to GNP, and the present value of debt service to exports—cast the level of indebtedness in terms of the country's potential capacity to service debt. If either of these ratios exceed a critical value—which is 80 per cent of the present value of debt service to GNP and 220 per cent of present value to exports, then a country is classified as severely indebted.[23] The NPV-based debt indicators for the year 2002 published by the IMF for PRGF-eligible countries shows that Nepal's NPV of debt to GDP was 29.6, and NPV of debt to exports was 122 per cent.[24]

There are also other benchmark rules governing the national debt management. It is said that the total outstanding debt should not exceed 60 per cent of GDP. Similarly, the foreign debt servicing should not exceed 20 per cent of the export value, and domestic debt servicing should not exceed 20 per cent of the domestic revenue. Even based on these criteria, Nepal's situation is within manageable limits. In 2003, Nepal's stock of external debt was around 50 per cent of GDP while overall debt in the public sector stood at 66.8 per cent. Likewise, its external debt servicing ratio as a percentage of internal revenue was 13.4 per cent, and external debt servicing as percentage of export earnings in the same year stood at 15 per cent. Based on these statistics Nepal's debt situation doesn't look as alarming as it is fashionably believed within academic and political circles.

Additionally, it may also be noted that Nepal's external debt stock is comprised mostly of concessional loans with long maturities and nominal interest charges. Some of the bilateral loans, like those from Japan and some Nordic countries are eventually converted into grant. This explains Nepal's low NPV of external debt and the comfortable debt servicing situation, although the total debt stock as percentage of GDP cannot be regarded as low. At present, the international climate for poor and indebted nations is very congenial as those advocating

TABLE 6.7
Trend of Public Debt in Relation to GDP
(1991–2003)

(1)	(2)	(3)	(4)	(5)	(6)	(7)	(8)
Year	*Domestic Debt*	*Foreign Debt*	*Total Debt*	*GDP*	*(2) as % of (5)*	*(3) as % of (5)*	*(4) as % of (5)*
1991	20865	59505	80361	120371	17.3	49.4	66.8
1992	23235	70924	94159	149487	15.5	47.4	63.0
1993	24456	87421	111877	171474	14.3	51.0	65.2
1994	30631	101967	132598	199272	15.4	51.2	66.5
1995	32058	113000	145058	219175	14.6	51.6	66.2
1996	34242	128044	162286	248913	13.8	51.4	65.2
1997	35891	132087	167978	280513	12.8	47.1	59.9
1998	38407	161208	199615	300845	12.8	53.6	66.4
1999	49670	173861	223531	342036	15.5	50.8	65.4
2000	54357	190691	245048	379488	14.3	50.2	64.6
2001	60044	201551	261595	410789	14.6	49.1	63.7
2002	73621	220126	293747	422301	17.4	52.1	69.6
2003	81703	221992	303695	454934	18.0	48.8	66.8

Source: IMF: *International Financial Statistics*, Year Book 2002/November.

debt relief are gradually being taken seriously. Nepal does not fall under the category of highly indebted countries and hence does not qualify for relief under the *HIPIC* initiative[25]. Nevertheless, demand for debt relief for poor countries is increasing. The UK government has already for agreed to pay back 10 per cent of Nepal's total debt to the World Bank.

This is not to suggest that Nepal can afford to pile up debt in an irresponsible manner. Despite the concessional nature of external debt, the exchange rate risk is high. Due to steady depreciation of rupee value in relation to convertible currency in the past, the pay back liability to the tax payers has mounted. This makes the soft loan 'hard' for all practical purposes to the debtor country. Therefore, a prudent public debt policy is necessary with adequate emphasis on the quality of debt. The borrowed amount should be able to create economic capacity for the future generations to repay the accumulated loan without additional burdens. It is therefore the moral responsibility of the present generation to apply the resources in building productive assets that enhance productive capacity, and increase income and employment opportunities.

SUMMING UP

Turbulent politics marked the democratic era of the 1990s. Unstable governments, intra-party feuds, extra-constitutional maneuverings, and the application of questionable methods to stabilize and destabilize governments characterized this period. In some ways, this was a period of 'growing pains' for a young democracy. The effect of violent Maoist conflict on the economy was even more serious and destructive. But, despite the unstable politics, the Maoist violence and the adverse impact they made on governance, the overall development performance during the period was not disappointing. It was short of the people's expectations and what could have been achieved with better governance and a single-minded devotion to the economic agenda, but it was much better than that of any period in Nepal's history and particularly compared to that of the three decades of *Panchayat* system that preceded the democratic rule. The macroeconomic performance was comparable to the South Asian norm of the last decade and public debt management was prudent and within sustainable limits. The virtuous combination of market friendly policies, expanded state role in the creation of infrastructure and social services, a liberal social policy to unleash the energy and potential of the non-government sector, and widespread political mobilization at the grassroots level helped bring about this progress.

Studies have conclusively shown that the intensity and scope of poverty went down considerably. The improved poverty level has been reflected in higher real consumption, income level, and the ownership of household durables. More importantly, people across all income groups, regions and ecological belts have better access to education, health and economic services. People's own perception about their welfare and well being has undergone positive change. The economy has also undergone structural changes, with an increased role of private sector in production, employment and income. The share of traditional agriculture in national production and employment has declined, while that of non-agricultural sources has made noticeable gains. Remittance income has emerged as an important factor in raising rural income and reducing poverty.

The experience has also shown weaknesses and unresolved problems of our society. Market forces increased the prosperity of relatively developed regions and income groups. Rural and geographically distant and difficult areas, where most poor people live remain backward. Agriculture, which offers employment to bulk of the population, despite some commercialization in relatively accessible areas, remains predominantly traditional and backward. A large section of our population, particularly the historically neglected and discriminated *Dalits*, indigenous communities, and women have not benefited from the fruits of development in an equitable manner. Economic disparities, instead of declining, have accentuated. More on this will be discussed in the next chapter.

NOTES

1. This seat won by UML leader Madan Bhandari in the 1991 general election had become vacant after his death in the Dasdhunga incident.
2. Among the various issues, Ganesh Man Singh strongly opposed this author's appointment as NPC Deputy Chairman over his favourite Durgesh Man Singh who had earlier served as NPC member in the *Panchayat* days. Singh's argument was that this author had lost the last Parliamentary election, and therefore, should not be given another responsibility. Similarly he charged Koirala for favouritism in other appointments. Koirala defended his selection based on merit and right commitment.
3. The Tanakpur agreement involved the use of a piece of Nepali territory, approximately 2.9 hectares, in the Kanchanpur district of far-western Nepal for the completion of the afflux bund of the Tanakpur Barrage constructed

on their side by India. The opposition contention on this was: this 'major agreement' involving the distribution of vital natural resources of the country, would attract Article 126 of the Constitution and therefore, required ratification by two-third members of the House. The government considered the agreement to be a simple Letter of Understanding. The issue went to the Supreme Court, which overturned the government position adding significant fillip to opposition's case.

4. Krishna Khanal, 'Parliament and Governance' in Baral (ed.) *Political Parties and Parliament*. 2004, Delhi: Adroit.
5. There is a theory that blames Deuba for acting as an instrument for the Palace design, taking the constitution to a 'dead-end' and creating space for the King to act. See, Khanal, ibid. His action was probably based on the assumption that he would soon be voted out as leader of the HOR. Deuba, however, became the victim of his own action subsequently. The king sacked him for failing to hold election.
6. The group included Ram Chandra Poudel, Tara Nath Ranabhat, Chakra Bastola, Ram Sharan Mahat, Bhim Bahadur Tamang, Mahesh Acharya and Nara Hari Acharya.
7. The data source here for the Eighth Plan performance is the Ninth Plan document.
8. The data source here for the Ninth Plan performance is the Tenth Plan document.
9. Ibid pp. 7–8.
10. Ibid, p. 10.
11. Central Bureau of Statistics, *Population Monograph of Nepal, Volume I*, 2003, Chapter 9.
12. Ibid, Chapter 10.
13. *Economic Survey 2003/04*, Table 4.1.
14. Ibid, Table 4.3.
15. UNDP, *The Macroeconomics of Poverty Reduction: The Case of Nepal*, 2004, Chapter 2. vp. 32. Kathmandu.
16. The World Bank, *Nepal: Poverty at the Turn of the Twenty First Century*, Giovanna Prennushi. May 1999. Report No. IDP 174, p. 6.
17. The report also says that an additional 28 per cent of the population would have fallen below the poverty line if the poverty level had been defined as one-and-a-half times the above poverty line.
18. The World Bank (1999), p. 111.
19. Based on Central Bureau of Statistics, *Statistical Report Volume I and II*. Also CBS and the World Bank, *Measuring Poverty in Nepal: results from NLSS I and NLSS I, 2004*.
20. World Bank, *Nepal Development Policy Review*, 2004, pp. 8–10.
21. The current account deficit for Nepal in 2003 was 3 per cent of GDP compared to 0.6 for India, 0.5 per cent for Bangladesh and 3.3 per cent for Pakistan. Source: IMF, *World Economic Outlook*, September 2003.
22. IMF, Nepal : *Request for three-year Arrangement on the PRGF*, 2003. Washington D.C. (Internal Document)

23. The World Bank, *World Debt Tables*, Volume I 1996, Appendix I.
24. The respective ratios for India were 17 and 112 per cent, Pakistan 42 and 221 per cent, Bangladesh 22 and 155 per cent, and Sri Lanka 47 and 129 per cent.
25. An international scheme designated to reduce the debt of Highly Indebted Poor Countries (HIPIC) to sustainable level. A total of 37 such countries were proposed to receive debt relief in two phases.

Chapter Seven

Performance and Delivery (II)

We reviewed the development performance at the macro level under the democratic regime of the post-Panchayat era in the previous chapter. Here, we review the development record in major sectors of the economy.

FINANCE AND BANKING

As a result of the liberalization measures introduced in finance and banking, this sector underwent rapid expansion after 1990. The expansion is reflected in the number and diversity of institutions and the nature of their assets and instruments. The number of commercial banks increased from 5 in 1990 to 17 in 2004. Their total assets grew from Rs. 26,854 million to 331,547 million. The capital base of the banks made a phenomenal jump from a level of Rs.130 million in 1990 to Rs. 13,823 million in 2004. With the growth of the financial sector, the financial products and services industry have also diversified catering to different needs, tastes, and preferences of the market. The overall financial sector expanded from 5 institutions in 1991 (excluding two public sector development banks) to 73 in 2000, and to 148 in 2004. These include commercial banks, finance companies, development banks and financial intermediaries registered with Rural Micro Finance Development Centre (RMDC) for the purpose of wholesale borrowing to be used for micro-credit. These intermediaries—that take the form of development banks, cooperatives, NGOs and other rural financing institutions—have access to RMDC funds for micro-credit operations.

This growth and expansion of the financial sector has led to a significant financial deepening of the economy as reflected in the ratio of total financial assets to the country's GDP—which rose from 26.9 per cent in 1990 to 62 per cent in 2000 and 87.6 per cent in 2004. A very healthy trend is also witnessed in the commercial bank/deposit ratio.

TABLE 7.1
Selected Indicators of Financial Sector Growth (1990–2004)

Year	*1990*	*2000*	*2004*
No. of Institutions	5	73	148
Paid-up Capital	130	5,713	13,823
Depositors	21,406	166,332	283,781
Total Assets/Liabilities	26,853	226,951	413,996
Assets/GDP Ratio	26.9	62.0	87.6
Of which Commercial Banking			
Year	*1990*	*2000*	*2004*
Number of Banks	5	13	17
Paid-up Capital	130	4,067	8,350
Deposits	21,407	154,943	233,665
Total Assets/Liabilities	26,854	209,471	331,547
Asset/GDP Ratio	26.9	57.2	70.2
Deposit/GDP Ratio	21.4	42.3	49.5

Note: Figures pertaining to paid-up capital, deposits, assets and liabilities are in million rupees.
Source: Data from the Nepal Rastra Bank and *Economic Survey* reports.

Another very important development of the last decade was the growth of micro/ rural credit institutions that target the poorest of the poor. Contrary to the urban bias of the commercial banks and finance companies, micro-credit institutions are making significant contributions towards meeting the credit needs of the rural poor. The most prominent institutions in the micro-credit sector are the five Grameen Bikas Banks in five Development Regions. Two of these banks were established in 1992 and the other three in subsequent years. The majority shares in these institutions is owned by the Nepal Rastra Bank and the His Majesty's Government. These banks were patterned along the model of The Grameen Bank of Bangladesh, targeting the credit needs of the poorest of the poor, based on the concept of group liability without any physical collateral. Similar institutions such as Nirdhan Bikas Bank, Swabalamban Bikas Bank, Deprosc Bikas Bank and Chhimek Bikas Bank aimed towards the most deprived population were promoted in

Photograph 8: Kaligandaki 'A' Dam Site

Photograph 9: Electricity distribution from a micro hydro

the non-government sector. After the enactment of the Cooperative Act of 1992, a large number of savings and credit cooperative societies were established to undertake limited banking activities.

Similarly, the enactment of Financial Intermediary Societies Act in 1998 has enabled the registered NGOs, with license from the Nepal Rastra Bank, to provide micro-credit services to communities below the poverty line. In addition to these, there existed some micro-credit schemes under a few established programmes such as the Deprived Sector Lending by commercial banks and the Small Farmers Development Programme. *Grameen Swabalamban Kosh* was started under the Nepal Rastra Bank in 1990 and the Western *Tarai* Poverty Alleviation Project was launched in 1998/99. The most important feature of the micro finance operation is that it provides loans without any physical collateral and offers door-to-door service to the poor people.

TABLE 7.2
Operation by Micro-Credit Institutions
As of mid January 2003

1.	Cumulative No. of Borrowers	716,000
2.	Cumulative Loan Disbursement	20,366
3.	Cumulative Loan Repayment	15,336
4.	Loan Outstanding	6,963
5.	Saving Collected	3,067

Note: All figures except under 1 denote rupees in millions.
Source: Nepal Rastra Bank.

Available statistics show that these micro-credit institutions provided a cumulative total of Rs. 20.3 billion in loans to 716,000 borrowers as of mid-January 2003. Of this amount, Rs.15.3 billion was repaid. The operation also created a savings pool of more than 3 billion rupees. The micro enterprises supported by the credit programme are employment intensive; in fact a study conducted in the Uttarganga VDC of Surkhet district shows that a micro-enterprise would, on average, generate jobs for 2.1 persons.[1]

The most conspicuous aspect of the micro-credit programme is high recovery: the repayment ratio of such lendings stands at 98 per cent. This shows that with proper supervision and under peer pressure, poor people can be good borrowers. One survey shows that in areas covered by micro-finance programmes, income of the borrowers has increased by 22 per cent.[2] Another positive side of some micro-credit programmes is they can serve as effective tools for social mobilization by encouraging a habit of saving, developing women leadership, and acting as catalysts for literacy, sanitation, drinking water and other socio-economic activities. But the drawback is its high operational cost. This is understandable in view of its social component, high administrative cost due to intensive preparation including the identification of target groups, group formation, training, supervision, and 'door-to-door-banking' nature of the programmes.

RURAL DEVELOPMENT AND EMPOWERMENT

Democratic exercises in the form of periodic elections gave strong voice to the rural population in the nineties. Rural people who had been traditionally neglected in socio- economic terms started exercising political power. Although this new empowerment still remained short of doing full justice to the historically neglected and discriminated communities such as the *Dalits* and women, the new dispensation made the elected representatives accountable to the general people. The national leadership, which assumed power under various governments in the democratic era, largely hailed from rural Nepal which was also their political support base. Most of the new political leaders came from rural areas with middle class and lower middle class backgrounds. This forced a restructuring and redistribution of state resources towards neglected rural areas. This explains the sudden spurt of rural development programmes in the 1990s, which contributed significantly to the creation of social and economic assets and services in rural areas.

Demand for roads and bridges, drinking water facilities, schools and health services, irrigation and river training by elected representatives in the parliament, local bodies and other forums forced the government to refocus and reprioritize public expenditure in favour of neglected rural areas. The expenditure pattern of the budgets in the 1990s bears testimony to this fact. The first budget allocated more than seventy per cent of the development budget to programmes located away from urban areas with this pattern being maintained in subsequent years as well. Programmes in such fields as roads and bridge construction, education and rural health, drinking water and other public health services multiplied. This restructuring of expenditure pattern resulted in perceptible improvements in rural life and significant strides were made in human development indices. Decentralization measures bolstered by financially empowered elected local bodies gave further boost to rural public works[3]. Many remote villages that had aspired for better access to market centres were now linked by fair weather roads—albeit of poor quality—built often with modest budget from the government and with community participation. The NLSS II shows a noticeable improvement in the rural people's access to modern economic services such as schools, health services, banks, road and transport services (Table 7.3).

Drinking water facility was extended to an additional 6 million people in the nineties. The proportion of households with access to safe drinking water increased significantly. According to the NLSS II findings, 81 per cent of the households get their drinking water from piped supply (44 per cent) and covered well (37 per cent). The rest, 19 per cent, depend on open well and other sources like pond, stream and river. The proportion of households with access to piped drinking water in 1995/96 was only 33 per cent.[4]

TABLE 7.3
Access to Facilities Within 30 minutes
(In % of Households)

	1995/96	*2002/03*
Primary schools	88.44	91.36
Health post/Hospital	44.81	61.84
Cooperative	25.90	33.72
Agricultural Centre	24.45	31.94
Commercial bank	20.71	27.84
Haat Bazar	41.38	81.93
Market Centre	24.21	34.36
Paved Road	24.19	37.2
Dirt Road	57.98	72.67
Bus Stop	33.07	52.98

Sources: NLSS I and II.

The new enthusiasm for rural works was also reflected in the over-fulfillment of planned targets in some activities like road and bridges in the Eighth and the Ninth Plans. Commenting on the road construction outside the plan framework, the National Planning Commission observed:

> In the road sector, a major achievement has been the active involvement of District and Village Communities in road construction, utilizing development grants from the central government. However, the quality of these projects is weak; and if appropriate measures are not taken to improve the quality, there is a danger of increasing environmental problems. Moreover, in the road sector, although the Plan target in terms of kilometers of road constructed has been exceeded, most of these roads are low priority roads.[5]

Photograph 10: A portion of the Karnali bridge: link with the Far West

There was also a negative side of the exercise of this new power. The multiplicity of projects was based on political and social considerations rather than on techno-economic rationale. Resources were scattered thinly and limited allocation over a large number of projects owing to budgetary constraints made their timely completion impossible.[6] Despite these pitfalls and limitations, the rural empowerment under democracy ensured a stronger flow of resources to the countryside in favour of development activities identified as priorities by the people themselves.

AGRICULTURE AND FORESTRY

Agricultural Growth

The aggregate increase in food production in the preceding decades was attributed largely to the expansion of new areas under cultivation as the average productivity did not increase. While the area covered by cereal crops increased by 2.2 per cent per annum over the period between 1961/62 and 1989/90, the production of principal cereal crops increased at an average of 2.1 per cent. The productivity, thus, declined by 0.1 per cent annually.[7] The main emphasis in the nineties and, particularly since the middle of the decade after the APP was formulated, was the commercialization and diversification of agriculture to transform the sector from a subsistence source to a modern enterprise. In the nineties, the acreage expansion was very limited. Hence, the production growth is attributable almost entirely to the improved productivity.

The government's Economic Survey reports have published data about the area, production and productivity indices with two base years. Treating 1974/75 as the base year, the indices for area, production and productivity of principal food crops for the year 1989/90 were 141.4, 151.5 and 107.14 respectively. In other words, in the last fifteen years of the Panchayat regime, the area under food crops expanded by 41 per cent and the production increased by 51 per cent, resulting in the productivity growth of only 7 per cent. The other set of data with 1994/95 as the base year shows that area, production and productivity indices for the year 2001/002 were 106, 134 and 126. In other words, area under cultivation rose by 6 per cent, production by 34 per cent and productivity by 26 per cent in this period of seven years. Similar trends are discernable with respect to cash crops: the productivity growth in the last fifteen years of the *Panchayat* era was 5 per cent, while it was 29 per cent in the last seven of the post-*Panchayat* democratic era.

TABLE 7.4
Area, Production and Yield Indices
(1974/75–2001/02)

	1974/75	1989/90	1994/95	2001/002
	Base year		*Base year*	
Food crops*				
Area	100.00	141.36	100.00	106.08
	(2142)	(3028)	(3107)	(3297)
Production	100.00	151.46	100.00	133.88
	(3778)	(5722)	(5413)	(7248)
Yield	100.00	107.14	100.00	126.20
Cash crops**				
Area	100.00	130.32	100.00	122.46
	(221)	(288)	(325)	(397)
Production	100.00	267.76	100.00	157.60
	(670)	(1794)	(2460)	(3879)
Yield	100.00	205.45	100.00	128.69

* Food crops include paddy, maize, wheat, barley and millet.

** Sugar cane, oil seeds, tobacco, potato and jute.

Note: Figures in brackets indicate area in '000 ha. and production in '000 mt

Source: Compiled from *Economic Survey* Reports.

The agricultural sector, however, did not perform as expected in the nineties particularly in the first half as compared to other non-agricultural sectors of the economy. The following paragraph has been reproduced from a UNDP report on the impact of policy reforms of the nineties on agricultural performance:

> Growth in agricultural domestic product was not significantly different from that of population. In addition, it is also important to note that agricultural growth has been highly variable in the 1990s, again indicating the failure of policy reforms to have consistent positive impact. Thus annual growth in real AGDP was highly variable with 104 per cent coefficient of variation (CV). During the period, cereal grain production grew by about 2.11 per cent and cereal yield by about 1.20 per cent, but again with high year-to-year variation. Growth in the production of cash crops was modest. Growth in the production of other crops (horticulture, pulses, and oilseeds) also remained low with a CV of 122 per cent. However, output growth in livestock production has been more stable (CV 56.9%) and higher than the population growth.[8]

TABLE 7.5
Other Crops and Livestock (in 000 mt)
(1989/90–2001/02)

	1989/90	2001/2002	
Other crops			
Pulses	129.10	163.23	250.40
Fruits	318.00	463.31	473.62
Vegetables	672.00	993.56	1738.09
Livestock production			
Meat	117.10	145.15	198.64
Milk+ milk products	711.54	859.36	1158.79
Fish	4.30	13.30	35.00
Eggs (in million)	219.60	342.15	538.42

Source: Economic Survey Reports.

Nevertheless, even in this otherwise critical report, there is an acknowledgement of the strong performance recorded in exports and high value crops in the second half of the decade. A study by the Asian Development Bank has noted that during the 1990s, the performance of cereal crops, except wheat, was weak and cash crops had a mixed performance. The production of potato and sugarcane grew rapidly, while that of jute and tobacco declined. But high-value crops like citrus, apple, mango, vegetables, tea, cardamom and others showed strong performances. In view of the small share of high-value crops, their performance was hardly noticeable in the overall agricultural performance. There were positive signs of increased productivity in major cereal crops. The report also acknowledged that the overall land and labour productivity was still low. The differences in the productivity among the quintiles of the farmer population revealed that rich farmers had higher productivity which was not only due to higher use of agricultural inputs like fertilizers, but also due to inferior quality of land owned by the poorer farmers.[9]

The report spoke of strong performance in the livestock sub-sector over the past decade, with total meat, milk, and egg production growing more rapidly than population. Owing to strong demand and investment by farmers, animal protein consumption was growing and inducing elaborate meat marketing systems in urban areas and commercialization of milk. The Dairy Development Corporation still dominated the milk market, but the share of private dairy was increasing. Livestock investment was increasing even among the poorest families who considered livestock as an important investment. Fishery, despite its

Photograph 11: A view of hill road

small contribution to the GDP, was a rapidly growing sub-sector with high potential.[10] In view of the importance of the study's findings on the overall agricultural performance against the prevailing atmosphere of pessimism, I reproduce here some paragraphs in their original form:

> Contrary to prevailing pessimism, during the period of the 9th Plan up to date, different indicators of performance have exhibited an upward trend. Even though the overall objective of the APP to accelerate agricultural income per capita to reach 2 per cent growth has not been reached, the agricultural income per capita has witnessed a turn-around when compared to the past. During the period 1990/91–1994/95, agricultural GDP per capita declined at an average rate of –0.6 per cent; during the period 1995/96 to 1999/00, it grew at an average rate of 0.7 per cent.
>
> During the most recent past, yield growth of cereals has accelerated and started to be the main factor of growth of cereal production—At the same time, agricultural exports growth has accelerated from an average of 3.2 per cent during the first half of the 1990s to 37.4 per cent during the second part of the 1990s. The acceleration of agricultural export growth has contributed to narrowing the gap in agricultural trade with India. The TA field data indicate that *(i)* investment in agriculture is still low but increasing in level; *(ii)* private sector expectations about the future outlook for agriculture and agro industry are positive; and *(iii)* most of the farmers consider their income and livelihood better than at the beginning of the Ninth Plan.
>
> One of the reasons for the prevailing pessimism about the performance of agriculture is the weakness of a regular, accurate and professional monitoring system. Moreover, the existing monitoring system has given almost an exclusive attention to performance of agriculture as measured by the gap between targets on the official data on achievements. As a result several improvements of performance have been missed, whereas non-compliance with some of the targets of the 9th Plan has been magnified and interpreted as overall lack of performance. The review has shown that some of the targets were not based on accurate analysis and some of the achievements were underestimated because of a lack of an appropriate monitoring system. Preliminary field level data even suggest that during the period 1995/96 to 2001/2002 farmer's income per capita has grown at 2 per cent.[11]

Forestry Management

The priority in the forestry sector was the expansion of community forestry programme through the introduction of innovative schemes like leasehold forestry, private forestry, and forestry management plans. At the end of the Ninth Plan, about 850,000 hectares of forests were under the management of 12,000 user groups. These community user groups are responsible not only for the sustainable use of the forest resources but also for their conservation. The participatory approach inherent in this concept also enables communities to exercise their collective energy to preserve the environment and bio-diversity associated with their local ecosystems. Democratic exercise at the local level is at the heart of the community forestry programmes. By empowering each and every member of the community regardless of gender, caste and ethnicity these programmes do more than just encourage sustainable management of forest resources: they provide a replicable model of development administration that is truly sensitive to local demands.[12] These programmes have visibly transformed the landscape of most hills in Nepal. Hills and valleys that used to be notorious for denudation, landslides and soil erosion are now lush green with community-protected forests and woodlots. Leasehold forestry scheme, which was introduced with the aim of supporting the livelihood of people below the poverty line, now covers an estimated area of 40,000 hectares of land. This land, which is now made available to various user groups, benefits about 12000 families.

It is interesting that although forests cover about 30 per cent of Nepal's land area, and the forests in *tarai* possess some of the best hardwood species in the world, they contribute very little to the national economy. The *tarai* forests offer tremendous economic and employment opportunity because of their deep soil, high ground water levels, warm climate and adequate rainfall. But the country has failed to exploit these potentials due to the lack of scientific management. Instead, this precious resource was getting depleted each day due to encroachment, illegal felling and smuggling of timber, lopping, grazing and fire damage. Therefore, an initiative for the scientific management of the *tarai* forests was started to make this sector an important source of industrial raw material, employment, national income and government revenue.

Assistance from Finland, which has enormous experience in this field, was received for this purpose. A study conducted under the Finland-assisted Forest Management and Utilization Project (1991–95) showed that with scientific management and commercial exploitation, 300,000 of the 546, 000 hectares *tarai* forest, could generate an annual revenue of US$ 300 million just by selling the forest produce. This was about half of Nepal's annual budget at that time. These forests possessed some of the best and most expensive wood on earth such as *sal* and *sisau*. If protected from fire, grazing and illegal felling, the *sal* in particular possesses a strong natural regeneration quality. Proper management of these trees, would not only yield good income, but also protect the forest wealth in a sustainable manner. The traditional emphasis on forest preservation through government mechanism had been unsuccessful and hence the new approach was on commercializing forestry. The idea was to protect and sell the annual growth of timber in a sustainable manner. The proposed vehicle to implement the plan was a private and autonomous commercial undertaking that would introduce modern commercial management techniques in forestry. The government would benefit from the royalty received from such undertakings.

However, forests are regarded as national wealth and are a sensitive subject in Nepal. Private entry in this field could easily provoke public outcry as it may be viewed as a sellout of national wealth for private gains. Therefore, despite the attractiveness of the plan, it was necessary to build a national consensus on this subject. This consideration prompted us at the National Planning Commission to present a paper on this subject at the National Development Council meeting on May 1994 for broader debate and approval. After a lot of deliberation, the participants supported the plan, but cautioned the government against the potential misuse and the play of vested interest in the otherwise attractive proposition.

As a test case for this new approach, Finnish consultants prepared a pilot project of the management plan of the forest area of Bara district. A joint venture company[13] was also identified for implementing the management plan and a proposal was sent to HMG for approval. However, some controversial conditions put forward by the Finnish side in the proposal ultimately led to the termination of the whole plan.[14] This author particularly recalls two conditions which the government was not in a position to comply with. First, they wanted an income tax waiver to the proposed joint venture commercial company. Granting such a waiver was against Nepal's income tax law. Second, they wanted permission to export lumber without sawing and processing inside the country, thereby, depriving the country of value added and employment benefits from the scheme. At the end, the Finnish decided to withdraw the proposal without offering alternatives.

INDUSTRY, TRADE AND BALANCE OF PAYMENTS

The economic growth of the nineties was contributed largely by non-agricultural sources. The non-agricultural GDP grew at an annual rate of 7 per cent during the 1990s, 8.1 per cent during 1991–96 and 6.0 per cent in 1996–2000. The growth rate of the manufacturing sector

◀ *Photograph 12:* Electricity through solar energy

Photograph 13: Increasing popularity of bio-gas in hills and *tarai* ▼

was even higher: 15 per cent annually in the first half, and 7.6 per cent in the second half of the 1990s. An indication of the surge of industrial activities in the initial years of the 1990s in response to the reform initiatives can be gauged from the following paragraphs summarizing the situation between July 1991 and May 1994.

> Since the initiation and implementation of a more liberalized policy, a total of 473 units have commenced production. These units have provided direct employment to 75,148 people and have invested over Rs.26, 319.7 million in fixed assets.
>
> How successful has the Government's liberal policy been in attracting foreign investments? A total of 153 units—62 per cent of the total since 1975—have been registered after the promulgation of the new Industrial Enterprise Act in March 1992. Of the total approved foreign investment, 129 are in operation, 28 are in various stages of construction, and 2 have closed down. The manufacturing sector accounts for 61 per cent of total foreign investment, followed by tourism (18 per cent), services (14 per cent), and energy-based (5 per cent).[15]

Treating 1987/88 as the base year, the industrial production index, which was 100.58 in 1989/90, shot up to 308.58 in 1999/2000 and to 334.58 in 2001/002. Among the main industry groups, the food manufacturing industry, which accounts for nearly 20 per cent weightage in the manufacturing production index, displayed the most phenomenal growth, from 133.63 in 1989/90 to 996.06 in 2001/002. Sugar, vegetable ghee, noodles and tea were some of the products registering a high growth in this group.[16] It may be noted that large sugar factories were started in Sunsari, Mahottari, Rautahat, Kapilbastu and Dhangadhi during this period. Their aggregate capacity exceeded domestic demand so they started exporting as well. Other industrial groups which registered high growth included paper and paper products, footwear, chemical products, iron and steel-based industries and dry cell battery. Some well-known multinational companies like Dabur, Hindustan Lever, Colgate Palmolive, and others started manufacturing joint ventures for domestic and external markets. The share of industrial GDP increased from 6 per cent in 1989/90 to 8.6 per cent in 2001/002.

Prominent export industries, which grew fast during the decade, were hand-knit carpets and ready-made garments. The carpet industry recorded an annual growth of 65 per cent throughout the decade. Their share in the global market increased ten-fold even after a slight decline towards the end of the decade.[17] The industry has recently stagnated in the face of static global demand, the issue of child labour and the lack of new designs and aggressive market diversification efforts. Similarly, the ready-made garments, which registered a phenomenal growth in the 1990s replacing carpets as the leading export commodity, have also slumped in recent years. Garments today face stiff competition in the United States—which is their principal market—from selected African and Caribbean garments that have been granted duty-free preferences. This industry suffered further setbacks due to increased competition from more efficient exporters in South Asia and China after the termination of quota facilities under the Agreement on Textile and Clothing at the end of 2004.

Following the market oriented reforms in the early years of the decade that increased Nepal's integration to the global economy, the country sustained a robust external trade position during the nineties. Deregulation, foreign exchange reforms including full convertibility in the current account, new trade treaties and the overall improvement in business environment led to an average annual export growth (in rupee terms) of 32 per cent over the first half and 24.5 per cent during the second half of the nineties. Imports increased at an average of 28 per cent in the first half and 12 per cent in the second half of the nineties. The trade to GDP ratio, which was about 29 per cent at the second half of the eighties, exceeded 50 per cent at the end of the nineties and even in subsequent years. Similarly, the export to GDP ratio, which was about 5 per cent in the late eighties, increased to more than 10 per cent in the nineties.

> Notwithstanding its narrow base, Nepal's growth in trade has been a driver behind accelerating per capita economic growth of 2.4% per year in the 1990s, compared to the less than 1 per cent growth rate for most of the country's prior economic history. Following trade liberalization in the early 1990s, Nepal?s exports grew at an average annual rate of 15%[18] throughout the decade, while the net exports of key items such as garments increased steadily, contributing to overall growth. Trade has stimulated demand-side growth by enabling Nepalese producers to access global markets and stagnant agricultural incomes. On the supply side, liberalization of machinery, eqüipment, and raw materials imports helped to boost growth. Imports of machinery and transport equipment grew at about 10% annually during the 1990s, enabling the growth of private investment.[19]

One distinctive development on the trade front in the 1990s was the export growth to India. This was due to improvements in the trade agreement between the two countries that eventually culminated in the trade treaty of 1996. The most important feature of the 1996 treaty that paved the way for higher Nepali exports was the access for selected Nepali manufacturing exports (except for those on the negative list) to the Indian market free of basic customs duties and quantitative restrictions. It may be noted that Nepal has always offered preferential access to manufacturing goods from India without any quantitative restrictions. However, the preferential access to Nepali goods in the Indian market was subject to the Rules of Origin condition. Under this rule and in the previous treaty regime Nepali goods had to satisfy the 90 per cent value-added condition to qualify for preferential treatment. This was reduced to 50 per cent in 1992 treaty, and removed completely in the 1996 treaty. It was replaced by a Certificate Of Origin condition under which a certification issued by an authorized body in Nepal would suffice.The FNCCI was designated for this task.

The new treaty which was the result of the efforts by politicians, officials and private sector representatives was a milestone in the trade relations between the two countries. It led to a phenomenal growth of Nepali products in the Indian market: Nepali exports to India rose from Rs.1.55 billion in 1980/91 to Rs. 3.68 billion in 1995/96, and a further Rs. 28.86 billion in 2000/01. Similarly, imports from India during the same period rose from Rs. 7.32 billion to 24.40 billion in 1996/97 and to Rs. 45.46 billion in 2001/02. The trade deficit with India narrowed down considerably in relative terms. The export to import ratio with India increased from 14 per cent to 64 per cent. Some of the products which registered unexpected export growth—particularly, vegetable ghee (which alone accounted for one fourth of Nepal's India-bound exports), copper wire, acrylic yarn, zinc oxide and mild steel pipes—had limited value added inside the country. These products depended on third country raw materials and only had a limited value-added domestically. Nepali manufacturers were taking advantage of the prevailing tariff differentials between the two countries as the Nepal's tariff on the third country raw material imports was very low compared to that of India.

The increased exports of these products proved to be transitory. The lucrative business of dumping low-value added commodities in Indian markets had started affecting India's certain domestic industries. India reacted by placing these products under 'surge' category. The trade treaty renewed in March 2002 placed restrictive conditions on such exports through more stringent Rules of Origin conditions (such as a minimum of 30 per cent value added condition) and other safeguard clauses such as the quantitative restrictions on the surge items.

The renewed treaty reduced Nepali exports to India. At the same time exports to third countries were also affected by external environment in the aftermath of 9/11 and the slowdown in demand owing to the global economic downturn. Internally, the weakened business environment caused by the Maoist insurgency, faltering

Photograph 14: Bee-keeping getting popular

Photograph 15: Community irrigation in the *tarai*

competitiveness and political instability took its toll. All these factors began having perceptible negative impact on Nepal's external trade since 2002. The growth momentum built up in the previous decade came to a halt. Consequently, the export to import ratio, which had risen from 31 per cent in 1990/91 to peak at 48 per cent in 2001/02, came down to 40 per cent in 2002/03. Trade deficit exceeded Rs. 74 billion in the same year from the level of 10 billion in 2000/01.

However, the significant growth recorded in transfer income, particularly workers' remittances, the current account position did not deteriorate much. This, coupled with a surplus in capital accounts helped in maintaining a comfortable foreign exchange position. The total foreign exchange reserves in the country as of March 2004 was equivalent to Rs. 124 billion.

Remittance income has emerged as an important source of foreign exchange earnings and balance of payment support in recent years. Separately classified data on remittances (available from 1999/2000) shows a consistently increasing trend from a level of Rs. 36.8 billion in 1999/00 to 46 billion in 2002/03. The estimated figure for 2003/04 is Rs. 70 billion. This was in addition to the Gorkha pension transfer that equaled Rs. 7.32 billion in 2002/03. The increased remittance earnings resulted from the deliberate government policy to encourage manpower export to the Middle East and the East Asia where the demand for Nepali workers is high. A liberal passport policy, together with the promotional measures and the entry of private manpower companies, contributed to this growth. In addition formal channels were opened up with attractive incentives which encouraged the people to use banking channels instead of the traditional *hundi* system to remit savings.

TRANSPORT[20] AND COMMUNICATIONS

There was 790 kilometres of road at the beginning of the *Panchayat* period in 1961. After thirty years of *Panchayat* rule, the total length of roads built had been extended to 7,036 km. The priority for the democratic governments in the road sector was to complete the remaining portions of the East–West highway, link all district headquarters with the strategic road network, build access roads to potential hydroelectricity project sites and provide market connectivity to farms. Maintenance of existing highways and other roads was also given importance. Emphasis was also placed on the construction of motorable and suspension bridges, local farm-to-market and intra district roads with people's participation under the aegis of local bodies like VDCs and DDCs.

Road construction received a big boost in the post-*Panchayat* era. The total road length increased from 7,036 km in 1989/90 to 15,308 in 1999/2000. Thus, a total of 8,300 kilometres were added to the country's road network in a decade, compared to a mere 2,096 kilometres added in the preceding decade of eighties under the *Panchayat* regime. Additionally, annual road construction in the nineties averaged 826 km compared to a meagre 209 km in the eighties (Table 7.6). The pace of construction slowed down in the first three years of the new millennium on account of the security threat posed by the Maoist insurgency and because of the absence of functioning democratic institutions, including the parliament, which would have created popular pressure for pushing forward the priority rural agenda.

Some of the districts connected by the road access during the nineties were Dhading, Ramechhap, Okhaldunga, Baglung, Myagdi, Parbat, Pyuthan, Arghakhanchi, Rolpa, Salyan, Rukum, Achham, Sindhuli, Lamjung, Dailekh, Taplejung and Tehrathum. Work progressed to connect other districts like Bhojpur, Solukhumbu, Diktel, Manang, Mustang, Darchula, Jajarkot, Kalikot, Jumla, Bajhang and Bajura. Many of these roads are yet to be blacktopped and made all-weather. A policy to blacktop all roads linking the district headquarters in the *tarai* and to ensure at least fair weather access to the hill districts was adopted and many other roads were upgraded. One interesting aspect of the road sector was that the construction targets were over-met both in the Eighth and Ninth plans. The Eighth Plan's target was to build 1,778 kilometres of road, but ended up building 2,863 kilometres. Similarly, the total target of the Ninth Plan was to build 1,920 kilometres of total road, but it ended up building 2,991 kilometres. The total road network in 2001/02 was 15,985 kilometres, of which 29 per cent was blacktopped, 24.3 gravelled, and the rest were fair weather earthen roads.[21]

The 1990s also saw the beginning of the use of the Royal Nepal Army in road construction. The role was not limited to supervision and management as was the case during the Panchayat period: RNA manpower was used to design and physically construct the road.[22]

The roads built by the RNA included Katari-Okhaldhunga, Hile-Leguwa, and later on, Musikot-Burtibang. The use of army personnel for road construction brought down the average cost significantly.

Another landmark development in the road sector was the eventual agreement reached with the Japanese government to build the long cherished Dhulikhel-Bardibas road after a few years of persuasion and

TABLE 7.6
Key Infrastructure Indicators (1979/80–2002/03)

S.No.		*1979/80*	*1989/90*	*1999/200*	*2002/003*
1.	Total Road Available in km	4,940	7,036	15,308	16,018
2.	Passengers in Domestic flight in '000'	228	291	1771	1209
3.	Cargo in Domestic flight in mt.	781	853	10,871	5,067
4.	Telephone line Distribution in '000'	11,812	57,320	255,777	371,816
5.	Electricity Generation in MW	57	176	352	550
Average Annual Extension					
S.No.			*1980-1990*	*1990-2000*	*2000-2003*
6.	Average Annual Road Construction		209	826	237
7.	Average Annual Irrigation Extension in ha.		27,035	33,215	19,690
8.	Av. Tel. Distribution		4,550	19,846	38,680

Sources: Economic Survey Reports.

Photograph 16: A community nursery

Photograph 17: Tea plantation covering eastern hills

lobbying. The initial hesitation on part of the Japanese was due to high costs and the long period of construction. The Japanese grant assistance is on an annual basis; therefore involvement in a long-term project would mean budgetary commitments on an annual basis. This important project, which at present is at advanced stage of completion, will reduce the motorable distance to eastern Nepal by as much as 130 kilometres. Besides, the districts of Kavrepalanchowk, Ramechhap, Sindhuli, Dhanusa and Mahottari will receive a big developmental boost.

The nineties also saw the application of labour intensive and environment friendly technology in the construction of some hill roads. This technology, initially applied by the Swiss to build the Arebhanjyang–Rampur road in Palpa district and was subsequently promoted by the GTZ in Dhading, Gorkha and Lamjung. The main features of this technology included the use of hand tools in construction and the employment with local participation of bioengineering techniques that would minimize damage to the environment. As this method relied mainly on labour and local materials, the money spent in the project remained within the community to help prop the local economy. This method, however, has one serious limitation. By its very nature, the construction process is slow and time consuming. This is primarily the reason why it did not become popular in most places including the Roads Department. The attraction of the bulldozer, which did quick work but at significantly higher financial and environmental costs, was too strong to resist even for the ordinary villagers.

Some institutional reforms were also introduced in this sector. The rapid expansion of road programmes mainly to the district and rural areas made the management and administration by a single organization difficult. Therefore, a new institution called the Department of Rural Infrastructure and Agricultural Road was created under the Ministry of Local Development to take over responsibility of rural roads from the Roads Department. The latter would now confine its responsibility to trunk roads, strategic network and urban roads. A policy to use DDCs, VDCs and local community in the form of user communities in road construction with the support of central grants was also initiated. A Roads Board Act was passed to make the maintenance of major roads self-financing with the use of road tolls and users fees.

Bridge construction also got a big boost during this period. Against the Eighth Plan target of completing 25 motorable bridges, 50 were completed. In the Ninth Plan, a total of 87 bridges were planned. But the popular demand and pressure led to the construction of 150 bridges which included, not just small and middle level motor bridges, but also the large ones like Trijuga, Rapti and Sunkoshi.[23]

Significant changes took place in the domestic aviation scene after promulgation of the open-air policy. Many private airlines and helicopter services started operation in various parts of the country. Air traffic along the existing routes increased many folds. An indication of the growth in the internal air traffic can be gauged from the fact that the total passengers in domestic flights increased from 2,28,000 in 1989/90 to 1,209,000 in the year 2002/003. The domestic air cargo shot up from 781 metric tons to 5,067 metric tons during the same period (Table 7.6).

Postal services were also extended to all VDCs of the country and big strides were made in the communications sector. At the end of the *Panchayat* regime, twenty seven districts of the country still lacked access to telephone services. These districts were brought under the telephone network in the Eighth Plan period itself. Rural telephone exchange system with capacity ranging from 150 to 300 telephone lines to service semi rural and market centers was introduced. By the year 2002, 1,800 VDCs had access to telephone services. A joint venture private company started providing Wireless Local Loop (WILL) based telephone services. As early as 1991, the government was consciously interested in maintaining Nepal's competitive edge over its neighbouring countries in telecommunication services. After necessary homework from the National Planning Commission and the Ministry of Communications, a policy to allow private sector in the telecommunications service was announced around 1993. Subsequently, proposals from interested parties were invited globally.

Many leading international companies from Denmark, Philippines and India along with a consortium of four leading Japanese companies showed interest and offered attractive proposals in competitive bidding. The companies were interested in a toehold in South Asia as Nepal was the first country to court international private investment in this area. However, a writ petition was submitted to the Supreme Court to stop the appraisal and selection process and the Court's delay in arriving at a decision ultimately killed the whole initiative.[24] Consequently, Nepal lost an opportunity to be the leader in the whole subcontinent in this field. It took Nepal a few years to come up with proper legislative provision and accompanying regulations to invite private investment in the telecommunications sector. By this time the neighbouring countries had made significant advances in this field. Unfortunately, Nepal became a late entrant in the field and lost some precious early opportunities.

IRRIGATION, HYDRO POWER AND ALTERNATIVE ENERGY

Irrigation Expansion

At the end of the *Panchayat* period, the total area under irrigation was 539,039 hectares accounting for 21 per cent of the cultivated land.[25] Average irrigation expansion during the last decade of the *Panchayat* era was 27,035 hectares per annum. It increased to 33,215 hectare in the nineties. Among the major irrigation projects were Mahakali Irrigation, Bhirawaha-Lumbini Groundwater Irrigation, Sunsari-Morang Irrigation, Bagmati Irrigation, and East Rapti Irrigation. Most of these projects were identified and put in process from the *Panchayat* days, and implemented subsequently with external assistance.

The policy orientation in the nineties was towards small irrigation with local participation and rehabilitation and the maintenance of the existing systems. Assistance from the World Bank and the ADB assistance was mobilized under the Irrigation Programme Loan and the Irrigation Sector Programme respectively for the development of small irrigation systems covering per scheme a few hundred to around thousand hectares per scheme with peoples' participation. Subsidized loans were channeled through the Agricultural Development Bank for the improvement and development of small-scale schemes with community participation. This modality became very popular and contributed significantly to the expansion of irrigation facilities. Of the 206,401 hectares of land brought under irrigation during the Eighth Plan, 76,098 hectares were covered under these programmes. During the Ninth Plan, a total of 110,465 hectares were brought under irrigation. Out of this 55,324 hectares were irrigated from new irrigation projects while the rest were from the improvement of farmers managed traditional systems. Here again, the contribution of the ADB/N's modality was significant. Another important feature of the new policy was the transfer of the irrigation management to the users' groups for maintenance and repair of the systems.

Hydro Power

Be it Trishuli, Kulekhani, or Marshyangdi, in the earlier decades, the country never implemented more than one hydropower project at a time. And, needless to say, all these projects were externally funded. In a country blessed with hydropower potential of 83,000 MW, the total power supply in 1961 was a meagre 7 MW! It increased to 227 MW in 1990 with the population with access to electricity increasing from 1 per cent to about 9 per cent during the same period.[26]

Photograph 18: Expanding cardamom cultivation

Photograph 19: An all weather hill airport

In the early nineties, a large number of projects were developed and promoted simultaneously for public and private sector investment. As described in the previous chapter, a new policy was announced and laws were enacted to encourage private investment. The projects developed for public investment during the period were Arun III (402 MW) and Kaligandaki A (144 MW). Mid Marshyngdi (46 MW) came into the portfolio a little later. Other projects promoted for private and joint venture investment were Jhimruk (12.5 MW), Khimti (60 MW), Bhotekoshi (36 MW), Puwa (6 MW), Chilime (20 MW), Indrawati (5 MW), and Modi (14 MW). All of these projects, except Arun III, were brought under implementation. Most of them have even been completed. Details about the aborted Arun III will be discussed in a separate chapter. Another project completed in the public sector with the help of World Bank credit was the upgradation of Trishuli-Devighat system that added 12.2 MW of power in the national grid. The total power generation capacity reached 550 MW in 2003.

One major project promoted for private foreign investment was the 750 MW West Seti Project—an attractive high dam project studied with the French assistance. An agreement was signed with the Snowy Mountain Engineering Corporation of Australia (SMEC) in 1994 to develop this as an export oriented venture to India. A long and protracted negotiation by the SMEC with the Power Trading Company (PTC) of India has now resulted in a power purchase agreement with India under which the latter will buy electricity at US $4.95 cents per unit. It has now also been reported that the project will be developed as a joint venture between the Snowy Mountain and the China National Machinery and Equipment Import and Export Corporation (CMEC), a Chinese company.[27] The main benefit to Nepal from this project will be 75 MW, ten per cent of the total energy produced or its monetary equivalent, free of cost.

Electricity transmission and distribution systems were upgraded and expanded with 132 KV transmission lines connecting major cities, business and industrial centers with the grid and 66, 33 and 11 KV lines connecting district headquarters and villages. The development of high voltage grid sub-stations, and the interconnection capacity between India and Nepal with double transmission line went side by side. Rural electrification programme was launched both through the expansion of transmission and distribution lines from the grid and the promotion of alternative energy sources like the solar, micro hydro and bio gas methods. By the end of the Ninth Plan, 1600 VDCs, and 58 municipalities of the 75 districts had access to electricity. By the year 2002, approximately 40 per cent of the total population had access to electricity, compared to only 9 per cent in 1990. Of this national figure, 33 per cent of the population benefited from the power supplied by the National Electricity Authority, and the remaining 7 per cent from alternative energy sources.[28]

One of the major issues of electricity consumption in Nepal is the high electricity tariff that averages 6.81 rupees per unit at present. The period of 1990s saw a series of power tariff increases from a level of approximately two rupees per unit in 1990. This has naturally added burden on the consumers, particularly the common man. Several reasons account for this increase. The hydro projects supported by external sources in Nepal have high costs. The losses in the transmission and distribution systems account for about one-fourth of the power generation. The donor community, before committing any support for new projects, insists on an evidence of cost recovery and a minimum of returns on past investment for a financially viable power sector. The financial burden arising from all these costs are passed on to the consumers. On the other hand, the attractive power price has encouraged new private investment in this sector. This has resulted in sufficient power supply as the consumers are no longer subjected to long hours of painful load shedding. The future challenge in this sector is to reduce energy cost and make it affordable to ordinary people while at the same time ensuring that it remains commercially attractive for new investment. For this to occur, one of the most urgent tasks is to reduce system losses of the NEA through increased efficiency. Promoting cheaper projects with innovative and cost effective methods is also an important way of reducing power tariffs. The prevailing power purchase agreements with private power producers are heavily loaded in favour of the producers and this calls for an urgent policy review. This subject is discussed in greater detail in the chapter on Arun III.

The biggest and the most controversial scheme approved in the 1990s was the Mahakali River Integrated Development Treaty with India. This treaty defines the bilateral utilization of the water in the Mahakali River, a river that is at the Indo–Nepal border in the west. The principal feature of this agreement is the construction of a multipurpose Pancheshwor Dam with the peaking capacity of 6,480 MW of electricity. This gigantic dam, approximately 315 meters in height, and to be built at an estimated cost of US dollars 10 billion would be one of Asia's tallest. The agreement was ratified by the Joint House of the Parliament on September 20, 1996 amid abstention from voting and floor crossing by a section of the Nepal Communist Party (UML) against the party whip[29] leading the party to break-up eventually. Although UML was the principal opposition party at the time of parliamentary approval of this project, it had supported the project. It is most unfortunate that the agreement, which was hailed as a major break-through in Nepal–India relationship for the joint harnessing of Nepal's water resources for mutual benefit, has yet not taken off. A detailed report of this project, which should have been completed within six months has still not been completed after eight years of its ratification because of differences between the two countries on various issues.

Alternative Energy

Innovative schemes were introduced and expanded in the field of rural energy. From the second year of the Eighth Plan, the government started to provide subsidies for micro-hydro schemes with the objective of encouraging local communities, private individuals and entrepreneurs to develop micro-hydro schemes from 1 to 20 KW capacities. The government provided the technical support and capital subsidy on Peltric technology. This was considered an effective way of providing electricity to far-flung areas, in view of the difficulty of supplying power through the electricity grids. The Agriculture Development Bank was designated as the executive agency for this programme and state subsidy to biogas plants in the rural areas has become a regular feature since the 1991/92 budget. A subsidy up to 10,000 rupees was provided to each biogas plant constructed. The monopoly access to these subsidies enjoyed by the government controlled Nepal Biogas Company was broken by allowing private companies to participate in the programme. This contributed to the rapid expansion of biogas in the countryside, making it an important source of alternative energy. The total number of biogas plants in the country presently approximate 140,000.[30] The proliferation of biogas plants has also helped forest conservation efforts, improved sanitation and organic manure, and more importantly, spared the women and children the drudgery of cutting and fetching firewood, and cooking in smoke-filled kitchen.[31] Similarly, the photovoltaic based solar energy system was the other innovative scheme popularized in the remote regions with state subsidy. A comprehensive study on the renewable energy systems in Nepal concluded that by the end of 2002/03 there existed 42,550 solar home systems generating 1,584 KW, 1,371 micro-hydro installations with 7,472 KW, 872 improved *Ghattas*, and 111,395 biogas plants throughout the country. Solar and micro-hydro schemes alone supplied electricity to approximately 3 per cent of the total households in the country.[32]

Unfortunately, an institutional vacuum existed in the promotion and coordination of the alternative energy sector. Responsibilities were scattered and disjointed with ministries and departments largely

Photograph 20: Nyatapola Temple, a world heritage site: renovated and maintained by the Bhaktapur municipality

preoccupied with bigger projects. The promotion of small sector did not receive the priority it deserved. To amend this, the NPC mooted the proposal of an Alternative Energy Centre under its own umbrella to promote and coordinate the alternative energy sector. The Centre was subsequently established under the Ministry of Science and Technology.

SOCIAL SECTOR DEVELOPMENT

The following paragraphs have been reproduced from a UNDP study to give an idea as to how the government's expenditure pattern evolved in the 1990s and began tilting towards social sector development:

> During the last twelve years, the budget allocation to economic sectors increased at an average of 15 per cent whereas the social sector budget allocation increased by an annual average growth rate of 21 per cent. This is in the context of a 14.4 per cent growth rate in the total budget expenditure.
>
> In a country where about 60 per cent of the development spending is donor financed, domestic efforts alone would be insufficient to allocate more resources to the social sector. Also, not all social spending can benefit the poor. Basic education, primary health care, and rural drinking water are the basic social services which can benefit the poor. That is the reason why UN agencies have endorsed the '20/20 Compact', which envisages 20 per cent of the Government budget to be allocated to the priority social sector with a matching share of the donors as well. Juxtaposing the budgetary performance against the 20/20 Compact, it can be observed that the budgetary process is heading towards that direction. In the government sector, resource allocation to social priority sector increased from 8.3 per cent of the total budget in 1976 to 17 per cent in 2001 whereas that on the donors side also went up from 7.5 per cent inn 1993 to 15 per cent in 2001[33].

One unknown aspect of Nepal's budget relates to the gap between the estimated and actual expenditure. There is up to 20–25 per cent shortfall in the actual expenditure that is generally known. But the unknown side is this—the expenditure shortfall is largely in economic sectors involving procurement and construction that requires elaborate decision-making process at various levels. This causes delay in programme implementation which ultimately results in slow disbursement. Furthermore, popular pressure for physically visible projects results in budgetary allocations for projects in economic sectors which typically suffer non-implementation. This also causes expenditure shortfall. On the other hand, allocation to the social sector from internal sources is almost entirely of recurrent nature in the form of salaries and office

TABLE 7.7
Some Education & Health Indicators (1980–2003)

A. Education					
S.No.	Year	1980	1990	2000	2003
9.	No. of Primary Schools	10,130	17,842	25,927	26,823
10.	No. of Lower Secondary Schools	3,501	3,964	7,289	7,954
11.	No. of Secondary Schools	785	1,953	4,350	4,369
12.	No. of Total School Teachers	44,181	94,033	142,752	162,627
	(of which public teachers)	N/A	N/A	(106,744)	(113,168)
13.	No. of Trained Teachers	17,477	35,844	71,977	37,302
	13 as % of 12	39.6	38	50	

B. Health					
S.No.		1980	1990	2000	2003
14.	Extension of Services*	1,096	1,096	4,421	4,401
15.	Skilled Man power**	767	27,948	81,381	89,311
16.	Hospital Beds	2,586	4,572	5,190	5,250

* Includes total number of hospitals, health centres, health posts, Ayurved centres, sub-health posts and primary health centres.

** Includes doctors, nurses, Kaviraj, Vaidya, health assistants and other health workers.

Source: *Economic Survey* Reports.

supplies, and is certain to be fully spent. Therefore, expenditure shortfall in the social sector is rather small. In other words, the actual expenditure pattern by sectors would show a higher social sector investment in relation to economic sectors than indicated by the budgetary allocation. The social sector expenditure in Nepal has shown a consistently increasing trend. The increasing investment is reflected in the expansion of basic educational and health facilities since 1990 as given in Table. 7.7.

It is remarkable that during the nineties the total health units increased from about 1100 to 4400. This dramatic expansion of health services became possible because of the government programme to set up at least one primary health unit in each of the country's 4000 VDCs and one health centre each in all parliamentary constituencies. Similarly, the total number of primary and secondary schools jumped respectively by 45 per cent and 122 per cent in a decade. The number of lower secondary schools increased by 83 per cent.

A temptation many Nepali academics generally cannot resist is to compare the Nepali situation with other South Asian countries whose social development status is considerably better. This is generally used to allege poor performance without considering the base level and the progress made over time. This becomes clear when one looks at the annual Nepal Human Development Report published by UNDP Nepal. If we look at the situation at a particular point of time without reference to Nepal's poor past, the position would appear very unfavourable. A balanced perspective emerges by reviewing the progress over time.

In this context, the global Human Development Report has done a commendable job and offers valuable insight into the progress made over time. The 1992 Human Development Report (HDR) had ranked

TABLE 7.8
Human Development Index Trends in SAARC Countries (1990–2003)

Year	*1990*	*2000*	*2002*
Maldives	0.719	0.735	0.753
Sri Lanka	0.698	0.719	0.740
India	0.514	0.579	0.595
Bangladesh	0.417	0.497	0.509
Nepal	0.418	0.448	0.501
Pakistan	0.444	—	0.497
Bhutan	—	—	0.536

Source: UNDP—*Human Development Report 2004.*

TABLE 7.9

Comparative HD Indicators in Four South Asian Countries

S.No.		Nepal	Bangladesh	Pakistan	India
1.	GDP per capita PPP	1350	1720	1940	2570
2.	Child malnutrition (%)	48.3	47.7	38.2	46.7
3.	Under-5 mortality rate	83	73	101	90
4.	Access to safe water (% of Population)	88	97	90.0	84
5.	Access to sanitation (% of Population)	28	48	62	28
6.	Net primary enrollment ratio	82.2	86.6	66.9	83.3
7.	% of Cohort reaching grade –5 male	57.2	63.4	—	59.2
8.	% of Cohort reaching grade 5-female	69.2	67.8	—	58.7
9.	Total fertility rate	4.2	3.0	4.5	2.9
10.	Maternal mortality ratio	539	380	500.0	540
11.	Life expectancy at birth, female	59.6	62.7	65.1	64.2

Source: The World Bank, *Nepal Development Policy Review* (2004, p. 9).

Nepal at the 152nd position among 173 countries in terms of its Human Development Index (HDI)—a low ranking even among countries with Low Human Development status. The 2004 HDR, however, elevated Nepal to Medium Human Development status: Nepal's HDI index had soared to 0.504 placing the country in the 140th position among 177 countries. Among SAARC countries, this position was slightly better than that of Pakistan (142nd position) but little worse than that of Bangladesh (138th). India with HDI 0.595 was placed at 127th position. Sri-Lanka and Maldives have much higher HDI scores.

The recent HDR has further refined the data and estimated the HDI index over time. Nepal's HDI has improved from 0.418 in 1990 to 0.488 in 2000 and further to 0.504 in 2002. Tables 7.8 and 7.9 provide a comparative chart on HDI and other selected social indicators with other countries of South Asia. Nepal's status is closely comparable to the conditions prevailing in the other three South Asian countries—India, Bangladesh, and Pakistan.

A study of the trend in selected social indicators shows that a significant progress was recorded with respect to child malnutrition, infant and maternal mortality, school enrollment, girl education, literacy, life expectancy and the access to safe water. Malnutrition of infant population came down from 57 per cent in 1990 to 44 per cent in 2000. Infant mortality came down from 107 per 1000 live births to 64. Similarly, maternal mortality more than halved during the decade. Contraceptive Prevalence Rate (CPR) went up from 24 per cent to 39 per cent. Ratio of girls to boys in primary education grew to 86 per cent from 56 per cent. Net enrolment in primary schools similarly increased. Adult literacy rate almost doubled. Average life expectancy increased from 53.5 years to 59.5 years. Access to safe drinking water facilities increased from 46 per cent of the population to 80 per cent.

This remarkable progress in aggregate terms, however, veils inter-caste and inter-ethnic disparities. Strong affirmative actions to address the problem of traditional social exclusion and discrimination were missing. Similarly, there was very little correction in intra-regional disparities. Some efforts were made to increase female and *Dalit* education in low literacy districts through modest cash incentive.[34] Institutions such as the *Dalit* Commission, the Women's Commission and the National *Janajati* Foundation were established to address the specific problems of the traditionally disadvantaged communities. Women's inheritance law was enacted to provide legal basis for women's right on parental property. Caste-based discrimination and social untouchability were made punishable by law. But these initiatives proved to be too few and too dispersed to make any noticeable dent on

TABLE 7.10

Some Selected Social Indicators(1990–2000)

S.No.		*1990*	*Mid-1990*	*Around 2000*
1.	Child malnutrition (1% of children under 3 years of age)	57	46.9	43.6
2.	Infant mortality rate (per 1000 live births)	107	78.5	64.4
3.	Under 5 mortality rate (per 1000 live births)	161.1	118.3	91.2
4.	Maternal mortality ratio (per 100,000 live births)	850	536	415
5.	Contraceptive prevalence ratio (% of women aged 15–49)	24.1	28.8	38.9
6.	Net primary enrollment ratio (% of relevant age group)	64	—	82.4
7.	Ratio of girls to boys in primary education	56	—	86
8.	Ratio of girls to boys in lower secondary education	41	—	81
9.	Adult literacy rate	25.6	36.7	50.7
10.	Average life expectancy	53.5	56.1	59.5
11.	Access to improved water source (% of population)	46	—	80

Sources: The World Bank (2004), *Nepal Policy Development Review*, NPC Plan documents and Human Development Reports.

the social conditions of these groups. The *Dalits,* or those belonging to occupational castes like *Kami, Damain,* and *Sarki,* traditionally treated as "untouchables", continue to be the most oppressed communities with the lowest human development indicators, in terms of income, consumption, education and health facilities. The ratio of *Dalits* HDI to national HDI is 74 per cent. Next comes the *Janjati* group which also comprises communities such as *Gurungs,* and *Rais* who score higher than other *Janjatis* in educational and income indicators because of their traditional service in the British and Indian armies. Similarly, *Thakalis* and *Sherpas* who have attained success in commerce and tourism are better off compared to others *Janjatis.*

Similarly, the regional disparities in human development opportunities remained unchanged. The far-western and mid-western regions, which have low HDI levels and have been traditionally neglected, showed less improvement in the situation than the country as a whole. The HDI in the hills is higher than in the mountains. The dispersed settlements in the mountains severely limit the access to educational and health services and, therefore, constrain opportunities. Looking at the ethnic groups, *Limbus, Tamangs* and *Magars* who largely live in the mountains and hills, and *Tharus* and *Musahhars* who live in the *tarai* are the most disadvantaged social groups.

Another noticeable development in the 1990s was the expansion of private education at all levels primary, secondary, higher, vocational, and technical education. There has been a tremendous growth of private and community participation in higher and technical education. Institutions like Kathmandu University, established in private but non-profit basis have excelled in quality education in a very short period. The total number of engineering colleges has reached more than thirty and the number of medical colleges has increased from one in 1990 to about a dozen. This includes the coveted and government-owned B.P. Koirala Institute of Medical Sciences in Dharan. It may be worth noting that the good reputation of these medical colleges has been able to attract a large number of bright students from abroad.

Questions, of course, continue to be raised about the profit motive of some of these private institutions. They generally serve the rich from within and outside the country with ability to afford the high cost of these institutions. A few points must be noted here. First, these medical colleges are bound by an agreement with the government to allocate at least 10 to 20 per cent of the seats on a fellowship basis to meritorious students selected by the Ministry of Education.[35] This provision has substantially expanded the access of meritorious but economically less well off students to medical education. In 1991, such arrangements

Photograph 21: Kathmandu University:
A community initiative on quality education

Photograph 22: A secene of community hill irrigation

were limited to a mere 40 seats available annually at the Institute of Medicine Campus at Maharajgunj. Second, the availability of medical colleges within the country has reduced the potential outflow of bright students for study in other countries. Third, the country reaps the income and employment multipliers from these investments in the country thereby helping the economy.

Similarly, the growth of private educational institutions, nursing homes and hospitals may be catering to those who can afford them or who prefer to access their services for various reasons. But, looked at differently, they have also helped relieve the pressure on the limited facilities at government health institutions. This is not to say, however, that the rate of private sector growth in the social sectors does not have negative side. It does and some of those have been discussed in the last chapter of this book.

SUMMING UP

The financial sector underwent rapid expansion and diversification. The expansion was not confined to urban-based banking and financial institutions. There was also massive expansion of rural and urban-based micro credit institutions catering to the needs of poorest segment of the population. Rural development received an overhaul under the new political structure dominated by rural constituencies. As rural Nepal represented the new base of political power, it received increased flow of public investment. Significant progress was made in laying down physical infrastructure like transport, communications and electricity in a country where such basic facilities were regarded remote 'luxuries'. Road and telecommunication networks expanded rapidly. Hydropower sector attracted investment from both public and private sector and as a result power generation more than doubled. Population with access to electricity jumped from 9 per cent to 40 per cent. People had better and closer access to services like the drinking water, irrigation and financial services. Modern sectors like the industry and services including air and surface transportation grew faster than agriculture. The growth of agriculture was slow, but the growth was attributed, unlike in previous decades, to rise in productivity rather than to acreage expansion. Commercialization of agriculture in cash crops, horticulture and livestock started making headway and investment in export-oriented industries grew. Exports showed a robust growth until 2002. The balance of payments remained favourable and foreign exchange reserves reached a peak of 124 billion rupees in March 2004.

Important strides were made in education, health and priority human sectors, which led to noticeable progress in human development indicators. Growth in private sector investment brought about qualitative and quantitative expansion in education and health services and relieved the pressure on government institutions. Incidence of malnutrition, infant and maternal mortality rates declined and average life expectancy and literacy rate increased. However disparities continued along regions, gender and ethnic lines. A large section of the population, particularly the traditionally neglected and discriminated *Dalits,* indigenous communities, and women, did not share the fruits of development equitably.

NOTES

1. Shalik Ram Sharma, 'Microfinance Against Poverty' in Nepal **Rastra Bank** (2003*), Economic Review Occassional Paper, No. 15.*
2. ILO Survey (2000) quoted in Kirti Bikram Dahal, 'Micro Finance in **Nepal'** *Mirmire*, a NRB publication No 217.2060.
3. A rough calculation shows that at present approximately Rs. 7.5 billion—which represents 15 per cent of the national development budget—is channeled directly to the local bodies to be spent under their discretion and management.
4. Based on data published in the *Economic Survey* reports.
5. NPC, *The Tenth Plan Summary*, 2003, p.12.
6. This problem, among others, forced the government to establish a Public Expenditure Review Commission as described in the previous chapter. One of the objectives of this exercise was to cut down the number of projects to bring them to a manageable level.
7. NPC (1992), *The Eighth Plan*, p.14
8. UNDP, *The Macroeconomics of Poverty Reduction: The Case Study of Nepal, 2004,* pp. 137–138.
9. ANZDEC Limited, New Zealand, *Nepal Agriculture Sector Performance Review* (ADB TA No.3536-NEP), 2002, p. x.
10. Ibid.
11. Ibid pp. xvi–xvii.
12. NPC *Tenth Plan*, 2002, p. 180.
13. The joint venture was to be led by a Finnish multinational forest company, Enso Forest Development Oy with three Nepali business houses. See, 'Missionary Zeal on Retreat' by Dipak Gyawali and Juhani Koponen in *AID under Stress*, Nepal: Himal Books, 2004, p. 245.
14. Some writers have attributed the demise of the plan to fierce protests by local NGO groups to which the government ultimately yielded. See ibid. But more important than the local protests were the unreasonable demands

made from the Finnish side to the proposed company, which the government was not in a position to accept.

15. Dixit (1995).
16. *Economic Survey* Reports.
17. HMG, Ministry of Trade, Commerce and Supplies, *Nepal Trade and Competitive Study*, 2004, p. xvi.
18. This was in US dollars.
19. Ibid, p. xi.
20. More discussion on the road development, particularly the donor policy towards it, has been discussed in a separate chapter.
21. *Economic Survey* reports.
22. During the *Panchayat* days, the Trisuli-Somdang road was constructed under army supervision and management, but private companies were used for actual construction.
23. NPC (2002), *Tenth Plan*, p. 352.
24. Going beyond the accepted norm, this author made a humble request to the then Supreme Court Chief Justice for an early decision on the issue, as it involved an important milestone in the country's telecommunications development. The decision came very late and in the negative on legal grounds.
25. NPC (1992), *The Eighth Plan*, p. 15.
26. Ibid. p.17.
27. *The Kathmandu Post*, 6 November 2004.
28. See NPC (2002), p. 289.
29. Of the 228 members present in the joint House, 220 voted in favour of ratification, and 8 against it. The 8 members included 2 from UML, 3 among King-nominated Upper House members and 3 from fringe left parties. 28 UML and 3 King-nominated members abstained from the voting.
30. *The Nepali Times*, 11–17 February 2005.
31. A new possibility of claiming compensation from Clean Energy Mechanism for saving carbon emission into the atmosphere has also opened up after the Kyoto Protocol. It is estimated that reaching a target of 200,000 biogas plants could result in a claim of $30 million annually. Quoted in Naresh Newar's article in Ibid.
32. CADC (2004), *Renewable energy data of Nepal, 2003* Kathmandu.
33. UNDP (2004), p. 77.
34. The budget for 1995/96 started a scheme to provide monthly stipend of Rs.25 to all Dalit children attending primary school. Allocation was made to provide similar incentive for girls' education in 10 districts with lowest literacy.
35. The provision of 10 per cent seats for scholarships in medical colleges with domestic investment, while joint venture medical colleges have to allocate 20 per cent.

PART III
CRITICAL ISSUES & FAULT-LINES

Chapter Eight

The Legacy of Exclusion and Neglect

Nepal is a country of human and ecological diversity. From the high Himalayas to the tropical plains, it has a variety of agro-climatic zones within a very limited space. The human diversity is reflected in its numerous ethnicities, languages, religions, cultures, and biological features. The Constitution of the Kingdom of Nepal recognizes the country as a multi-ethnic and multi-cultural Hindu Kingdom.

The 2001 national census has classified 98 caste/ethnic groups and sub-groups, with an almost equal number of languages and dialects. The country has three distinct ecological and cultural belts—the mountains, mid-hills and the southern *tarai*, all stretching from east to west. The sparsely populated northern mountain region is basically an extension of the Tibetan civilization inhabited by ethnic groups of Tibeto-Burman origin practising Tibetan Buddhism. The southern *tarai* on the other hand, is an extension of the Indo-Gangetic civilization and is home to predominantly Hindu settlements with various caste groups speaking different languages and dialects of the Indo-Gangetic plains. The belt also has a high concentration of various indigenous ethnic groups,—predominant among them being the Tharus —again, speaking different languages and dialects. The Muslim population predominates in certain pockets. The *tarai* belt, endowed with fertile plains, has also been the centre of other industrial and economic activities. This region has attracted migration from the hills in recent decades, particularly following the eradication of malaria in the 1950s. The mid-hills are inhabitated by a mixture of Nepali speaking Indo-Aryan Hindu caste groups and various casteless Tibeto-Burman ethnic groups who speak their own languages. As the King is a Hindu and the state power has traditionally been exercised by high caste Hindus, orthodox Hinduism has traditionally been practiced as the basis of state policy and inter-ethnic relations.[1]

The *Mulki Ain* (Civil Code) during the time of Jang Bahadur in 1854, formally codified the caste system in Nepal. Under this Hindu stratification of social relations, the priestly *Brahmins* were accorded the top position, followed by the warrior/ruling class *Chhetris*. The various casteless Tibeto-Burman ethnic groups who follow differing religious and cultural practices were accorded the middle rung. At the bottom of the hierarchy were the *Dalits*—traditionally neglected, discriminated, and treated as "untouchables". Although, the practice of untouchability was legally abolished in 1963, its social practice is still prevalent, and *Dalits* continue to remain neglected in practically all spheres of public life. The Panchayat rule also adopted a homogenization policy to assimilate the multi-cultural society into a mono-national culture in the name of modernization. The slogan of one nation, one dress and one language was promoted as state policy.

Some scholars have blamed the contemporary state attitude for not recognizing the discrimination and domination between groups and by doing so, helping maintain the dominant group's superior position. They refer to the prevailing discrimination on two fronts: cultural and in accessing resources through institutions and attitudes. The constitutional provisions relating to the Hindu Kingdom, imposition of dominant language on the society, Hindu ideology-based state laws, the absence of minority heroes and symbols in the national pantheon, and cultural and gender related discrimination in the distribution of public goods are shown as forms of institutional and cultural discrimination. Similarly, the demeaning social attitudes, practices, and non-recognition are seen as examples of attitudinal discrimination.[2] Other ethnic scholars blame the ruling high caste groups for oppressing and suppressing the various indigenous, ethnic, and depressed caste groups to eliminate their language, culture and religion through a variety of "coercive methods" such as Hinduization, Sanskritization and Nepalization.[3]

It was only after the People's Movement of 1990 and the restoration of multiparty democracy that the indigenous ethnic and depressed communities started voicing their discontent over their rightful place in Nepali society. Demands coming from such communities at present, among others, include: the ethnic autonomy or right to self-determination, federalism, equal status to all languages, government support for education in mother languages, news broadcast in all languages, secular state instead of the present "Hindu" state, right to slaughter cows, and rights to form ethnic-based parties.

ETHNIC EXCLUSION

Nepal has never witnessed the type of ethnic or communal conflict and violence seen in many other countries, and the cultural harmony within the broad framework of nation-state is not fragile. However, with education and the freedoms afforded by democratic exercise, there is an increasing ethnic and minority consciousness of this disparity. Recognizing their unequal access to state power, governance, and public goods, the minorities have leveled charges of discrimination and suppression on the dominant groups. It is also important to note that the unequal access to political and socio-economic power is not limited along ethnic lines, but also by gender and geographical regions. The prevailing distribution of social, economic, and political power make this very clear.

Historically, political and administrative power in Nepal has largely been monopolized by the *Brahmins* and *Chhetris*, the two upper caste Hindus, and the *Newars*—the culturally, educationally and commercially advanced ethnic group largely concentrated in Kathmandu and other urban centres. The *Dalits*, the ethnic hill groups of Tibeto-Burman origin, the *tarai Madhesis*, and other indigenous groups have negligible share in the country's administrative and political power. The *Dalits* bear the case of extreme exclusion with all the disadvantages of caste discrimination, low literacy, landlessness, and lack of political voice. Similarly, the *Janjatis* clamour against subjugation mostly manifested through cultural and religious domination. In addition, they also suffer from low literacy and an unfavourable economic base. The *Madhesis* have particular grievances of being subjected to linguistic discrimination, hill domination, and employment restrictions, particularly in the military establishment.[4]

Available statistics show[5] that the *Brahmin-Chhetri-Newar* combination, who make up 37.5 per cent of the population, have control over 82 per cent of the 'integrated national governance'.[6] The extreme case of non-representation in national governance is that of *Dalits*, who constitute 9 per cent of the total population but have no representation in any of these institutions, except in the Parliament and a token representation in the education system. Their share in the integrated national governance is a mere 0.3 per cent and their position is nil in almost all influential spheres of Nepali society. Their extreme exclusion can be gauged from the fact that there has not been a single *Dalit* cabinet minister in Nepal's history. They remain the most subjugated community of the country and this status quo is perpetuated by a hierarchical caste structure and discriminatory social and political practices. It is interesting that the practice of discrimination and untouchability prevails even within the *Dalit* sub-groups thereby further complicating the problem.

The other non-represented communities are the *Madhesis* and the *Janjatis*. *Madhesis* constitute 31 per cent of the total population, but account for only 11 per cent in the overall governance. Their share in the primary index of national governance (cabinet, judiciary and parliament) is 17 per cent. Within the *Madhesis*, the exclusion of *Dalits* and *Janjatis* is even more serious. Similarly, the *Janjatis* account for 21 per cent of the population[7] but have control over only 7 per cent of governance. However, their position improves to 13 per cent in the primary index of governance. The overall governance index does not include the army and the police where the representation of hill ethnic groups is sizable in view of their martial tradition and fighting qualities.[8] Similarly, hill *Janjatis* have a strong presence in the police. However, the representation of the *Dalits* and *Madhesis* is marginal even in the army and police. Gurung explains the disparity in education and employment indices among social groups in the following words:

> In a way such a chasm is the making of social discrimination, that perpetuates economic inequality. Therefore, the Khas-Bahun hegemony in politics and Sharma-Shrestha (Bahun-Newar) supremacy in intellectual pursuits. These have historical and occupational underpinnings in that the extended Nepal was basically a Chhetri-Bahun construct while Bahun's priestly vocation and Newar's bazaar location imbued them with access to knowledge.[9]

Disaggregated data on human development indicators shows that the *Brahmins* and *Newars* are way above the national average in practically all aspects including, per capita income, education, literacy and life expectancy, while the *Chhetris* are just a little above the national average. The hill *Janjatis* are below the national average, while the *Dalits* are significantly below the national average in every respect. The HDI positions of the advantaged groups are as follows: the *Newars* above the national index by 41 per cent, *Brahmins* by 36 per cent, and *Chhetris* by 7 per cent. The HDI of the *Janjatis* is 8 per cent below the overall national index, while the *Dalits* are 26 per cent below (Table 7.1). A distinction between *Bramins* and *Chhetris* has to be made as well. The control of *Brahmins* within the *Brahmin-Chhetri* combination would appear very stark, even in the administrative and professional life of the country. In the numerically the larger *Chhetri* category (17 per cent of the population as against the second largest 13 per cent *Brahmins*), the *Thakuris* are doing well, whereas the *Chhetris* as a group are not in an enviable position. The position of the *Chhetri* group may in large part, be influenced by the extremely high position of the *Thakuris* in the establishment as well as their easier access to resources.

All indicators of human development such as life expectancy, adult literacy ratio, years of schooling, and per capita income indices, show the *Chhetris* below the *Brahmins*. The prevalence of *Chhetris* in positions of leadership as indicated by their presence in the parliament, political party central committees and the administration is also much below the *Brahmins*.[10]

An analysis of the pattern of representation in the various legislative bodies indicates a continued domination by the same caste groups of middle class background. During the party-less regime, the *Chhetris* dominated the National Panchayat, followed by the *Brahmins*. In the 1991, 1994 and 1999 House of Representatives (HOR), the *Brahmins* displaced the *Chhetris* with 42.7 per cent, 48.2 per cent, and 47.3 per cent of the seats, while the *Chhetris* had only 20 per cent, 18 per cent and 17.3 per cent of these seats. [11]

Harka Gurung's analysis[12] of the social composition of the House of Representatives in the last three general elections also shows the continuing predominance of the hill caste groups. In the 1999 election, the hill caste groups comprising 40 per cent of the total population won 57.6 per cent seats in the HOR. The hill ethnics (including the *Newar*) representing nine language groups and 20 per cent population controlled 22 per cent, while the *tarai* caste groups with 16 per cent population had 14.5 per cent seats. Similarly, the *tarai* ethnic groups with 7.9 per cent population had 5.4 per cent, while the Muslims with 3.5 per cent population had 1 per cent representation. Gurung concludes that despite the rhetoric of increasing ethnic activism, the share of ethnics remained unchanged in the three general elections.

Unsurprisingly, an analysis of the educational attainments of the Nepali population based on the 1991 census also shows that the three elite groups—*Brahmin, Chhetris* and *Newars* accounted for 70 per cent of all graduates in Nepal. The natural consequence of this is reflected in their domination in professional occupations. The social composition of Tribhuvan University teachers and the government bureaucracy makes this clear. Of the 3871 University teachers, 80.9 per cent came from the three elite groups. The hill ethnics comprising 20 per cent of the total population account for only 2 per cent of graduates and 3.2 per cent of the university teachers. The imbalance is even more pronounced in the civil service. The social and economic entrenchment of the dominant groups tends to further enhance their position and accentuate these disparities.

TABLE 8.1

Human Development by Caste and Ethnicity

Human Dev. Indicators	*Average Nepal*	*Brahmin*	*Chhetri*	*Newar*	*Hill Janajatis*	*Hill Dalit*
Life expectancy (yrs)	55.0	60.8	56.3	62.2	53	50.3
Adult literacy(%)	36.7	58	42	54	35.2	23.8
Mean yrs schooling	2.3	4.7	2.8	4.4	2.0	1.2
Per capita income (NR)	7,673	9,921	7,744	11,953	6,607	4,940
Per capita PPP (US$)	1,186	1,533	1,197	1,848	1,021	764
1. Life expectancy index	0.500	0.597	0.522	0.320	0.467	0.422
2. Educational attainment index	0.295	0.490	0.342	0.462	0.280	0.186
3. Income index	0.179	0.237	0.181	0.289	0.152	0.110
Human Dev. Index	0.325	0.441	0.348	0.457	0.299	0.239
Ratio of national HDI	100	135.9	107.3	140.7	92.2	73.6

Source: World Bank (2004), *Nepal Development Policy Review*, p. 11.

REGIONAL DISPARITIES

The country has been divided into five Development Regions—Eastern, Central, Western, Midwestern, and Farwestern. Each of these five regions contains the three distinct ecological belts of the country—the mountains, mid-hills and the *tarai*. Wide disparities exist between these regions in terms of their economic conditions, human development status, and other opportunities. Similarly, there is a serious urban-rural dichotomy. In fact, there are two Nepals reflecting a dualistic character—rich urban centres with modern facilities and opportunities, and the poor rural Nepal deprived of even the most basic socio-economic amenities.

Particularly conspicuous is the position of the rich Kathmandu valley, the country's capital, where the incidence of poverty is only 4 per cent against the national mark of 42 per cent[13]. The vast majority of the households in Kathmandu fall in the upper quintile of national consumption distribution. The overall poverty level in urban areas is 23 per cent, while it is 44 per cent for rural areas. Urban Nepal is also marked by higher income inequality than rural Nepal. The gini coefficient for urban areas is 0.43 as compared to 0.31 in rural areas. Also, the higher level of inequality in Nepal compared to other countries is manifested in the slightly higher national coefficient, 0.34 per cent, compared to 0.32 for South Asia. A further breakdown shows that the poverty level is particularly high in the Mid and Far-Westen regions, both in the *tarai* and hills/mountains, the incidence being as high as 72 per cent in hills and mountains. Similarly, the poverty level in the central hills and mountains is particularly acute. Among the ecological belts, the poverty level in the mountains is the highest.

An insight into the social and human development status and unequal living conditions between various regions can be observed from the disaggregated human development indices. Nepal's Human Development Index, according to the global Human Development Report prepared by UNDP stood at 0.547 for 2001. Using a different methodology, the national HDI calculated by Nepal Human Development Report was 0.446 for the year 2000. Further breakdown showed that the HDI for urban and rural areas stood at 0.616 and 0.446 respectively, clearly indicating an urban bias of development activities. Classified by ecological regions, the HDI for mountains, hills and *tarai* were 0.378, 0.510 and 0.474 respectively. The difficult geography and highly dispersed population in the mountain region makes access to public resources extremely difficult. Understandably therefore, this region has the lowest HDI. Among the development regions, the Central

Development Region—where the nation's capital is located—has the highest HDI with 0.493, closely followed by Eastern (0.484), and Western (0.479) regions. On the other hand, the mid-western and far-western development regions, with respective HDI scores of 0.402 and 0.358, remain economically and socially the poorest regions. If one looks at the statistics by eco-development regions, the mountain parts of these two regions emerge as the most backward parts in the country with 0.322 and 0.286 HDI (Table 8.3).

TABLE 8.2
Poverty and Consumption Inequality by Region

	Poverty	*Gini Coefficient*
Nepal	42	0.34
Urban	23	0.43
Rural	44	0.31
Kathmandu Valley	4	0.37
Other Urban	34	0.43
Rural Eastern *Tarai*	39	0.29
Rural Western *Tarai*	46	0.26
Rural Eastern Hills/Mountains	33	0.32
Rural Western Hills/Mountains	40	0.35
Tarai	42	0.29
Hills	41	0.39
Mountains	56	0.35

Source: World Bank (1999), pp. 94-95 based on *NLSS I*. Rural East includes central and eastern parts, while Rural West includes western, mid-western and far-western parts.

It is not mere coincidence that the launching pad of the Maoist movement was the mid-western hills which ranks amongst the lowest in HDI. The HDI in the mid-western hills in 1996, about the time the insurgency started, stood at 0.276 compared to the national average of 0.325. The average HDI of the five mid-western districts most affected by Maoist activities—Rukum, Rolpa, Salyan, Jajarkot and Kalikot—was 0.234.

It may also be noted that some progress has definitely been made in various aspects of human development over the years as discussed in the previous chapter, which is reflected in the overall improvement in the national HDI. But what is clear from this analysis is that the benefit has not been shared equitably by all regions. Most of the mountain areas, except the central mountains, have lagged behind significantly. In fact, the human development situation in the far-western mountain region seems to have deteriorated. Among the *tarai* regions,

TABLE 8.3
Disaggregated Human Development Status in Nepal: 2002

Nepal	**0.466**	**Eco-Development Regions**	
Rural	0.446	Eastern Hills	0.513
Urban	0.616	Central Hills	0.510
		Eastern *Tarai*	0.488
Ecological Belts		Western Hills	0.487
Mountains	0.378	Central *Tarai*	0.462
Hills	0.510	Central Mid-Western *Tarai*	0.458
Tarai	0.474	Central Mountains	0.437
		Western *Tarai*	0.435
Development Regions		Mid-Western Hills	0.433
Eastern	0.484	Far-Western *Tarai*	0.425
Central	0.493	Eastern Mountains	0.424
Western	0.479	Western Mountains	0.414
Mid-Western	0.402	Far-Western Mountains	0.393
Far-Western	0.382	Mid-Western Mountains	0.322
		Far Western Mountains	0.286

Source: Nepal Human Development Report 2001.

the western and far-western *tarai* and central hills have also lagged behind in accessing proportionate benefits (Table 8. 4).

TABLE 8.4
Percentage Change in HDI during 1996–2000 by Eco-Development Region

Eco-development Region	*% Change*	*Eco-development Region*	*% Change*
Central Mountains	25.9	Eastern *Tarai*	7.5
Central *Tarai*	19.1	Western Mountains	5.6
Mid-Western *Tarai*	18.7	Far Western *Tarai*	4.7
Far-Western Hills	16.3	Western *Tarai*	1.9
Eastern Hills	15.0	Mid-Western Mountains	1.3
Western Hills	13.5	Eastern Mountains	1.0
Mid-Western Hills	11.3	Central Hills	0.8
		Far-Western Mountains	-14.6

Source: Nepal Human Development Report 2001.

GENDER DIVIDE

In recent years, a Gender-related Development Index (GDI) has been developed to measure gender disparities. In the Nepali context, gender-related exclusion covers factors like physical survival, health and educational opportunities, ownership of assets, mobility, and overall cultural status. Statistics show that the country's GDI of 0.452 is closer to equality (HDI 0.466), but disparities persist across the variety of human development parameters. At 0.494, the GDI is highest in the hills while women continue to suffer exclusion in the mountains (0.355), and the mid and far-western regions (Table 8.5).

TABLE 8.5
Disaggregated Gender-related Development Indices: 2000

Nepal	**0.452**		
Urban	0.605		
Rural	0.426		
By Ecological Belts		**By Development Region**	
Mountains	0.355	Eastern	0.465
Hills	0.494	Central	0.476
Tarai	0.456	Western	0.463
		Mid-Western	0.376
		Far-Western	0.356

Source: Nepal Human Development Report 2001.

Another indicator developed to measure women's participation in economic, social and political decision making is the Gender Empowerment Ratio (GEM). This indicator is derived as a composite of variables like women's participation in elections and their shares in administrative, managerial and technical jobs. Nepal's overall GEM is 0.385 and the extent of female participation in the political process is one fifth of what it is for men. Similar pattern is observed with respect to professional and administrative jobs. Their share in earned income is one-third of that of men and they are generally worse off compared to men with respect to life expectancy, literacy, and average school years in all regions. This is evidenced from the figures presented in Table 7.6. But the good news is that the gender gap is narrowing. This was also the conclusion of the NLSS I data which showed that though significant disparities existed in education and health indicators, the trend was towards a narrowing of the gap.[14]

In terms of empowerment, Nepali women are still without voice and influence in the public domain. Their representation in Nepal's influential civil service and all three levels of elected governments remains nominal.Women make up less than 8 per cent of the overall staff of the civil service and only 4 per cent of the officer level staff. These numbers are starkly lower than those of other South Asian countries. Women were also under-represented in Nepal's elected governments. After the last elections, they made up only 6 per cent of the Lower House and 15 per cent of the Upper House members (where some of the seats can be nominated by the King). The representation of women in the district and village level bodies is even lower.[15]

The exclusion and voicelessness of women provided fodder for radical slogans of the Maoists, especially in the earlier years of their revolution. On her field visits to the insurgency-affected areas, the chairwoman of the National Commission for Women found that the majority of women who had joined the Maoist militia cited ill-treatment by abusive husbands, alcoholic fathers, practice of polygamy, exclusion from mainstream parties, and lack of freedom of sexuality and safe sex as their primary motivations.[16] Another report by the National Commission for Women states that the chief attraction for women was the Maoist slogan of *Mahila Mukti* (Women Liberation). Having come from a background of social exclusion and neglect, these women raised issues that were legal, political, humanitarian, social, and financial in nature. Their primary assertion was that under the traditional system they were nobodys, whereas now they have 'the status' and 'the responsibility to accomplish tasks'.

TABLE 8.6

Gender Disparity in key Human Development Indicators (1996–2000)

	Life Expectancy in Years				*Adult Literacy in %*				*Average School Going Years*			
	1996		*2000*		*1996*		*2000*		*1996*		*2000*	
	Male	*Female*	*Male*	*Female*	*Male*	*Female*	*Male*	*Female*	*Male*	*Female*	*Male*	*Female*
Mountain	52.7	50.4	48.6	51.1	44.2	11.8	61.9	26.6	2.27	0.71	3.71	1.33
Hill	58.0	55.5	65.4	64.7	58.4	24.3	72.3	39.5	3.42	1.61	3.97	2.18
Tarai	59.5	57.0	61.7	63.2	52.3	19.9	60.2	32.5	3.10	1.25	3.71	1.93
Urban	63.2	60.3	71.4	70.8	76.7	51.5	81.2	56.9	5.63	3.88	6.01	3.80
Rural	53.7	51.3	58.2	59.3	52.0	19.5	63.6	32.3	2.93	1.15	3.40	1.66
Nepal	55.0	52.4	59.3	59.8	54.3	21.3	65.8	35.4	2.55	1.13	4.45	2.25

Source: World Bank (2004), *Nepal Development Policy Review*, Page 11, Compiled from *Nepal Human Development Reports*.

AFTER DEMOCRACY

Open democratic exercise since 1990 provided political and social space for the disadvantaged and the culturally diverse communities to articulate their grievances, and assert their identities and rights. The Maoists have exploited the ethnic problems to their advantage with promises of distribution of power along ethnic lines and draw large proportions of their cadres from the *Dalit* and other disadvantaged ethnic groups. The demands for a secular state, the right to education in one's mother language, right to cow slaughter, etc. are becoming more pronounced. Such voices have prompted the state to announce some reform measures to rectify the traditional injustice and discrimination that prevailed in Nepali society.

Since 1991, various governments have taken different measures and enacted legislations in response to such demands. It is now mandatory to have woman representatives at all levels of the elected bodies like VDCs, DDCs and the national legislature. This, by itself, creates a minimum body of about 50,000 women representatives at the local level and offers a solid foundation for leadership development. At the national level, a permanent Women Commission has been formed to look into women issues and concerns, and initiate appropriate actions. Similarly the National Foundation for Upliftment of Nationalities has started work for the presevation of languages and cultures of indigenous groups. The *Dalit* Commission was established to deal with cross-cutting issues concerning the *Dalits* and a *Praja* Development Programme has also been under implemetation for the upliftment of the *Praja* community.

In accordance with the recommendation of the National Language Policy Recommendation Committee in 1993, more languages are now being encouraged to develop and assert their rightful roles in national life. Consequently radio news can now be heard in at least 13 native languages and text books for primary education have been prepared in 11 indigenous languages by the Ministry of Education.[17] The *Mulki-Ain* abolished the practice of untouchability a long time ago, but such practices still prevail. To reinforce efforts against such social evil, the practice of untouchability, including caste-based restriction of public places has been made legally punishable. Furthermore, the 2001 amendment to the Education Act 1971 and other regulations introduced in 2002 have stipulated free education to indigenous as well as *Dalit* children below the poverty line, and also the reservation of 5 per cent scholarships to disadvantaged groups[18] Barring the extreme exclusion of Dalits and low representation of women, the representation of the hill ethnic groups and the *Madhesis* was slowly becoming visible at least in the legislative body of the government. With a view to correct the legal discrimination against women, their right on parental property has now been guaranteed by law. Judicious representation in legislative bodies does give proper voice to disadvantaged groups and foster an environment that can be conducive to redressing the existing social inequalities. But political presence of the ethnic representatives alone is not sufficient condition for the resolution of the problem of exclusion which has deep historical roots.

There are proposals put into place for special provisions like quotas and reservations in civil service, educational institutions, army and police for the under-privileged communities. A major programme has recently been started with international financial support to provide a 250 rupees monthly stipend to all *Dalit* children and the poor girls up to class 5 under the Education for All Programme. The stipend is given directly to the students through their schools for purchasing school uniforms, and the reading and writing materials. The programme has met with good response: the number of participating *Dalit* children from grade I to V has now increased to 559,000. Similarly, there were 635,000 eligible girls studying in primary schools. The total amount of scholarship money released in this fiscal year (2004/05) alone amounted to Rs. 139 million for *Dalit* children, and Rs. 159.5 million for poor girls.[19]

Though these well-meaning reforms are in the right direction, they are not sufficient. It would take a long time to bring these communities, particularly the *Dalits* and some other ethnic groups at par with the dominant groups. This is mainly because of factors like low levels of educational attainment and the lack of visionary leadership from within these communities. Moreover, there is an absence of well organised political entities pressing for reforms, or a strong social and political movement for the assertion of the *Dalit* rights and status. Such a scenario makes it even more important for the dominant political class and the government to lead the process of social change within the constitutional framework in order to prevent a situation of potential unrest which could occur in a situation of continuous marginalization and exclusion.

A very positive aspect of the Nepali polity has been the capacity of national parties to manage ethnic politics within their ranks despite the continued dominance of a few high caste elites in politics.[20] In fact, most of the times, the high caste political leadership has provided significant impetus to this aspect of internal reform. Many of the well known ethnic leaders have come from mainstream parties and, in fact, every member elected to the parliament from disadvantaged communities has been on the platform of the major political parties. No party trying to capitalize on purely communal and ethnic issues has won a seat in the parliament so far. Even the *tarai*-based Nepal Sadvabana Party has fared poorly in its own territory, where the position of the two major parties remains predominant. There is now a growing consensus among major political forces for a more radical reform in the distribution of power to properly reflect the diversity of Nepal's plural society.

Democracy ultimately draws its strength from the people and for the people to take ownership in the political process, their participation and involvement in decision making is necessary. As this calls for the broadening and deepening of the democratic process, the traditionally rigid and centralized state structure is now giving way to a more decentralized governance. Nepal enacted the Local Self Governance Act, 1999 to institutionalize the devolution of authority to local bodies. This makes the local governments responsible for such areas like the health, education, drinking water and sanitation, social development, and a number of other economic and community development activities. The Act empowers the local bodies to generate revenue through various taxes, fees, and rents. The Act also has provision to ensure the representation of women and disadvantaged groups in local governance. This democratic exercise has helped improve redistribution of state resources in favour of rural areas and some changes are evident through increased socio-economic opportunities and developmental benefits.

The process of empowering people does not stop at the level of local government; it goes further and deeper to the level of societies, communities and individuals. In a situation where the socio-economically disadvantaged communities have remained powerless under elite domination for centuries, social mobilization has emerged as a powerful tool for their upliftment. It is only through collective action that the marginalized groups can develop their self confidence in asserting and claiming their rights. One can see genuine social mobilization efforts targeting the women and deprived population taking place in various parts of the country under committed local leaders. Women have proven to be more committed and enthusiastic participants in such activities. These efforts are bringing improvements in the access to resources without regard to gender, social class, ethnicity or religion, and also have helped in social and economic upliftment.

NEEDED: MORE THAN A REPRESENTATIVE DEMOCRACY

Democracy is essential but not necessarily the sufficient condition to prevent a sense of injustice and exclusion for marginalized groups. Redressing the cultural exclusion of the minorities and other marginalized groups requires more than providing for their civic and political freedoms and socio-economic policies through the instruments of a majoritarian democracy. The Maoists' creation of ethnic autonomous regions and the attendant opportunity for self-determination has given a fresh impetus to ethnic concerns and grievances. The fact that seven of the eight 'liberation fronts' of the Maoists have an ethnic basis clearly points out the latent national fault-line. Perhaps inspired by the Maoist appeal, other ethnicity-based militant organizations like the Madhesi Tigers have taken birth. These bodies are trying to cash in on the existing exclusion and disparities that the deprived communities suffer from. The solution to this serious problem lies in specific multi-cultural policies to ensure cultural recognition, and strong affirmative actions to address the problems of socio-economic exclusion, and the discriminatory language and religious practices. More importantly, an equitable participation of the diverse cultural groups must be ensured in political decision making. The conventional colour-blind approach to ensuring equality before law 'irrespective of caste, creed, sex and tribe' is insufficient at a time when the 'deconstructionist movement' emphasizing ethnic and sub-national identities is having an increasing appeal. The new emphasis should be on 'impact equality' through a policy of deliberate 'minority preference'.

Nepal has adopted the Westminster model of pluralist democracy – majoritarian in character and with political parties as principal actors for organizing and mobilizing people around policies, programmes and platforms. The classical majoritarian political democracy, designed for generally homogenous societies, is not always capable of handling the demands of a multi-cultural and plural society like that of Nepal. Institutions of a representative democracy, therefore, call for adjustments and modifications to mitigate its inherent institutional biases. In the absence of appropriate adjustments, the formal state structure tends to favour the predominant groups. Political pluralism requires institutional arrangements for ensuring an active involvement of all communities in decision making. Nepal's political process has yet to fully indigenize the specific character of the country's diversity.

A national consensus is emerging around the recognition that in addition to positive socio-economic measures, substantive political reforms to restructure the state power is also required. Opinions vary regarding the exact nature of such restructuring. A constitutional guarantee of political power sharing by the disadvantaged minorities and a greater devolution of power are more frequently mentioned areas for constitutional reforms. The improvement in the electoral system is necessary to prevent the chronic under-representation of the excluded communities, and the creation of an autonomous regional administration is emphasized to put an end to Kathmandu's monopoly over state power and resources. More radical proposals such as a federal political structure and power sharing along ethnic and communal lines are also being made. This would involve the establishment of territorial sub-units within a state where the minorities could exercise considerable autonomy. These are difficult propositions whose applicability would be complicated by the fact that ethnic heterogeneity characterizes all regions and districts in Nepal. Even nationally dominant ethnic groups are minorities in regions, where minority ethnic groups are numerically dominant. On the demand for federalism based on ethnic/linguistic division, Gurung writes;

> This seems to be fraught with problems of area demarcation and the sustainability of Nepal itself. While large-scale inter-regional migration of people has eroded discrete cultural areas, a federal structure could encourage centrifugal forces. Some reorganization seems economically justified since most of the present administrative districts are too small to be economically justified. Such a regrouping, however, should be for decentralization purposes that would ultimately lead to the devolution of power at the local level. [21]

The debate is between a radical restructuring of the state along federal lines and regional governance with devolution of power and a reformed electoral system. What is beyond controversy is the imperative of ensuring equitable representation of all communities to ensure the empowerment of the neglected communities, regions, and a wider political participation. This can only be addressed by a multi-cultural policy and effective power-sharing institutions where the country's diverse communities would have adequate space and voice. The perception of the majoritarian imposition and the domination by culturally dominant groups must be put to an end without contradicting or weakening the goals of a capable state. A strong democracy ensures equal opportunities to all citizens.

NOTES

1. See Bihari K. Shrestha, 'Conflict Resolution Through Governence Effectiveness' in *Conflict Resolution and Governance in Nepal, 2002,* Kathmandu:NEFAS.
2. See Mahendra Lawati, 'Defining Minorities' in *Nepal Journal of Contemporary Studies*, March 2002, Kathmandu : NCCS.
3. See Krishna *B.* Bhattachan, 'Challenges of Ethnonationalism in South Asia' *Journal of Contemporary Studies* Vol I, No. 2 Sept., 2001.
4. Harka Gurung, 'Trident and Thunderbolt', *Cultural Dynamics and Nepalese Politics,* M.C. Regmi Memorial Lecture, 2003.
5. Mahendra Lawati, (2002), cited from Govinda Neupane (2000), *Nepalko Jatiya Prasna.*
6. A composite indicator of overall governance comprising institutions like the cabinet and the parliament, the judiciary and constitutional bodies, the leadership in political parties, local government and public administration, industry and the education system, science, technology and culture
7. Ibid. It may be noted that the *tarai Janjatis* and *Dalits* are not included here, but lumped together with *Madhesis.*
8. Out of the present 18 army generals ranked two-star and above, 6 are from the hill *Janajatis.* See Subas Devkota and Sarad Bhattarai's report in *Samaya,* Mansir 10, 2061.
9. Harka Gurung, Nepal: *Social Demography and Expressions*, Kathmandu: New Era, 1999, p.125.
10. Mahendra Lawati, (2002) op.cit.
11. Lok Raj Baral, 'Govemance and Security in Plural Society: The Case of Nepal' in Chari (ed) *Security and Governance in South Asia*, Colombo: Regional Centre For Strategic Studies 2001.
12. See Harka Gurung, 'General Election—1999' in *Nepali Journal of Contemporary Studies* Vol. 1. No. 2, Kathmandu, Sep 2002.
13. Based on NLSS I findings for the year 1995/96.
14. World Bank (1999).
15. World Bank (2004), p.11.
16. See Durga Pokhrel's eyewitness report on field visits to insurgency-affected areas (unpublished).
17. *Nepal Human Development Report 2004*, (Draft) p. 53.
18. Ibid.
19. *The Kathmandu Post*, 18 November 2004.
20. Baral, op. cit. (2001).
21. Harka Gurung, op.cit. p. 204.

Chapter Nine

The Arun III Debacle

Perhaps no single develoment issue attracted as much attention, controversy, and debate in the early nineties as the Arun III Hydroelectricity Project planned on Arun river in Sankhuwasabha district. This project was identified by a JICA reconnaissance study in the Koshi basin, and screened further on the basis of energy capacity, distance from the load centre, accessibility, and a rough cost-benefit analysis. As one of the four attractive projects identified by JICA, it was subsequently studied upto the pre-feasibility level. In 1987, a Least Cost Generation Expansion Plan (LCGEP) was prepared with the help of a Canadian firm called Canadian International Water and Energy Consultants based on the inventory of projects studied upto the pre-feasibility level. The Plan concluded that the most economic generation sequence to meet the forecast demand through 2005 would be a combination of load management, thermal power, and a two-stage Arun III project. The study had considered various options including both thermal and hydro projects ranging in size from 10 MW Modi to 660 MW Kaligandaki II. An update of LCGEP in 1990 reconfirmed that Arun III was part of the least cost plan. The total generation capacity of the project was 404 MW of electricity.

THE PROJECT

This background information shows that when the elected government of Nepali Congress took over in mid-1991, Arun III had already been developed as an essential part of Nepal's least cost energy plan for the medium term. In response to the concerns about macro-economic affordability, this project was redesigned in 1992 as a two-stage project of 201 MW each. This was again reconfirmed as part of the least cost plan in 1994. Fed by mountain glaciers and aquafiers, the most attractive feature of the project was the firm energy it produced throughout the year. The other projects developed and identified for the future generated very low firm energy, ranging from 15 to 60 per cent of the installed capacity in lean seasons. Compared to those, Arun III would provide about 85 per cent of the firm installed capacity even in the dry season of December–April, when the need for load-shedding normally became acute in Nepal during those days.

The total estimated cost of the project as of 1994 was US $1.08 billion, of which about two-third was committed by external agencies entirely in the form of grants and soft loans. The principal donors included IDA ($ 175 million), ADB ($127 million), Germany ($125.4 million), Japan ($150 million), and France, Switzerland and Finland ($ 46 million).[1] Of the main sources, the German assistance was an outright grant. The Japanese commited soft loans convertible into grants and the World Bank and the ADB loans represented soft credit payable over a period of 30–40 years at less than one per cent service charge. Others were grant-cum-credit. A rough calculation showed that the foreign assistance package had a seventy per cent subsidy element in it. The annual power generation from the project at the prevailing power tariff at that time would yield approximately five billion rupees. The debt servicing obligation and operational costs of the project would take about one fifth of this revenue, leaving approximately four billion rupees as net revenue to the government for investment in other priority sectors.

One important component of the project was the 122-kilometre access road to be completed at the cost of $124 million. The high cost of the road was mainly attributed to its design, and the methods of construction. It involved simultanous construction at different sites, transportation of construction materials by helicopters in view of their locations at inaccessible places, and extreme sensitivity to environmental concerns.[2] Highly capital intensive methods were used with the objective of shortening the period of road construction. Delay in completing the road would affect the construction of the power project, which, in addition to pushing up the normal project cost, would mean sacrificing power revenue. The value of this road development should be seen from another perspective as well. Beside its importance from social and regional development standpoints the road would facilitate the development of second phase Arun III, Upper and Lower Aruns with an identified power capacity of 844 MW—making the overall power generation among the cheapest in Nepal.

The Nepali Congress government supported and approved the

project after being satisfied with its attractiveness. This was confirmed and reconfirmed after being subjected to rigorous appraisal and scrutiny at various levels from technical, economic, environmental, social, and regional considerations by national and international experts. The country had already spent US $20 million for pre-feasibility, feasibilty, and engineering designs. Various other studies concerning the impact on environment, seismology, hydrology, resettlement, and GLOF (Glaciar Lake Outburst Flood) had also been completed as prescribed by experts and incorporated into the project design. Dozens of public hearings and consultations were conducted at the national level and with local bodies, user groups, and other stakeholders including the inhabitants of the project-affected areas. The support was enthusiastic, particularly from the affected areas mainly due to the perceived benefits from the access road.[3]

A period of approximately eight years was spent in these activities as well as in negotiating with various donor countries and institutions with varying mandates, programmes and budget cycles. Each participating donor had made thorough appraisal of the project and found it attractive. Furthermore, the donors have their own parliaments, boards and other bodies where development projects are scrutinized and debated based on various considerations. The Arun III project had passed through all these tests and financial assistance had been committed after a long and arduous process.

CONTROVESY AND CANCELLATION

Unfortunately, the project attracted unprecedented debate and controversy within the country as well as from a powerful network of international non-governmental organizations. A lot of arguments were made and written on the issue of Nepal's hydropower in general and the Arun III in particular. The opposition instigated by business interests and the thermal lobby was natural. However, the staunchest anti-Arun campaign was launched by international NGOs and their local counterparts.[4] The campaign was launched particularly in various financial capitals including Washington D.C., Manila, Tokyo, and Bonn, aimed at negatively impacting the decision of the project financing partners.

The controversy took a political turn when the UML criticized the G.P. Koirala-led Nepali Congress government for promoting the project without creating national consensus and studying alternative scenarios. They were also suspicious of the role of 'commission money' behind the project. We, at the National Planning Commission, became the target of much criticism for pursuing a wrong 'mega projects'-policy in the hydro sector, and negotiating this 'expensive project'. In a haste to find fault in our approach, facts were mixed with fiction, blurring their distinction. The climax was reached when the UML General Secretary Madhav Kumar Nepal shot a letter dated 18 October 1994 to the World Bank President expressing "serious reservations about the way the project has been designed and proposed". He also wrote that his party would undertake a fresh review of the cost-benefit and the environmental side of the project before taking any final decision, "if elected to form a new government in Nepal". The letter also questioned the competence of the then 'caretaker' government to decide on this vital project. This happened at a time when Nepal was preparing for the mid-term elections for a new parliament, and the World Bank Board was scheduled to give final approval to the project on the 3rd November 1994.

It is absurd that the letter mentioned the lack of project debate in Nepal's parliament, and challenged the competence of the 'caretaker' government to take a decision. Both these assertions were at variance with the truth. First, the project was debated in the parliament based on the Motion of Public Importance tabled by a prominent UML leader.[5] Second, the question of the competence of a 'caretaker government' was not valid, since the project had already been negotiated and processed by the full-fledged cabinet before the announcement of the election.[6] The only formality remaining was the approval by the World Bank Board of Directors. Naturally, the World Bank took the content of the letter seriously, as it came from the leader of the major opposition party which stood a chance of winning the election. Consequently, it deferred the final decision on the project.

The mid-term elections in November produced a hung parliament with no party winning majority seats. The CPN (UML) which emerged as the single largest party formed a minority government. In view of the party's earlier position on the project, it tried to procrastinate a decision on the project. In the meantime, the anti-Arun campaign was gaining strength. Similarly, a new management had assumed office in the World Bank and they did not share the same commitment to the project as their predecessors. Sensing the seriousness of this turn of events, this author, as a member of opposition, tabled a Motion of Public Importance in the House of Representatives demanding an immediate government decision on the project. This author warned that any delay in taking the decision could potentially lead to the loss of the project, on which the nation had invested so much time, energy, resources. The debate on the Motion drew unprecedented participation and continued until late at night. Practically all party leaders, including some members of the ruling party, spoke in favour of an immediate decision. The response from the Minister of Water Resources was non-committal; he raised several questions about the design and cost of the project, which according to him "needed to be sorted out" before any decision was made. Subsequently, the Minister dashed off to Washington D.C., naively believing that he could reduce the project cost by redesigning a project which was already processed for final formal approval. The project had already been subjected to thorough scrutiny from all possible angles by the brightest minds in the profession.

The World Bank was not convinced of the government's commitment to the project. On 3rd August 1995, the new World Bank President, James Wolfensohn cancelled the project "in agreement with the Government of Nepal". Referring to his telephone conversation with Prime Minister Mana Mohan Adhikari, he said priority would now be given to "devising and implementing alternative strategy of meeting its (Nepal) needs for electric power".[7] In cancelling the project, the President gave three reasons, namely :

(i) concern regarding Nepal's management capability to meet the demands and long list of actions which the project of this size and complexity would involve;
(ii) difficulty in gaining popular support in implementing a number of measures including power tariff and prioritization of public expenditure and;
(iii) difficulty in mobilizing additional $ 30–40 million cost overrun as a result of the delay in project implementation.

The arguments were not very convincing. The first two concerns were raised many times before, and were fully addressed. The Inspection Panel which the Bank had set up to review the social and environmental questions raised by NGOs found no fault in the way the project was designed. The President had cancelled the project even without discussing with the Board of Directors, where other cofinancing partners would have presented their respective positions. In fact, some of the concerned financing partners were surprised at the World Bank management's decision. The decision was particularly surprising since the Bank itself had championed this project for about a decade. The Bank had virtually led the country to a 'no option trap'.

One immediate fallout of the project was the joy and celebration by the anti-Arun NGOs. The World Bank management had been repeatedly attacked by this group for promoting 'destructive megaprojects', and its new President, who came from an investment banking background, was equally criticised. The President's decision pleased this group tremendously. It is sad that even Joseph Woods, a World Bank Vice President who had worked hard to promote this project, fell in line with the new management's approach. He said, "the signal we would send out is that the Bank no longer supports infrastructure projects like this".[8] Ironically, just a few months after this decision the World Bank approved a mammoth 1450-MW Ghazi-Barotha hydroelectic project in Pakistan and an 11-km Jamna Bridge in Bangladesh. This only indicates how a small and poor country tends to fall victim to a changing approach of mega institutions influenced by a network of interest-groups.

ALLEGATIONS AND FACTS

Let us now review the allegations to the project against the facts. The criticism of the project was based mainly on the following grounds relating to its size, cost and environmental impact.

The first criticism was that Arun III was a huge project costing more than Nepal's annual budget. It was alleged that Nepal did not have the management capacity to implement big projects and only the big international contractors and their local commission agents would prosper. It would crowd out small scale projects and Nepal would not be allowed to promote project above 10 MW after accepting Arun III. Therefore, an alternative approach was necessary with emphasis on smaller projects to be implemented by indigenous capacity. The government was also criticised for advocating big projects at the expense of small ones.

Second, this project would cost $3,800 per installed KW, whereas private companies could produce power at half that price. The project would make the power tariff unaffordable, and the loan component of the project would impose a huge debt servicing burden on the economy.

Third, the project would have adverse effects on natural resources such as land, forests, fisheries, and the socio-cultural environment of the Arun basin where 450,000 population of 10 ethnic groups lived. Parallels were also drawn with the controversial Narmada project of India.

Small Vs Big Debate

The charge that Arun III's cost was equivalent to one year's national budget did not make economic sense. First, the project expenditure was spread over eight years and second, it would not crowd out other priority development activities. The allegation that the Nepali Congress government favoured only big projects was not valid. One of the important policy departures made by the National Planning Commission in the early nineties was the emphasis given to smaller initiatives, particularly in energy generation, irrigation, roads and similar development projects. Programmes were formulated to implement small hydro and other schemes for districts which had no access to electricity. We even invited agencies who were advocating small projects to take up the challenge of implementing mini hydro schemes in such districts for which government would provide every conceivable support.[9] Actions were undertaken to promote indigenous capacity in hydropower. The most outstanding example of the domestic capacity was the Butwal Power Company. Through their untiring efforts and quest for building up domestic capability during the last three decades, they had reached a stage to execute a project of the scale of Khimti (60 KW), after completing Tinau (1 MW), Aandhi Khola (5 MW) and Jhimruk (12 MW). The NC government gave recognition to the legendary contribution made by Mr. Odd Hofton in pioneering these projects by extending him national honors.

This author, himself, called several meetings at the NPC inviting banks and other financial institutions to find ways of mobilizing resources from the national financial system to support the Khimti project. The government developed the Kali Gandaki A project and brought it to the bankable level. A number of other smaller projects such as Modi Khola, Bhotekoshi, Puwa Khola were pushed forward for further investigations and detailed engineering studies to bring them to implemention stages. The Hydro Power Act enacted by the NC government paved the way for all these projects because the Act made it possible for private parties, local and/or foreign, to invest in hydropower. It was a very sensible move in the context of increased global competition for soft credit and limited investment capacity of the government.

The proponents of the alternative approach had proposed to transfer the planned Arun III funds for the construction of ten different smaller scale projects to spread the risk. This looked fine in principle, but experience showed that the process of developing alternative hydropower projects is far more difficult and time consuming. They take a long time for investigation, feasibility, detailed engineering, financial mobilization, and subsequently implementation. Furthermore, donors consider financing only identified and studied projects after their own careful appraisal. It was naive to believe that the funds committed to Arun III would easily be transferred to other projects.

The duration for implementing one medium hydro project from the stage of investigation to implementation and final commissioning ranges from 6 to 10 years, even if the whole schedule is strictly followed with clock-work precision.

Even as Arun III was under negotiation, we, in the government, thought it wise to promote another medium-sized project, Kaligandaki A, to meet the intermediate power needs. But, the World Bank was against this if we were to proceed with Arun III. They opined that Nepal's macroeconomic situation could not afford both projects, and that it would be difficult managerially as well. We rejected this proposition and went ahead with developing this project further with UNDP and subsequently Nordic assistance. Thanks to the hard and excellent professional work done by our experts, we were ultimately able to convince the World Bank and others about the macro affordabilty of both projects. Kaligandaki A consequently became part of the agreed investment plan and was included in the future resource envelope. Therefore, the conditionality prohibiting NEA from taking up projects above 10 MW without prior World Bank consultation became redundant. The main purpose of that conditionality had been to block Kaligandaki A, which was subsequently approved as part of the investment plan. The clause was not in a position to prevent the government from starting other projects if one could show that the project would not divert resources from Arun III, and jeopardise its implementation.

In a country with such a high degree of underutilization of hydropower potential, the question of big versus small is rather academic. For Nepal's hydropower development, a one-dimensional approach is simply insufficient and wrong. There should be space for projects for all sizes. The small is of course beautiful, and is the only answer to provide electricity to remote mountains and the hills, hence the programmes of micro-hydro and other sources of decentralized energy schemes. Some of the programmes implemented in this field in the 1990s have been dicussed separately.[10] The micro hydros are needed to electrify small distant villages and the mini hydros for hill district headquarters and growth centres not connected by the grids. Similarly, the medium and large hydros are essential for our grid systems and export purposes. In the first half of the 1990s, Nepal's energy demand was increasing at the rate of approximately 15 per cent, i.e. about 40 MW annually. It was simply impossible to meet this ever-increasing demand by limiting our options to small projects. Furthermore, more power supply was required to meet the existing unmet demand as 90 per cent of the population had no access to electricity. The liberalization policy initiated by the NC Government had set in motion a surge of industrial initiatives but power supply still remained a constraining factor. Many investors visited Nepal with investment proposals, provided the government would assure them of the required amount of reliable power supply. The historical electricity sales curve also showed big sales growth in years when major hydro projects were commissioned. Therefore, the challenge for policymakers and planners is developing projects of all sizes and from all sources—private, public, internal and external. Without such an approach, meeting the ever increasing electricity demand would not be possible, let alone exporting it and making it the engine for growth.

Debt Burden, Power Tariff and Project Cost

The allegation that the project would impose a huge debt burden on the economy was false since even skeptics accepted that the most attractive feature of Arun III was its financial package. Over half of the external assistance was in the form of grants. The remaining debt portion was of a concessional nature and carried around 1 per cent interest rate and was payable over a period of 40 years. If needed, a grace period of an additional 10 years was available. As noted above, the project would have generated a minimum of five billion rupees ($100 million) annual revenue at the prevailing tariff at that time. At the present price it would be about eight billion. Not more than 20 per cent of the revenue generated by the project would have gone to service debt, the rest being available for investment in other priority areas such as poverty alleviation, rural development, education, and health. So far, of all the investment projects supported with external credit in Nepal, it is mainly the investments in hydropower and telecommunications that have generated revenue sufficient not only to service debt, but also produced a large amount of 'social profit' for government investment. Even a relatively small hydropower complex like Kulekhani I presently generates an annual revenue of Rs 828 million, of which 160 million is used to serve debt, thus generating a net revenue of Rs 668 million annually. Similarly, Marshyangdi generates a net revenue of Rs. 1010 million annually.[11]

It was amusing to see some critics belabouring to present a high energy cost from Arun III by adding elements not permissible in normal economic practice and conventional project analysis. Financial costs were combined with economic costs and the cost of installed capacity was calculated instead of the cost of energy generation, particularly that of firm energy. Arun III had an edge on the question of year-round firm energy. Others calculated the investment at future prices, and compared its economics with past investment and prevailing tariffs without price adjustments. Such estimates were obviously misleading.

Despite the continued reminder of load shedding, one often forgotten aspect of the Nepali power scenario is the mismatch between the energy demand and supply, particularly when examined on a seasonal basis. As the bulk of the power supply is derived from the existing run-of-the-river projects, the power supply during the dry season is much below the installed capacity and results in huge power deficit in the dry season. This problem could be remedied either through the development of large storage projects or projects which give firm energy throughout the year. Another alternative to this would be to generate power through diesel-fired thermal plants or imports from India. Arun III could generate firm energy throughout the year, thereby precluding the need for importing large quantities of fossil fuel. Such imports would pose logistical problems, increase external dependence, cause environmental damage, and drain the foreign exchange reserves. It is also important to note that the cost per unit of thermal power is much higher than the normal hydro-based tariff rate.

In fact, of all the projects studied until then, Arun offered the cheapest firm energy, that is at the rate of 5.94 cents per kw/hr. This cost was to the Nepal Electricity Authority, not to Nepal as the external assistance received by the government in grant and concessional loans is subsequently re-lent to NEA at the rate of 10.25 per cent interest. If one takes into account only the cost of the project to the national economy, the production cost of both firm and average energy by Arun III would be less that 2 cents per kw/hr. We did not come across any firm proposal which would generate power at a cost even remotely close to this figure. This cost would come down further if one were to consider the common infrastructural facilities such as roads, dam/intake, transmission lines, camp facilities etc whose costs were fully absorbed by the proposed project. These facilities accounted for nearly 50 per cent of the total project cost. As these facilities would have been available for the subsequent phase of Arun III and other projects in the Arun valley, the implication was "higher energy cost now for lower cost in future". If one were to further take into account the use of the access road and transmission lines for other projects including the Lower and Upper Arun, with total the generation capacity of 643 MW, the energy generation cost would come down to being among the cheapest in the world.[12]

Some critics raised the issue of affordable energy price, which was reasonable. The issue of affordablity ultimately depends on the cost of energy generation which varies from one project to another. One question was often asked: if Arun III could generate cheap energy why was a tariff increase of approximately 88 per cent required over a period of nine years from 1996? The tariff question is related to an arrangement between HMG and the NEA, under which HMG treats all investment on Arun III as well as past investments as loans to NEA at the rate of 10.25 per cent interest. This requires NEA to increase the tariff rate in order to ensure that sufficient resources are generated to pay back the loan to HMG at the agreed rate of interest. The rationale behind this arrangement is two-fold. First, this is to ensure that NEA generates necessary resources to finance local costs of Arun III, as well as other power projects so that HMG does not have to divert its resources from other priority sectors to finance the hydro power development programme. Second, the purpose is to impose some financial discipline in our public undertaking by charging tariffs which reflect the cost of production so that the grant or soft money provided by the international community are not treated as free gifts to be squandered by providing cheap utilities.

In sum, the question of tariffs is not linked with the energy generation cost of Arun III. Any government serious about tariff issue would consider other feasible means to moderate it. Such possibilities include reducing system losses, increasing the efficiency of NEA, reviewing the valuation of past investment and bringing them to realistic levels, and capitalizing of some of NEA's debts which would reduce the interest burden. Even one per cent reduction in the interest rate could bring down the electricity cost by 22 paisa per unit. These are all internal things which could be done by any government in due course without complicating project negotiations with the donors. The main point is that the NEA should become a commercially viable and efficient entity capable of generating a minimum internal rate of return on its investments after servicing its debt.

Criticism was also made that implementation of projects such as Arun could lead to concentration of wealth in the hands of a few, as it would enrich big contractors and commission agents. Contractors and businessmen play their roles in any commercial endeavour, big or small, even in closely-held economies, and tend to benefit financially. But it would be impractical to stop a road or irrigation or a power project simply because some contractors, agents or businessman could benefit from them. There are some accepted rules of the game. If there is international capital coming from agencies like the World Bank or the Asian Development Bank, one has to accept international competitive bidding to the member countries for major contractual and procurement works. Under bilaterally-funded projects, contractors from the concerned donor countries will get the contract. If we do not accept such conditions, the recipient countries are free to choose a different type of financing model, and we might as well forget about foreign assistance. One cannot avoid big contractors in such projects, but any government worth its salt has the responsibility to bring these contractors and agents under the its tax net, and make them pay in line with their true earnings.

Environmental Opposition

Some critics abroad were exaggerating the environmental and cultural damage from this project. Comparisons were made with the controversial Narmada Dam of India without considering the fundamentally different natures of the two projects. A group of Western NGOs said:

> The threatened area is one of the last virgin forests in the Himalayas. The road would endanger a proposed national park, the Milke Danda area, as well as the Hurure-Chilchia cloud forest. Three sal forests would also be at risk...the dam will destroy fisheries...21 bird, 42 plant, and 13 fish species, including the migratory Copper Mahseer are among the endangered or threatened plant, mammal, butterfly, reptile, bird, and fish species.[13]

One has to accept some trade-offs between the environment and modern development. Construction of infrastructure projects like hydropower, roads, and irrigation create negative environmental impacts but such projects are also vital to improving the living conditions of the poor people. Otherwise, poverty itself will destroy the ecological balance. What is important is a proper mitigation plan to minimise the negative environmental impact from such projects to maintain a balance between environment and development. This was adequately done in the case of Arun III. This was not a reservoir project involving large scale displacement of families, but a simple run-of-the-river project. The simple 50-hectare reservoir proposed in the project did not displace any family or submerge farm land. The construction of the access road and the transmission lines to evacuate the power to the national grid created some resettlement and compensation problems. The total affected families numbered 958 of which only 119 were seriously affected. The project had provisions for an attractive compensation package that included substitute land, cash, and employment for at least one member of the seriously affected families.

To compare Arun III with the Narmada Dam, which involved the construction of a a huge reservoir displacing a population of about 67,000 largely indigenous tribals, and submerging approximately

11,000 hectares of forest land was simply ridiculous. The Arun III project had the Regional Action Plan and Environmental Mitigation Programme with a total budget of US $ 18.6 million to mitigate the negative impacts on the environment. Adequate provisions were made under the project for forest conservation, environmental mitigation, preservation of biodiversity, religious monuments and artefacts, and the development of microhydro and rural roads.

A NATIONAL LOSS

Arun III was lost and it took away with it an attractive financial package for a project that would have brought about improvements in the lives of poor Nepalis. In particular, the project would have also given a massive boost to national revenue. The Eastern Development Region has particularly been robbed of the precious developmental opportunities which the multiplier effects of this project would have created. For the poor people of the Arun valley—who continue to bear the pain of carrying bags of salt, fertilizer, and other essentials for several days and yearn for a more efficient way out of their drudgery—it was a dream that came close to materializing into reality before being shot down.

It may be a long while before the project is brought back for implementation. Internal capacity to develop the project does not exist and the possibility for availing grants and soft loan packages is extremely remote. Accessing concessional loans for a capital investment project of commercial nature like electricity will be increasingly difficult in the coming days. Such credit is in short supply, but in high demand from other high priority sectors of noncommercial nature throughout the developing world. It is also estimated that about a trillion dollars will be required for financing the power sector expansion plans of low income countries during this decade. As the international financial institutions are unable to meet this requirement with soft loans, alternative sources including the commercial loans and private capital will have to be mobilised under harder terms, and with higher repatriation of dividends and debt servicing requirements. Even this does not seem remotely possible under the country's present investment climate and in the absence of access road in place. Even in the unlikely scenario of getting the capital investment, the project cost will be several times higher.

The naïve belief that the funds committed for Arun III could be transferred to an alternative approach did not materialize. The World

Bank had promised to fund an alternative power generation plan, but in the eight years after the cancellation of Arun, not a single power generation has been supported by this institution. An umbrella project called Power Development Fund with IDA credit of US $75 million (compared to $ 175 million committed to Arun III) was approved recently with the objective of supporting private sector projects. But the implementation is yet to take off. Thanks to the Nepali Congress government's foresight in promoting the Kaligandaki A, the country did not go dark. The Asian Development Bank and the Government of Japan were successfully pursuaded to jointly support this project. This support was irrespective and independent of Arun III and therefore, there was no transfer of funds committed to Arun. Only the funds committed to Arun III by Germany were transferred to Mid Marshyangdi Hydro Project, and that too, after a lot of persuasion.

One positive development in the last decade has been the development of private sector power generation. But the foreign exchange implications and other unfavourable aspects in the power purchase agreement due to poor negotiations have caused tremendous financial burden on the NEA. The total sales proceeds from the power procured from the private producers called Independent Power Producers (IPPs) is less than what the NEA pays as the procurement price. The NEA is obliged to buy all power produced from these schemes irrespective of their marketabilty, particularly in the surplus season. The annual loss to NEA on account of the difference between buying and selling costs alone approximate Rs. 850 million. Am even more serious problem has emerged because of the seasonal mismatch between the demand and the power supplied by the IPPs. Out of the total installed capacity of 140 MW by the IPPs, only 60 MW represents the firm capacity available during the critical dry season when the power demand is the highest. On the other hand, the NEA is compelled to shut down its hydro electric plants partially during the wet season, when all plants normally run on full capacity, in order to receive electricity procured from IPPs under power purchase agreements.[14]

The debacle of Arun III has a lesson if only we are prepared to learn it. Preparation and mobilization of investment for projects that are of Arun III's scale take a lot of time, money and effort, even when goodwill and a congenial atmosphere for development assistance prevails. But it takes only a few months of determined activism to destroy it in this world of instant global communications. Opposition to such projects can always be expected from the global network of organizations driven by ideological and other consideartion. But when national policymakers themselves fall prey to wrongly motivated advice, the nation suffers. And, once undone, recovery is not always swift and easy.

NOTES

1. The project figures in this section are mainly based on the World Bank Staff Appraisal Report of the project.
2. Restrictions were placed on helicopter flying to ensure safe distance from the river bed so that the mating habit of rare fishes is not disturbed. Ajit Thapa, former MD of Nepal electricity Authority quoted in a weekly magazine *Spotlight*, 8–17 October, 2004.
3. See, *The World Bank Staff Appraisal Report, Arun Three Hydro Electric Project,* 29 August 1994.
4. Some of the lead international NGOs opposing this project were UK and USA based International Rivers Network, International Technology Development Group, the Globe International, Greenpeace, Environment Defense Fund and Friends of the Earth. Prominent Nepali NGOs opposed to the project included Alliance for Energy, INHURED International, and the Arun Concerned Group.
5. UML leader Jhalanath Khanal had tabled a Motion of Public Importance on the subject.
6. Government assumed the 'care-taker' status after the announcement of the election date.
7. *The World Bank News Release No.96/Soo8.* August 3, 1995.
8. See press release of 4 August 1995 by International River Network. Joshep Woods together with Binayak Bhadra, then NPC member responsible for the energy sector, had visited various donor capitals holding interactions to address the concerns raised by the civil society organizations about the project.
9. Some of these NGOs were invited in the National Planning Commission at my inititive seeking their expertise in developing small scale hydros for districts like Kalikot and Khotang still without electricity. They replied that their job was advocacy and therefore would not be involved in implementation side.
10. See, Hydro Power and Alternative Energy in Chapter VI.
11. Figures are for Fiscal Year 2003/04 available from the NEA.
12. It is roughly estimated that the cost would be $ 2,221 per kw installed capacity and $ 3.21 per kw hour.
13. Extracted from the presentation made by the NGO delegation to the 27th ADB Annual Meeting in Nice, France.May 1994.
14. See A.B.Thapa, Why Is Electricity So Expensive in Nepal? in *Spotlight* , 6–12 May 2005.

Chapter Ten

The Refugee Impasse

In recent years, Nepal has played host to more than a hundred thousand Bhutanese, the largest refugee population in South Asia. With the help of international agencies including the UNHCR and WFP, these victims of Bhutan's ethnic policy have been settled in eight refugee camps in Jhapa and Morang districts. Efforts towards finding a negotiated settlement to facilitate their early repatriation to Bhutan have not yet succeeded. Furthermore, Bhutan's insistence on treating the issue as a purely bilateral matter has meant that the involvement of the international community in mediating a mutually agreeable solution to this serious humanitarian problem has been limited.

Bhutan's reluctance to resume even the bilateral process is the latest blow to the efforts aimed at negotiating a smooth repatriation of these refugees. For this reason, Nepal is considering abandoning the bilateral route in favour of an international campaign to pressurize Bhutan to take back its citizens.[1] The Khundabari incident of 22 December 2003 had earlier provided an excuse for Bhutan to further prolong this already protracted issue.[2] All these have come as an anti-climax from the earlier euphoria after the last Joint Ministerial Committee (JMC) meeting culminated in Bhutan reportedly agreeing to take back all refugees, except the 20 per cent who were not found to be bonafide Bhutanese citizens.

At various earlier occasions, optimism was expressed about the early settlement of the refugee issue, both at the government level and by international institutions. After completing her landmark trip to Bhutan, India, and Nepal in mid 2000, the UN High Commissioner for Refugees, Sadako Ogata had been convinced of Bhutan's commitment to find an early resolution to the problem. She even assured the refugees that they were welcome in Bhutan and their return was imminent. Prior to Ogata's visit, a European Parliamentary delegation led by Jerard

Collins had also visited Nepal. The EU attitude, as expressed during their interaction with the Nepali parliamentarians in Kathmandu, was very candid. They considered this problem as a serious breach of basic human rights and strongly believed in the refugees' right to return home with honour and safety. It was noted that the denial of this right could invite international condemnation and Nepal was assured that the European Parliament would campaign in favour of early repatriations.

Preceeding these developments, the US Assistant Secretary of State for Population, Refugees and Migration, Julia Taft, visited the refugee camps and appreciated Nepal's generous asylum to the refugees. Subsequently, her boss Madeleine Albright wrote to this author in his earlier capacity as the Foreign Minister of Nepal assuring US interest and support in promoting a resolution to the problem. The then Norwegian Foreign Minister Knut Volleback, on his January 2000 visit to Nepal and Bhutan, took a special interest in this problem as well. He was kind enough to call me from Oslo giving a brief on his meeting with Bhutan on the refugee matter. He even offered to play the mediator's role if both sides so wished. This, of course, did not transpire.

BILATERAL MEETINGS

Bilateral meetings between Nepal and Bhutan have been taking place since 1991 to come to a closure on this issue. So far, fifteen JMCs have been held on the exclusive agenda of refugees. The Prime Ministers of the two countries have met, and numerous other meetings have been held at the official level but with little progress. As Bhutan maintained that the refugees were not Bhutanese citizens and therefore it was not bound to take them back, it became necessary to verify the refugees' identities. On Bhutan's insistence, the JMC meeting in October 1993 made a controversial decision to classify the refugees into four categories, namely: (*i*) bonafide Bhutanese forcefully evicted from Bhutan; (*ii*) Bhutanese who "voluntarily migrated"; (*iii*) "non-Bhutanese" people, and; (*iv*) those who committed "criminal acts". Subsequently, they agreed to set up a Joint Verification Team (JVT) to confirm the authenticities of the refugees.

Although Nepal wanted to start the verification immediately, there were differences between the two countries on the definition of the various categories of refugees, particularly on those "who were forcefully evicted" and those "who migrated voluntarily". A compromise looked difficult, especially since Bhutan insisted that all those who had signed the Voluntary Migration Form had left the country voluntarily and Nepal held that the refugees were compelled to sign the forms under duress.

Relations started to thaw in September 1999 when the Eighth Joint Ministerial meeting took place in Kathmandu after a *hiatus* of about three and a half years. Some progress was made on the interpretation of Category II, and Bhutan showed a willingness for a liberal interpretation of their citizenship laws to facilitate the transfer of these people into Category I. It was agreed that if there was any evidence that bonafide Bhutanese were made to leave the country under "compelling circumstances"[3], they would be included under Category I. Nepal, on the other hand, agreed that Bhutan was not compelled to accept the refugees who did not wish to return to Bhutan. It would be an international responsibility to deal with such cases. The Bhutanese side also moderated the stance on their earlier position regarding Nepal's proposal for third party mediation. They agreed that the issue of third party reference could be examined at an appropriate time, if the differences of positions between the two countries could not be reconciled. The departure from the earlier rigid positions brought the two sides a little closer.

The next task was to start the verification and proper categorization of refugees. Bhutan proposed to start the verification process on the basis of a sample list of 3056 refugees prepared by an UNHCR official. Nepal rejected this proposal, and proposed the verification of all refugees inside the camps with the condition that it could be started with any camp chosen by the Bhutanese side. Subsequent ministerial meeting held in Thimpu towards the end of 1999, and the two secretary level meetings thereafter, resulted in Bhutan agreeing to Nepal's proposal on the camp-by-camp approach.

In the Thimpu meeting, Nepal also suggested that all pending issues be resolved at the following JMC meeting so that the verification and the subsequent repatriation process could start in the first year of the new millennium. The Bhutanese side looked positive. Following this meeting in Thimpu, this author returned to Nepal by road, visited the refugee camps in Jhapa, and gave cautious hope to the refugees.

The tenth JMC[4] agreed on the establishment of a Joint Verification Team for the verification of the refugees and their classification into four categories. After spending a lot of time on these and other procedural steps, the verification started on 26 March 2001 in the Khundabari refugee camp. The verification work of 3,158 families of 11,182 refugees was completed by December of the same year, but it took another six months to declare the results. The results were quite unexpected. Although the result admitted that about 76 per cent of the refugees were Bhutaneese citizens, only 2.5 per cent were considered forcefully evicted. The rest 70.5 per cent had "voluntarily" emigrated, and 2.8 per cent had criminal records. Obviously, the liberal interpretation of category I, earlier agreed by Bhutan, that refugees who were "made to leave Bhutan under compelling circumstance" were not classified under category I.

The Bhutan side was represented in the JVT by the same officials who were involved in the 1988 controversial population census of Bhutan, which had arbitrarily denationalized a large number of *Lhotsampas* (Southern Bhutanese). There existed a clear conflict of interest on the part of the verification team. Furthermore, the verification process did not involve any representation from the refugee community, the real victims, nor the representatives of an independent third party, such as the UNHCR. The Nepali government made no objection to this in the interest of pushing the process forward. Naturally, the result evoked protests from various quarters, and massive appeals were submitted against the arbitrary categorization. Then the news came that Bhutan had agreed to take back all the refugees including those who, in its version, had emigrated "voluntarily". Naturally this was good news and it was welcomed by all sides. However, based on earlier experience in dealing with the issue, this author for one, had alerted the government against being unduly optimistic on the matter as there still remained some space between the proverbial 'cup and lip'. I remarked that the universally accepted principles for refugee repatriation are honour, safety, and dignity, and it was not clear whether Bhutan was ready to accept these refugees under such conditions. The JMC was silent on the issue. The Nepali delegation was saying that the manner in which Bhutan treats the returnees would be their 'internal matter'.

Meanwhile, Bhutan had adroitly persuaded the Nepali delegation during the Fourteenth JMC, after the Royal takeover on 4 October 2002, into considering Nepali citizenship for those Bhutanese who were not willing to return to Bhutan. This was clearly a deviation from the position Nepal had taken earlier that the problem would be addressed separately as an international humanitarian issue. Since granting citizenship to the refugees was against existing constitutional provisions, this decision created a lot of controversy in Nepal resulting in a dampening of the earlier optimism regarding refugee repatriation.

MOTIVE AND HISTORY

It is clear that in order to take as few refugees as possible, Bhutan was playing a 'push game' in Bhutan, and persuading Nepal to create a 'pull' factor. Amid this scenario, it went a step further in Khundabari on 22 December when the Bhutanese delegation was setting conditions for the refugees once they returned. Seventy five per cent of the refugees who were classified under category II had to reapply for citizenship. They would have to remain in the transitional shelters for two years during which they had to give evidence of their 'good conduct' and their children would have to learn the *Dzongkha* language. During this period, the government would not bear any responsibility for these people and only the head of the family would be allowed to work. As for those facing criminal charges in Bhutan, they would have to remain in police custody until the time the court acquitted or convicted them. As all these conditions were stated in an abusive and provocative manner, the refugees were enraged. Their hope of returning home after a long patient wait was being dashed again.

The happenings inside Bhutan indicated no evidence of an atmosphere conducive to receiving the refugees. On the contrary, a push factor was clearly being created. First, the government had already launched a resettlement programme on the land and property of the *Lhotsampa* refugees. The refugees could neither return to their homes nor get back their landed property. Second, Bhutan was not willing to accept the presence of UNHCR or any international humanitarian or human rights organization to support and oversee the repatriation process to ensure that minimum humanitarian conditions were met.

Third, a strong public opinion was being built inside Bhutan against accepting the refugees. It would be interesting to study what transpired during the 2003 summer session of the Bhutan National Assembly to sense the atmosphere[5]. Hurling a variety of abuses against the refugees who were called *Ngalops* (traitors), members of the Assembly belonging to the majority *Ngalongs* ethnicity were saying—"the idea of their return has outraged people", and "accepting them back would be a great security risk; the *Ngolops*, after their return would sow discord within our peaceful society". Even the response of then Home Minister Jigme Thinley, who, in his previous capacity as Foreign Minister had led Bhutan in most ministerial meetings, was not very helpful. His reply included remarks like—"the easy life in the refugee camps encouraged local Nepalese to enroll as refugees" and, "(the) bulk of the people in the camps are not genuine Bhutanese and *Ngalop* leaders want to establish multi-party system and grant amnesty to all criminals after their return".

The Nepali side, impatient to resolve the problem, did not want to provide any excuse for Bhutan to further complicate and prolong the issue. It, therefore, did not want to discuss how the repatriation and resettlement process would take place and it was left entirely as Bhutan's internal matter. This was a serious lapse. Such a position could have been perfectly understandable in a normal bilateral framework. But the refugee issue has not only a long and painful history, but also international and humanitarian aspects. The refugees had been living in the camps for fourteen years with international support. There are universally accepted principles to govern repatriation and resettlement of refugees, such as—the return must be voluntary, safe, dignified, and honourable. It is incumbent on the negotiating parties to ensure that these principles are adhered to.

Bhutan is trying to paint its ethnic Nepali populace as economic immigrants who entered the country in recent decades for jobs and economic opportunities. This assertion contradicts historical facts. Nepalis have been living in Bhutan for centuries; in fact, some of their ancestors came to Bhutan as early as the ruling *Ngalongs* community who came from Tibet in the seventeenth century. As early as 1624 A.D, even before the unification of present Nepal, the king of Gorkha, Ram Shah had dispatched a team of artisans, construction workers, and agriculturists to Bhutan at the request of Shabdrung Nawang Namgyal, the Dharma Raja of Bhutan, to train Bhutanese in construction techniques, agricultural practices, arts, and crafts. The Nepali artisans built fortresses and several famous monasteries such as the Kichu of Paro valley and Jambay of Bumthang. There is also evidence of Nepali influence in Bhutanese symbols and names.

Following the loss of one-third of its territory to British India after the war of 1864–65, Bhutan started a deliberate policy to encourage organized migration of Nepali population from Nepal, Sikkim, and Darjeeling. This was primarily done to reclaim the inhospitable territory of southern Bhutan with a view towards raising new sources of state revenue. The settlement started in the 1860s and 70s in the inhospitable southern Bhutanese foothills that were infested with malaria and tropical diseases. What started as a small number of settlements received a big boost after 1887 when a royal decree was issued authorizing two prominent Nepalis, Dalchan Gurung and Garja Mann Gurung to settle ethnic Nepalis in the Sibsoo and Samchi areas, and Sarbhang, Chirang and Dagana districts. In 1898, a separate Liaison Office called Bhutan House was established in Kalingpong to administer the state-sponsored settlements and revenue collection from the settlers.[6] As Rijal further observes:

> British India encouraged and supported this arrangement as the settlement of hardy Nepali people provided a safety buffer zone against the marauding Bhutanese from the north. The Dorji family, in alliance with Wangchuck family and British India, actively promoted the settlement of Nepalese people, their culture, ethos and value system as the former as well as the British wanted a legitimate base for the monarchy as against the past theocratic set-up which did not provide stability to the country.[7]

There was a separate administration for the areas newly opened up for Nepali settlements. They remained exclusively Nepali-speaking areas with no interactions with other communities in northern Bhutan and northern Bhutanese were required to obtain permits to enter the Nepali settlements. This contributed to the preservation of language, culture, symbols, and religious practices of the people of Nepali ethnicity. Very soon, the hard work of this community turned the inhospitable terrain into lush agricultural areas enabling the state to extract heavy revenue. In the 1950s and 60s, heavy taxes, the increasing pressure on limited land, a variety of compulsory free labour arrangements imposed by the state, and the lack of access to educational and health facilities led the Nepali population to start migrating to Nepal and neighbouring Indian states of Assam and Bengal. During this time, the king of Bhutan, Dorji Wangchuk and Prime Minister, Jigme Dorji made a special appeal to the Nepalis not to migrate. On promise of basic development facilities, the Nepalis were encouraged to stay on and work towards nation building. To stem the outflow, the Bhutanese government also put restrictions on land transactions and out-migrations.[8]

The Nepali language was accepted for official transactions and most government officials, including the king and his ministers, spoke the language. The Citizenship Act of 1958, resolutions of the National Assembly, land tax receipts, and other official documents were made available in Nepali. All Hindu religious festivals were celebrated with much fanfare and gusto. The Nepalis also learnt *Dzongkha* (national language), wore *Kho* and *Kira* (male and female national dress) in schools and offices, and participated in Buddhist prayers. Inter-communal marriages were encouraged to develop a cohesive society in Bhutan and for national integration.

The Nepalis made valuable contributions towards Bhutan's nation building efforts. Conscripted Nepali labour was used for the construction of schools, health units, irrigation systems, and the road connecting north and south Bhutan. With their industry, hard work, and education, the Nepalis started making their marks in various walks of life. They assumed positions in sensitive state organs including the bureaucracy, cabinet, National Assembly, royal guards, army, and police, and continued to provide exemplary contributions. The representation of the Nepalis in such positions was generally in line with their share in the total population: they comprised more than their 40 per cent of Bhutan's total population. Their representation in the realm of politics, however, was very low—14 in the 100-member National Assembly, and 2 in the 9-member Royal Advisory Council. In northern Bhutan, one Assembly member represented 5000 people, while the member from the South represented 20,000. Even this arrangement was changed later on under various pretexts thereby making the representation of the ethnic Nepali extremely difficult.[9]

The situation changed, particularly since the mid 1980s. The 1980-81 census revealed that the Nepali-speaking population of the South was increasing at a faster rate than in other parts of the country. This probably prompted the rulers to reconsider their ethnic policy. There was fear of increasing influence from the better-educated and harder working southerners who had witnessed democratic practices through living along the Indian border. This demographic threat was perceived at a time when new developments were taking place in the region. It is said that the Sikkim's amalgamation to India had a positive impact on Bhutan into correcting its in-built discriminatory policy against ethnic Nepalis which was previously similar to that of Sikkim's Chogyals. But the violent movement in Darjeeling for a separate Gorkhaland, and the recognition of the Nepali language in the Indian constitution negatively impacted Bhutan's rulers into reconsidering their policy towards the *Lhotsampas*. Especially after Indira Gandhi's death in India, Bhutan started a more assertive foreign policy by sending its first ever delegation to China for border negotiations.[10]

Under the Sixth Plan, it made further departures from its past policy of ethnic harmony by introducing the controversial 1985 Citizenship Act and its Bhutanization programme. The slogan of One Nation One People was adopted in a multi-ethnic and multi-cultural country. A new code of ethics called *Driglam Namza* was introduced with a purpose of enforcing new social and cultural rules, and marginalizing the ethnic Nepalis by promoting a monoculture. The dress code of *Kho* and *Kira* respectively for men and women were made compulsory at all places and at all times without any sensitivity to the hot climate of southern Bhutan. Nepali language was abolished from the school curriculum, the practices of Hindu religious rituals restricted, and their temples desecrated.

A new Citizenship Act with a retroactive effect from 1958 was introduced to further marginalize the ethnic Nepalis. It classified the Bhutanese into seven categories and required them to produce documentary evidence of their permanent residence since 1958. This Act made the process of acquiring citizenship by naturalization very stringent even for children who were born to one Bhutanese parent. In 1988, a biased and manipulative census succeeded in denationalizing *Lhotsampas* on a massive scale. Thousands of families who had already received citizenship identity cards were forced to forfeit their status and were arbitrarily placed in Seventh Category of non-nationals, i.e. migrants and illegal settlers. Appeals for justice including those to the king to review the provisions of the Act and the way it was implemented were ignored. This provoked a large-scale uprising in Southern Bhutan by the Lhotsompas in 1990 giving the regime further pretext for brutal suppression and eventual eviction.

Prominent ethnic Nepalis who petitioned their grievances were imprisoned and tortured. The most prominent among them was Tek Nath Rijal, a member of the Bhutan's Royal Advisory Council. In his earlier capacity as the coordinator of the bureau to investigate corruption cases, he had unearthed massive high-level corruption involving prominent members of the royal family and had invited considerable wrath from the regime. Rijal was stripped of his position and branded a 'traitor'. Fearing for his life and further prosecution, Rijal fled to Nepal. But under the autocratic Panchayat regime, Rijal, along with his colleagues were bundled up at night and sent back to Bhutan where he spent 10 years of prison life in the most inhuman and torturous conditions. In the intervening period, thousands of *Lhotsampas* were denationalized and deported. This created a large-scale exodus of ethnic Nepalis from Bhutan. The number of refugees to Nepal numbered 84,000 by the mid-1990s. The deported and fleeing Bhutanese were forced to sign the Voluntary Migration Form stating that they renounced the citizenship 'voluntarily'.

Among those who became refugees include many prominent members of the *Lhotsampas*—Hindus and Buddhists, who served in high positions of the government, including the army, police, National Assembly, government ministries, and as secretaries and department heads. This very fact negates Bhutanese claims that they left the country voluntarily.

QUIET DIPLOMACY AND INDIA FACTOR

Bhutan's quiet and subtle diplomacy has attempted to project itself as a pristine Shangrila dedicated to preserving its traditional Buddhist heritage and a country committed to 'spiritualism, tranquility, and happiness'. Its theory of Gross National Happiness encompasses the four tenets of self-reliance, environmental protection, cultural promotion, and good governance. It has been able to preserve its pristine environment in a commendable way. But the ethnic discrimination and humiliation of cultural minorities in the last two decades betrays all symptoms of its cleansing drive against cultural minorities. According to a scholar:

> The treatment meted out to approximately 100,000 refugees dragging out their lives for the last ten years in camps in Jhapa, Nepal, by the government that we all had to believe was concerned with GNH rather than GNP, is unforgivable.[11]

Another observer of the Bhutanese scene writes:

> Bhutan on the excuse that Nepal is passing through a political turmoil has sought to win over senior politicians of Nepal by wining and dining with them, including the "Charm offensive', audience with the King. Bhutan has gone about a systematic way to destroy all houses, gardens, fields, and remnants of dwellings of the refugees and has coerced the northern Bhutanese to occupy their places. By any international standards, the process of forcibly evicting citizens of specific ethnicity and making the lands and places available to another group of different group of different ethnic origin is nothing but ethnic cleansing.[12]

Even on the face of these truisms, efforts were made to create an acceptable façade and interpretation to the whole problem. Even scholars of the eminence of Bhabani Sen Gupta have fallen prey to parroting the official Bhutanese version. In what looks like a sponsored project, Gupta in his book, *Bhutan: Towards a Grassroots Participatory Polity*, quotes extensively from the official mouthpiece Kuensil, endorsing the official line without verifying the facts.[13] He speaks of Prime Minister G.P Koirala's expression of sympathy to the cause of popular movement in Bhutan, and argues that this encouraged Bhutanese dissidents to go to Nepal and devise a strategy of attracting 100,000 *Lhotsampas* in order "to exert international pressure". Even more absurd is his claim that the entire Nepali-speaking population in North Bengal, Sikkim and part of Assam "has long been fed on the concept, crafted and nourished by Nepali Congress leaders and intellectuals affiliated with the party, of a Greater Himalayan State or a Greater Nepal". He further states that the West Bengal Government "had deployed additional security forces to prevent the movement of Southern Bhutanese to Nepal and vice versa" much against the Nepali will. The reality is that Nepal has always opposed the West Bengal government's role in facilitating the refugee movements to Nepal. Evidence shows that trucks and buses packed with Southern Bhutanese came to Nepal's border under protection of the Bengal police.

Gupta's endorsement of the official propaganda is evident from his anti-*Lhotsampa* tirade in the book. He frequently uses the term *Ngalops* (anti-nationals)—a word used against the *Lhotsampas* in state propaganda, and blames them for seeing themselves as part of the larger Nepali community spread across the northern districts of India and Nepal. He also finds fault in their maintaining extra-territorial social and cultural linkages in the form of marriage, rituals, and cultural affiliations.

The refugees in Nepal feel that Indian intervention could contribute in resolving the issue, even though India wants the problem to be resolved bilaterally. One may be inclined to respect India's policy of non-intervention, especially when a bilateral mechanism is in place between its two neighbours. But the reality is that India is the preeminent power of the region and its own role is very much linked with the present problem. When a country like Norway from Nordic Europe can show interest and mediate between the Tamil Tigers and the Government of Sri-lanka in a purely internal matter, there is no reason why India cannot mediate on an issue which could have repercussions to Indian interests as well. A potential nexus between the insurgency groups in India, Nepal, and the frustrated young refugees could be a reality at any time.

Moreover, Nepal does not share a border with Bhutan and it is not the first asylum destination for the refugees. There is evidence that the refugees' passage to Nepal was facilitated by the West Bengal administration but obstructions were placed when they wanted to return. Furthermore, India's special relation with Bhutan, particularly with regards to the latter's external relations as defined by the India-Bhutan Treaty of 1949 is well known. There is a widely held view in the refugee community that Bhutan's new ethnic policy would not have been possible without India's turning a blind eye. Bhutan also took advantage of India's strained relation with Nepal in the late 1980s, which culminated in its trade embargo on Nepal. It was during this time that the king of Bhutan forged a bond of personal friendship with Rajiv Gandhi and his family, and India's tacit assent encouraged Bhutan to proceed with mass eviction of ethnic Nepalis. [14]

Looking from the perspective of Indian foreign relations, its 'hands off' policy on the issue may have been prompted by the fact that Bhutan has been its loyal ally and has strictly supported Indian position in international forums, unlike Nepal which has followed an independent line. By disturbing the Bhutanese rulers' ethnic interests, India probably does not wish to risk Bhutan's moving closer to China. Even the pro-Hindu BJP-led government, for pure nationalistic interest, did not show interest in pressurizing Bhutan on the issue despite its apparent concern on the matter.[15] On the other hand, India feels obliged to the Druk regime for its assistance in driving out the ULFA and BODO militants from Bhutanese camps. The king of Bhutan was honoured as the Chief Guest of India's Republic Day celebrations of January 26, 2005. Besides, Bhutan has given enough hints that when necessary, it could quietly play the 'China Card'. Voices for closer ties with China are occassionally heard in the National Assembly[16] and a Chinese Deputy Minister visited Bhutan in 2001 ostensibly to discuss border issues.

TOWARDS THE FUTURE

The problem of Bhutanese refugees is a humanitarian problem of serious proportions arising from the state policy of blatant ethnic discrimination and a drive to reduce the population of an ethnic minority. The state has tried to impose a monoculture in a multi-lingual and multi-ethnic nation. The refusal by Bhutan to involve a credible third party is due to the fear of its discriminatory ethnic policy being exposed before the whole world. By involving a third party in the repatriation process, it will be duty-bound to create conducive conditions to the refugees' return for which it does not appear prepared.

Nepal agreed to put this problem in the bilateral format in the hope of resolving it in an amicable manner, and thus being relieved of the burden of hosting a large refugee population. However, this has not been of much help. Bhutan has continued its delaying tactics for repatriation. Due to its insistence that Nepal accept refugees not willing to return, while at the same time adopting a hostile policy within Bhutan for those who dare return, Bhutan has dampened the prospect of the bilateral mechanism from succeeding. It could be calculating that the delay in arriving at a solution would eventually lead to the assimilation and integration of the refugees in Nepali society. To some extent, this has been happening. For Nepal, the refugee problem has created social problems leading to crime, displacement of local jobs, and environmental degradation. The futureless refugee youth are vulnerable to crimes, and militant revolutionary appeals, from which the country has already been suffering.

The efficacy of the bilateral mechanism to represent the interest and concerns of the refugees is now under question mark. The Government of Nepal cannot be party to any decision which the refugees cannot accept. The refugees are asking for an international conference to solve their problem and this demands serious attention. The uncertain future for the refugees languishing in the camps is an unacceptable situation as their future cannot remain hostage to the intransigence of government policy. Nepal just cannot agree to treat this as Bhutan's internal affair. Sadly, Nepal's own internal problems and turbulent politics have prevented the country from according the issue as much priority as it deserves and Bhutan continues to exploit this situation to its full advantage.

The Nepali side should now press and insist on the involvement of a neutral third party such as the UNHCR, particularly in the repatriation process. The UNHCR has not only the right mandate, but also worldwide experience and knowledge in such matters. As Bhutan has agreed to take back the refugees willing to return, it is the responsibility of the international community to ensure that the repatriation process follows the universally accepted principles of human rights. Bhutan has always been against third party mediation on the issue but the envisioned role of the international intermediary is not mediation per se. What is really sought is technical and logistical support in order to expedite the repatriation and resettlement of people whom Bhutan agreed to take. The third party involvement would also bring international financial support, which Bhutan has been wanting. It is worth restating that the issue of third party involvement had been discussed at earlier ministerial meetings when this writer had led the Nepali side. At that time, it was agreed to keep this issue at the margin so that it could be considered as and when necessary, particularly when the two sides could not resolve the issue bilaterally.

On the political front, what happens inside Bhutan is something to be decided and resolved by the Bhutanese themselves. Though it is doubtful that in today's global society, one can remain untouched from such happenings anywhere—particularly when the victims happen to be the people of ones' ethnicity and one has to bear its direct impact. However, the issue of human rights, ethnic discrimination, and exclusion is more of a concern for the international community of the rich and powerful countries, than it is for Nepal. The country is excessively preoccupied with its own internal problems of conflict, and poverty. Nepal's only concern at the moment is the early repatriation of the refugees with dignity and honour.

There are also proposals for resettlement and burden-sharing, which call for distributing the refugee population between various countries, including the integration of a portion in Nepal. Bhutan could be banking on this option as well. This is probably the reason why it is stalling the repatriation of verified refugees and moving on to other camps for verification. It is for the international community to decide whether to accept this or not. The refugees have every right to return to the country of their birth, reclaim their homes and property and enjoy their rightful status at proper citizens of the country. As far as Nepal is concerned, it should strongly oppose any proposal for integration of the refugees in Nepal. This would be akin to penalizing the country for no fault of its own, and letting Bhutan go scot-free for their policy of ethnic cleansing against its citizens.

NOTES

1. *Kathmandu Post,* 13 December 2004.
2. On December 22, 2002, the refugees, under provocation of objectionable and derogatory remarks from the Bhutaneese delegation, had pelted stones at the joint verification team officials. Nobody was hurt.
3. This included situations such as administrative coercion, physical torture, intimidation, psychological pressure, family breakdown and threat for life, which compelled the people to leave the country.
4. This JMC from the Nepali side was led by Chakra Bastola, then Minister of Foreign Affairs.
5. See http:www. Kuenselineonline.com/ assembly on 80th Assembly discussion on the joint verification of refugees.
6. Tek Nath Rizal, *Ethnic Cleansing and Political Repression in Bhutan: The Other Side of the Shangrila.* Kathmandu: SAP-Publishing House, 2004, pp. 5–6.
7. Ibid., pp. 6–7.
8. Ibid.
9. *See* for details, C.L. Timsina, 'Option for Peaceful Bhutan', Hari Prashad Adhikari, 'Sons of Soil in Southern Bhutan', in *Bhutan Political Problem* (2003), edited by R.B. Basnet and D.N.S, Dhakal. Also, Rijal (2004), p. 22.
10. Timsina; Ibid.
11. Prof. Jack D. Ipes, in key note address on Bhutan seminars *at* Interlaken, Switzerland.
12. S. Chandrasekharan, 'Bhutanese Brand of Ethnic Cleansing' in (2003) (ed) R.B.Basnet and D.N.S. Dhakal.
13. *See* Bhabani Sen Gupta, (1999) *New* Delhi: Konark Publications Chapter 6.
14. Tek Nath Rijal (2004), pp. 28–29.
15. During this author's meeting with Prime Minister Bajpai in 2001 in New Delhi, the latter clearly indicated his concern at the reported religious conversion of the poor Hindu refugees in the camps.
16. S. Chandrasekhar, (2003).

Chapter Eleven

Corruption Perception

Defined simply, corruption is the abuse of public office for private gain. Private gains occur in the form of bribes, personal benefits through patronage and nepotism, theft of state assets, and the diversion of state revenues. Bribery, the primary means of corruption, is used to 'buy' many things provided by the central or local government. Here, public officials may seek bribes to supply these things. The World Bank lists a number of government actions for which bribes are used. These include: to win government contracts, influence allocation of benefits, reduce the amount of taxes or fees, get licences, speed up decisions, and influence legal outcomes.[1] The report further points out:

> The government benefits purchased with bribes vary by type and size. Contracts and other benefits can be enormous (grand or wholesale corruption) or very small (petty or retail corruption), and the impact of misinterpretation of laws can be dramatic or minor. Grand corruption is often associated with international business transactions and usually involves politicians as well as bureaucrats. The bribery transaction may take place entirely outside the country. Petty corruption may be pervasive throughout the public sector if firms and individuals regularly experience it when they seek a license or a service from government. The bribes may be retained by individual recipients or polled in an elaborate sharing arrangement. The sums involved in grand corruption may make newspaper headlines around the world, but the aggregate costs of petty corruption, in terms of both money and economic distortions, may be as great if not greater.[2]

Corruption erodes public trust, and if unchecked and unpunished, will undermine political legitimacy to the extent that even honest people will see little point in playing by the rules. Corruption undermines development and reduces the effectiveness of internal and external resources used to improve the living conditions in poor countries.

Corruption not only misallocates the distribution of resources and increases the cost of development, but by distorting social values, justice, and merit, it ultimately penalizes the poor.

Transparency International (TI) has devised a tool called the "Corruption Perception Index" to measure the degree of corruption as perceived to exist among public officials and politicians. It is a composite index drawing on corruption related data in expert surveys carried out by a variety of reputable institutions. TI, in its 2004 Report, ranks Nepal 94th globally, with a score of 2.8 (10 indicating highly clean and 0 highly corrupt).[3] Among the four other South Asian countries, Sri Lanka has the best score with 3.5, followed by India 2.8, Pakistan 2.1, and Bangladesh 1.5. As Table 5.1 indicates, studies by TI suggest that Nepalis experience fewer incidences of corruption than most other South Asian countries. In fields like education, health service, power, land administration, police, and the judiciary, the ratio of respondents reporting corruption in Nepal, is relatively less than its neighbours. However, the high cost of corruption in public administration paints a very bleak picture. For example, the average cost of a bribe paid to the police is Rs.1,637, which is ten per cent of the annual per capita income.[4] Based on user feedback, the top three corruption-prone sectors in Nepal are: police, judiciary, education and tax.

TABLE 11.1
Comparative Corruption Scorecard for the Sectors
(Percentage of respondents reporting corruption in their interaction with the sectors)

Country	*School*	*Health*	*Power*	*Land admin.*	*Tax*	*Police*	*Judiciary*
Bangladesh	40	58	32	73	19	64	75
India	34	15	30	47	15	100	100
Nepal	25	18	12	17	25	48	42
Pakistan	92	96	96	100	99	100	96
Sri Lanka	61	92	—	98	—	100	100

Source: Transparency International Report 2003, p. 38

CORRUPTION IN DEMOCRACY

The growing concern about bad governance and corruption in developing countries has increased to an almost unprecedented level. The concern and debate is no longer confined to affected countries, but also to the international community which until recently treated it strictly as an internal matter. Until the early 1990s, issues of governance and corruption were treated as taboos or 'off-limits' by the donor community. The subject has now become an important element in their country assistance strategies, aid considerations, policy dialogue, and in the choice and design of their projects. International aid agencies are becoming increasingly vocal on the issue. At the Nepal Development Forum meeting of 2002, Mieko Nishimizu, the World Bank Vice President for South Asia made a very scathing remark:

> What ails Nepal is a crisis of governance, corroding the nation's economy, finances, and once proud institutions. Crisis of governance, distorting the distribution of income, wealth and human capital. Crisis of governance, threatening social justice, harmony and the very soul of any nation states—hope and happiness of the sovereign people.

The acidic remark was not without controversy. The Bank official was trying to throw a challenge to the leadership to emerge as real agents of change. However, she also had some good words about how leaders in Nepal were trying to resurrect good governance and reduce poverty. In the statement made immediately afterwards this author, as Finance minister, highlighted several facts which defended positive developments after the restoration of democracy in Nepal while pointing out weaknesses and challenges the country faced. However, the general perception still remains that Nepal suffers from bad governance and increased corruption in the post-*Panchayat* era. To quote a harsh indictment on the state of affairs:

> Since 1990 all previous records of corruption have been broken as far as scale, categories, the status and number of personalities involved were concerned. Nepali parliamentarians have set such despicable examples of corruption that they were prepared to 'devour' any thing they came across, ... A few ministers and parliamentarians who presented themselves as saleable commodity during the infamous horse trading of 1996/97 were whisked away to Bangkok at public expense for 'medical treatment' ...As a result of several scams insidiously hatched by leaders belonging to most of the political parties, the poor kingdom has been recurrently swindled to the point of bankruptcy. We need either the donor community or visiting dignitaries to point out the extent of foul smell of corruption that our public figures are emitting.[5]

A recent study entitled The 'State of Democracy in South Asia Poll' coordinated by the New Delhi-based Centre for the Study of Developing Societies has brought to light several interesting findings. One of the results of the survey was that 56 per cent of Nepali respondents feel that the thing they most disliked about democracy in Nepal was the increase in corruption. Despite this, 62 per cent of the respondents agreed that democracy is preferable to any other form of government and a full 80 per cent felt that democracy is suitable or very suitable to Nepal. 18 per cent were indifferent on the subject, while only 10 per cent preferred dictatorship.[6]

Part of this perception is the result of a premeditated propaganda crafted and unleashed by people, who even now, are trying to discredit the democratic polity in an attempt to justify an authoritarian regime. But to be fair, even a large part of the citizenry and the international community involved in Nepal's development efforts genuinely share this perception. This is due to various factors including the acts of omission and commission under various governments, the public love for sensational stories, and the overall climate of negativism among the elite. This impression has increased particularly after the prosecution of some high profile politicians and officials by the CIAAA in recent times.

Nevertheless, corruption does exist, in systemic and isolated forms, in various walks of our civil and development administration. People have to pay bribes to move files for timely action. They suffer from having to bribe officials to access services ranging from public utilities like electricity and water supply, to land administration, police, financial institutions, court, customs, and taxes. Underhand payments are a widely used practice to receive timely payments on procurement and contractual jobs, loan approval from banks, income tax and customs clearance, and timely release of contractual payments. Bribes are paid not only for accessing normal services as a matter of right, but also in return for undue advantage, such as reducing the assessed tax, avoiding police action, and escaping punishment. Government facilities are misused for purposes not allowed under normal practice. The vehicles of development projects and public enterprises are abused by unrelated officials including politicians. Foreign jaunts are made under various pretexts with public money. Excess payments are made to contractors under variation orders, pushing up project costs. The taxpayers' money is often spent on expensive buildings, high-cost luxury vehicles, and other similar unjustified facilities.

Public trust erodes and government revenue suffers when underhand payments are used to distort justice, misclassify and undervalue goods for customs payment, cheat income taxes, and reward the undeserving. Many public sector enterprises have become financially bankrupt for reasons of mismanagement and corruption. Public deposits are used to finance unviable projects and banks consequently suffer from defaults and non-performing loans. Instead of reaching their proper beneficiaries, money meant for local development often ends up in the pockets of contractors, technicians and officials. Corruption takes place in the form of kickbacks in larger procurement decisions, award of contracts, and the issuance of licences in lucrative business. The amount of money illegally exchanged would depend on the perceived value of the service received in return by the bribe payer.

What is beyond doubt is that corruption has been afflicting Nepali society and eroding public confidence on its vital institutions including the government, legislature, judiciary, and other important bodies. But this author disagrees with the proposition that it has intensified under democracy. This, however, is not to justify the various unpardonable acts that happened under democracy.

The rot started to quicken after the country saw the era of coalition governments when some parliamentarians and ministers were seen indulging in activities incompatible with their status. The frequent switching of sides, state-financed foreign jaunts to avoid crucial parliamentary voting, misuse of diplomatic passports, and doctoring of medical bills for monetary benefits were some of the infamous reported activities which ridiculed the status of people's representatives to the highest body in the land. The damage inflicted by such actions on the reputation of democratic institutions is serious and will take a long time to salvage. Similarly, appointments and transfers of officials in public corporations and government offices, breaking with official norms is simply indefensible.

People took such acts under the *Panchayat* system for granted as there was no popular ownership on the government. The system was seen as autocratic and transparency did not exist. Under democracy, everything became transparent. Corruption by the same elected officials who had fought for democracy was simply unacceptable. Those who misused the authority followed the culture of Panchayat regime, thinking that the powerful could get away with any crime. One need just recall the widely reported culture of gold smuggling by members of *Rastriya Panchayat*, some of whom were caught red-handed at Tribhuvan International Airport. Also, the real, perceived, and concocted stories in the media of under-hand dealings involving high-level functionaries contributed to the widespread disenchantment. The general public is not aware that against a few hundred elected representatives who allegedly misused their position for personal gains, there exist thousands of others at various levels who have maintained their integrity in public lives and done a commendable service to the nation. This becomes obvious when one looks at the miserable living conditions of most of the elected representatives of the post-*Panchayat* era.

The fact that the abuses of authority after 1990 were brought to light by parliamentary committees, parliamentarians, and the media speaks volumes for the strength of the democratic order to punish wrong doing. The legislation to curtail such activities, including laws to prevent parliamentary defection and empowerment of the CIAAA to prosecute suspected wrong-doers, were also enacted by the elected institutions. In fact, these acts were initiated by the very people who have become their first victims. Indeed, democracy is a self-correcting system, and takes time to mature. Even developed democracies in other parts of the world have passed through such stages.

It was again under democracy that various measures to minimize corruption were introduced through amendments in financial regulations. Now, all procurement decisions are taken by department heads without going to the ministries. Variation order in government contracts are now limited to a maximum of 15 per cent. Measures were introduced to compulsorily complete all tendering processes on contracts within the first quarter of the fiscal year and start construction within the second quarter. Instead of the annual systems, multi-year tendering systems were introduced for core projects. These measures were necessary because the practice of delayed and annual tendering resulted in the actual construction taking place during the monsoon towards the end of the fiscal year leading to enormous wastage, leakage and corruption.

What happens in the absence of democratic institutions, including elected government and parliamentary oversight, is evidenced from the developments which took place after the dissolution of the House of Representatives in 22 May, 2002 and the subsequent Royal takeover of 4 October 2002. One need only have glanced as the news trickled down in the media. A huge amount of public money was being spent on military hardware with increased budgetary allocation to modernize the army. Such procurement has a high propensity for commission money which should be legally declared and taxed. Yet, no voices were raised. This author had publicly demanded that the Prime Minister and the Defence Minister disclose whether any commission agent existed behind the gun deal with the Belgian company in the latter part of 2002. However, the government was mute on the matter. Similarly, the money allocated to the Royal Palace tripled for the fiscal year 2002/03 budget while the economy was languishing and had registered negative growth.

The cabinet sanctioned an extra budgetary allocation of around Rs.15 crore for the Royal Palace to buy, among others, a Jaguar and a

Rolls Royce. Another Rs.1.25 crore was sanctioned for the medical treatment of a certain Royal family member. An ordinance was passed authorizing the Royal Palace to decide its own budget without parliamentary control and scrutiny. The beverage bill of the Prime Minister's residence for the month of August 2004 was Rs.175,181, against a Rs. 200,000 hospitality bill for the previous month. The allowable monthly limit for overall hospitality was Rs.40,000, and an earlier decision to ban alcohol in government parties, as an austerity measure, was still applicable. The cabinet approved Rs.4.2 million for distribution to the ruling party cadres in Dashain 2004. The issue was subsequently questioned by the Supreme Court and the CIAAA. Furthermore, the cabinet decided to give ministerial-level facilities to members of the Peace Sub-Committee. Under political pressure, it also planned to bring an ordinance to open seven new universities. This was happening despite objections from the University Grants Commission and the academic community, and at a time when the government-funded Tribhuvan University was suffering from a serious financial crunch. These were just tips of the iceberg. Many more would have come to light under the gaze of the parliament and the mere possibility of their existence would have been nipped in the bud.

The Ministry of Local Development proudly mentioned that Rs. 127 billion out of the 187 billion allocated for grants to VDCs in the year 2003/04 had been spent, despite the fact that these institutions are bereft of elected representatives.[7] Those who are familiar with the conditions of rural life in Nepal know very well that rural development has come to a virtual standstill because of Maoist insurgency. What is reported as development expenditure is in fact 'account fixing' and procurement-related expenses that have a high propensity for 'under-hand payments.' This explains the pressure from the parties in the government to have their cadres nominated as 'peoples' representatives' to fill up the vacant positions of local bodies despite the imminent threats to their lives. Quite a few of the nominated functionaries including mayors of Birgunj and Pokhara municipalities were murdered by the Maoists during the government led by Surya Bahadur Thapa. The motivating factor for the nominations, as this author wrote then, was the resources available at the local bodies served as "barn for the mice", at a time when no accountability system existed. Again, most malpractices and misuse of authority go unnoticed in the absence of democratic institutions.

A further example of the intensity of corruption in the absence of democratic institutions was succinctly brought out by a leading Nepali journalist after visiting the district of Kalikot. To quote him:

> Since 2002, the people's representatives have been in limbo, this means no accountability in public spending. "We saw the Panchayat, we saw multi-party democracy, but never have we seen corruption as bad as this", says Tula Raj Bista of the UML who has kept careful record of the Rs. 500,000 that Kathmandu doles out to each VDC. No one from Manma can go to the villages, so the bureaucrats and officials have pocketed the Rs. 15 million meant for 30 VDCs this year by faking suspension bridges, apple orchards and roads. "On paper they showed 100 per cent target met and collected the money, not even the zero per cent of the work has been done", Bista asks angrily".[8]

One can assess the extent of leakage and corruption taking place at various levels by looking into the output of various development ministries in recent years against the financial disbursements that were made. The average construction of such public works like road, irrigation, and drinking water has nose-dived since 2001/02, while their budget expenditure has not declined. The average annual road expenditure is still between 3 to 4 billion rupees, but the actual construction in terms of mileage is less than one-fourth compared to pre-2002 years. Where has all the money gone? A similar phenomenon plagues other areas like irrigation and drinking water.

DONOR RESPONSIBILITY

For a country like Nepal, an important aspect of development is the need for collaborative work with external agencies. In response to donor allegations of corruption in one of the pre-consultation meetings of the NDF 2002, this author responded by stating that corruption takes place in various ways in our revenue and expenditure systems, but the biggest corruption takes place in big projects funded with external assistance. Hence, it would be naïve to believe that it could be controlled without cooperation from the donor side as well. Corruption has significant transnational dimensions which cannot be controlled by poor countries with weak governance. To attribute the problem entirely on the recipient side by ignoring the partnership character of the whole relationship is to acknowledge an unequal donor-recipient partnership. As Devendra Raj Pandey stated, "a donor can easily invoke partnership to claim its right in the programme and then suggest ownership (by the government) to vacate its accountability towards it". In a special luncheon address to the NDF 2002, Pandey, in his capacity of the Chairman of Transparency International, suggested a four-point unilateral action on the part of the donor community to fight corruption:[9]

(*i*) Limit possible leakage at the conceptualization and design phase of the project. There is suspicion that primary objective of the project can be achieved at much lower cost than what is programmed and allocated in many aid agreements. Huge cost of technical assistance comprising big remuneration and perks not only approximate corruption, but also have a demoralizing effect on national institutions.

(*ii*) Do not short-circuit the government's system by providing extra-legal and extra-budget payments in cash or kind to public officials for services rendered. The practice is self-defeating in terms of self-respect, self confidence and the moral capacity to negotiate with the latter on equal footing.

(*iii*) Ensure that procurement transactions are fully monitored to ensure OECD convention guidelines that criminalizes bribery of public officials in the importing countries by suppliers.

(*iv*) Apply the tool of Integrity Pact devised by the Transparency International under which the international procurement bidding is made fully transparent by making room for peer monitoring by the competing suppliers themselves with the civil society exercising its oversight role.

The government is no longer the sole player in the game of development assistance, as was the case until a decade or two ago. Assistance is now channeled through a variety of sources—central and local governments, municipalities, civil society, non-government organizations, and the private sector. This is in part, the reflection of the realization that state institutions are, by themselves, insufficient mechanisms to deliver public services and carry out development activities. Therefore, the domain of partnership, policy dialogue, negotiations, and the sharing of responsibilities in the drive towards anti-corruption has naturally expanded. The government still remains the principal actor and the leader of the process, but does not represent the whole. Payment of extravagant salaries and vulgar use of expensive facilities that are out of line with national conditions may not be corrupt practices in the strict sense of the word, but they still lead to distortions in the market and encourage corruption.

BRIBERY BY MNCs

Corrupt practices by powerful multinationals, that bag most of the big procurement contracts for developmental works, cannot be controlled by weak governments of the recipient countries. Despite stringent laws against bribes, the prevalence of a kickback culture among companies in leading industrial countries is an acknowledged fact. In a scathing attack on the double standards of rich countries on the eve of OECD Ministerial meeting in May 2002, Peter Eigen, Chairman of the Transparency International (TI) noted:

> Politicians and public officials from the world's leading industrial countries are ignoring the rot in their own backyards and the criminal bribe-taking activities of multinational firms headquartered in their countries, while increasingly focusing on the high level of corruption in developing countries.

He alleged that these companies were using a criminal course to win contracts in emerging economies. The Bribe Payers Index Survey (BPI) is the most comprehensive set of opinion polls on perceptions about sources of corruption undertaken by the Transparency International. Its results show that even American MNCs which face criminal prosecution under Foreign Corrupt Practices Act of 1977 have a high propensity to pay bribes to foreign officials. The BPI for the US for the year 2002 was 5.3 out of a best possible 10. This matched BPI ratings of Japanese companies but was worse than that of most European companies.

Similarly, despite the OECD Anti-Bribery Convention of 1999, no criminal persecutions have been reported in any of the signatory countries until now. TI, in its report blames the rich countries for not doing enough to curb bribery by their companies to public officials around the world. It posits that corruption and bribes by big companies to corrupt officials and politicians are undermining the prospects of sustainable development in poorer countries. TI further found that most of the business sector was ignorant about the Convention and the risk of criminal prosecution for being a party to bribery. TI finds the most flagrant cases of corruption in public works, construction, and arms sector. Experts estimate that systematic corruption can add as much as 25 per cent to the cost on government procurement, resulting in inferior quality construction materials and unnecessary purchases.

In one of my meetings as Nepal's Finance Minister with the World Bank President in Washington D.C in October 1999, this author had proposed an independent post-project evaluation of the procurement and construction projects completed with IDA assistance in recent years to assess the performance of the concerned parties. However, this proposal was not followed up primarily due to a change in government almost immediately afterwards.

I was particularly troubled by the poor quality of work even by international contractors selected under competitive global bidding, and whose works were supervised and given good performance certificates by reputed international firms. One conspicuous case related to the bursting of the "butterfly valve" in the Trisuli Hydro. This incident disrupted the plant's power supply for most parts of a year and caused huge financial losses. The incident was especially strange in light of the fact that the system was upgraded less than a year prior to the incident with IDA money under the Power Sector Efficiency Project. There are, of course, many cases like Narayani Irrigation and Battar Lift Irrigation, which are living monuments of poor and faulty designs by international consultants and for which we continue to service debt. Studies show that even relatively successful projects like the Bhairahawa Lumbini Groundwater, Sunsari-Morang and Mahakali irrigation projects suffer from extremely high investment in relation to returns.

A recent study of the Bhairahawa-Lumbini Irrigation concludes that tube-wells have been erected in sites where alternative sources were available. Twelve deep tube-wells completed under the project have now been abandoned due to wrong location and a randomly selected tube-well which was designed to cover a command area of 120 hectares was found capable of commanding only 13 hectares.[10] High cost and low returns in such projects is the result of an affinity to choose expensive technology and design without giving sufficient consideration to local conditions, maintenance capability[11], and of course, misuse of funds.

The government and concerned officials cannot be exculpated for not giving sufficient attention from identification to design, and subsequently to construction and maintenance. After all, the recipient countries will have to service the credit and it is they who must ensure that the aid money is put to optimum use. The problem is attributed to insufficient attention given by national technical professionals who have a tendency to rush the project to meet deadlines and to readily accept expatriate advice. People with real competence and integrity are in short supply in most government offices, and such people are overstretched or not properly utilized due to bad management and nepotism. The inclination to question expatriate advice is weak. Even in government bureaucracy, the tendency to opt for expensive solutions without considering cost effective alternatives, and professionally reward employees in expensive construction projects is very high. Most of the projects this author came across in the National Planning Commission and the Ministry of Finance at their last stages were still in the form presented by the experts with practically no revisions or comments. I remember intervening from the NPC and the Ministry of Finance to alter project designs in a few cases.

Procurement, construction and consultancy represent bulk the of the project budget in externally assisted projects. The suppliers or service providing foreign companies appoint their local agents to act as intermediaries with the recipient country's functionaries. The advantage of this system is the savings in time, expense, and efforts of buyers and sellers in dealing with each other. It is suspected that huge amounts of commission money changes hands in such sectors as aviation, telecommunication, and defence procurements. Much of the high-level corruption in countries like Nepal is attributed to the invisible nature of dealings by these agents, who often transfer a part of their commission to the buyers who happen to be government officials. In the business world, it is perfectly normal and legal to pay commission money to the authorized agents for promoting sale of their product. But there is very little transparency in their dealings. In most procurement, no agent is declared; in others where agents are declared, the true magnitude of the transaction is not declared. It is this undeclared money that invariably becomes the source of corruption to public officials, and results in tax evasion.

During the *Panchayat* days, public scrutiny of these aspects was glaring in its absence. After the restoration of democracy, questions were raised on this issue and the House of Representatives passed a resolution asking the international companies to compulsorily declare their local agents in all procurement deals, and subsequently laws were revised to make the act of false declarations punishable. But this parliamentary stricture did not evoke favourable response from donor institutions.

In addition, through an act of the Finance Bill introduced with the budget, an opportunity was provided to those who evaded tax through such and other methods, to become good citizens by paying the evaded amount under the Voluntary Disclosure of Income Scheme (VDIS) within a certain period, or face the consequence later. The offer evoked a good response, and on two occasions netted about a hundred crore rupees to the treasury. Political instability due to frequent government changes prevented the logical follow-up on this by nabbing and punishing those who still did not avail of this offer.

TOWARDS NON-DISCRETIONARY REGIME

The root cause of corruption is the officials' power to dispense favour in a discretionary manner. They control access to valuable benefits, and can also impose private costs at an individual and societal level. Corruption is also a function of expected benefits of breaking law against the expected cost of being caught. The high probability of being caught will discourage corruption. The restoration of democracy in Nepal also saw the initiation of economic reform measures which led to the dismantling of most of the licensing and permit systems in economic and social fields which previously gave enormous discretionary power to government officials and ministers.

The licensing practice with respect to establishment of industries, import of merchandise, access to foreign exchange, which represented a prominent source of corruption by politicians and civil servants during the *Panchayat* regime were scrapped. In its place, a transparent rule-based non-discriminatory system was started. All imports were brought under open generalized licensing. Foreign exchange for all imports is now made automatically available. It is no longer necessary to obtain licenses to start industries except for those on the negative list. Discriminatory tax laws which brought distortions in economic activities were replaced by non-discriminatory tax laws. Public corporations which offered enormous scope for misuse of authority for personal gains to ministers and bureaucrats were streamlined, and the privatization process was accelerated. The breaking up of public sector monopolies in fields such as aviation, telecommunications, trading in goods like fertilizer, and to a large extent, even in the banking sector, considerably reduced the scope for corruption while improving the quality of services at the same time.

Some people have also blamed privatization in Nepal for corruption. This allegation is wrong and comes from interest groups or from people who have very little knowledge about the privatization process in Nepal. Nepal's privatization process is extremely transparent, undertaken on an open competitive bidding basis, and has to pass through various stages, often scrutinized by various agencies including the parliamentary committees. The scope for underhand payment for undue favour simply does not exist. On the other hand, after their privatization, the PEs will no longer serve as boundless pastures for unscrupulous managers, civil servants, and ministers for personal benefit.

While even democratic polity is not immune from corrupt practices and misuse of authority, the scope for the same is much less here compared to under an autocratic system. The causes of corruption are related to the country's social practice, culture, history, bureaucratic traditions, government policies, and political development. It tends to grow when formal institutions are weak, undemocratic, non-transparent, and where leadership is poor. Despite all its shortcomings, corruption can be best fought under democracy in view of the built-in mechanism for public scrutiny and control. Corrupt practices which were invisible under autocratic and undemocratic regimes, or are hidden in the absence of elected bodies, come to light when there are vibrant and functioning democratic institutions. The very fact that there has been a perceptible improvement in development performance in practically all sectors during 1990–2002 with comparable volume of public investment in other years indicates better resource management under democracy.

NOTES

1. The World Bank, *Helping Countries Combat Corruption*, 1997, p. 9.
2. Ibid, p. 9–10.
3. Transparency International (2004), *Corruption Perception Index 2004*, p. 5. Berlin.
4. Ibid.
5. Bharat Pokhrel, 'Commissions, Kickbacks, and Bribes in Nepal' in D.B. Gurung (ed) *Nepal Tomorrow: Voices and Visions,* Kathmandu: Koselee Prakashan, 2003.
6. Krishna Hachhethu, *The State of Democracy in Nepal: Survey Report.* The State of Democracy in South Asia/ Nepal Chapter in Collaboration with International IDEA, 2004, Kathmandu.
7. *See Kantipur,* November 12, 2004.
8. Kunda Dixit's report, *The Nepali Times*, 29 October–4 November, 2004
9. Ministry of Finance, *Chairman's Report on the Proceedings, NDF 2002*, Annex V. Kathmandu.
10. *See* HMG/World Bank/SAPROS, *Delivery of Rural Development Services*, Kathmandu, 2000, p. 36..
11. One example of high capitalization is the Inland Container Depot Project in Birgunj (discussed in the last chapter under the section on external assistance).

Chapter Twelve

The 'Development Catalyst'

An interesting report on the history and dynamics of the Maoist insurgency in Nepal's Rapti hills came out in 2002. This report entitled "Sowing the Wind" was based on the field assessment by an individual named Robert Gersony, a Mercy Corps International (MCI) consultant supported by the USAID. MCI is an INGO specializing in humanitarian and emergency assistance in war-torn societies. This author is personally familiar with their work in other conflict-ridden situations, particularly in Afghanistan. The report is based on the interviews of some 250 individuals including 150 local residents in 6 districts of mid western region including its four hill districts, namely, Rolpa, Rukum, Surkhet and Salyan which are hardest hit by Maoist insurgency.

The report has done a commendable work in delving into the root causes of the Maoist revolt, providing a realistic assessment of their support base, the role and conduct of HMG's armed forces, and future prospects. It is not my intention here to summarize this report but only to highlight an important finding. The report posits that it was the state's inability to deliver an important development priority as perceived by the people that fostered an environment for the insurgency to spread in these districts.

ROAD : THE DEVELOPMENT CATALYST

The report hits the right chord when it states that the highest development priority of the area was access to roads. To quote the report, "its best economic activities, the off-season vegetable and vegetable seed initiatives, which sustainably multiplied the income of thousands of families, illustrate why roads are important". Social, economic, and infrastructural development activities become more economical and more sustainable once roads are built. Similarly, roads increase the disposable income of families as the products they buy become cheaper, and they themselves receive more income from what they sell. Understandably, people perceived roads to be the common development denominator in the region. In contrast, micro projects such as "chicken, goats and advocacy" efforts were of very little significance and without durable impact. They succinctly declared, "without road, every thing fails".

Apart from the economic perspective, rural people consider roads as a catalyst for social progress. Change immediately becomes visible in areas with roads, people become more dynamic, forward looking, and gain confidence to change things. They also become less vulnerable to manipulation by feudal lords and Maoists as roads diminish the power of oppression. A wonderful correlation is also visible between Maoist influence and the distance from roads—the Maoists have less influence in areas with road access.

The above observation, of course, is not a new finding. Road access remains a prominent election issue in virtually all constituencies at all levels, and even more so in the hills and mountains. Much of the blame hurled on successive governments is partly due to their inability to deliver on this critical front. If the demands made by the members of Nepal's parliament since 1991 is any indication, this is the highest development priority identified by the people. The key role of transport in economic development is, of course, well recognized in development literature.

> Transport is crucial to development—without access to jobs, health, education, and other amenities, quality of life suffers; without access to resources and markets, growth stagnates and poverty reduction cannot be sustained.
>
> ...Studies by the World Bank show that transport generates growth by facilitating trade, both nationally and internationally, and increasing access to health and educational facilities as well as local and national facilities. At the macroeconomic level, cross-country studies have confirmed that investment in transport raises growth by increasing the social return to private investment without "crowding out" other productive investment and inadequate transport infrastructure is an important constraint on aggregate agricultural productivity. At the micro-economic level, transport improvements directly lower agricultural input prices and hence production costs, increase access to markets and hence diversification of outputs, and indirectly facilitate the development of the non-agricultural rural economy.[1]

Apart from reducing transaction costs in economic activities, roads are also pre-requisites to ensuring proper returns on investment in the social sector. Key social institutions such as the schools and health centers need qualified teachers and health personnel. However, such people are not willing to work in remote places that are without roads. The general perception of the common man is that without roads, development will have bypassed them, and they will not be linked to the national mainstream.

Despite this well-known reality, the issue of road construction has not been without controversy and debate, especially in the donor community. In the early phase of development efforts, Nepal's request for assistance in this sector was met with good response from bilateral donors. However, in the recent past, in the early nineties, the donor community did not show the same enthusiasm as the government. This mostly affected the hill districts where the need for road access was acute. This is not to say that there has been no donor-financed project in such areas, but what we received was too little to fulfill the necessity felt by the people. Let me share some of my own experiences in this matter.

NATIONAL PRIORITY Vs DONOR APPROACH

Back in 1991, when the first elected NC government took office, the construction of North–South roads linking the inaccessible districts was declared as a priority. The government even committed itself to link all district headquarters to the national road network within fifteen years. The Eighth Plan (1992–97), with whose formulation this author was intimately associated with, declared the reduction of regional disparities as one of its principal objectives. The development of infrastructure and social service facilities was particularly emphasized in the relatively underdeveloped far-western and mid-western development regions. A strong emphasis was placed on exploiting regional complementarities and inter-relationships between the hills and the *tarai* arising out of the different agro-ecological conditions. The extension of rural roads would go side by side with facilities like primary health care, education, and drinking water.

The most important components of the road development programme were the North–South roads, and other feeder roads connecting remote areas. Road projects like Salyan-Musikot, Chhinchu-Jajarkot, Silgadi-Sanfebagar-Mangalsen, Bhalubang-Pyuthan, Surkhet-Jumla, Surkhet-Dailekh, Ghorahi-Holleri, Khodpe-Bajhang, Sahajpur-Dipayal, Patan-Baitadi-Darchula, Daiji-Jogbuda, and Baitadi-Jhulaghat were among those which particularly featured in the mid-and-far-western development regions by the Eighth Plan.

In view of the limited internal resources available for these and other North–South roads, we approached the international community for assistance. However, seemingly influenced largely by a British ODA-supported study on the impact road projects in the West-Central Nepal in the mid-seventies, the response of the donor community did not match the government enthusiasm.[2] This controversial study undertaken by Blaike, Cameron and Seddon had used a neo-Marxist dependency perspective to show how the road construction had increased not only Nepal's dependence on India, but also the internal centre-periphery relationships at local and regional levels. It had highlighted the impact of road construction on the growth of socio-economic and spatial inequalities and environmental degradation. It argued that roads facilitated the penetration by Indian merchant capital at the expense of domestic capital; and Indian manufactured products replaced local artisan and manufactures. Its conclusion was the road construction benefited a tiny population leaving the vast majority of the people untouched.

The British government had built the Dharan-Dhankuta road, but was concerned about its poor maintenance. Although it still showed interest in new projects, it was confined to the upgradation and periodic maintenance of some portions of existing highways such as the Mugling-Naubishe. On the other hand, USAID was not ready to commit to any more road projects after the Dhangadhi–Dadeldhura road and German assistance in the road sector was limited to labour intensive 'green roads'. The Japanese, after much persuasion, agreed to take up the Banepa-Sindhuli-Bardibas road. Although the Asian Development Bank was involved in projects in the Far West and Eastern Regions, mostly in the upgradation and maintenance of existing roads, it also agreed to take up rural road projects in the three hill districts of Kavre, Tanahun and Baglung. The World Bank's assistance in this sector was confined to the periodic maintenance and rehabilitation of existing highways. Nevertheless, after much dialogue, they agreed to upgrade the Dumre–Besisahar road to all-weather asphalt—an important contribution that was made possible by using the funds saved from Marsyangdi hydro. The Swiss, who had constructed Lamusanghu–Jiri road, were mainly preoccupied with its proper maintenance.

The World Bank came up with its road sector policy for Nepal in 1993, which considered most North–South and hill roads planned by the HMG to connect hill districts as economically unfeasible in view of their low economic rate of returns. We questioned this position and tried to justify the program from the National Planning Commission (NPC). I still recall the long telexes and faxes sent to the World Bank with critical comments on the draft version of the Bank's policy document. We argued that the roads proposed by the government had strong social value, and their priority was identified by the people themselves. Even to raise the productivity of existing trunk roads, the North–South and other feeder roads were important. If we wanted to alleviate poverty in the hills and mountains, it was necessary to commercialize and diversify the agriculture sector and for that, market accessibility was crucial. Furthermore, we felt that the potential of Nepal's hill agriculture, if properly exploited, held numerous advantages in the vast Indian market. The diverse agro-ecological zones of Nepal would produce a number of high quality farm products which would have a ready market in India. It was impossible to exploit this comparative advantage without an adequate road network. To address the donor concern regarding the high cost of the hill roads, we initially proposed the construction of low cost dry weather roads.

But our arguments did not change the position of the World Bank's experts. The policy paper, which came in its final shape, was not much different from the initial draft. The document advised that the basic strategy for the road sector should be confined to the maintenance and improvement of the existing strategic road network, improved connectivity between the central hills and the *tarai*, Indian gateways, and short farm-to-market roads in the *tarai* connected to the East-West highway. As for the North–South roads, its conclusion was:

> Additional North South roads (parallel to the existing corridor between the Birgunj-Kathmandu-Kodari) have in the plans for many years to connect the hills and the *tarai*. The high cost of these projects makes less than one-third of these new corridor projects feasible under the most positive traffic growth scenarios.
>
> ...the total investment requirements of these expensive roads total at least Rs. 7.7 billion. These roads' high cost makes their construction a low economic priority in most cases ... It would therefore be of paramount importance to drop at least two-thirds of all new kilometers undertaken in on-going projects to avoid financing the lower priority projects in the current portfolio.[3]

With regard to the backward mid-western and far-western regions to which the government plan had accorded highest priority for road construction, the report prescribed:

> ...The western and far-western regions would require further developments of trials and suspension bridges, since road construction is expensive and uneconomical in many instances. The high costs of transport would

> therefore continue to make the case for air transport as the only mechanized form of transport to the important settlements[4].

I recall long meetings at the NPC, when my colleagues and I would try to persuade the reluctant donors in favour of road assistance to Nepal. Our country is perhaps the most road-deficient country in the world with only 0.4 km of road per 1000 population, as compared to 1.89 km in India and 1.8 in Bangladesh. If one looks at the road situation in relation to its geography, the position is even more acute. Nepal has 5.0 km of road for every 100 square km as compared to 112 km in Bangladesh and 41.3 in India.

The buzzword in those days was 'social sector investment'. This term was borrowed heavily from the experience of other developing countries, which unlike Nepal, already possessed basic transport and other infrastructural network. Nepal had already been increasing investment in the social sector from about 22 per cent of the development budget in 1990, to about 35 per cent by the end of the decade. The social justification for hill roads and the argument that even social sector investments would not yield proper results in the absence of minimum physical facilities like road and electricity did not cut much ice.

HMG, however, did not change its strategy and went ahead with the road development program with internal resources—apart from the few exceptions of external assistance already indicated. In the nineties, approximately 1,000 kilometres of mostly dry weather roads were built in districts like Surkhet, Jajarkot, Rukum, Salyan, Rolpa, Pyuthan, Dailekh, Dang, Achham, Doti, Baitadi, Dadeldhura and towards Kalikot and Jumla. During this decade, a total of about 8,300 km of road was added to some 6,700 km that Nepal had at the end of the Panchayat regime. In the process, it even made use of the skills of the Royal Nepal Army (RNA) in constructing the roads for Okhaldhunga and Bhojpur in the East. With the support from Prime Minister Koirala, this author, on behalf of the NPC, offered five possible road projects to the RNA to choose from for implementation.[5] They chose Katari–Okhaldhunga and Hile–Bhojpur roads in view of their better command over logistics in those areas.

Most of the construction, especially in the hill districts, was internally funded. It would be interesting to see the budgetary breakdown within the road sector in those years. The road budget in those years was characterized by a long list of internally, but inadequately funded new construction projects, and a few adequately funded with external support the rehabilitation, reconstruction, and maintenance projects. It was well understood that economic prudence would dictate concentration of the limited resource to a fewer projects rather than scattering them widely. But this was not possible due to popular pressure. I am mentioning these historical facts here with the view of stating the truth on record. This is because it has become fashionable to blame democratic governments for doing nothing for the poor people of the regions that gave rise to insurgency. In one of the sessions that I chaired at the NDF 2002, some donors blamed the government for the lack of visible development actions in the mountain regions. My extempore response in relation to the road sector, among other things, was:

> ...changes are seen even if you go to the mid-western region, which is the hotspot of terrorist activities. In the last ten years we have built three to four hundred kilometers of road in some of the most difficult terrain of the country. This was regarded as the most backward region, difficult to work. But we have worked there...
>
> When we asked for international assistance to build roads in these areas we were turned down. I was the Deputy Chairman of the Planning Commission then, ...colleagues who were working with me then are here. We were turned down because it was felt that roads in these areas are not economic propositions; they do not make economic sense; you must invest in social sector, not in infrastructure building (we were told). So we used our domestic resources in building roads in these areas. Now after some time there is a realization in the international community that roads in these areas make sense and we are now getting assistance to build them.[6]

NEW DEVELOPMENTS

The donor approach changed somewhat towards the latter part of the decade. A major cause of this change was the influence of the Agriculture Perspective Plan prepared under the aegis of the NPC. The project had received financial support from the Asian Development Bank. John Mellor, who supervised and guided the study, fully understood and appreciated the government's road policy. A Nepali team was even flown to Himachal Pradesh of India to show, among other things, how proper road access could help in revolutionizing the agricultural potential of a hill economy. The APP had argued for roads to facilitate the drilling and maintenance of shallow tube wells in the *tarai* and to promote the marketing and agro-business activities associated with the high-value commodities in the hills. That represented the foundation for a growth in income. The APP further observed that even the *tarai* region of Nepal had less than a quarter of the road density per square kilometre and less than a fifth per thousand of population, than Bangladesh. Uttar Pradesh of India had twice the road length per thousand of population and four times the road length per square kilometre of area, compared to neighbouring Nepal.

The APP called for a doubling of the length of roads added annually in Nepal, with emphasis on proper maintenance of existing roads. It gave priority to providing a full grid of agricultural roads around the existing trunk roads—the existing East–West highways and North–South roads, and the roads to district headquarters. The APP also proposed the construction of 6,200 kilometres of agricultural roads—3,400 in *tarai* and 2,600 in hills and mountains. It recommended a road density of 22 km of all-weather road per 100 square mile of mapped agricultural area in *tarai*, 11 km in hills, and 4 km in mountains. In addition, it stressed the completion of an additional 1,837 kilometers of roads to connect district headquarters on an all weather basis and an early completion of the Karnali Highway to connect Kalikot and Jumla.

The World Bank also revised its earlier policy with regard to hill roads and new construction. In 1999, the HMG-IDA approved a Road Maintenance and Development Project at the cost of US $64.40 million, of which 45.8 million was to be spent on completing the construction of 197 km of dry weather feeder roads and upgradation of 253 km of other hill roads to gravel standard. Most of these projects were intended to complete the road links already started by HMG in hill districts. This was the first time the Bank came up with such a large programme of hill road construction. The North-South roads that were regarded as economically infeasible in its earlier report were now accorded priority. The new study also showed that their ERR ranged from 12 to 95 per cent.

Interestingly, most of the new North–South new construction projects planned under the new IDA credit were in the mid-and far-western regions. In these regions, the previous policy document had only recommended the development of 'trails and suspension bridges,' and air service as the only mechanized transport system in view of the 'high construction costs of roads'. The roads proposed under the IDA credit were: Chamelia-Darchula, Sanfebagar-Martadi, Sanfebagar-Mangalsen, Kalikot-Jumla, Chedegad-Jajarkot, Surkhet-Kalikot, Dharapani-Chedagad and Gorusinghe-Sandikharka. In the absence of external support, these roads had been initiated by the government from 1991 entirely with its internal resources. In addition to the quantifiable economic benefits, the new policy talked of the social and economic impact, almost exactly along the line articulated by the NPC before. The Appraisal Report of the new project said:

> New north-south feeder roads are necessary condition for promoting growth in hill districts still characterized by: *(1)* dependence on subsistence agriculture; *(2)* trade based on barter exchange system; *(3)* economy supported by high seasonal migration to *tarai* and India; and *(4)* the majority of the population not having sufficient food for more than six months in a year. To utilize the comparative economic advantage of hill regions, investments in new roads are needed where justified. They will promote strong complementary support existing between the hill and the plains.[7]

This was followed by new commitments from the ADB and DFID, mostly in central and eastern Nepal. The Chinese agreed to build the Shyabrubesi–Rasuwagadhi road. These were positive developments and also vindication of government policy. Projects that had been poorly funded earlier, found new hope of early completion with external support. The budget figures of the last few years show a substantial increase in allocation to the earlier prioritized district roads. Unfortunately, the timing of the new donor support coincided with increased intensity of Maoist violence, resulting in security risks in the construction areas. The Maoists, knowing the conflict prevention impact of road access, have successfully stopped further construction work in most districts. Consequently, the enhanced road budgets in these areas remain unspent.

The paradigm shift in recognition of the tremendous importance of infrastructure development, particularly roads, is evident in other policy papers also. A recent World Bank policy document on Nepal states:

> Transport remains the defining constraint to growth, public services, and poverty reduction in Nepal as recognized in the 10th Plan/Poverty Reduction Strategy. Nepal has one of the lowest road densities for a landlocked country. As roads are the main arteries of the economy in Nepal's terrain, the lack of roads makes connectivity a significant constraint. An estimated 3.5 million people (15 per cent of the population do not have road access in Nepal: some villages can be up to 13 days walk to the nearest road head.[8]

The new strategy of the Bank, in addition to the support for the maintenance of existing road network, is an increased investment in the road sector that will enable Nepal to expand its road network. The increased network will include the completion of the North–South corridors, a fast track Kathmand–*Tarai* link, and upgrades on village roads. The total length to be completed in western Nepal alone was 1184 km, of which only 581 had been open at the track level or under construction. Hence, completing these roads was given primary priority.

PLANNING IMPERATIVES

Nepalis are the best judge of their priority needs and know what works best in their situation. However, limited internal resources constrain their abilities to act on these priorities. Theoretically, international support is supposed to flow to areas identified as priority by recipient governments; but in practice, this does not happen. Donor agencies are guided by their own mandate, defined by respective governing boards, executive and legislative branches, with regard to the nature, methods, and areas of assistance. The influences of themes and policies emerging from contemporary development literature and global development institutions are other strong determinants. Thus, the perception of priority does not remain consistent all the time. The vulnerabilities of a poor country desperately needing assistance everywhere are well known. Weak administrative capacity, limited manpower, and the need for resources make them susceptible to go by donor wishes. In practically every field, there is need for higher investment, but investment in well chosen under-funded areas would yield higher returns.

Road development will continue to be important in Nepal for some time. Many remote districts still lack roads, and people have to walk several days to reach the nearest road head. Even where they exist, the network is of low quality and generally limited to fair weather. Lack of road access is also the biggest hindrance on the farmer's ability and willingness to the shift from subsistence to commercial farming. In the absence of roads, transportation costs of essential goods, including agricultural inputs like fertilizer, becomes prohibitively high. Therefore, the prospects of small industries and commercial activities are automatically restricted. The remote areas without roads are also devoid of development personnel, teachers and health workers, despite the fact that they exist on government payroll. Even attracting development personnel in areas without proper physical infrastructure is an impossible task. Studies done in Bangladesh show that road access increases the productivity of social and economic institutions by 32 per cent.[9] It is possible that the figure could be higher for Nepal because of its difficult geography and acute remoteness. Even in their otherwise critical evaluation, Blaike, Cameron and Seddon spoke of the positive impact of road construction in land prices, growth of towns and administrative centres. They further acknowledged:

> ...physical access by motorised transport has reduced the chances of food deficits turning into famines. Monopolies and monopsonies enjoyed by traders in hitherto remote centres have fallen, to the general benefit of

> poor consumers. Also, the real personal and social value of improved travel and transport by much faster and less onerous means must not be underestimated. Better physical access to health and educational facilities and to a wider range of goods and services can only help improve real access for poor people in rural areas. But all the evidence indicates that roads alone are not enough to bring about significant change in the rural areas[10].

Investment in this sector, however, needs careful planning, prioritization, and management. The expensive nature of investments in Nepali hill and mountain terrain, ecological vulnerability, and the need for adequate and proper maintenance make this all the more difficult. Due to a lack of adequate feeders and links with principal market and production centres and the lack of proper maintenance, even high investment in some roads have failed to give adequate returns in the past. On the other hand, roads with low investments but built with peoples' participation have brought about transformations in rural life. Thus, a road needs to be treated as part of the package with other complementary activities to maximize its developmental impact.

At present, the problem of Maoist insurgency and the popular desire for peace have given the impetus for spending billions of external assistance in the name of peace, conflict prevention, crisis management, advocacy, and empowerment. One cannot underestimate the importance of such efforts in generating awareness and inculcating better management skills. But in a country where resource is scarce and competes for more urgent human needs, the opportunity cost of resource thus spent should be seriously weighed before an investment decision is made. For people living in rural areas, development means education, health, road access, electricity, drinking water, irrigation, and better income. Development expenditure has no meaning for them unless there are visible improvements in the fulfilment of these necessities. This reality needs to be appreciated and internalized while making decisions in the name of poverty and conflict prevention. That is where the role of a strong and accountable government, capable of defining and articulating one's priorities and requirements becomes necessary.

NOTES

1. The World Bank, *Sustainable Transport Sector Review and Lessons of Experience*, 1996, p. 1.
2. The study report by the Overseas Development Group at the University of East Anglia did not come out in full form because of the controversy it generated. The revised and reconstructed version of the report was published

in 1980 as *Nepal In Crisis,* authored by P.M. Blaike, J. Cameron, and David Seddon (the three were co-directors of the project), by Oxford University Press.

3. The World Bank *Nepal Expenditures in the Road Sector, 1993,* p. 57.
4. Ibid, p. 55.
5. The productive discussion this author had with the then COAS Gadul Shamsher Rana, and General K.N.S. Thapa in various meetings at the NPC is recalled here. The RNA showed good cooperation and agreed to build the road with the technical and other manpower available with RNA, using contractors at the minimum.
6. *See* Finance Minister's remarks in response to comments made during the first session of NDF 2002, *NDF Bulletin-2* Kathmandu.
7. The World Bank, (1999) on *Road Maintenance and Development Project:* Project Appraisal Document, p. 36.
8. The World Bank, *Nepal Development Policy Review*, 2004, pp. 28–29.
9. APROSC and John Mellor Associates, *Nepal Agricultural Perspective Plan: Main Document*, 1994, p. 124.
10. P.M. Blaikie, John Cameron and John David Seddon, *Nepal In Crisis: Growth and Stagnation At The Periphery*, Delhi: Adroit Publishers, (Enlarged and Revised Edition) 2001, p. 303.

Chapter Thirteen

Security Cost : On the South Asian Path?

The nature of war has undergone a significant transformation in recent decades. The Cold War has ended, but the transition to the new millenium has been marked by deadly conflicts which are overwhelmingly concentrated in developing countries. During 1987–1997, more than 87 per cent of the wars were fought within national borders—14 in Africa, 14 in Asia and 1 in Europe. Similarly, the nature of war victims has also changed.[1] A vast majority of the casualties are no longer combatants. Those who suffer the most are civilians—mostly children who are at the formative and productive period of their lives, women, elderly, and the infirm.

After more than a decade of reductions, the world military expenditure started rising since 1998. The Stockholm International Peace Research Institute (SIPRI) estimated the world military spending in 2001 at US $839 billion, representing an increase of 2 per cent in real terms compared to the previous year.[2] As a global average, it accounted for 2.6 per cent of the world GDP and US $137 per capita. Even these figures are an under representation, since supplementary spending since 9/11 and subsequent war on terrorism are not properly reflected in them. The regions with the strongest growth in military spending are: Central and Eastern Europe, Africa, South Asia, and the Middle East, where real aggregate growth of more than 25 per cent has been recorded between 1998 and 2001. The main reasons for this increase are internal and external armed conflicts, threats of new conflicts, the war on terrorism, and continued modernization of the military. The US-led war on terrorism marked the start of a new approach to combating terrorism with a heavy emphasis on military force. This will involve heavy increases in internal security costs which would include strong measures for counter terrorism. By contrast, the worldwide spending on weapons and forces had fallen by one-third between 1987-97, reflecting not only the disarmament after the Cold War, but also a higher efficiency in the use of resources for military purposes.

SOUTH ASIA DEFIES

Defying the global trend, the military spending in South Asia shows a consistently increasing trend. Military spending in South Asia increased from US $11.3 billion in 1992 to US $13.8 billion in 1998. During the same period, global spending on defence declined from US $847 to US $719 billion. The region's share in the global military spending during this period increased from 1.3 per cent to 1.9 per cent. South Asia's military budget further rose to US $17.4 billion in 2001, accounting for 2.3 per cent of the global military expenditure.[3] Tensions between India and Pakistan largely determine the total shape and size of military spending in South Asia as their military expenditure accounts for 93 per cent of the region. Furthermore, India and Pakistan belong to a group of countries which boast the 10 largest armies of the world. With an annual spending of US $12.9 billion on military, India also ranks 11th among the major military spenders.[4]

The South Asia Human Development Report in 1997 pointed out that South Asia is one of the most militarized regions in the world. In marked contrast to the global trend, the region is expanding the standing armies at the time when other nations are reducing them. The region is acquiring a range of modern weapons when military holdings of combat aircraft, artillery, ships and tanks have declined elsewhere. Although both India and Pakistan carry a heavy burden of defence expenditure, the overall impact is much heavier on Pakistan in view of its smaller size. Pakistan's economy is roughly about one-fifth of the Indian economy and it contains one-seventh of the population of India. India spends 3.6 per cent of its GDP on defence, while for Pakistan it is as much as 7 per cent. In per-capita terms, India's defence expenditure is US $10, while for Pakistan it is US $26.

Increasing security expenditure in South Asia, however, is not a phenomenon limited to India and Pakistan. Smaller countries like Bangladesh, Sri Lanka and Nepal also follow this general pattern. The increase in military expenditure for Bangladesh, Sri Lanka and Nepal during the period 1987–94 were 7.5 per cent, 108 per cent and 43 per cent respectively. Faced with continuing ethnic insurgency over the last twenty years, Sri Lanka's security spending has dramatically increased to 5 per cent of its GDP; and its per-capita defence expenditure is higher than that of Pakistan. South Asia is the home of the largest number of 'non-state armed groups' of any region in the world. Out of the 18 such armed groups identified by the Military Balance 2002–2003 of the Internatioanl Institute of Strategic Studies, 3 are in Bangladesh, 8 in India, 5 in India/Pakistan, and one each in Nepal and Sri Lanka. Most of these armed groups are trans-national in character, which often leads to accusations of cross-border terrorism. About 63 per cent of such armed conflicts are of protracted nature and their duration is at least three times the global average.[5]

SECURITIZATION IN NEPAL

Traditionally, Nepal's defence expenditure has been one of the lowest in South Asia. Nepal's share in total military spending in South Asia was 0.2 per cent in 1991. Similarly, according to the World Development Report 2000-1, Nepal's military spending as a percentage of GDP was 0.8 per cent in 1997 compared to 5.7 for Pakistan, 2.8 per cent for India, 5.1 for Sri Lanka, and 1.4 per cent for Bangladesh. The Human Development Report in South Asia 1997 showed that its share in the total government expenditure in 1995 was 5.9 per cent, as compared to 17.6 per cent for Bangladesh, and 11.6 per cent for Sri Lanka. Its defence expenditure as percentage of health and education expenditure in 1991 was 35% compared to 41% for Bangladesh and 107% for Sri Lanka.

Nepal's budgetary pattern has undergone significant changes since the outbreak of Maoist insurgency. The combined police and army budget, which never exceeded 10 per cent of the total government spending in the 1990s, is now about 20 per cent. The figures presented in the budget are an under-representation since a significant portion of the additional security demand is met through extra-budgetary arrangements. Since 2002/03, about 20 per cent of the security expenditure has been met in this way. This figure further excludes the hardware and technical assistance received under bilateral assistance as part of counter-terrorism measures. Assistance has come from India in the forms of arms and ammunition, mine-protected vehicles and trucks, advanced light helicopters, and communications system. The UK has provided MI-17 non-lethal helicpters and the American assistance consists of guns, communication systems and other logistics assistance. Since 1996, the total strength of the army and police has increased by about 80 per cent.

The turning point occurred on 23 November 2001 when the Maoists, in a daring attack, destroyed the Royal Nepal Army garrison in Dang and looted sophisticated arms and ammunitions. After this massacre, the issue which was previously viewed as a problem of law and order, became a national security concern. The Nepal Police, which had been deployed to resolve the issue, was now replaced by the expanded Royal Nepal Army (RNA). The expansion of the RNA has taken various forms.[6] First, the size of the army has recorded significant growth from about 50,000 in number to 85,000 by 2004. In recent years, the RNA has added 3 new divisions and five brigades. Second; the increased number has been accompanied by a sophistication in its arsenal and improvements in its facilities. Third, a concept of Unified Command, under which all security forces including the civil and armed police come under the overall command of the army, has been introduced. The concept was mooted to optimise the capabilities and resources available with the government forces from the centre down to the district level under the army's operational control. The total size of the civilian police is about 50,000 and that of armed police 18,000. The most serious aspect that distinguishes Nepal's situation in the current political scenario from that of other South Asian countries, particularly India and Sri Lanka, however, is the absence of elected civilian government, and the attendant parliamentary control. Such a situation tends to encourage the propensity for militarism and militarization. A political analyst observes:

> This is exactly a situation in which a weak and fragile government can be forced to comply and made subsevient to the interest of armed forces. This situation has therefore given rise to militarism in Nepal. Militarism begins with the threats of sanctions (non-cooperation), if the government does not cooperate to the military demands. This is, in other words, the high-handed technique that the military uses when the reliance of the government increases on the armed forces. Nepal provides an ideal situation for the army to bankroll its needs, as the government is unpopular, illegitimate, isolated and moribund that cannot survive a day the army pulls out its support. This is the classic situation of "blackmail' that Samuel Finer had noted by suggesting that the "armed forces in fact begins to rule covertly, either by exercising a veto or by substituting policies and personnel of their choice for those of the de jure government" (Finer 1962). The RNA, as it should be noted, has already acquired such an extreme position in the national decision making process through the developoment of the Unified Military Command System.[7]

In all fairness, the situation is not the making of the army or any member of Nepal's security apparatus. The militarization from the Maoists' side has been more serious. The government's military operation was simply a response to the Maoist offensive since the attack on Dang, followed by similar adventurism in other police and army installations. In fact, a section of the Nepali opinion never favoured the mobilization of the army to counter the Maoists even when the latter were organizing themselves along military lines. They naively believed that the police force on its own could deal with the problem. I recall an occasion in 1999 when I was invited at the Army Headquarters, together with the Prime Minister and Home Minister for a briefing about the army prognosis and assessment of the Maoist problem. The Chief of Army Staff expressed his readiness to offer any service that the government may decide in this respect. The proposal was not immediately followed up since the police force was expected to deal with this problem. When the problem appeared beyond police control, the government was considering the army deployment. But then the Chief of Army Staff threw a spanner by talking of an 'all party consensus' and the declaration of a state of emergency as preconditions before any army mobilization.

As described in a separate chapter, the Maoist military strength has undergone phenomenal growth and expansion—graduating from a rag-tag militia numbering a few hundred equipped with looted country guns to become an effective force with the capabilty of inflicting heavy damage on the state. The estimates on Maoist military strength includes 4000 armed guerillas, 5000 militias trained as guerillas, and 20,000 unarmed militias. They have three Divisions in Western, Eastern and Central regions, with three brigades each. There are 29 battalions each with the strength of 300 to 350 combatants. Their weapon holdings comprise a total of 3300 units, including 322 7.62 mm SLRs, 9 mm SMG, 132 7.62 SMGS, 42 7.62 LMGS, 1370 303 Rifles, INSAS, pistols, revolvers, shotguns, home-made guns, AK 47s, and various forms of mortars and rocket bombs.[8] Their arsenal was sourced primarily from their loot from security forces, indigenous manufactures, and clandestine commercial purchases. They have extensively used landmines, improvised country bombs, electronic detonators, and explosives against the security forces. In 32 armed combat operations with the security forces starting from the first attack in Ghorahi of Dang to the attack in Mugu in October 2004, the Maoists have made their mark by looting arms and ammunitions from the state forces which has raised their possession of the Galil, M16s, and INSAS rifles along with expensive weapons, including 81 mm mortars.[9]

SECURITY: A BROADER CONCEPT

This phenomenon of increased militarization and security spending is most unfortunate at a time when the emphasis is on the broader concept of security with people at the centre stage. The traditional definition of security with a focus on military and strategic consideration is no longer considered sufficient. The UNDP Human Development Report of 1994 broadened the definition of human security by focussing on such aspects as security from hunger, disease, malnutrition, natural calalmities, crime, joblessness, and fear. National security, therefore, is increasingly dependent on human security, which in turn is linked with job security, income security, environmental security, and security against crimes. Mahbub Ul Haque says:

> Ideally, there need not be a conflict between national and human security, since the essence of real security lies in safeguarding peoples not just in safeguarding borders. But a conflict can arise if the military/social spending tilts in favour of military spending and if a delicate balance between defense and development is disrupted.[10]

The mighty Soviet Union crumbled when human aspirations for more freedom, better jobs, and economic well-being could not be met. Other countries which invested heavily in the armies rather than in their people have met similar fate. For example, the military to social spending ratio in 1980 was among the highest in Iraq (8 times), Somalia (5 times), and Nicaragua (3.5 times). All three countries failed to protect their national sovereignty, territorial integrity, and the welfare of people despite the liberal acquisition of arms and expansion of their armies. On the other hand, Costa Rica, which spent nothing on its military, having abolished it in 1948, spent one-third of its national income on education, nutrition, and health during the last few decades. It now remains the only prosperous democracy in a troubled Central America. South Asia today is one of the most militarized regions of the world, but that does not make the region any more secure. National security cannot be achieved in a situation where people starve and arms accumulate and where the state spends more on defence and less on social development. Like the concept of development, the concept of security too has increasingly become people-centred.[11]

It is observed that insecurity emanates from vulnerabilities which need not necessarily be related to inter-state or intra-state conflicts. It could come from from a variety of other sources and still destroy vital institutions, political order, and national sovereignty. The weaknesses of South Asian countries, and more so of Nepal, arise from their internal problems—failure of the state, poverty and unemployment, slow development, poor or non-delivery of essential services to the people, exclusion and deprivation, and minority discrimination. The increasing disparities and dualism in the distribution of national wealth and income, rampant corruption, erosion of institutions, and the increasing influence of external forces in decision making are other sources of insecurity. Security of a nation state, therefore, depends on the extent to which the basic needs, desires and aspirations of the people are met, and when a sense of justice and equality is meted out to diverse communities and regions.

> South Asia is equally deeply engulfed into human security concerns. All the three concerns of human security namely; security of life and freedom from fear, freedom from want and search for quality of life, and lastly, security of environment are present in South Asia. Loss of life in raging insurgencies like the Maoist rebellion in Nepal and the ethnic war in Sri-Lanka has been phenomenal. Communal antagonism has played its ugly role in internal violence in South Asian countries like in India's Gujarat state...The instances in South Asia of poor farmers commiting suicide and families selling their daughters for prostitution due to poverty are galore. There are also food riots and hunger deaths. And such instances are not confined to single country.[12]

SOCIAL COST AND SUSTAINABILITY

High security spending has its own economic and human costs. Excessive military spending preempts resources from more productive investment in social and economic sectors. Consequently, the share of scarce public resources available for sustainable development is reduced. This in turn fuels economic insecurity, which could be the source of internal instability, thereby leading to a vicious circle of enhanced military spending to contain social unrest. A disproportionate share of public spending on defence will mean foregone social and economic opportunities for people, leading to lower economic growth, higher levels of illiteracy, infant mortality, and short life expectancy. Therefore, higher military spending is also recognized as one important factor in limiting poverty reduction.

On the positive side, military spending can offer some economic improvements through technological innovation, modernization of civilian industries, and building of physical infrastructure. However, this is possible only in countries with a relatively developed military industry and a good manufacturing base. In a small country with a low industrial base and a high propensity to import military hardware, such positive impacts are negligible.

Furthermore, corruption in arms procurement deals is a well-known phenomenon. Nation states have a tendency to treat security spending with secrecy. Procurement decisions are often based on foreign policy preferences rather than technical criteria. This allows the military decision-makers and their civilian counterparts to hide financial interests behind the claim of national security. "The global arms bazaars, underpinned by powerful economic interests, reinforce excessive secrecy and corruption in many countries' security sectors".[13] Questions are being raised about the lack of transparency in hardware procurement by the RNA leading to purchase of materials motivated by ulterior financial interests rather than by their appropriateness to the Nepali conditions. A lot of communications equipment and other materials are reported to be lying unused. In Nepal, relatives of the Palace functionaries and military top brass often act as commission agents in such procurements.[14]

It would, of course, be simplistic to attribute South Asia's poverty and underdevelopment entirely to its conflict situation and militarization. There are also other good reasons behind its backwardness. However, it would be interesting to make a comparison with East Asia which, starting on the development path under similar conditions in the 1950s, has now given a higher standard of living for its people and boasts one of the highest economic growth rates in the world.

South Asia today is the most populous and poorest region of the world. With 22 per cent of the global population, it contains 40 per cent of the world's absolute poor. Its adult literacy rate of 48 per cent lags behind 55 per cent in Sub-Saharan Africa, and 98 per cent of East Asia (excluding China). South Asia's per-capita income is US $309, compared to $555 in Sub-Saharan Africa, and more than US $10,000 in East Asia (excluding China). The gap in the per-capita incomes between South Asia and East Asia (excluding China) has widened from US $200 in 1960 to US $9,700 in 1993. While factors like higher investment in human capital, outward looking trade strategies, land reforms, prudent fiscal and monetary management, and investment friendly policies explain the success stories of East Asia, another important factor contributing to its growth is the high priority given to economic and development issues. In 1992, public expenditure on education in South Asia as percentage of GNP stood at 3.4 per cent, compared to 2 per cent in 1960. Comparatively, East Asia was already spending 3.7 per cent of GNP on education in 1960 and by 1992, it had already risen to 4.4 per cent. Military spending as percentage of combined expenditure on health and education in South Asia stood at 72 in 1991, down from 113 in 1960. In East Asia, the decline was much sharper from 273 in 1960 to 49 in 1990.[15] The World Development Report 2000/01 estimates that military spending as percentage of GNP in South Asia has remained constant at 3.1 per cent during 1992–97, while it declined from 2.9 per cent to 2.5 per cent in East Asia and the Pacific.

Conditions such as deprivation, economic and social exclusion, and a sense of discrimination among excluded groups offer fertile ground for radical ideas and philosophies which lay down the foundation for conflicts. Conflict and deprivation are mutually reinforcing. Conflict destroys the productive capacity, distorts resource allocation, and hampers future growth thus resulting in more deprivation and poverty. This further intensifies the conflict. Conflict is openly violent and economic deprivation is potentially so. South Asia has the highest concentration of global poverty and human deprivation, yet it continuously invests a disproportionate amount of resources on security. With such uneven distribution of development benefits, it is no surprise that the region is one of the conflict-prone hotspots on earth.

The armed conflict and the consequent physical insecurity in all aspects of national life in Nepal has led to a reordering of national priorities. Instead of economic development, security through militarization has assumed the centre stage. The large security expenditure has put heavy pressure on fiscal resources. To meet these costs, the government has raised taxes, diverted funds from the development budget, and resorted to extra-borrowings. This has placed the economic reform process in jeopardy. Macroeconomic stability has been disturbed due to rising fiscal deficit, widening current account deficit, discrepancies in trade account, and an increasing debt burden. Thankfully, large-scale programme lending and extra budgetary support from the donor community have somewhat eased budgetary pressure.

Statistics based on budgetary figures that were published by government sources show that the combined police and military expenditure as percentage of GDP increased from 1.8 per cent in 1990/91 to 2.3 in 2001/02. However, the actual expenditure is far greater than that shown in the budget. There is a proclivity to under-report defence spending and camouflage defense-related expenses under civilian headings. Allocation for various items including arms, ammunitions, communication equipment, flying equipment, and new recruitments are made through extra-budgetary arrangements, which in recent years have represented an additional 20 to 30 per cent of what's reported. In the current fical year 2004/05, the additional security budget of 8 billion rupees was demanded, which is equivalent to 50 per cent increase to the budgeted figure. The per capita defence expenditure including non-budgetary allocation is approximately US $4 at present. Although this figure is not high by South Asian standards, it should nevertheless be viewed against the traditionally low military spending of Nepal, and the displaced social investment in a country whose per capita income is already the lowest in the region. Furthermore, the assistance extended under bilateral arrangements are not reflected in these figures either. The expanding size of the armed forces and police has not only meant additional allocations, but also added a huge budgetary liability with implications for future sustainability.

Given the limitations of the existing system to deal with guerilla warfare, the need for a strengthened security force capable of stronger counter insurgency operations can hardly be exaggerated. This will require proper weaponry and logistics suited to the kingdom's terrain. A paramilitary force in the form of armed-police has been set up. There are plans to increase the size of the army to 100,000, with simultanous increases in police and the armed police. The question, however, is one of the sustainability of rising military spending against competing claims from critical social sectors. A recent decision by the RNA inviting tenders to supply military hardware including tanks and armoured gunship helicopter/aircraft has already provoked controversy and debate.[16]

The implications of a large army and unsupervised weaponry is not confined to questions of its immediate rationale and long-term sustainability. The increased firepower and the nationwide deployment of the army are giving them a status in national affairs which it never enjoyed in the recent past. Several controversial statements on political matters attributed to a past Army Chief raised serious questions about the army's political neutrality, and confirmed the widely-held suspicion that increased military strength enhances the aggressive behaviour of regimes. Furthermore, one of the principal demands by the Maoists for settlement is the integration of their own 'people's army' into the RNA to transform the present army into a true national army under civilian control. This proposition is questionable on political, practical, and economic grounds, and may not find acceptance across political lines. Nonetheless, these are not good signs. The country cannot sustain such a huge army and therefore, some scholars have already started making proposals for de-militarization. They think that the best option will be a significant reduction in the defense forces, and demobilization of insurgents, either unilaterally or through negotiation between the warring parties. Others have proposed a third option of total demilitarization, demobilization, and democratization (a la Costa Rica) for Nepal's peaceful future.[17]

PEACE DIVIDEND!

Resources are often fungible and easily transferable to other uses. Defence spending has alternative uses that involve significant opportunity costs. Every rupee spent on defence implies foregone economic and social opportunities. Naturally, a decline in military expenditure will release resources for other priority programmes. Mahbub Ul Haque estimated[18] that India and Pakistan increased their military budget at the rate of 6 per cent per annum over the five decades since their independence. A freeze or a cut-down in military expenditure by 5 per cent through mutual agreement, would release a peace dividend of US $80 to 125 billion over a period 1997–2010. If a Mirage 2000–5 is not purchased, it would be possible to extend primary education for 3 million children with that money. A similar estimate for Nepal shows that the cost of an M-16 gun would be enough to supply medicines requirement of a village dispensary for one year, or to immunize 900 children against a deadly disease.[19]

South Asia is the home of 44 per cent of the world's poorest who live on less than US $1 a day. In recognizing poverty as the most serious problem of modern times, the UN General Assembly has committed itself to the objective of halving the global poverty by the year 2015. The other components of the Millenium Goals are universal primary education, the elimination of gender disparity in primary and secondary education, the reduction of infant and child mortality by two-thirds, maternal mortality by three quarters, universal access to reproductive health, and the reversal of the loss of environmental resources.

To achieve these goals, we require actions that accelerate growth, reduce income inequality, and increase investments in human development programmes. Securitization and militarization in the midst of extreme poverty is not only ironic but also anachronistic. The security of human beings against poverty, hunger, malnutrition, and illiteracy are no less important than security against lethal enemy attacks. A state, while protecting its citizens against conflicts, also has the responsibility to address the causes of such conflicts. Poverty is not just an economic issue but it is also a result of social, political, and cultural processes whose interactions could worsen or ease the deprivation of the poor. Therefore, anti-poverty goal calls for actions to enhance opportunities, empowerment, and security in political, social, and economic contexts.

Investment in armed forces will have to be balanced with provisions for human development needs. An imbalance between defence expenditure and human development programs will only deepen poverty, the root cause of instability. Conventional military security is necessary, but not at the cost of social concerns. Inefficiency, wastage, and wasteful practices will have to be reduced and eventually eliminated. If political determination is forthcoming for mututal restraints of military build-up, estimates show that a potential peace dividend in the order of US $5–8 billion would be possible in South Asia. In Nepal alone, a proper restructuring of security budget could release a peace dividend of Rs.3–4 billion if the security strength could be reverted to the pre-insurgency levels. However, this is only possible with a commitment from all sides to settle for a genuinely sustainable peace within the framework of a representative and participatory democracy capable of addressing the legitimate aspirations of all communities.

NOTES

1. The World bank, *The World Development Report 2000-2001*, p. 50.
2. SIPRI *Yearbook 2002.*
3. Numbers reflect 1998 prices.
4. Ibid.
5. Sridhar Khatri, 'What is the 'New' Security Agenda for South Asia?', paper presented in the seminar on Non-Traditional Security in South Asia, organised by NCCS in Kathmandu, 16–17 November 2004.
6. For an elaborate discussion on the subject, see Druba Kumar, 'Trenches of Violence: Militancy, Militarism and Militarization of Social Sphere in Nepal', paper presented at the seminar on Non-traditional Security in South Asia by NCCS on 16–17 November 2004 Kathmandu.
7. Dhruba Kumar, ibid.
8. Gen. Sadip Shah's presentation at the India International Centre Conference on 7–8 December, 2005.
9. Ibid.
10. Mahbub Ul Haque, *Human Development Report in South Asia,* Oxford University Press, 1997, p. 84.
11. Ibid.
12. S.D. Muni, 'Human Security in South Asia', paper presented at NCCS seminar in Kathmandu 16–17 November 2004.
13. UNDP, *Human Development Report, 2002*, p. 89.
14. Report by Subash Devkota and Sarad Adhikari, *Samaya,* Nepali weekly, Marg 10, 2061.
15. Mahbub Ul Haque (1997), p14.
16. Kanak Dixit, a leading journalist wrote: The country seems to be caught in headlong rush towards an unsupervised, unrestricted military build-up that it can ill afford. One wonders if there is proper discussion even within the military command about the need for and implications of adding tanks, helicopter gunships or bombers to the arsenal. What seems to be deliberate

plan to acquire such weaponry must be questioned primarily because of the lethal internal consequences, both in military terms and the larger inter-institutional equilibrium of the state *The Nepali Times*, 16–22 May, 2003.

17. Dhruba Kumar, 'The Necessity of Choice: Demobilization, Demilitarization and Democratization in Nepal,' *Journal of Contemporary Studies*, Kathmandu, March 2003.
18. Mahbub Ul Haque (1997).
19. Dhruba Kumar, op. cit

Chapter Fourteen

The Maoist War

In an interview to a revolutionary magazine on 20 February 2000, Prachanda, the supreme leader of the Communist Party of Nepal (Maoist) boasted: after the counter-revolution in China, Nepal's People's War may be "a spark for a prairie fire". In a desert of revolutionary war, he added, "it offers a glass of water for all revolutionary people". According to him, Nepal has now become "a country of proletarian heroes". Further, he proudly asserted: soon the revolutionary red flag would be flying on top of the Mount Everest, the highest peak in the world.[1]

Prachanda's optimism was based on the initial success of the Maoist war, which made progressive growth in subsequent years. A movement, which started from a very rudimentary form, has grown by astronomical proportions and now threatens to effectively challenge the power of the state. Although the Maoists planned their offensive meticulously from the very beginning, based on their knowledge and thorough analysis of the theoretical and practical sides of the Maoist war in other countries, much of their strength accrued in the process of war itself. Denouncing the intellectual's tendency of studying and learning before going to war, Prachanda said:

> This is not dialectical materialism. This is not according to the scientific theory of knowledge. The issue is that of learning of war through war itself. Comrade Mao said 'we had nothing first. We had only millet. We ate millet. We had some rifles. And we fought and we captured all these things. We were not clear at that time what to hit and what not to hit.' We went to hit and we learned how to hit. We also tried to do things in this way.[2]

DYNAMICS OF GROWTH

Progression

The Maoists started their People's War from 13 February 1996 with raids on the police stations in Rolpa, Rukum and Jajarkot and capture of the Small Farmers Development Programme offices in Gorkha and Sindhuli. The land ownership documents of the farmers used as collateral for loans were captured and distributed to the farmers and loan records were destroyed. Prior to this, a leaflet was distributed throughout the country calling the people to 'march along the path of People's War to smash the reactionary state and establish a democratic state'. The stated objectives of the War were to confront 'three mountains', namely, (*i*) remove the bureaucratic-capitalist class and the state system; (*ii*) uproot semi-feudalism, and; (*iii*) drive out imperialism, in order to establish a New Democratic Republic with the view to establish a new socialist society. To achieve their objective, they adopted the Maoist strategy of establishing bases in rural and remote areas aiming to eventually surround the urban centres and seize state power. Another Maoist military principle they adhered to is the Protracted People's War consisting of three strategic stages, namely, strategic defense, strategic balance and strategic offence. Each strategic stage was further divided into sub-phases and within these, tactical action plans were defined.[3]

During the second stage, they started developing guerilla zones, capturing weapons, and annihilating selected 'enemies'—local tyrants, policemen, and informers. Attacks on police stations and the looting of weapons from the village population went side by side. In the third stage, the guerilla war was further extended with programs to boycott the local election and force the resignation of elected officials. Buoyed by the fair degrees of success achieved at this stage, they then started installing their own peoples' governments to take over the functions of the Village Development Committees (VDCs).

The formation of the Central Military Commission was announced in February 1998. During the fourth stage in February 1999, they formally announced the formation of the People's Army. They were also forming strategic base areas to launch military offensives that gradually began increasing in scope, scale and intensity. They started forming three distinct fighting forces—the main force at platoon level under a commissar, a secondary force at the squad level, and a stationary base force comprising of the militia. At the political level, the principle of three-in-one committee, i.e. the party, the fighting force and the united front consisting of members of frontal organizations was applied. The fifth plan period saw the purification process when the 'rightist deviations' were eliminated. During the sixth sub-phase, the Maoists launched a large number of guerilla raids, sabotage, annihilations, ambushes and kidnappings. The process of strengthening the base areas continued. A number of surprise raids were launched against the police stations with increasing precision and sophistication.

It was during this phase on 25 September 2000 that about 1000 Maoist guerillas successfully attacked Dunai, the district headquarters of Dolpa, in which 14 policemen were killed, 41 wounded and 12 missing. This was until then the biggest and the most successful military operation from their perspective, and they still consider it of 'universal significance among the successes gained after the restoration of capitalism in China'.[4]

The Second National Conference of the Maoists in February 2001, held against the backdrop of these successes, elevated the position of Prachanda from the General Secretary to the Party Chairman. The guiding principle of their revolution was now christened 'Prachandapath', which represented "the centralized expression of collective leadership and Prachanda's correct and continuing leadership". This doctrine, according to them, represents a set of ideas and experiences from Nepal's five years of revolution in the sense that it is an embodiment of creative Marxism, opposed to right revisionists and sectarian dogmatists and an enrichment of Marxism-Leninism and Maoism.

Subsequent to that, more daring attacks were mounted on army barracks and armed police concentrations. Most notable offensives took place in Salleri of Solukhumbu district, Ratamata of Rukum, Bhakundebesi of Kavre, Sanfebagar and Mangalsen of Achham, Sitalpati of Salyan, Gam of Rolpa, Khara of Rukum, Sandikharka of Arghakhanchi, Ghorahi and Satbaria of Dang, Bhojpur, Okhaldhunga and Beni in which massive human and material losses were reported on both sides. In September 2001, the People's Army was renamed People's Liberation Army, and a central headquarters set up with "general staff and logistics department" under the supreme commandership of Prachanda. A fighting force that began with a few rifles now boasts three divisions, nine brigades and 29 battalions, equipped with semi-automatic SLRs and rocket launchers looted from the police and the army barracks, and some even procured from abroad.[5] The Maoists announced formation of 37-member United People's Revolutionary Council under the leadership of Babu Ram Bhattarai. This was in practical terms an alternative government of the Maoists.

Subjective Preparation

A section of the Nepali society has always been attracted to the radical communist philosophy. Inspired by the Chinese revolution and radical communists in India, the Communist Party of Nepal was founded as early as September 1949. However, the Nepali communists soon started a moderate line, a 'revisionist deviation' in the radical lexicon. The Cultural Revolution in China greatly inspired the Nepali youth. Nepal was the centre and conduit of radical literature coming from China in those days. The Naxalite Movement of West Bengal led by Charu Mazumdar was another source of inspiration that led a radical communist group in Nepal to launch an armed uprising against the landed interest in Jhapa district in the early seventies to eliminate 'class enemies'. This radical communist group formed a nucleus of what was to become the largest communist party of Nepal, the Communist Party of Nepal (ML), now UML. At that time, the prominent Maoist leaders of today were still part of the mainstream Communist Party of Nepal, fighting against its 'revisionist' leadership. The internal rebellion by a radical group led to the formation of the Communist Party of Nepal (Fourth Congress) in 1974, under the leadership of Mohan Bikram Singh, a legendary communist leader from the hill region of the mid-west, an area which presently remains the base of the People's War. The Thawang village of Rolpa district, which is the epicenter of the Maoist movement, was Singh's operational headquarters from as early as 1955. He used the place for spreading the communist ideology, developing the party organization, organizing peasant movements and embracing *Kham-Magars*, one of the most neglected and isolated ethnic communities which would later become the most ferocious Maoist fighting force in that region.

From the very beginning, the party believed in armed rebellion. In 1979 Nirmal Lama, another veteran communist, took over party leadership from Singh. The party split again in 1983, with Singh making his own party NCP (*Masal*). It was in this year that Revolutionary International Movement was founded, with *Masal* as one of the founding members. There was further break-up in 1985 between NCP (*Masal*), led by Singh and NCP (*Mashal*) led by Mohan Vaidya. The latter branded the Singh group as a revisionist, and adopted the doctrine of violent armed movement for mass uprising. Subsequently, Pushpa Kamal Dahal (now known as Prachanda) took over the party leadership from Vaidya as the General Secretary. The RIM membership was also given to this faction (*Mashal*), as RIM considered the *Masal* as revisionist. This group, presently under the name of Communist Party of Nepal (Maoist), represents the nucleus of the leadership of the People's War. During the People's Movement of 1990, the three radical left parties including the Fourth Congress, *Mashal* and a breakaway faction from Masal led by Dr. Babu Ram Bhattarai formed a new party, the CPN (Unity Centre), with Prachanda as General Secretary. Even as the Unity Centre and its hardcore leaders remained underground, it formed United People's Front Nepal (UPFN) as a political front to contest in the parliamentary election with the objective of 'exposing parliamentary inadequacies and hypocrisy'. This front won 9 seats in the 205-member House of Representatives. In December 1991, the "unity congress" of the Unity Centre passed a resolution for a "protracted people's war for carrying out the New Democratic Revolution in a country with a Marxist–Leninist–Maoist ideological perspective".[6] The Centre further split in 1994, one led by Prachanda and the other by Nirmal Lama. Their political front, the UPFN, was also divided between Babu Ram Bhattarai and Niranjan Govinda Vaidya factions. The Election Commission recognized the Vaidya faction as the legitimate UPFN. Following this, the Unity Centre gave up its electoral politics through UPFN and went underground completely. In its third plenum in March 1995, the party renamed itself the Communist Party of Nepal (Maoists) and decided to concentrate all efforts for the development of the people's war for the "true liberation of people".

Poverty and Remoteness

Describing the economic conditions of the small area in Mid-Western Nepal considered the Maoist heart-land, an area he calls the Red Zone, Robert Gersony says:

> The Red Zone is heavily forested, mountainous area, which achieves a maximum altitude of almost 6900 meters ...The Red Zone comprises 1600 kilometers, 1% of Nepal's territory...
>
> Not a single motorable road serves the Red Zone. Thawang is a two-day walk along the mule track from the Ropla district headquarters, Liwang. Until 2003, there was not a single road anywhere in Rukum district. In May 2003, the first road to serve the district, constructed by Royal Nepal Army (RNA) was completed, connecting Rukum's capital, Musikot, with an existing road in neighboring Salyan District.
>
> Since the 1980s, Rolpa's Southeastern corner has had a few agricultural feeder roads connecting it to neighboring districts and perhaps one-track leading to Liwang. Its first major road from Dang to Rolpa's capital, Liwang was inaugurated in 2002. Both the fractured terrain and lack of road access made these districts, and the Red Zone in particular, advantageous for a rural insurgency'. The Red Zone's population is overwhelmingly *Magar* ethnic group'. But the terrain is so fractured, and the population so isolated, that the *Magars* of the Red Zone and its

> surrounding areas speak a different language—called *Kham*—which is distinct and mutually unintelligible from mainstream *Magar.*
>
> Historically, the population of the Red Zone's northern reaches was engaged more in sheep herding than farming, and the religious faith of most is described by local residents as more animist than Hindu?Only about 10 per cent of Rolpa and Rukum 's land is considered arable. In the Red Zone, local population farm parcels of a quarter or half hectare, eking out of poor quality rain-fed manure-fertilized soil just enough basic grains and potatoes to feed their families for three to six months. In these chronic food-deficit areas, as in most hill area of western Nepal, they must rely on other sources of income to bridge the food gap and to but salt, oil, clothes and educational supplies for their children, In a country among the poorest in the world, Red Zone residents consider themselves among the most deprived.[7]

Sheep farming as a profession was declining with the diminishing volume of grazing land due to overgrazing and expanding population. Other sources of income were mining (for iron), the British Gorkha service, and hashish cultivation. Iron mining started getting difficult in the 1970s, as the hardwood needed for charcoal (used in smelting raw iron) became scarce because of increasing deforestation. This, coupled with the availability of cheap industrially produced iron products, forced the iron mines to close. Recruitment in the British Gorkha and the Indian army, which offered some employment, was also diminishing. For a long time until the early 1970s, cultivation of hashish offered an important source of income for the people of this area. The marijuana harvested here was renowned for its quality all over the world. The passage of the Drug Act in 1976, however, prohibited the production, sale, and distribution of hashish. After that, whatever little was produced illegally was taxed heavily by the police and the corrupt elements in the administration, effectively depriving families of the Red Zone of what used to be a lucrative income source. In recent years, the harvest and sale of *yarshagunbu* (cordyceps *sinensis)*[8], a tiny insect (used as energy enhancer and anti impotency substance) that grows underneath high altitude meadows in winter has emerged as a substitute for the traditional hashish cultivation as a source of local cash income. In its season, thousands of residents from northern Rukum and Rolpa flock to the highland meadows to harvest the product, which is ultimately marketed to China and India. The Maoists have now interposed themselves as intermediary dealers in the trade and have profited from the business[9].

Whether it is the core Red area or any other region where the Maoists have influence, remoteness and economic backwardness are the principal characteristics. Nepal's rugged geography of mountains and

Photograph 23: Teacher Mukti Nath Adhikary
of Lamjung killed by the Maoists

deep valleys, extensive forest cover, scattered settlements untouched by modern transport and communication facilities offer an excellent habitat for the Maoist guerillas to operate and expand. The midwestern hill region, which is considered the stronghold of the Maoists, is the most inaccessible region of Nepal: people have to walk for numerous days to reach the nearest road head or even an airport. Even the district headquarters of the midwestern hills were not connected by road until the early nineties.

This remoteness is accompanied by the virtual absence of civil and security administration of the state which makes it easy for the Maoists to operate unchallenged. Even where some security administration existed, surprise guerilla raids on the security posts forced them to retreat and withdraw to more secure places like the district headquarters. The administrative void thus created was then filled by the rebels. They started making people's committees and people's government in such areas to run their own administration in "an exercise of people's power". These committees handled most functions of the local government—administrative, social, cultural and educational. The land captured from the absentee landlords and feudal interests were distributed on cooperative basis to the people. They also collected taxes from everybody including the tourists. Extortion money was collected from practically everybody—school teachers, government employees, traders, and farmers.

Radical philosophy draws strong appeal in a poor society. When poverty is accentuated by perceptible neglect from the state, the appeal grows stronger. Even if the state had been more sympathetic, Nepal's difficult geography, particularly in the remote Midwestern hills would have presented, and continue to present a formidable development challenge. In the absence of the basic infrastructure like road access, access to other social and economic services is also restricted in these far flung regions. Even when state-provided services can be accessed, the quality of delivery of these services has been poor and ineffective. Implementation of successive development plans since 1956 has not brought about significant change on the lives of the people, especially at a time when the communication revolution and democratic exercise have inflamed popular expectations of the population. The economic growth and development have not been sufficient to create enough job opportunities to the labour force that enters the job market. The Maoists find easy recruits in these unemployed, and subsequently, disenchanted youth.

Forty-two per cent of the population was below the poverty line in 1996. This aggregate national figure, however, veiled sharper spatial disparities as the prevalence of poverty in the underdeveloped mid-western and the far-western regions were 56 and 46 per cent respectively. Disaggregated human development data show that the mid-western and far-western regions remain economically and socially the most deprived regions of the country with HDI scores of 0.402 and 0.385 respectively, against the national average of 0.466. Data by eco-development region shows that the mid-western and far-western mountains remain the most backward zones with 0.322 and 0.286 HDI respectively. Around the time when the Maoist movement started in 1996, the HDI in the Rapti Zone of mid-western region stood at 0.276. That same year, the average HDI of the five hill districts most infested by the Maoists—Rukum, Rolpa, Salyan, Jajarkot and Kalikot—0.234, and their respective ranking among 75 districts of Nepal were: 58th, 60th, 63rd, 71st and 73rd.[10]

Ethnicity, Gender and Exploitation Theory

The Maoists have correctly identified the weaknesses and fault-lines of the Nepali society and used them to their advantage. They have exploited the feeling of discrimination and exclusion among the *Dalits,* the ethnic *Janjatis*, and the *tarai Madhesis.* The monopolization of the state and administrative power by the urban-based socially advanced caste groups has led to the neglect of the geographically remote regions, which traditionally enjoyed autonomy and independence in their administration. The *Brahminical* Hindu tradition, by imposing social restrictions on women, has provided cultural foundation for gender discrimination. The Maoists have particularly targeted the *Dalits* in their political mobilization as the *Dalits*, among other disadvantaged groups bear the greatest brunt of caste discrimination, low literacy, landlessness and lack of political power. In order to sharpen social cleavages and mobilize the ethnic frustrations and aspirations to their cause, they have formed various front organizations along ethnic and regional lines. These include the *Kirat* National Liberation Front, the *Magarat* Liberation Front, the *Tharuwan* National Liberation Front, the *Tamuwan* National Liberation Front, the *Tamang* National Liberation Front, the *Majhi* National Liberation Front, the *Thami* National Liberation Front, the *Madhesi* National Liberation Front, and the Karnali Regional Liberation Front. All these fronts have been promised the right to self-determination. Organizationally, these fronts are coordinated by the CPN (Maoist) Ethnic and Regional Coordination Council. It is not mere coincidence that most of these ethnic groups are of Mongoloid origin; they have been carefully chosen, not only because of their traditional exclusion and neglect, but also in view of their martial tradition. That they do not suffer from caste and other Hindu inhibitions is an added bonus.

Serious doubts, however, exist about the Maoist commitment to the minority cause. There are indications of emerging conflicts between the large ethnic base in the Maoist War and their upper-caste dominated leadership on the one hand, and the ethnic emphasis on pluralism as opposed to the communist centralization and absolute intolerance to opposition on the other. The Maoists have also been blamed for failing to raise the *Madhesi* issues effectively and for promoting the cult of violence. Recently, the ethnic organizations like the *Tarai Mukti Morcha* and the *Kirat* Workers Party have broken off alliance with the Maoists. Another splinter group called *Madhesi* Tigers has emerged. Prominent ethnic scholars argue that the sole rationale behind the Maoists championing minority issues was the calculated need to expand their limited political base. The Maoists have exploited the frustrations and grievances of the minority to overcome the difficulty of narrow base. When they started the insurgency in a patrimonial society, most of political activists were already aligned with major political parties. Therefore, they had to raise new issues in order to recruit members for their organization. It is also noted that the ratio of indigenous nationalities killed by the Maoists is the same as by the government forces. Of the total number of people killed by the security forces in the insurgency, the indigenous community accounted for 32.5 per cent, while among those killed by the Maoists the same subgroup represented 33.2 per cent.[11] The Maoists have not spared the *Dalits* and minority ethnic groups from their atrocities either.

Female participation remains one major highlight of the Maoist war in Nepal. Women are active participants in all fields—political, military and front organizations. They also participate in company, platoons, and battalions. Precise ratio of their participation is not known and is estimated to vary from 12 to 40 per cent. If the number of Maoists killed in combat by the police can be used as a proxy, women represented 96 of the 702 persons killed until February 2002 (12 per cent). Given the fact that women normally are not traditionally involved in violent operations, this is a high proportion.[12] The high female participation is attributed to the patrimonial nature of the Nepali society that subjects women to economic, social, and political discrimination and oppression. As Marx said, the root of slavery was born in the womb of the family structure itself as it is from the family that the ill-treatment and subordination of women begins. Therefore, they believe that women themselves must be involved in the destruction of existing values and order.

Some of the women's issues raised by the Maoists to attract their participation are: the absence of women right on parental property, high level of women involvement on both farm and household chores, unequal payment for equal job, and the vulnerability of low caste women to sexual exploitation. The high level of son preference because of the prevailing inheritance law, female discrimination resulting in high maternal mortality, early marriage, restricted female mobility under Hindu tradition, and extremely low level of female participation in social and political life are the other issues championed by the Maoists to enlist female participation. Although the discrimination along cultural and other issues such as access to household resources is not uniform among ethnic and cultural groups, the discrimination with regard to access to personal property cuts across all groups. The conservative Hindu social practices such as the arranged marriage, and the prohibition of remarriages after widowhood have further helped propagate the Maoist message. Additionally, the sexual freedom, the right to choose husbands, and the attraction of revolutionary culture and life style are also important attractions for the women joining the Maoist militia.[13]

As the Maoist movement is directed against the feudal *Brahminical* Hindu rule, the People's Democracy promises them complete emancipation from all social, economic, cultural and political suppression and discrimination. They have targeted the ethnic communities of Tibeto-Burman origin, particularly the *Magars*, and the *Dalit* communities for their recruitments where the social rigidities of the Indo–Aryan Hindu tradition do not exist. Prachanda has acknowledged that they were not so serious about the women issues in the beginning. The true potential of women as militants and active members of the revolutionary force was realized in course of the struggle itself, and subsequently the question was seriously debated and recognized.[14]

The woman participation in the Maoist war has not been without negative consequences. Sexual abuse and unwanted sex is a common complaint made by the women who have escaped the Maoist camps[15]. Women and children are generally used as human shields when attacking police posts and military garrisons. Women are often used to carry heavy loads of arms, food and other war materials. The pain and agony suffered by pregnant militia women, and health care problems during and after childbirth in the midst of violence and terror offer the other side of the story.[16]

The Maoists have also used the theory of imperialist and capitalist exploitation–historically by the British colonialism through the Treaty of Sugauli of 1816, and since the 1950 by various imperialist powers and Indian 'expansionism' through the Peace and Friendship Treaty of 1950—to justify their war. The destructive effects of expansionary and imperialist forces have been blamed for stunting Nepal's internal development process and by implication, for aggravating the poverty and backwardness. They maintain that the uninterrupted semi-colonial relations with India have had a very negative and destructive effect on the development of class relations and socio-economic structures and, in essence, on the development of national capitalism in Nepal. Therefore, one important objective of the People's War is to break the shackles of semi-colonialism, and usher in a new national capitalism (and a new democracy) by mobilizing people of all ranks and classes suffering under all forms of semi-colonial exploitation and oppression. They use similar semi-colonial and feudal exploitation theories to explain the regional disparities in the development of Nepal—characterized by the existence of vast areas of poor rural areas and limited urban centers and islands of extraverted development. They reconcile the rampant poverty in rural areas with the extravagance seen in urban centers by attributing this phenomenon to the extraction of the surplus product from backward regions, their accumulation in the hands of a few in the urban areas and their ultimate transfer abroad as proceeds for imported foreign products.[17]

METHODS AND RESISTANCE

Despite the strength of their progressive socio-economic agenda, the principal reason for their growth remains their methods, which are coercive, cruel, and mostly brutal. Gersony's observation,[18] based on field interviews in the Red Zone and other outlaying areas, was that outside the Red Zone there was no evidence of critical mass support and substantial political constituency for the Maoists. The apparently unchallenged presence of the Maoists outside the Red Zone was attributed to total absence of stable police or military. The Maoist intimidation and terror made obedience to their instruction the only logical choice as non-compliance was punishable by beatings, abductions, amputation of limbs, and murders. Cutting off the tongue, ears and lips, hammering the teeth, cutting the victims' bodies in half, burning dissenters alive, etc. are normal punishments meted out to suspected informers or 'class enemies'. In some gruesome cases, children were forced to watch as their fathers were tortured to death. A general pattern was found in their methods and this was repeated in a ritualistic manner. The objective of these gruesome 'mutilation atrocities' are mostly demonstrative.[19] These brutalities are meted out also to the *Dalits* and poorest of the poor if they do not subscribe to the Maoist diktats. Political activists, local leaders in the rural areas are selectively targeted for physical liquidation, abduction, physical cruelties, and other punishments in the name of '*Jankarbahi*' (people' action). This has forced a large number of local leaders, school teachers, and social workers to leave the countryside and migrate to more secure areas. Those who remain in the villages are forced to pay protection money and do as the Maoists say.

The terror tactic to force obedience in far-flung villages is accompanied by the complete withdrawal of government security apparatus in these areas. Landmines, ambushes, and booby traps along major highways and routes have curtailed the mobility of security forces to a significant extent. All these have made the isolated countryside virtually the Maoist areas of control. They have successfully established intelligence networks, mobile bases away from the striking distance of the security forces—generally in confluence between three or four districts—and developed elaborate supply lines for the replenishments and evacuation of casualties. Their method of geographically dispersed attacks compel the government forces divide their limited combat power. The modus operandi starts with decentralized actions (ambushes, small raids, extortions, sabotage and assassinations) in the first phase, relatively centralized actions in the second phase, and big scale attacks with maximum force in the third phase to humiliate the government, make the population insecure and apply pressure on the government.[20] Other methods include sabotage, bandhs, and blockades on major supply arteries to cities and towns causing economic destabilization and panic among the population.

Monetary power is one prominent source of Maoist strength. Protection money is raised through extortion from rich businessmen, industrialists, government officials, and practically from everybody with means. Civil servants and teachers who work in places other than secure urban centers are forced to pay monthly levy. This is supplemented by looting banks, financial institutions and households. Kickbacks and levies are raised locally from traders and businessmen regularly. All this has made the Maoists amongst the richest 'terrorist groups' in the world with the 'money bag' of Rs. 5 to 10 billion rupees in the year 2000. The fling with monetary benefits may become a temptation to continue violence and intimidation as has been witnessed in countries engulfed in conflicts.[21].

At places, people have dared to come out openly against the Maoist atrocities. Resistance and protest programmes at the local level took place in the past in places like Tara Khola of Baglung, Dohali of Gulmi,Titeria of Morang, and others. But in the absence of security protection from the state, ultimately they fizzled out when the Maoists began slaughtering the prominent resistance leaders. However, an open and unprecedented defiance on a large scale was organized by women of the Dullu region of Dailekh, one of the districts hit hardest by the Maoist insurgency. The protest spread like wildfire in 15 VDCs of Dailekh. Thousands of women rose, and took out rallies on 18 November 2004, chanting slogans against the Maoist terror and atrocities, beating Maoist area leaders and forcing dozens of office bearers to resign and surrender. Women formed local security committees themselves and began staging round-the clock patrols and vigils. Maoists who harassed local women were hounded and punished. The anti-Maoist movement spread fast in other neighbouring areas also, including in such 'base' and 'model' villages like Naumule, Toli and Salleri VDCs. Armed Maoists retaliated against the leaders of the protest rally the following day by secretly surrounding and storming into the house of Bir Bahadur, where villagers were detailing the structure of retaliation committee against the Maoists. The Maoists killed three locals, including an eight year-old boy in cold blood, injured many and abducted two dozen others. Not to be cowed down, thousands of locals, mostly women, took out anti-Maoist protest rally the very next day.[22]

Immediately following this event, a large-scale anti-Maoist demonstration took place in Baglung district. When the Maoists began drilling (with wood drills) the bodies of some women leaders who had resisted their diktats, the rural women could not tolerate the atrocities any more.[23] An even more daring incident broke out in Sirsihawa and Ganeshpur VDCs of Kapilbastu district on 17 February 2005 when about 5000 local people revolted against the Maoist atrocities by swarming the Maoist hideouts and beating to death 22 Maoists including a district leader[24]. While isolated instances of resistance are heart-warming and encouraging, how long they can sustain without fool-proof security protection remains to be seen.

There has also been negative consequence of this development. The mob in Kapilbastu got out of control and led to vigilant violence with government encouragement, resulting in further killings in front of the security forces and burning of 318 houses of ordinary people. A total of 47 of the 77 VDCs of the district were affected. To escape Maoist retaliation, thousands of villagers fled to India.[25] Resistance and retaliation committee to fight Maoist atrocities were formed with

Photograph 24: Policemen killed by the Maoists

Photograph 25: Maoist guerillas killed by the security forces

government encouragement and support in a number of villages of Nawalparasi. But the ultimate victims of this act have been the innocent civilian people. About 200 armed Maoists attacked the Bargadhawa village at the mid-night of 14 April 2005 killing 10 innocent villagers, torching and destroying their property and houses on suspicion of their being involved in the retaliation committee. The armed members of the retaliation committee, however, escaped[26]. The retaliation committees comprised vigilant groups with criminal records. In the name of fighting the Maoists, they have become a new source of terror for the common people. The gun-totting vigilantes have subjected the innocent villagers to house search, interrogation, torture, extortion and killing. They have also started creating communal rift between the hill and *tarai* populace[27].

COST OF CONFLICT

Widespread poverty and backwardness, ethnic and gender exclusion, difficult geography, youth unemployment, and other issues provided the perfect incubator for the spread of Maoist appeal in Nepal. The socio-economic cost of this conflict has been devastating. Poverty and conflict reinforce each other. The Maoist war has destroyed the productive capacity of the country, distorted resource allocation, and helped create further poverty and deprivation, setting in motion a vicious cycle of poverty-conflict-and-further poverty. Because of data limitations and serious methodological challenges, the precise quantification of the cost of war is practically impossible. However, some of the manifestations of the socio-economic cost of this conflict are reflected in the following forms:[28]

- An average of 2.5 per cent GDP loss since the fiscal year 2000/01. Decline in non-agricultural GDP from an average of 7 per cent annual growth to 3 per cent in since 2000/01.
- Steady decline in tourist arrivals from a peak of 492,000 in 1999 to 335,000 in 2003.
- Decline in development expenditure from an around 10 per cent to 6 per cent of GDP at present.
- Sharp decline in additional road construction from an average of 800 km annually during 1994–2000 to an average 231 km since 2000-1.
- Increase in transport cost and time. Transport disruptions have lowered the rural sales by private firms by 20–25 per cent.
- Decline in export/GDP ratio from an average of 13 per cent

during 1996/99 to an average of 9 in subsequent years.

- Shifting government expenditure from development to defence. Security expenditure rose from 1.6 per cent of GDP in 1994/95 to 3.2 in 2004/05.
- Decline in additional public sector health units from an average of 1,309 annually until the year 2,000 to a mere 11 after that. Immunization of children in conflict areas has gone down drastically.
- Decline in the growth of primary schools from an average of 1,011 per annum to only 130 after the fiscal year 1999/2000. Most private schools in Maoist-affected areas closed. School children abducted in masse for forced indoctrination. School facilities are often used for militia parade, and training and associated activities.
- Decline in the extension of drinking water facility from an average of 689,000 population per annum to 308,000 population since 2000/1.
- More than 10,000 deaths. Of the 10,112 killed as of first week of August 2004, 3469 were killed by the Maoists, and the rest by the security forces. Of those killed, 4,141 were civilians, 1,478 security personnel, 400 political workers, and 4,000 Maoists.[29] Increasing number of violence-victims, handicapped, and displaced population. Countryside stripped of local leadership and youth population.
- Wide use of women and children as human shields in most offensives.
- Cases of extra-judicial killings and human rights abuses by the government forces. Illegal detention, disappearances, fake encounters and human rights abuses with impunity are widespread.
- Large-scale destruction of the development infrastructure including bridges, telephone towers, power stations and transmission lines and government buildings valued approximately Rs.18 billion.

What's more poignant than this laundry list of damages to the country's economy and society is perhaps the fact that the highest incidence of damage and economic loss from the insurgency has been in areas and regions which were already poor and deprived. Over 700 private schools in the countryside have been closed and 3,000 schoolteachers displaced from rural public schools. In effect therefore, the insurgency has further accentuated regional disparities. There are indications that the improvements witnessed in alleviating poverty and improving the human development indicators across regions and agro-ecological belts in the 1990s[30] have been wiped out in recent years, particularly in the rural and backward regions where the incidence of Maoist violence is higher.

EXTERNAL DIMENSION

As founding member of the RIM, the Maoist party maintains constant ideological and political exchange with this organization. The Maoists proudly acknowledge the fact that it was from RIM that they gained knowledge about the experience of Peru, the Philippines, Turkey and Iran. They benefited from interaction with their counterparts in Sri Lanka, Bangladesh and from direct and continuous dialogue with the People's War Group(PWG) and the Maoist Communist Centre (MCC) of India. After the setback in Peru, Nepal's success came as a big boost to the RIM, and the international proletariat movement. They claim there is a dialectical relationship between Nepal's People's War and the new wave of international communist movement.

Prachanda has declared that the People's war in Nepal is part of the international proletariat movement, and the objective is to contribute towards the attainment of glorious communism by ending all forms of human exploitation from the face of the earth. This philosophy is fully aligned with the true spirit of the Leninist principle of the fusion of national liberation movement with the international proletariat movement.[31] The party's Second Convention also advanced the idea of new Soviet Federation at South Asian level as part of the strategic objective of providing leadership to the national liberation aspirations of the people of the region. The continuous debate and interaction with the RIM throughout the whole process of the preparation, initiation and development of the People' War is considered an important aspect of the movement in view of South Asia's growing importance as a center of world revolution. The Maoists view South Asia's economic, political, cultural and geographical conditions ideally suited for revolution. Therefore, in order to benefit from synergies, they felt the need to coordinate the revolutionary processes in these countries. Towards this end, they have formed a regional alliance with other Maoist parties of the subcontinent called the Confederation of Communist and Maoist Parties of South Asia (CCOMPOSA). The Maoists maintain strategic relations, particularly with the militant groups in India, particularly ULFA, MCC, PWG, North Bengal Liberation Front,

Kamatapur Liberation Organization, National Democratic Front of Bodoland and Indo-Nepal People's Democratic Front.[32] It has also been reported that Maoist leader Prachanda was instrumental in effecting the merger of the two prominent Maoist organizations in India, the MCC and the PWG.

The Indian leaders have expressed increasing concern about the Maoist nexus with the Indian militant groups. Prime Minister Man Mohan Singh himself spoke on 5 November 2004 about the growing strength of the Maoists in Nepal and its links with the left extremists along the Indian borders.[33] A meeting in Calcutta around October 2004 attended by the Nepali Maoists with their regional and international counterparts is reported to have mooted the concept of a Himalayan Revolutionary Zone from Kashmir, through Nepal, Bhutan and into Assam. In their analysis, the topography, ethnic exclusion and poverty in the Himalayan arc make it an ideal location for a trans-boundary revolution in which the guerillas can move freely across borders. They propose to convert the ethno-separatist agenda of militants in India's Northeast to fight a united class war. Following this meeting Maoist activities have increased in western Bangladesh, and a new Maoist party has been formed in Bhutan.

Nepal's Maoist revolution is now part of a regional strategy coordinated with international revolutionaries. It is also reported that the rebels are engaged in frenzied tunnel digging activity in various parts of Nepal to thwart possible Indian air raids.[34] This report coincided with a lecture by Indian Air Chief Marshall S. Krishnaswamy in the Indian Institute of Defence Studies and Analysis in which he warned that the Marxist-Maoist movement might one day threaten the region's security 'vertically down from Nepal to Andhra Pradesh' in South Asia. Emphasizing the optimization of the air force crew to support counter-insurgency operations, he said the Indian air force has excellent ties with the Royal Nepal Army, and has developed flexible command and control means 'such as UAV's and other sensors' for enhanced effectiveness.[35]

GOVERNMENT RESPONSE AND PEACE ATTEMPTS

The Maoist threat was not taken seriously in the beginning, because the rebels did not enjoy much popular support. When they participated in the first parliamentary election as the United People's Front, they could only win nine seats in the 205-member House of Representatives, and that too, only when they formed electoral adjustment with other communist parties, particularly the CPN (UML). Even this United Front was divided; one group deciding to remain within the parliamentary politics. The UPF had strong base in a few districts like Rolpa and Rukum. But their ability to make an impact elsewhere was beyond anybody's imagination. The government responded to their activities with police operation codenamed Operation Romeo, confined to a few districts in the West. The second phase of operation, which started in 1998, was codenamed Kilo Sierra 2 was extended to 18 Maoist-affected districts in the Mid-West, West and Central regions. These operations resulted in serious casualties not only on the Maoist side, but also took serious toll on ordinary people. These strategies turned out to be counterproductive for the government as much to the Maoists' delight. Arbitrary arrests, harassment, torture and mistreatment of innocent people antagonized the local population.

Questions started being raised about the efficacy of the untrained and ill-equipped civilian police to deal with the Maoist guerillas who were being organized along military lines. Deployment of the RNA was proposed and an Integrated Internal Security and Development Plan (IISDP) for the Maoist-affected districts was being mooted. The Plan was to be implemented with security provided by the RNA. But the then Army Chief of Staff Prajjwal Rana's insistence on an all party consensus and the declaration of the state of emergency as prerequisites for the deployment of the army postponed any progress on this. These conditions were not easy to meet in view of the highly divided political opinion. A plan to strengthen the police force with modern arms and improved logistics like helicopters could not materialize in the face of RNA's opposition. Their contention was that the police force was not properly trained for this and the equipment could fall into the Maoist hands.

In 2001, a decision was made to form a para-military force in the form of the armed police. In July 2001, when the Maoists attacked a police post in Holleri killing 31 policemen and taking 69 others hostages, the army was sent to help. But after a brief clash, they came back without major offensive. G.P. Koirala who was the Prime Minister at that time resigned protesting non-cooperation from the army, which owed its de facto loyalty to the king. The government had also complained earlier of army's non-cooperation during Dunai incident also. A company level detachment located 40 minutes away did not come to rescue the police force when the Moist guerillas had raided the Rolpa district headquarters leaving dozens of policemen killed and wounded.

Peace talks were initiated during Deuba's premiership, who took over from Koirala. A ceasefire was declared and most of the Maoist

Photograph 26: Civilian victims of the Maoist landmine

leaders were released and court cases against them withdrawn. The Maoist leaders and cadres came over ground holding public meetings and rallies in many places, including Kathmandu, at places displaying arms and expanding their organizational network. After two rounds of talk, Maoists walked away abruptly, and declaring an end to the ceasefire unilaterally, launched a series of daring attacks in Dang, Surkhet and Syangja, inflicting heavy casualties on army personnel. Sophisticated arms and ammunitions were looted. The government declared a state of emergency immediately. The Terrorist and Disruptive Activities Ordinance was promulgated and the CPN (Maoist) was declared a terrorist organization. The army was brought into action. International support was requested. The United States, India and the UK responded promptly by offering to help strengthen the logistics and communication systems, firepower, and provide technical assistance in various areas.

After King Gyanendra took over the country's state power on 4 October 2002, the peace process was initiated for the second time with Prime Minister Chand's short-lived government at the helm. This process continued under Chand's successor Thapa. As preconditions for talks placed by the Maoists, the government removed the terrorist tag, and the international red corner notice on the Maoists, and subsequently also withdrew court cases against their leaders. A large number of Maoist cadres were released from jails. But again, the Maoists unilaterally broke off the talk when the government refused to accept their key demand—the constituent assembly.

As described above, the Maoists have skillfully and shrewdly used the ethnic issues to their advantage, and made a determined attempt to involve the minorities in their war. The progressive agenda calling for the restructuring of the state power to properly reflect the country's plural society has now become almost the common agenda of Nepal's mainstream parties. This is obvious from the 18-point programme announced by the five agitating political parties[36] in July 2003 and the Reform Proposal put forward by the government during the second peace negotiation on 27 April 2003. In the words of a scholar:

> The historic and contemporary trends of apathy of the government and the dominant group toward the minorities makes it plausible to assume that they would not have recognized the minority issues, if a growing alternate force had not espoused the minority causes. The Maoist insurgency may also have sensitized a section of the government and the dominant group by showing that violent conflicts, including ethnic, is possible in Nepal, which otherwise was popularly perceived and promoted as a peaceful country.[37]

However, the Maoists have not shown interest in discussing the socio-economic agenda over which a broad national consensus has already emerged. Their primary concern, as expressed during the peace negotiations, was the political agenda where the principal demands were: a round-table conference, an interim government under their leadership, and the election for the constituent assembly under the international supervision to write a new constitution. They were not ready to discuss the issue of renouncing violence, laying down arms, and decommissioning their army and militia. Obviously, their calculation was that with the interim government under their leadership or with the preponderance of their military might they could easily win majority seats in the election for the constituent assembly. This would enable them to write a constitution of their choice. Furthermore, accepting their demand for the constituent assembly and concomitant demise of the present constitution would give them tremendous psychological boost to sway the voters on their side. By following this road map, they probably believe that the goal of People's Republic would come nearer. The Maoists walked away from the peace process, when it became obvious that the government would not concede their demand for constituent assembly and a government under their leadership.

It is questionable whether they will renounce violence and lay down arms even if the demand for the constituent assembly is accepted. Judging by their official resolutions and statements, they may not be ready to dilute the revolutionary objective so easily. They are the true believers in the Mao's theory that everything else is illusionary except state power, and that power comes from the barrel of the gun. They are proud of their 'People's Liberation Army'. Prachanda once remarked—without the People's Army people have nothing. The talk of an interim government, a round-table conference, and the constituent assembly may just be calculated tactical steps towards their cherished goal. Otherwise, how would one link their demand for constituent assembly with the systematic killing of innocent local leaders, social workers, teachers, and others? They have made no secret of their hatred towards multi-party polity, as to 'expose the parliamentary hypocrisy' is among their most popular rhetoric. In one of his interviews with an international revolutionary magazine, Prachanda said: 'the parliament and the parliamentarians are the sheep-hold and sheep of imperialism and feudalism'.

True to their revolutionary goal, the Maoists have successfully applied their divisionary tactic 'driving a wedge in the enemy camp' among and between the political parties and the Palace. During G.P. Koirala's last premiership, he was their sworn enemy. Calling him Hitlerian, the Maoists urged everybody to fight his leadership and even made overtures to Deuba. In the aftermath of the Palace Massacre, the Maoist ideologue and second-in-command Babu Ram Bhattarai cleverly talked of an 'undeclared working relationship' on some national issues with the dead king. He alleged the massacre to have been engineered by RAW(with backing from the CIA) with the aim of Bhutanizing Nepal. This, according to him, would ultimately lead towards the Sikkimization of Nepal, whereby the new monarch would serve as Jigme Singhe and Koirala as Lendup Dorje. Their attitude transformed drastically after Deuba became Prime Minister, and effected the state of emergency after the failure of the first peace negotiation. The Maoists raised an olive branch to Koirala, and met him in New Delhi. They played a similar divisionary game between Madhav Nepal and Oli camps of the UML. They willingly started the peace negotiation with the Chand government, but raised the question of legitimacy of the Deuba government, when the latter appealed for dialogue. Both the Prime Ministers were nominated by the king under Article 127 and if there was any difference between them, it was in the size of their respective power bases: Deuba government had a broader popular support than that of Chand.

When the Maoists sat for the peace talk, their international ideologues 'who are fundamentally against the idea of exit through negotiated settlements and convinced that real class struggle cannot conclude in a tie leaving no clear winner or loser' were opposed to it. They considered peace negotiation an anti-insurgency tool invented by the imperialists with the objective of destroying the subversive groups in general, and in the American continent in particular. In various countries of Latin America and elsewhere, peace negotiations were deliberately used to dilute and erode the progressive and revolutionary stances of the insurgents, while simultaneous military actions were used to destroy the movements. They argued that the process of dialogue only strengthens the military and oppressive character of the reactionary regimes. Criticizing the peace process in Colombia and Nepal, Louis Arce Borga wrote:

> The nature and essence of the wars in Colombia, and in Nepal or in any other country is: those are class wars, that is, the struggle between exploited and exploiters. These kinds of wars are social phenomena which come up and mature in a large process of acuteness of the antagonistic contradictions between rich and poor. Those contradictions will only be solved by a violent political and military confrontation with the local groups and imperialism. Out of this absolute truth are left only political fantasies that come involved in a bourgeois idea, which plans to solve the armed conflict through peaceful negotiations. This updated idea,

> either as tactical or strategic movement, is the safest road to capitulation? It becomes of utmost importance in strategic order for the revolution to show the masses that 'the pacifist ways out of the armed conflicts,' or 'the peace agreements' with the oppressors are political illusion brought into being with the intension of defeating the armed processes.[38]

How did the Nepali Maoists justify the short-lived peace process then? They rationalized it by citing the Maoist philosophy of 'fighting tit for tat'. Faced with the clamour for peace by the urban middle class and to win over a large section of the masses, they agreed to sit for talks to "fight and defeat the enemy at the negotiating table". This was the adoption of the policy of maximum tactical flexibility of "advance and retreat" with the objective of advancing 'people's war' and revolution to victory. The Maoists were not oblivious of the fact that the peace process could be utilized against their objective to engineer splits within their ranks and to dilute the revolutionary stance. Aware of the negative experience of Peru, they had even calculated the risk of their negotiating team falling into the enemy's hands.

The Maoist leaders on various occasions have made reference to the Brest–Litovsk Treaty of 1918 under Lenin and the Chunking Negotiations in 1938 under Mao Tse-tung as the guiding principles for their peace negotiations. The first refers to the treaty with Imperial Germany and its allies, which resulted in the surrender of Ukraine, Finland, and Balkan Provinces by Russia to preserve the October Revolution in the face of advancing German troops to St. Petersburg. The treaty was rendered inoperative very soon after the new Soviet Union consolidated its position. The second refers to the negotiations under Chairman Mao with the Kuomintang leadership, which brought the Chinese communists to the centre-stage in the fight against Japanese occupation. This eventually led to the communist takeover of China, by pushing out the demoralized Kuomintang.

The Nepali Maoists have proven their international skeptics wrong by using the two failed negotiations as a battle strategy for tactical gains without diluting any of their revolutionary fervour. They successfully arm-twisted the government into meeting their pre-conditions before sitting for talks. They were able to get their detainees released, court cases withdrawn, come over-ground to expand their organization, enhance acceptability among the people, and mobilize huge financial resources. Their military strength and organizational capacity is believed to have grown several-fold during the two 'cease-fires' and the negotiation process. They quietly walked out of the peace process, when they realized that they would not make any further gains.

UN MEDIATION?

Meanwhile, expressing concern at the deteriorating situation in Nepal, the United Nations has expressed interest several times to assist in the peace process. Kul Chandra Gautam, a high-ranking Nepali in the UN, through an article in the *Kathmandu Post*, made a case for an enhanced, preventive and pro-active UN role in Nepal to stop it from disintegrating into a failed state. He warned that if the situation is allowed to deteriorate further, the international community would one day have to invoke the principles of "responsibility to protect the civilian population" from untold suffering, and rescue the country from violent anarchy. Samuel Tamrat, a special envoy of the UN Secretary General, visited the country several times with the Secretary General's message. I had the benefit of several meetings with him at my home. Some European countries have also expressed their readiness for any appropriate role in peace negotiation. Understandably, the Maoists have also shown readiness for a UN-brokered negotiation.

The Maoist eagerness for a UN role can be explained for several reasons. First, it would accord them the much-needed legitimacy and recognition—a big morale boosting opportunity at a time when they have been branded as terrorists. The Western countries, particularly the United States consider them the equivalent of Al Qaida, Abu Sayaf, Shining Path, and Khmer Rouge, bent on forcibly imposing their beliefs on others. The Maoists are one of the 37 terrorist groups placed under their "international terrorist watch list" by the US. The Maoists may be fighting for a political cause, but the methods they use are terroristic and condemnable. Various international resolutions and conventions testify this. The UN General Assembly Resolution 51/210 of 17 December 1996 condemns all acts of terrorism as "criminal and unjustifiable", irrespective of the motive behind it. It says:

> Criminal acts intended or calculated to provoke a state of terror in the general public, a group of persons or political group are in any circumstances unjustifiable, whatever the considerations of a political, philosophical, ideological, ethnic, religious or any other nature that may be invoked to justify them."

The UN Security Council Resolution 1373 passed unanimously in the aftermath of 9/11, also clearly rules out the claims of political motivation as the ground to condone "perpetrators, organizers or facilitators of terrorist acts". The SAARC Regional Convention on Suppression of Terrorism signed in 1987 during the SAARC Summit in Kathmandu is even stronger and specific on this subject. It declares:

> Activities including murder, man slaughter, assault causing bodily harm, kidnapping, hostage-taking and offenses relating to firearms, weapons, explosives and dangerous substances when used as a means to perpetrate violence as terroristic, and for the purpose of extradition will not be regarded as political offence or inspired by political motive.

With UN mediation between the two warring parties, the Maoists may also be expecting to validate their theory of "two regimes" —with "two armies" and the two "areas of control"—which they claim exists in Nepal. The "old regime", according to them, is the one which the king and other constitutional forces represent, and the "new regime" is the one they represent. Their claim is that the entire countryside except the nation's capital and district headquarters remain under their control. It may be noted that unlike in Sri Lanka and other conflict-ridden situations, where the insurgents control a defined territory, there is no such area, which can be called militarily controlled by the rebels in Nepal. Their control of some areas is by default, that is, in the absence of the government's security presence. In every negotiation, the rebels want recognition of their 'control area'. This was one bone of contention between the two sides, which complicated the implementation of the 'ceasefire' during the second peace process. It may be recalled here that a meeting during the second peace process took place, at the Maoists' insistence, at Hapure of Dang district, which they claim as their area. The members of the negotiating team were politely told not to use the government helicopter and security personnel in that area.

Regardless of the bitter experiences of the past, the Maoists' eagerness for talk—whatever their ulterior motive—should be interpreted in a positive perspective, and taken as an opportunity to test their sincerity and commitment to peace. However, rather than a high-profile formal mediation, quiet diplomacy could be used to explore a solution. In view of the UN's position on terrorism, there is no way they could start formal mediation until the Maoists express commitment to give up their terrorist methods. In that vein, if the UN really wants to broker negotiations, they should persuade the rebels to renounce violence as a tool to achieve political objective. I had proposed a six-point formula[39], if the UN's good office is to be used:

- *(a)* Restoration of democratic institutions, which could offer the only framework for peaceful handling of conflict.
- *(b)* Monitoring of human right violations from both sides.
- *(c)* Using international leverage to pressure the Maoists to renounce violence, extortion and intimidation to achieve their objective.

(*d*) Humanitarian assistance for the conflict victims,

(*e*) Use of quiet informal diplomacy rather than high-profile publicized negotiations. Most successful negotiations are always conducted behind the scene until they reach an advanced stage.

(*f*) Peace process should proceed without pre-conditions.

However, the government's position regarding third-party mediation has not been favourable. Their contention has been that the problem is internal, and it can be resolved internally. The option of using the UN or any credible third party should be kept open, but under a well-defined national policy, which unfortunately is lacking at present. No serious attempt has been made so far to arrive at a consensus on this important issue that could eventually pull the country out of a quagmire of violence and further crisis.

CONCLUSION

Nobody believes that the Maoist war will achieve its goal by overpowering the state. The military successes achieved earlier by the Maoist seem to have tapered off. They have failed to register any major success to their credit in recent times. On the other hand, in the last one year they have suffered heavy losses at Ganeshpur of Bardia, Pandun of Kailali and Khara of Rukum at the hands of much strengthened and well equipped government forces. Voluntary recruitments to the Maoist ranks have stopped. One fallout of this and their inability to mobilize people in the absence of popular support is the shift in their tactic. Highway blockages, setting off landmines, torching public transport vehicles[40], ambushes to army convoy and other hit and run tactics are being used as the principal strategies.

Furthermore, the intra-party power struggle which has now come out in the open is certain to weaken the Maoists. In an apparent bid to centralize all powers at the hands of the party supremo Prachanda, the last central committee meeting removed Babu Ram Bhattarai from the leadership position in the party's United Front and transferred it to the party standing committee[41]. With this Bhattarai also lost his position as the head of the Peoples Revolutionary Council. He called the decision 'immature' and 'unprincipled' which would weaken the struggle. Accusing the party leadership of promoting groupism and deviating from the principle of 'democratic centralism', he resented the growth of personality cult in the party and centralization of all power in one individual. He also demanded intra-party publication of 'two line struggle' to institutionalize healthy debate on political and ideological differences[42]. In response, Prachanda accused Bhattarai of his unruly working style, self-centred thoughts and indulgence in unprincipled factionalism. Bhattarai was blamed for promoting parallel party headquarters, making the party internal matters public and helping the cause of expansionism, imperialism and RNA. Questioning his understanding of Mao's teaching, Prachanda suspected that Bhattarai was preparing a background to disassociate himself from the party and People's War. Bhattarai was asked to undergo a process of self-correction and transformation[43]. Babu Ram was removed also from the membership of the Standing Committee.

It will be premature to assess the extent of damage on the Maoist war as a result of this development. At the same time it would be foolish to think that the Maoists can be contained easily through military methods. They continue to inflict heavy damage to the state, strangulate the economy and make lives miserable for the majority. This scenario has given them tactical advantage to negotiate. Public opinion, internal as well as external, favours a peaceful settlement. Major political parties including the Nepali Congress and the CPN (UML) have expressed their readiness to accept even the Maoist demand for the constituent assembly, if that can make the rebels renounce violence and join multiparty politics. The Monarch, who is an important actor in any future settlement, is not ready for this. He seems to fear this could be a prelude to the end of monarchy itself. Nevertheless, there is little guarantee that the Maoists would give up violence and decommission their army even if the state were to meet the three political demands, including that of the constituent assembly. The three demands understandably are only tactical steps towards achieving their main goal.

The prospect for peace negotiation has become even more remote since the 1st February action of the king. The king formally called them terrorists, strongly condemned their actions of terror, intimidation, extortion, kidnapping, destruction, and other atrocities, and promised to deal with them effectively. After he expressed his determination to mobilize security forces for this, the reaction from the Maoists was even harsher and stronger. Contrary to their earlier response to the peace appeal by the previous Deuba government,[44] the Maoists ruled out any peace negotiation with the king. They called the royal action an exhibition of "feudal fascist brutality" and appealed to everybody, including the political parties, to create a broad front to unitedly fight against what they called "the last lunacy of the feudal clique that had lost its necessity and credibility in history". They vowed to continue the People's War until "the total defeat and dissolution of the royal army".[45] It is clear that both sides now seem determined to pursue the military means to defeat each other.

A common national approach to the Maoist problem is lacking because of the division among political forces. With their shrewd manipulation, the Maoists have succeeded in dividing and confusing other political forces. The democratic institutions, which could have offered a mechanism for conflict resolution by giving political space to all forces, have been decimated and this has dimmed hopes for an early solution. The suppression of political liberty, denial of legitimate role to political parties, and the large-scale detention of political leaders and workers have created the risk of pushing the constitutional forces closer to the Maoists in forging a common cause. This is the type of opportunity the Maoists were looking for to polarize the political forces against the monarchy. The middle ground between the two extremes—a republican agenda and an executive monarchy—the political parties could have offered, is being eroded. All this has been to the supreme advantage of the Maoists.

NOTES

1. *See* interview with Li Onesto in *The Revolutionary Worker*, 20 February 2000.
2. Ibid.
3. See Deepak Thapa with Bandita Sijapati, *A Kingdom Under Seige*, Kathmandu: the printhouse, 2003, pp. 98–102.
4. Ibid, p. 102.
5. More details on this discussed in a separate chapter entitled Security Cost: On the South Asian Path?
6. Cited in Deepak Thapa with Bandita Sijapati, op. cit., p. 43.
7. Robert Gersony, *Sowing the Wind: History and Dynamics of the Maoist Movement in Nepal's Rapti Hills*, 2003, October 2003, pp. 7–8. Report submitted to Mercy Corps International, October 2003.
8. The product is used in the traditional Chinese medicine with multiple uses. A kilogram of this product was sold for Rs. 200,000 in 2004.
9. Gersony, op. cit.
10. Ram S. Mahat, 'Economic Dimension of Conflicts in South Asia, A Case of Nepal', paper presented to seminar on Comprehensive Security: Economic Perspective from India organized by DGP on 23–24 September in New Delhi.
11. For an enlightened discussion, see Mahendra Lawati, Maoists and Minorities: Overlap of Interests or A case of Exploitation? in *Studies in Nepali History and Society*, June 2003.Kathmandu: Mandala Book Point.
12. Ibid.

13. *See* Eyewitness report by Durga Pokharel, Chairperson of the National Women Commission based on her field observations, 2003.
14. Prachanda's interview with Onesto.
15. *See* Watchlist on Children and Armed Conflict, *Caught In the Middle: Mounting Violence against Children*, January 2005, pp. 38–39 for reported testimony about sexual exploitation and abuse.
16. See for detailed discussion, Sujita Sakya, 'The Maoist Movement in Nepal, An Analysis from Women Perspective' in Arjun Karki and David Seddon ed. *People's War in Nepal: Left Perspective*, New Delhi: Adroit Publications, 2003.
17. *See*, Babu Ram Bhattarai, *'The Political Economy of People's War'*, ibid.
18. Gersony, op.cit. Section three.
19. Ibid.
20. General Sadip Shah's presentation in the IIC conference in New Delhi on Democracy and Peace in Nepal, 6–7 December 2004.
21. Dhruba Kumar, 'Trenches of Violence: Militancy, Militarism and Militarization of Social Sphere in Nepal', p.11. Paper presented at NCCS *seminar 16–17, November 2004, Kathmandu.*
22. See *The Kathmandu Post*, 19 to 23 November.
23. Civilians protested against Maoist atrocities in Ratanganj of Nawalparashi district, which was followed by Maoist retaliation in which three Maoists and two civilians were killed. *The Himalayan*, 26 December 2004.
24. The incident followed the abduction of a former sub-inspector of the police from the area by the Maoists. *The Kathmandu Post*, 18 February 2005.
25. The National Human Rights Commission strongly urged the government not to instigate "anti-Maoist" vigilante in future to prevent loss of life and property. *The Kathmandu Post*, 7 April 2005.
26. Report by Dipak Gyawali in *Samaya*, a national weekly, 15 Baisakh 2062.
27. See J. B. Pun's Report in *Himal Khabar Patrika*, 29 April–14 May 2005.
28. Drawn from various sources including HMG's annual economic survey reports, budget speechees, and assorted sources.
29. *Nepali Times* #209 13–19 August 2004.
30. Various surveys including *Rural Household Consumption Survey 2001, Demographic Household survey 2001* and *Living Standard Measurement Survey 2003*, indicate a reduction in poverty levels across regions as indicated by increased consumption, ownership of household durables and human development indicators. See, World Bank report *Nepal Development Policy Review*. June 2004.
31. See, *A World to Win*, 28 May 2001.
32. Sadip Shah, op.cit.
33. The *Kathmandu Post*, 6 November 2004.
34. Puskar Gautam, Tunnel Vision, *in Nepali Times* #220, 5, 11 November 2004.
35. See, *The Kathmandu Post*, 13 November 2004.
36. More on this in Chapter 15.
37. Lawati, op.cit.

38. Luis Arce Borja, 'Criticisms of the Peace Negotiations,' Brussels, 2003.
39. Ram S. Mahat, UN Mediation for Peace?, *The Kathmandu Post*, 19–20 April 2004.
40. 18 trucks were set ablaze by Maoists on 22 December 2004 on the Manahari–Hetauda section of the Mahendra Highway, followed by similar incidents subsequently.
41. The 'centralization' and 'integration' of 'the proletariat leadership' to the five-member Politburo Standing Committee headed by Prachanda was justified by the Central committee on the ground that the party was in a sensitive 'counter offensive phase' and the national and international reactionaries were hatching conspiracies. Prachanda said — in a special and sensitive process like strategic counter offensive, if all power is centralized in the standing committee, there will be greater clarity in the party and the movement. See Prachanda's response to Babu Ram Bhatarai, published in *Jana Dharana weekly,* 22 Baishakh, 2062.
42. Babu Ram Bhattarai's letter of 26 Kartik and 15 Marga, 2061 published ibid.
43. Stated in Prachana's press release of Baishaks, 2062 published in *Jana Dharana weekly,* 22 Baishakh 2062.
44. The Central Committee of the Maoist party had said the talks would not be held with the servants of the old regime, but with their owner (i.e. the king) with the help of reliable international mediation. *The Kathmandu Post,* 3 September, 2004.
45. Prachanda's press statement of 1 February 2005.

Chapter Fifteen

Political Deadlock

In recent years, the country has been mired in an unprecedented political stand off. As if the pains and agony to the nation from the Maoist war were not enough, the Royal takeover on 4 October 2002 created a constitutional crisis and paved way for further uncertainty and political deadlock. The process of taking over political power reached its culmination on 1st February 2005, when King Gyanendra took direct charge of the country's administration, bringing an end to the rule through his nominated Prime Ministers. The *de facto* character of the king's rule after October 4 assumed the *de jure* form also in February 1. The Constitution became defunct in the absence of legislative bodies. The country continues to be entrapped in a triangular political struggle–between the Maoists waging a violent war, an executive monarchy, and the political parties fighting to restore the constitutional process.

King Gyanendra sacked his third nominated Prime Minister, Sher Bahadur Deuba, on 1st February and formed a cabinet under his own chairmanship. Justifying his action through a televised address to the nation, he blamed political parties for political instability, abuse of authority, vandalism, and indifference to the welfare of the people. He accused them of failing to make a unified approach against terrorism, when bloodshed, violence and devastation pushed the country to the brink of devastation and human suffering. The last Prime Minister was blamed for giving only lip service on the urgency of holding early election. The king promised "to restore multiparty democracy and peace with the implementation of effective reforms" within three years. He appealed those who had "gone astray and taken up arms" to return to the mainstream of national politics peacefully and at the same time, vowed to use security forces effectively to defeat terrorism.

The king's proclamation was ridden with clichés and platitudes—

malgovernance and corruption by the parties in power, breakdown of law and order, threat to national unity and sovereignty—and betrayed uncanny similarities with late King Mahendra's speech on 15 December 1960. Although the king cast his action "to protect multiparty democracy and constitutional monarchy", the move had all the ingredients of a familiar and indefensible coup: political leaders detained, key constitutional rights suspended, army censorship on press and communications cut off.[1] Fearing popular protests, most leaders and activists were immediately put under house arrest or detained. A state of emergency was declared throughout the country and fundamental rights including the right to property and privacy were suspended to defend the "sovereignty, integrity, and security" of the nation. Internal and external communications were cut off. Telephones, faxes, e-mail, Internet, and other means of communications were closed immediately. External TV news channels were also closed. Press and media came under heavy censorship. Anybody defying the official order was threatened with dire consequences.

The national and international reaction to the king's action was negative. G.P. Koirala called it the beginning of absolute and authoritarian rule. Madhav Nepal condemned the step as an attack on the sovereignty and political rights of the people. The Maoists called it the imposition of "medieval feudal autocracy". India called it a '"serious setback to the cause of democracy in Nepal" and a matter of "grave concern to India". Even while Nepal's new Foreign Minister was announcing that King Gyanendra would lead Nepal's delegation to the SAARC Summit scheduled the following week in Dhaka, India announced it would not be participating in the Summit on the scheduled date in view of the "grave developments in the neighbourhood".[2] The Summit was postponed. Great Britain lamented the action saying it "would increase the risk of instability in Nepal, undermining the institutions of democracy and constitutional monarchy in the country". The United States' reaction was that it was a "step back from democracy" which would undermine the struggle with the Maoist insurgency. Similar reactions came from the EU presidency. The UN Secretary General Kofi Annan called for "the immediate restoration of democracy". The reaction from the international press was even more bitter and hostile.[3] The UK announced freeze on military assistance. India said its military assistance to fight insurgency is being reviewed.

Donor countries also threatened to review the development assistance. The first country to announce suspension of aid was Denmark. The new Finance Minister who had gone to Paris to participate in the donors' meeting to solicit development assistance was told that

Photograph 27: Political leaders at the anti-regression rally

Photograph 28: Top leaders on *dharna* in front of the Royal Palace

the donors wanted the lifting of the state of emergency, release of political prisoners and restoration of civil and political freedoms to continue their support. Under this circumstance and also because of its failure to meet the commitments made during aid negotiations before, the government was forced to scale down the planned foreign aid by 37.5 per cent for the fiscal year 2004/05.[4]

Another fallout of the royal action was the tough time Nepal faced in the 61st session of the UN Human Rights Commission in Geneva when Switzerland brought a resolution to appoint a Special Human Rights Rapporteur in Nepal under Agenda 9 as a mechanism for credible, impartial and independent monitoring of human rights violations in Nepal. The government avoided the ignominy of being placed under the category of Burma and North Korea after the two sides found a face-saving formula. The government signed a Memorandum of Understanding with the UNHRC under which a 50-men UN mission would be stationed in Nepal with field offices to monitor, investigate and verify human rights violations.

The new regime had not expected the hostile reaction it received from the international community. The king, in his interview with Alex Perry of the US magazine *The Time*, said that he was disappointed by the international reaction[5]. The international community continued their pressure on the king. On 19 April 2005, expressing concern at "the King's refusal to restore constitutional liberties and democracy despite condemnation of his action and suspension of military aid to Nepal by India and Great Britain, and similar actions by the US" and satisfied that his "actions would further strengthen the Maoist insurgency", the US Senate passed a unanimous resolution asking the king to "immediately release all political detainees, restore constitutional liberties, and undertake good faith negotiations with the leaders of Nepal's political parties to restore democracy"[6]. Eleven congressmen of the US Congress wrote to the king in a similar vein.

Practically all political parties except the RPP came out on the streets protesting the royal action. The RPP did not directly oppose the king's move. It did not support the same either. Forgetting their past differences, Nepali Congress together with Jana Morcha Nepal and NSP joined hands with UML and NC (D) to hold joint rallies. NPWP and the United Left Front joined later. The government responded with heavy hands arresting political leaders and workers in large number. Cases of physical assault and custodial torture were also reported from various parts of the country. In a bid to unify and rally all political forces around common platform, the seven parties signed a common agenda on 8 May 2005 vowing to fight collectively to bring the king's direct rule to an end through a popular movement. The agenda, among others, called for the revival of the House of Representatives to activate the constitution, form an all-party government and hold peace negotiation on the basis of a progressive agenda to resolve the Maoist insurgency.

BACKGROUND TO THE DIRECT RULE

The king's latest action followed an experiment with three governments under three Prime Ministers chosen by himself, since he took over executive power by sacking an elected Prime Minister on 4 October. All political parties except the RPP and a faction of NSP had termed the royal action of 4 October an unconstitutional and regressive act. The RPP termed the action the 'product of compelling circumstances'. The first Prime Minister chosen on 11 October 2002 was Lokendra Bahadur Chand, RPP leader and a royal yes-man who had lost the parliamentary seat in the last general election. His cabinet consisted largely of technocrats, and some deserters from the NC and the UML. It was during Chand's time that the five parties, including the NC, CPN (UML), NSP (Anandi Devi), Janmorcha Nepal (JM) and NPWP, started street agitation against the king's 'regression' under the banner of the People's Movement. They demanded a restoration of the constitutional process.

In the process of the Peoples' Movement, the agitating parties also developed and agreed on an 18-point future agenda. This agenda not only called for the restoration of the constitutional process, but also included other political and socio-economic reforms aimed at addressing the issues raised by the Maoists. These included a limitation on the royal authority and privileges to confine the monarchy to a purely constitutional status, an inclusive polity to reflect the plurality of the Nepali society, a greater decentralization and devolution of power, and an effective civilian control over the Royal Nepal Army. However, the immediate and the interim demand was the restoration of the constitutional process. It was proposed that the king appoint a Prime Minister based on the recommendation of the five agitating parties, who would then form an all party government, restore the House of Representatives, and initiate dialogue with the Maoists based on the 18-point programme.

The only landmark act, or achievement if it may be called so, of the Chand government was the ceasefire with the Maoists and an initiation of the peace negotiation. Unfortunately, this only ended up helping the Maoists consolidate their political and military strengths further. The government liberally met all of Maoists' preconditions for the talk[7], and later backtracked under popular pressure. Faced with increasing street protests, Chand resigned on 30 May 2003. The five agitating parties had recommended Madhav Kumar Nepal as their choice for the Prime Minister's post. But the king appointed RPP's Surya Bahadur Thapa, an old war-horse of the Panchayat fame as the next Prime Minister.

This government was also found seriously handicapped in the face of the anti-regression agitation by the five political parties. The protest was now joined by professional organizations and civil society. The isolation of the government became complete when even the RPP (Thapa's own party) came out on the street demanding his resignation. This ultimately led Thapa to resign. Following his resignation a Royal communiqué - without specifying any political party or group—made a public appeal to recommend names for his successor. The communiqué also defined the terms of references of the new Prime Minister, which were, broadly, to restore peace, and hold general election. Differences surfaced among the five agitating parties on the issue of responding to the communiqué. The UML wanted to recommend a name for the Prime Minister but the remaining four parties were against it, because they were not specifically asked to recommend a candidate. Furthermore, the four parties also felt that there was no assurance that the king would accept their recommendation. After all, the consensus candidate of the agitating parties had been turned down by the king in favour of Thapa in the previous occasion. Also, the parties felt that under the Constitution, the king had no authority to define the Prime Minister's job. Because of this difference, the UML decided to break from the five-party agitation. The king nominated Sher Bahadur Deuba as the next Prime Minister, although nobody had formally recommended his name. In deciding to join the Deuba government, the UML asserted that Deuba's reappointment, after being sacked earlier on ground of 'incompetence', was a partial rectification of the October 4 action.

The remaining four parties decided to continue the agitation. Although Deuba's government—which was an alliance of the UML, RPP and NC(D)—had a broader participation compared to the previous RPP government's there were no substantive differences in the functioning and authority of the government. Some of the government's actions were contrary to the position taken by the UML earlier. This caused major resentment within the Party.[8] Particularly the new Royal Household Expenses Ordinance, which authorized the palace to decide its own budget, an increase in the palace budget, and other decisions which openly promoted palace interests were contrary to the UML's publicly stated positions. The repeated hikes in the price of petroleum products was justifiably motivated by compelling economic reasons but they were so poorly handled that the decisions invited strong resentment from the UML party cadres. The government also failed to initiate the peace process with the Maoists. Its repeated appeals for peace talks were spurned by the Maoists who questioned the government's legitimacy and status to hold substantive dialogue. The UML was torn between a dilemma of playing its traditional populist policies and the imperative of acting as a responsible partner in the government. In the words of a political analyst:

> The present government headed by Deuba faces a number of hurdles and cannot make headway for a negotiated settlement with the Maoists. Some of these constraints are: the power of the Government in question because of the central role of the King. The previous government headed by Deuba had no problems of taking other coalition partners together despite internal problems of the ruling NC Party. Today, the UML's own predictability and credential is challenged because it wants to enjoy best of both worlds—being a partner in the government and also its critic. The utterances of senior UML leaders and the demonstration staged by its student wing against the recent price hike in petroleum products show the cruel dilemma faced by the party. The UML seems to play football in both A and B team or the government and the opposition at the same time.[9]

The dilemma was reflected when the UML ministers abstained from the meeting of *Raj Parishad* in October 2004. The student and youth wings of UML launched street protests against the petroleum price increases. Madhav Nepal charged that the price hike was unjustified and he was not consulted on this. The ministers representing his party retorted that he had been fully informed. The controversy over the appointment of the Nepal Rastra Bank Governor further soured the relation between Deuba and the UML. The Prime Minister refused to accept the preferred candidate recommended by a panel, which the Deputy Prime Minister-cum-Finance Minister had headed.[10] Furthermore, serious differences emerged within the ruling coalition when the Prime Minister wanted to declare the election date. The security situation was not getting any better with the rebels threatening a bloodbath in case of a parliamentary election. A total of 22 army personnel had been killed in an ambush by the Maoists in Puwa Khola of Illam, and another eight, including a Major, had been killed in Byaphle of Parbat district. News of hundreds and thousands of students abducted by the Maoists were coming from different parts of the countryside.[11]

The king's mandate to the Prime Minister was to start the election process by March 2005. It was obvious that Deuba had to implement his election commitment (to preclude the possibility of being labeled "incompetent" for the second time) even when ministers and leaders of the ruling coalition, including the leaders of his own party, were speaking against it.[12] The UML leaders, including the Deputy Prime Minister, openly questioned the Prime Minister's plan to hold election without restoring peace. Even the Election Commission and the Royal Nepal Army were talking about the absence of necessary preparations for the election.[13] In the wake of all round opposition to the planned election, and sharp escalation of Maoist violence, most leaders of the ruling coalition were favouring the restoration of the House of Representatives, rather than polls, as the tool to revive the constitutional process. UML General Secretary, in accordance with the decision of the Standing Committee of his Party, is reported to have insisted the Prime Minister to recommend the restoration of the dissolved HOR.[14] Pressure on the UML leadership was mounting from party workers and prominent leaders to withdraw from the government[15].

It was obvious that the election as per the royal mandate was becoming an unrealistic proposition. Even if elections could have been held, given the level of violence and militarization, the legitimacy of the results of such an election would have been questionable. National and international opinion was aligned against the continuation of a government without legislative accountability. Public opinion was fast moving in the direction of the revival of the dissolved parliament in order to activate the functioning of democratic institutions. Initially a Nepali Congress agenda for all practical purposes, the House revival had now received a broad consensus. Leading constitutional experts, civil society leaders and newspaper editorials were openly supporting the proposal. Arguments favouring the immediate revival of the House were based on several advantages.

First, it was expected to put an end to the triangular power struggle by confining the king to the constitutionally defined role. A revived parliament was seen as a better mechanism to politically tackle the Maoist threat, as it would bring all forces back on a single forum to debate, discuss, and put up a common front. Even the Royal Nepal Army's battle would be made easier with the opening of the political front.[16] And any political solution to be negotiated with the Maoists would derive legitimacy with the parliamentary backing. Second, the derailed constitution would be back on track. A functioning legislature would act as an insurance against the royal encroachment on the Constitution and state power and executive authority would revert to the elected representatives. Third, political activities and development works stalled in all 205 constituencies in the absence of elected representatives would be restarted. Lastly, the country would be spared of the prospective bloodbath and huge electoral expenses in the alternative scenario of holding election whose fairness would have been greatly suspect.

Some opined that the dissolved House could not be revived since the Supreme Court had upheld the Prime Minister's recommendation to dissolve the House in 2002. However, leading constitutional experts, including the Nepal Bar Association, had spoken strongly on this issue.[17] Their conclusion was the Court had upheld only the Prime Minister's prerogative to dissolve the House to hold election within six months. In the event of elections not taking place, the Court ruling did not prevent the possibility of revival of the House. Furthermore, since the core spirit of the Constitution stipulates that there can be no parliamentary hiatus for more than six months, the House could be revived on political and constitutional grounds. A statement issued on 31 July 2003 by the six members of the Constitution Recommendation Committee, which drafted the constitution, said:

> In the interest of maintaining a healthy democratic tradition and the doctrine of necessity, it makes it imperative to resort to Article 127 to activate the entire constitutional mechanism...The Supreme Court has not given any verdict to prevent or not to recognize the revival of the House of Representatives. The verdict upholding the dissolution was situation-specific, on the assumption that the election would be held within six months. The decision cannot apply in the case of election not being held.... There can be no doubt that all constitutional obstacles will be removed once the House of Representatives are restored and an all-party government is formed.[18]

The Bar Association of Nepal made a special demand before the Supreme Court of Nepal to expedite the hearing on the writ petition pending at the Court to review its earlier verdict on the House dissolution.[19]

The revival of the House was clearly something the monarch did not want. He probably feared the restoration of the House could lead to the revival of the 18-point agenda, which proposed curtailment of royal power and privileges and the RNA's full accountability to the parliament. Second, a parliamentary presence would confine the king to his constitutional role and thereby curtailing the degrees of freedom he was exercising after its dissolution. In fact, the royal action of 4 October and 1 January would not have been possible with a functioning parliament. This probably explains the haste the king showed in dissolving the House within minutes of the Prime Minister's recommendation on midnight of 18 May 2002.[20]

Not being satisfied with the functioning of post-1990 democratic governance, the king was aspiring for a bigger role for himself and looked for an appropriate opportunity to strike. Ever since his enthronement, and more so after 4th October, the king, by style, expressions and actions, had given enough indications of his desire to play a wider and active role in governance. A number of remarks attributed to him in formal and informal occasions indicated his disillusionment, and even dislike, towards Nepal's multiparty politics and politicians. In an interview with a local daily on 19 August 2001, he had said:

> Unlike my brother, I cannot keep quiet even while witnessing such a plight of the country and countrymen...I am determined to play optimum role that a King can play for the good of the country and countrymen.[21]

In another interview to the Time magazine on 26 January 2004, he blamed the political parties for not being pro-nation and pro-people, and denied that the constitutional monarch's role is limited "to suggest, warn and be informed". He spoke of his accountability to the people and to play a "constructive"' role.[22] In his public reception in Nepalgunj, he also blamed politicians for not being pro-people. Invoking the traditional king-people bond, he asserted that the monarchy is not just to be seen but also to be heard when the countrymen are in distress.[23] In his choice of political managers, he showed a particular fondness for the politicians of the Panchayat era. Some important executive decisions made after 4 October clearly showed that he wanted to have a final say in important matters. A decision by the Chand cabinet made the prior royal approval mandatory for any cabinet decision on matters relating to transfers and appointments of special class civil servants, police, army, and ambassadors. Prior to 4 October immediately after the dissolution of the House, the palace budget was raised from a level of 11 to 39 crore rupees through the ordinance budget in July 2002. Even after appointing Thapa as the Prime Minister with 'full executive power', the king made intervention in vital appointments for constitutional positions.[24] The king was also giving personal audience to assorted personalities from various walks of life to gauge public opinion and feel the pulse.

Following the royal action of 4th October, *Raj Parishad* (the State Council) was activated to hold regional consultations and meetings on political affairs of the country. The *Parishad* has not been given such function by the Constitution. Its defined role is related only to the announcement of Royal successor in the event of the king's demise or abdication. But soon it began passing resolutions commending the 4th

Photograph 29: G. P. Koirala addressing the mass against royal rule

Photograph 30: A student demonstrator hit by the police *lathi*

October and subsequent royal actions, expressing unflinching faith at the farsighted and noble leadership of the Monarch "in defense of the country's unity, sovereignty, democracy, peace and development". Lately in November 2004, the king had indicated his intention for direct rule to some friendly countries including India, United States, and the UK. These countries advised him against any such move warning him that it would remove the buffer between the Maoist insurgents and the monarchy.[25]

INSURGENCY AND REGRESSION: MUTUALLY REINFORCING

The instability, political horse-trading, and weak governance of the nineties have often been cited as the reason for the royal takeover. The king certainly used these factors to his advantage. But more importantly, he was concerned about the increasing intensity of the Maoist insurgency and their republican agenda, which provided the rationale for his action. Their misplaced adventure, terrorist methods, attempts to decimate political opponents and the republican agenda led the monarch to believe that only he, with the support of the RNA which remained loyal to him, could effectively respond to the Maoist challenge. In fact, a question often raised was whether the RNA was being used to its full might against the Maoist War. Some suspected that they were made to wait deliberately for the king's takeover.[26] Externally also, the Maoists rescued the king's present position. Despite the initial hostile reaction of the international community, the king was convinced that the Western powers would eventually accept an active monarchy to take on the Maoist threat; much in the same way they accepted the Musharraf regime in Pakistan to fight the Al Qaida after 9/11.

Furthermore, Maoist atrocities, terror tactics and intolerance to other views considerably weakened the organization of political parties in rural areas and thereby prevented a large-scale mass mobilization against the Royal action. The Maoists have targeted the Nepali Congress workers in particular and other activists in general for physical elimination in the countryside. The revival of democratic institutions through election of local bodies and national legislature could have put an effective check on the Royal ambition. But the Maoist threat of bloodbath for any such exercise made the royal takeover an extremely easy proposition, especially after the dissolution of the House of Representatives. At the same time, as the Maoists grew stronger the government's own security apparatus, particularly the RNA, had to be strengthened to match and counter the rebel forces. The consequent militarization of the regime proceeded without much protest and scrutiny. This naturally helped in strengthening the king's position.

On the other hand, and quite interestingly, it is the royal takeover on 4 October and subsequent actions that gave validity to the Maoist theory that the so-called 'people's sovereignty' established by the Constitution of the kingdom of Nepal 1990 is just an illusion. The Maoists maintained all along that the real power rested with the king who, with the help of the RNA, could usurp the people's power at will. The Maoists have been justifying their republican agenda on this ground. They consider the monarchy as the root cause of Nepal's underdevelopment and poverty. They were particularly emboldened after the Palace Massacre when they said the traditional monarchy has already come to an end, and a republic was born. According to Dr. Babu Ram Bhattarai:

> Subsequent events, particularly those after the infamous palace massacre of June 1, 2001, and more specifically the dramatic dissolution of parliament on May 22, 2002 should, however, dispel all illusions and establish beyond doubt how the monarchy controls the real power of the state...the continued allegiance of the RNA to the feudal palace have enabled the monarchy to retain absolute power and for ever dangle a Damocles' sword over the parliament. Recent course of events have fully corroborated this and some more are more likely to follow in the near future.[27]

The 1st February action gave fresh ammunition to the rebels to mobilize opinion for their republican agenda. The Maoists called it the revival of "the medieval feudal autocracy". They appealed all political parties, intellectuals, civil society, and common masses to create a broad front against the 'feudal autocracy' for the establishment of a 'democratic republic'.

Thus, for different and antagonistic reasons, the actions of the king and the Maoists have reinforced each other. Actions from both sides are intended to gain space at the expense of the middle ground represented by the constitutional forces. The Maoists are making the normal democratic functioning impossible with the help of arms and violence. This has given the monarch an alibi to usurp the sovereign rights of the people and his actions have reinforced the Maoist thesis that democracy under monarchy is not a functioning proposition.

CONSTITUTIONAL AVENUE

Is there a constitutional solution to the crisis? The constitutional parties still believe that the solution can be found within the constitutional and democratic framework. For this, the reactivation of the constitutional process is necessary. The arguments for this school of thought are based on the fact that the present constitution is fully democratic as it recognizes the people as the ultimate source of sovereignty and state authority. It is flexible enough to accommodate all reforms, while keeping its basic structure intact. It allows freedom for people to discuss the monarchy and even hold republican views. A well-known constitutionalist wrote:

> The Constitution of the Kingdom of Nepal 1990 is the only constitution in our history, which places the people above all others, above any sections of it and any institutions of the country.... Power to the people is the main spirit and has been inviolable and not amenable to constitutional amendments. It is the first constitution in Nepal's history that has acknowledged the right of the people's movement to bring about constitutional changes and declared the people to be the source of sovereignty.
>
> ... Other values such as multiparty democracy, human rights, rule of law, adult franchise and parliamentary system of governance are there to strengthen the people and the citizens...
>
> People through their representatives in parliament have decisive say in running the affairs of the country including its finances and military apparatus. The King has decisive say only on the provisions regarding employees of the Royal Palace (Article 121) and the laws of succession to the throne (Article 28). Even the articles of the Constitution can be changed if parliament so desires in normal procedures of amendments.... Content and shape of the constitutional monarchy can be changed by the parliament through the normal amendment procedure of the Constitution without any extraordinary revolutionary process[28].

Article 126 of the constitution allows amendments in all provisions except those that will compromise the basic structure of the constitution as enshrined in the preamble of the constitution. The basic structure of the constitution as defined in the preamble includes: people-centred sovereignty, multi-party democracy, commitment to universally accepted human rights, and the constitutional monarchy. Issues like gender and ethnicity-related discrimination and exclusion, regional autonomy, and status of a truly constitutional monarch, which are often cited as areas calling for redress by the protagonists of a new constitution, can be addressed within the present constitutional framework. The 18-point platform of the five agitating parties, among others, included the stripping of some of the royal privileges. This, they believed, would represent a compromise in answer to the republican agenda of the Maoists in order to bring them to the political mainstream. They see a risk of falling between two stools in proposing a new constitution at a time when the present constitution itself remained encroached upon. Therefore, the present constitution should represent the basis and the anchor for any future political set-up and arrangement.

CONSTITUENT ASSEMBLY AND BOURGEOIS REVOLUTION

There is, however, another school of thought that considers constitutional rigidities as impediments to progress in this dynamic world. Proponents of this view opine that one should march forward with the emerging realities and demands of time, by moving beyond the basic structure of the constitution and this, according them, will be made possible only by a new constitution. They argue that the present constitution is already dead in the wake of the king's action, who instead of performing the constitutionally defined role of protecting it, has chosen to destroy it. They feel the time has come to write a new constitution. Another justification for the need of a new constitution is that the present constitution, which was drafted in 1990 based on the compromise of the political forces existing at that time, has lost its validity, in the context of the Maoists emerging as another major political force. They insist that new constitution should reflect the realities of this new power equation. It is also alleged that the present Constitution has failed to address the country's pressing problems including its poverty, backwardness and poor governance.

Opinions differ as to who will draft the new constitution and how. The predominant opinion is in favour of the election for a constituent assembly—as demanded by the Maoists—which would institutionalize the sovereign right of the people to decide their political future themselves. The advocacy for an elected constituent assembly for a new constitution is based on the following grounds.

First, it is the supreme exercise of the peoples' sovereign right. Ultimately, it is the peoples' legitimate representatives who should decide the type of political and government system for their country. Only that will establish the sovereign right of the people. It may be noted that the subject of the constituent assembly has not been raised in Nepal for the first time. In his first speech after the successful anti-Rana revolution in 1950, King Tribhuvan had promised that Nepal would be governed under a constitution framed by the peoples' elected representatives. B.P. Koirala was the strongest advocate of the people's right to draft their own constitution even in the subsequent years characterized by confusion and uncertainty. But political developments took a new turn after 1958 when King Mahendra declared the election for the parliament instead of the constituent assembly.

Second, the present Constitution has not sufficiently addressed the issue of minorities and the traditionally neglected communities through a provision of equitable sharing of state power. The diversity and plurality of the Nepali society should be sufficiently reflected in the political power structure.

Third and most important, the election for constituent assembly is the only way out of the violent conflict as this is the minimum condition set by the Maoists for their joining the mainstream politics. The Maoists have blamed the monarchy as the principal impediment to the democratic rights of the people, and feel that their own struggle since 1996, the Palace Massacre and the regressive steps of 4 October and 1 February, have heightened the anti-king and anti-monarchy sentiments in Nepal. The Maoists, therefore, consider the republican form of state through the constituent assembly as the principal political agenda. They have demanded elections for such an assembly 'under reliable international supervision'. It may be noted that the constituent assembly is a bourgeoisie concept and not generally on the communist agenda. However, they have proposed it for Nepal 'keeping in view Nepal's peculiar situation'. The Maoists consider this as a concession made to the constitutional forces. Yet, they have never said they would renounce violence and ultimately lay down arms if this principal demand is accepted. They probably believe that in the event of such an election taking place without decommissioning (although silenced) their People's Liberation Army, the result would go in their favour, and they could write a constitution of their choice in a democratic way.

Another important aspect of the Maoists' prime agenda, as they have put it, is—the destruction of the feudal production relations to create the foundation for a "bourgeois democratic revolution". This is a classic Marxist doctrine, but it is not followed anywhere. Under orthodox Marxism, the proletarian revolution does not take place in a society characterized by feudal production relations. Such a revolution will follow the development of bourgeois productive forces. But in its revolutionary history, communism has not followed the classical linear path, where bourgeois revolution precedes the proletarian revolution. Communism has been forced into predominantly agrarian societies. Even in Russia, the bourgeois productive forces had not fully developed for a proletarian revolution. Lenin defended his October Revolution as the "merging of two revolutions simultaneously"—a combined peasant war with the working class movement under the special emergency conditions created by the World War. Leon Trotsky had seen such a possibility much earlier, and had advocated the "telescoping" of the two revolutions.

In other communist countries including China under Mao, the proletarian revolutions were forced into agrarian economies even before passing through the phase of developing capitalist production forces. Experience shows that agrarian societies, rather than industrialized nations, have been the typical habitat for communist movements in recent history. The thesis that the development of the forces of production parallels the development of socialism has been tacitly abandoned. Socialism no longer needs to be nurtured by capitalism.[29] Judged against this context, the talk of bourgeois democratic revolution could be a Maoist tactical ploy intended to assure the people that they need not fear the harsh and radical political and economic programme typified by other communist regimes after taking over state power. Similarly, the agenda of the constituent assembly may also be a strategic step towards achieving their ultimate goal.

Against this backdrop, the Central Committee meeting of the Nepali Congress, after a series of marathon sessions, passed a political resolution on 17 July 2004 which could have important bearing in the country's search for political solution to the national stalemate. Given the unprecedented controversy to which the monarchy has been subjected to after 4 October, and the agenda of exclusion and centralized governance, which has been exploited by the Maoists to gain strength, the NC emphasized the imperative of a refined agenda. The refined national agenda, according to the resolution, includes—strong Constitutional safeguards against any future regressive action by the Monarch, restructuring of the state power to ensure fair representation to Nepal's neglected communities, and putting an end to the Maoist violence through negotiated settlement. Towards achieving this objective, the resolution puts forward three options as a means, namely: *(a)* constitutional reforms; *(b)* an exercise of people's sovereignty by putting the basic constitutional provisions before the referendum; *(c)* and a new constitution by an elected constitutional assembly. The Nepali Congress expressed its readiness to discuss any of the three options as a way out of the present crisis.

However, common riders were placed while resorting to any of these options. These were: *(a)* the restoration of the House of Representatives, *(b)* acceptance of the principle of people-based sovereignty; *(c)* multi-party system and full observance of universally accepted human rights; *(d)* renouncement of violence as a means of achieving political objectives and laying down of arms, and; *(e)* an all party government to conduct free and fair election under international supervision.

Another important development that took place along this line was the announcement of a common agenda by the seven political parties on 8 May 2005, as mentioned above. While committing itself to the revival of the HOR and an all party government, the agenda kept open all democratic options including the constituent assembly to resolve the problem of insurgency. It also stressed the constitutional means to address the crisis, and proposed to hold election under international supervision after the crisis is resolved. The seven parties reinforced their commitment in no uncertain terms to the supremacy of parliament with sovereignty based on the people. It is evident that political parties still favour a constitutional solution; they expressed readiness to consider the option of constituent assembly if that remains the only way to pull the country out of the vortex of violent conflict.

It may be pertinent to mention that the product of a constituent assembly in itself is no guarantee for a fully democratic constitution capable of addressing the country's myriad problems. History is full of instances when even the constituent assembly has failed to solve the problem; in fact they have ushered dictatorship and instability. In Pakistan, army generals repealed the constitution prepared by the constituent assembly to start military rule. In Soviet Russia, Lenin's Bolshevik Party dissolved the constituent assembly and scraped the draft constitution prepared by it. Ultimately, the communist party of the Soviet Union made the new constitution. Even in France, the constitution prepared by the constituent assembly could not provide stability. On the other hand, constitutions prepared through other means have proved to be democratic and offered stability in many other countries.

There is also a misconception in some quarters that many of the problems faced by the country, including its poverty and backwardness, is because of the failure of the present constitution. This is a flawed view. A constitution in itself or the modality to formulate it is not the panacea to all problems. It is only a document that defines the basic rules of governance, the functions and organization of various state organs, and the rights and obligations of its citizens. A constitution does not automatically guarantee good governance, economic development, and justice and equity to the neglected and disadvantaged communities. It is also no substitute for hard work, discipline, entrepreneurship, and right policies, which are the ultimate determinants of economic growth and development. The constitution cannot be blamed and faulted for the shortcomings of its practitioners.

LIBERAL DEMOCRACY SANS VIOLENCE

The 1st February action has removed the civilian veil of a royal regime of the previous two year and four months. The king has taken full responsibility to fix up the mess. The justification for his action was the promise "to restore peace and democracy". Peace is indeed everybody's prime concern. A diplomat, who met the king immediately after the takeover to express his concerns over the royal action, subsequently told this author that the king considered himself a champion of democracy. The US Ambassador to Nepal publicly said the king promised him to restore democracy in three months. The king's confidence in playing a savior may have been misplaced. His ability to rescue the country from the Maoist violence and the democratic shortcomings may have been exaggerated. But the people would be prepared to give him the benefit of doubt, if he really could deliver what he promised. Despite general skepticism from the intellectuals and the politicos, a section of the society pinned cautious hope on the potency of the king's action to rid the country of anarchy, violence, and instability.

But judging from the actions till these lines are written, the government seemed bent more on discrediting the previous governments, delegitimizing the political parties to justify the takeover, and indulging in populism to consolidate political power than in containing violence to restore peace and create conditions for democratic exercise. The government was quick in announcing a number of socio-economic programmes of populist nature, but had nothing substantial to restore peace and security. Meanwhile, the news of Maoist violence is continuing. A daring attack by the Maoists on a prison in Dhangadhi—the principal commercial and administrative hub of the Far-Western region—freeing 165 prisoners, including 60 Maoists on 10 February, the blockade of all major highways choking the Kathmandu valley for two weeks since 13 February and in subsequent occasions, and several other incidents that have gone unreported in the heavily censored media are not encouraging symptoms. The king promised to deploy the security force more effectively against the insurgents, but this has not happened. The forces seem preoccupied with putting down peaceful opposition and more busy "arresting dissidents, censoring the news, nationalizing property, scattering demonstrations, disbanding organizations, generally evading the laws".[30]

There was massive reorganization at the top echelon of the government bureaucracy. Much against the civil service norm and regulation, seven permanent secretaries serving in major ministries were sent to the reserve pool; some others were shunted to unimportant jobs[31]. A massive reshuffle was undertaken in district administration involving the transfer of 52 Chief District Officers. Seven joint secretaries and over two dozen CDOs were sent to the reserve poll. The civil service regulation does not allow civil servants in reserve poll for more than 30 days. New posts were created to consolidate administrative and political power. Pro-palace political workers and previous Panchas were nominated to act as district development monitors. A new ordinance was promulgated to enable the king to directly appoint regional and zonal administrators "to reach out to the people by expanding the administrative mechanism". [32] The posts of regional administrators have now been filled by loyal political appointees instead of civil servants as provided before. The zonal commissioners have been drawn mainly from RPP and former Panchas. Preparation is also underway to fill the DDCs and municipalities with trusted nominees. Out of the six vacant ambassadorial posts, four have been filled by former army generals.[33] The Civil Service Act is being amended through royal ordinance to enhance the royal administration's discretionary power in appointments, transfer, dismissal and other matters.

The 21-point programme announced by the first cabinet after the royal takeover addressed issues like anti-corruption, special provision to children from the *Dalit* and other backward communities, decentralization, land distribution to the landless, special package for the Karnali Zone, a policy of positive discrimination to favour the backward communities, and religious tourism.[34] These are familiar clichés borrowed from previous governments. The government also reduced the price of kerosene and cooking gas marginally, a month after the previous government had raised the prices of all petroleum products to align them with international market prices. Another prominent measure was the executive decision to form the controversial Royal Commission on Corruption Control empowered to probe corruption cases and take decision on the spot. Its power includes confiscating and nationalizing the property earned through irregular means. This Commission—defying basic norms of natural justice and rule of law—amalgamates into it the authorities of investigation, prosecution, and judiciary; any criticism against it is punishable up to six months of imprisonment and heavy fine. Armed with such power and under conditions of a police state, the legitimacy of this body's action is bound to be questionable.

As for the Maoists, there is growing consensus on a number of socio-economic issues they have raised. But this is not what they are interested to negotiate about. Their main agenda is political. Their demands of the constituent assembly, a round-table conference, and an interim government are both tactical and political. The acceptance of these demands does not appear too heavy a price, if that can bring about a lasting peace and violence-free politics, which is the overriding concern for everybody. The important question, however, is the future of the Maoist arms. No real solution will be possible without confronting the issue of their violent methods and armed organizations which will have to be demobilized, and eventually decommissioned.

The offer to discuss their political demand in lieu of their readiness to renounce violence is also necessary to test the Maoist commitment for peace and preparedness to join peaceful political process within the framework of a liberal democracy. The various resolutions passed by their party forums leave one suspicious on whether they are at all prepared to accept multiparty democracy. The Maoist leader Prachanda's meteoric rise to power and eventually the adoption of his doctrine *Prachandapath,* is attributed to the leadership he consistently provided in fighting revisionism and revisionist tendency, and his successful application of the Maoist doctrine of People's War to the Nepali conditions. The Maoists who have waged armed struggle to attain their 'democratic and republican goals' have no faith in reformism and parliamentarism, which they consider symptoms of rightist and petty bourgeois order.

Peace, however, is worth any effort and should be given every chance. After the direct rule of the king from 1st February, the Maoists have ruled out any possibility of peace negotiation. They are talking of final assault for the establishment of a 'democratic republic'. One unfortunate fall-out of the royal takeover is the removal of the buffer zone between the monarch and the Maoists. With the monarchical regime suppressing genuine political activities, and suspending multiparty politics, the popular pressure on the political parties to positively respond to the Maoist call for a broad front against the monarchy is increasing. Such a possibility will signal the demise of both monarchy and democracy. For the monarchy's own survival, the development of a genuine multiparty democracy is necessary. One cannot fight the insurgency by suppressing political freedom and mutilating democratic process. The political parties are still committed to the middle path—democratic and constitutional. Their recently announced common platform opposes the king's direct rule but does not reject monarchy. It rejects Maoists' armed violence, but expresses readiness to discuss political solution including the constituent assembly. Authoritarian and violent means will bring neither peace nor democracy. The solution lies in democratic and constitutional route. The route may be bumpy, long-winded and fraught with occasional faltering and shortcomings, but remains amenable to self improvement and course correction.

At the same time, the Maoists should realize the futility of their violent struggle, if the one-party proletarian dictatorship still remains their goal. With India tightening the noose around their neck, and adversarial international conditions, they must be reconciled to push their agenda through peaceful means in a competitive democracy. If the objective is to ensure justice to the downtrodden and the people at the margin and guarantee the sovereign rights to the people, then political settlement can be arrived at. But the violent methods must be discarded. The bottom line is—a violence-free liberal democracy where all ideologies and ideas are allowed to compete peacefully without intimidation and fear.

NOTES

1. International Crisis Group, *Nepal's Royal Coup: Making a Bad Situation Worse*, Asia Report No. 91, 9 February 2005.
2. It was clear that the development in Nepal was the main reason behind the decision. The Indian Foreign Secretary clarified this in New Delhi.
3. This was stated by Finance Minister Madhukar Rana to the media men on his return at the Tribhuvan International Airport. See *The Kathmandu Post*, 7 March 2005.
4. The total foreign aid figure was scaled down from the estimated Rs. 32.3 billion 20.4 billion. See *The Himalayan Times*, 22 April 2005.
5. 25 April 2005 Issue of *The Time*.
6. Amendment No. 492 proposed by The Senator Cochran from Mississippi , for Senator Leahy, Chairman of the Foreign Relations Committee.
7. Their demands included, among others, removal of the terrorist tag and the red corner notice on the Maoists, release of all their detainees, withdrawal of court cases and confinement of the RNA within five kilometres of their barracks.
8. The student wing of the party ANFSU formally passed a resolution to this effect, while prominent leaders demanded the withdrawal from the cabinet in the Central Committee meeting. *The Kathmandu Post*, 29 November 2004.

9. Lok Raj Baral, 'Security, Democracy and Pluralism: The Case of Nepal' paper presented in NCCS Regional seminar 16–17 November 2004, Kathmandu.
10. The panel headed by Bharat Mohan Adhikari had recommended Yub Raj Khatiwada, a member of the National Planning Commission for the job. On being asked by the Prime Minister to review the legality of the recommendation, the Attorney General declared that Khatiwada was not eligible for the job, as he still was holding a relatively junior position in the Nepal Rastra Bank. The concerned Act allowed only a Deputy Governor to be considered for the Governor's job.
11. What had almost become a routine feature in many hill districts, in the last week of January 2005, a total of 1,150 students were abducted in Dhading and Sankhuwasaba districts for their orientation programme (*The Himalayan Times*, 28 January 2005)
12. UML Deputy Prime Minister Bharat Mohan Adhikari considered polls impossible (*Kantipur,* 27 January 2005) and RPP senior Minister Balaram Ghartimagar ruled out immediate election (*The Himalayan Times,* 1 February 2005).
13. Chief Election Commissioner Keshav Raj Rajbhandari said at least six months were needed to make preparation to hold election, and his Spokesman said there was no possibility of polls before October 2005. (*The Kathmandu Post*, 11 January 2005). Deepak Gurung, the spokesperson of the RNA said the government had not formally discussed the polls with the RNA (Kantipur, 29 January 2005).
14. *The Himalyan Times* 18 January 2005). Other leading members such as Bam Dev Gautam and Pradip Nepal were openly advocating the HOR restoration. Even within NC (D), majority of Central Committee members spoke in favour of the House revival rather than polls in the Central Committee meeting held in the last week of December 2005.
15. A three-day national meeting of zonal and district lead workers of the UML in Kathmandu urged the leadership to withdraw from the government, if the peace process with the Maoists could not start afresh. They also urged the party not to go ahead for polls in view of the security situation. (*The Himalayan Times,* 28 February, 2005 and *The Kathmandu Post,* 27 January 2005).
16. Kank Mani Dixit, 'Exit Strategy, Nepal Quagmire' *The Kathmandu Post*, 30 October 2004.
17. Veteran constitutional lawyer like Ganesh Raj Sharma, the most consistent advocate of the Prime Minister's right to dissolve the House, also admitted that the restoration of the House would be the best way to revive the Constitution under the scenario of the election not taking place within the stipulated period. Also, see interview of Sambhu Thapa, the Chairman of the Nepal Bar Association, *The Kathmandu Post,* 28 November 2004 making a case for the revival.
18. The statement was issued jointly by the Chairman of the Constitution Drafting Committee Biswo Nath Upadhyaya and members Bharat Mohan Adhikari,

Madhav Nepal, Daman Nath Dhungana, Mukunda Regmi, Laxman Aryal, and then Minister for Law and Justice and Coordinator of the Cabinet Sub-Committee on Constitution Nilambar Acharya.

19. See *The Himalayan times*, 25 November 2004.
20. On every previous occasion when the Prime Minister made such recommendation, the King took time holding consultations regarding the constitutionality of the move.
21. *Nepal Samacharpatra*, 19 August 2001.
22. Online Interview with Thomas L. Kelly for *Time*, 26 January 2004.
23. There is a historic similarity of this speech with that of King Mahendra in Nepalgunj itself on 30 January 1960, when he said that he would not hesitate to take drastic action in the interest of the country and the people. (See relevant section in Chapter III).
24. The Constitutional Council's formal recommendations of Bhoj Raj Pokhrel for the post of Chief Election Commissioner and Usha Nepal for Commissioner were changed after intervention from the Palace. Similarly, the recommendations of Sri Kanta Regmi and Ram Kaji Bantawa for the vacant membership positions of CIAAA were overruled by the Palace.
25. See Swapan Dasgupta, 'Kingly Faith' in *The Telegraph*, 11 February 2005. This was corroborated to this author from other sources also, particularly by the diplomatic representatives of the countries concerned.
26. The RNA did not make an effective move for days when hundreds of school children were abducted from Pharping of Kathmandu district. The Maoists were openly raising 'taxes' from trucks and buses plying in major highways, under the nose of security force. It seemed the latter were turning a blind eye.
27. Babu Ram Bhattarai(2003) 'A Rejoinder on Current Issues' in *The People's War in Nepal*, Arjun Karki and David Seddon (ed.), op.cit.
28. Nilambar Acharya, 'People and Parliament', *The Kathmandu Post*, 29 November 2004. Acharya was the Minister of Law and Justice and the Coordinator of the Cabinet Sub-committee on the Constitution to monitor and liaise with its Drafting Committee in 1990.
29. See R.S.Mahat, 'Peasantry as a Revolutionary Force in a Proletarian Revolution: A Possibility' *Arthavijnan*, June 1978, Gokhale Institute of Politics and Economics, Poona.
30. Manjushree Thapa, *The New York Times*, 12 February 2005.
31. The secretaries thus affected were: Bijaya Raj Bhattarai, Shashi Kanta Mainali, Bhoj Raj Ghimire, Dinesh Chandra Pyakurel, Tika Datta Nirola, Narayan Silwal, Umesh Mainali and Bidyadhar Mallick.
32. This was revealed by the Minister for Information and Communications in a press meet on 31 March 2005. *The Himalayan Times*, 1 April 2005.
33. The posts of Permanent Representative of the UN in New York and ambassadors to France, Thailand, and Myanmar have been filled by former army generals.
34. See Nepal's national daily newspapers on 5 February 2005.

Chapter Sixteen

Fault Lines

In the preceding chapters, we reviewed and analyzed the historical evolution and dynamics of the political economy of Nepal since its emergence as a nation about 240 years ago. The state of the political economy as it exists today is the outcome of socio-economic factors and events interacting with the political developments over the period. Some of the emerging controversies, debates, and critical issues of the Nepali society, which surfaced particularly in the last decade after the restoration of democracy, have also been highlighted. Before concluding this book, we propose to flag a few more fault-lines and challenges that have an important bearing on the future course of Nepal's political economy.

'SOFT STATE' GOVERNANCE

The Nepali society suffers from what Gunnar Myrdal called the 'soft state' character which is manifested in the secular lack of social discipline and weak implementation of state laws and regulations. Myrdal saw little hope for South Asia's development and any measure of social upliftment without greater social discipline. He lamented the fact that in South Asian countries, governments required extraordinarily little from its citizens in terms of obligations in the interest of the community or to avoid actions opposed to that interest. The low level of social discipline is what distinguishes South Asia today from the European societies at the early stage of industrialization. Laws and regulations that will impose citizens' obligations to the society and state are enacted, but the regulations are not backed by compulsion. As Myrdal points out, nothing is more dangerous for a democracy than lack of discipline. By refusing to accept a limited, democratic coercion, the community may make necessary for itself the unlimited coercion of totalitarian government.[1]

Nepal has not lagged behind in introducing modern and innovative principles in various instruments of its governance. This includes a modern constitution, organs and institutions of government at national, municipal and local levels, civil and development administration, and associated laws and regulations. But laxity and casualness in their enforcement have rendered them largely ineffective.

An example of this is provided by the recent World Bank assessment on Nepal's financial accountability. The study considers Nepal's accounting and reporting system—statutory and legislative framework, bookkeeping and accounting, manpower, financial reporting, procurement and asset management—well defined and elaborate. But the challenges are in its implementation, including a failure to link the expenditure with outputs as required by the system.[2] The failure to comply with the impressive legal and fiduciary framework has resulted in the country being categorized as 'high risk' by the standards of the study's framework.

Myrdal's soft state concern mainly relates to a lack of enforcement on citizens' obligation to the society. The traditional practice of contribution for the maintenance of trails, canals, bridges, and other community assets has largely been discontinued, while in Western Europe, the long-term trend has been towards perfection of these systems, and transformation from the network of individual relationships into community obligations. Even the development of the welfare state concept has not affected this trend; instead the trend is towards a more precise definition, a reduction of laxity and arbitrariness, and a more just distribution of the burdens in accordance with the abilities to shoulder them.[3]

In principle, there is unanimity on the need for community participation, obligation, and ownership in local development matters. In fact, community participation has been an important theme of the current development literature, and Nepal is no exception in this regard. Elaborate regulations and manuals governing the formation, operation, accounting and auditing of the users' committees to implement such projects as irrigation, road, and drinking water have been enacted in Nepal. Part of the total project cost has to come from the community contribution in cash or labour. But what happens in most cases is : a deal is struck with the prospective contractor to assume the responsibility for the community contribution out of his profits in return to the contract award, thus diluting and abusing the whole concept of community participation. In other instances, the users' committees, instead of performing the job themselves, subcontract the work to the professional contractor in return for a small commission.

Nothing would highlight the soft state character in the Nepali governance more prominently than the practically inoperative Consumer Interest Protection Act that outlaws cartels and syndicates in the supply of goods and services. Furthermore, there exists a Vehicles and Transport Management Act that bans cartels in transport services. But these laws have not made any difference in the existing syndicate system in the transport business along major highway routes. This has prevented possible competition in the area, which would not only have reduced the prevailing transport fare, but also improved the quality of services. In 2004, the country faced a sugar crisis in the eve of *Dasain* and *Tihar* festivals despite the fact that the total production capacity of the country's sugar industry is higher than domestic demand. The tight sugar cartel deliberately kept the production low while successfully lobbying to impose high sugar import tariff in the name of protecting 'infant domestic industry'. The result was sugar shortages and high prices at the festive season penalizing millions of hapless consumers, while the sugar lobby reaped huge profit in connivance with the establishment.[4]

The creation of institutions with public money at the slightest excuse, without appraising their substantive merits and financial sustainability, is a tendency seen practically in every government in varying degrees. Towards the end of 2004, the government proposed to set up seven universities through ordinances, mainly on political considerations. The University Grants Commission (UGC) had already drafted an Umbrella Act to govern the policy and regulations of establishing universities in Nepal. Needless to say, there was no proper homework and preparation regarding the rationale of these universities in relation to manpower planning, sources of funding, the type of manpower proposed from these universities, the management system and so on. Following protest from all quarters, including from the UGC, all former University Vice Chancellors, and the education community, the ordinance was limited to only one university. But nobody knows when the other ordinances will be promulgated. This development is taking place at a time when the two full-fledged universities—Purbanchal and Pokhara universities—established in the last decade with state funding have failed in meeting their original objectives of serving as regional universities by shedding the present unwieldy size of Tribhuvan University.

The number of public holidays in Nepal has perhaps no parallel in the world. Out of 365 days in a year, there are 132 days of public holidays including the weekends. In addition, public officials are entitled 12 days of casual and festival leave, 30 days of home leave, and 12 days of sick leave. This excludes the 'deemed' off-days on account of *bandhs*, strikes, and blockades. Calculating all these, the actual working days in the public offices in Nepal would not exceed 165! Another typical characteristic is the underutilization of personnel in most public offices. It is normal to see the staff attending only a few hours in the office and spending most of their time gossiping or on personal business. In most other countries, it is customary for professional staff to stay extra hours in offices for serious professional work, but our government offices look like graveyards after 5 p.m. Additionally, frequent calls for *bandhs* and strikes, obstruction of public traffic without permission, destruction of public and personal property are all further symptoms of a soft state.

The concept of civil disobedience and *Satyagraha* methods are perfectly justified when fighting against autocratic and undemocratic rule. However, the extension of this technique to pressurize the democratic administration even on trivial issues not only promotes social indiscipline, but also harms the interest of the nation and its people. The well-known Indian jurist N. Palkhiwala observed, "Work is not a curse to be kept at bay by holidays and *bandhs*".[5] But wastage and loss in our economy on account of excessive holidays, *bandhs,* lockouts, *dharnas*, and physical blockades have now been accepted as part and parcel of the normal way of life. Nepal is too poor a country to afford losing millions of man-days each year on account of such disruptions.

Our public administration is another area which betrays the character of indiscipline and lack of commitment. In the very first session of parliament after democracy, a section of civil servants was being used, with political backing, for street demonstrations, pen downs, and disruption of normal government functions. Actions under various governments, including excessive political interference in their day-to-day functioning and arbitrary mass transfers have further demoralized the civil service.[6] An even more disturbing phenomenon is the unattractiveness of the civil service, unlike in the past decades, as a career for the best and brightest. This is not only because of uncompetitive incentives in the public sector, but also because the examination and recruitment practices of the civil service are too arcane and haven't kept pace with time. This does not augur well for the quality of future governance.

Public sector enterprises have been the living monuments of inefficiency, nepotism, and anarchy since long. Public enterprises are often criticized for serving the interest of politicians, senior officials and influence peddlers by offering ready employment to cronies and relations, borrowing vehicles for indefinite periods, and enjoying the hospitality at the expense of the respective Ministries or Departments. With every change of government, there is change in chairmen, the composition of the boards, and general managers of these enterprises.[7] The soft management of the public enterprises in Nepal can be gauged from the fact that even a relatively well managed and prestigious PE like the Nepal Electricity Authority, which is under constant scrutiny of the international community, loses 23 per cent of the total electricity generated to system loss, evaporation, and pilferage. Equally irresponsible is the manner in which the management of some PEs decide to increase unfunded long-term liabilities without considering their financial sustainability. Many public corporations have pension provisions for their employees after retirement without creating a pension fund for the purpose. The capacity of these enterprises to meet these obligations is bleak and the burden ultimately is passed on to the government treasury. The government took some stringent decisions to stop such tendency in the past but the problem is far from over.[8]

POLITICAL BEHAVIOUR

Over the years, Nepali politics has exhibited symptoms of a culture of 'political underdevelopment'. Especially since 1994, unstable governments have been the hallmark of Nepali politics. Although elected for a period of five years, no House of Representatives (HOR) has completed its full term. All general elections called and/or conducted are of mid-term nature. Generally speaking, whenever any Prime Minister has sensed a threat to his government, he has recommended the dissolution of the HOR as an 'exit strategy'.[9] Practically every Prime Minister of the post-*Panchayat* era has resorted to this technique. Despite intra-party fighting within the NC, the first government after the general election was generally stable in the sense that there was only one government in the first HOR, which lasted for about three and a half year. In the second HOR, which produced five Prime Ministers, the making and unmaking of cabinets became very frequent. The NC had a comfortable majority in the third HOR, but even this period saw three Prime Ministers due to serious party in-fighting. The changes in Prime Ministers also produced a large number of ministers. During the second HOR, of the 265 members of the two Houses, 121(45.7 per cent) became ministers. Even the third HOR saw the making of some 79 ministers in three cabinets out of the total NC strength of 112.[10]

Resorting to extra-constitutional methods to force opposition demands was another perversity frequently witnessed during this period. Practices such as the physical blocking of parliamentary proceedings, '*gheraos*' of the Speaker by slogan-shouting opposition members almost became accepted behaviour. This reached its culmination in March/April 2001 when the opposition physically obstructed the parliamentary business for 57 days rendering the entire winter session of the parliament futile. Whenever the opposition wanted to force its agenda on the government, the threat of obstructing parliamentary proceedings was generally the tactic of choice. The aggressive oppositional fight was taken beyond the halls of parliament and to the streets under the slogan '*Sadan-Dekhi-Sadak-Samma*' operationalized by demonstrations and nation-wide shut downs that led to the loss of life and property. If street politics begins determining the behaviour of the parliament, then it is a clear departure from the accepted parliamentary tradition and makes street the locus of parliamentary norm.[11]

Another important phenomenon that was witnessed during the period was that practically every political party, including the Nepali Congress, UML, RPP and NSP, went through a period of serious internal turmoil that lead to party splits. The UML, which had split over the issue of Mahakali Treaty, has now been reunited. The RPP and NSP were divided, reunited, and divided again. The MPs of the Peasants and Workers Party became the victim of poaching from big parties. Periods of political turmoil, instability, and uncertainty, marked by frequent changes in government and untimely elections create fertile grounds for malpractices, populist policies, and corrupt behaviour. It was during such periods that the allegations of corruption, malpractices, and scandals involving ministers, Members of Parliament, and politicians became newspaper headlines threatening to shatter popular faith in the people's representatives. Increasing perks and privileges of the lawmakers, including the duty-free imports of vehicles and lucrative pension schemes, became the subject of deep criticisms. These privileges were subsequently withdrawn. Such behaviour naturally weakens the moral authority of political leadership and erodes democratic values and ethos. The effect of this in civil and development administration and overall governance will be even more serious. Such an environment reduces people's faith in democratic governance, offering an excuse for the emergence of authoritarian regimes.

The political behaviour did not become any better after the Royal takeover. Many of the personalities who were rewarded under the new dispensation were the people who were the initiators and perpetrators of such malpractices under democratic governance. Some of the decisions of the regime to raise financial privileges and budgets of the Palace, unjustified grants-in-aid on partisan and personal considerations, extravagance on taxpayer money and other malpractices have been noted elsewhere. Even from the perspective of political stability, the record of this period is worse. After the royal take over there were four governments in two and half years.

The political forces also had difficulty in internalizing the culture and basic values of the multi-party politics, and the underlying principle of King-in-Parliament in a constitutional monarchy.

> One of the new features of Nepal's parliamentary experiment is that actors who introduced the system themselves are unclear about the basics of parliament and parties. Political parties did not develop out of their long involvement in the parliamentary processes.... Parties were created first for bringing about a change, then for participation in elections, and eventually for claiming a share in power either singly or as partner in coalition politics.[12]

There were problems of adjustments and reconciliation with the new political arrangement. Particularly, the agenda propagated by the left parties for more than forty years appeared too radical to be compatible with the spirit of the parliamentary process. Despite occasional revolutionary rhetoric, the UML did its best to project the image of a moderate left party. Even their methods, however, remained aggressive and obstructionist. There were other radical parties like the Unity Centre and the *Mashal* brands of leftist politics. Constitutional monarchy and parliamentary democracy were frequent targets of attacks from these groups. Although their ideological postures did not directly disapprove of the ongoing experiment with the parliamentary system, it created suspicion and confusion among people and the king.[13]

Finally, there were also instances that led people to question the king's real commitment to act according to the letter and spirit of the constitution. The king's nomination of ten members of the Upper House without consulting the Prime Minister, seeking judicial advice on the Prime Minister's recommendation to dissolve the House, and the bills passed by the Parliament[14] are examples which do not strictly conform to the constitutional spirit. None of the Prime Ministers took objection to these acts, preferring to play safe by not annoying the monarch. It should be noted, however, that this behaviour must be seen in light of the transitionary nature of the Nepali political process as at the time, monarchy had just been forced out of an authoritarian mould. But, despite these isolated instances, politics under King Birendra was generally a smooth affair as he seemed reconciled to playing a limited role. The search for a more assertive monarchical role became obvious under King Gyanendra when he started expressing his dissatisfaction with the democratic governance in press interviews and public speeches. The actions of 4th October, the subsequent changing of Prime Ministers, and eventually the start of direct rule invoking historical obligation to "defend democracy" and "restore peace" were contrary to the accepted norms of constitutional monarchy.

PRIMARY NATIONAL AGENDA: ECONOMY OR POLITICS?

South Asia and East Asia started the development journey under similar initial conditions after the colonial era. The per capita income difference between South Asia and the East Asia (excluding China) in 1960 was around US $200. At present, the difference is around US $10,000.[15] What explains this extremely unequal performance? It is believed that the excessive preoccupation of South Asian countries with political rather than economic agenda is responsible for this disparity. The East Asian countries have devoted, and continue to devote, most of their energy to economic issues. These countries followed policies which would create economic opportunities to improve the living conditions of their people. More growth-oriented and human-centred policies were followed with positive results. In essence, the order of national priorities for these countries—first, second and third—were all economic.

The South Asian priorities, on the other hand, have been predominantly political. Even under the partyless *Panchayat* system, which was introduced with the declared objective of accelerating economic development in the country, the national resource and energy were devoted mainly to protect and consolidate an authoritarian regime. In the contemporary world, economic and development issues dominate the national agenda, and competition between nations centres around growth, development, poverty reduction, and human prosperity. The alignment and realignment of international relations among and between nation states are determined largely by economic and commercial interests.

Globally, democracy, human rights, and multi-party democracy are now the accepted principles of political governance. In Nepal, these issues were settled after the People's Movement and the promulgation of the Constitution of the Kingdom of Nepal 1990. But unfortunately the armed Maoist insurgency and the monarchial activism have now opened up the same political question and we are again debating and struggling on the issue. This is very unfortunate at a time when we should have been channelling our national attention, resources, and energy towards economic development and nation building. Politics and political process are important for economic development. The political system must guarantee the inherent political rights of the people and broad-based participation of all communities and regions.

There is also a school of thought that a new constitution or a constitution drafted through a new mechanism would solve all the country's problems including economic ills and exclusion. This is wrong. Beyond a democratic and inclusive political system, there is no alternative to a right policy environment, pro-poor development strategy, hard work, discipline, and entrepreneurship to address the problems of poverty. Nepal is a poor country by any standards, and poverty cannot be banished without increasing productivity and creating new opportunities. To expand opportunities, a right policy environment is a prerequisite.

Similarly, there is also a doctrinaire approach to the problem—a misconception that unquestioned adherence to a particular political ideology would offer solution to the country's myriad ills. The communists with their indoctrination on state-controlled economy see the solutions of the country's problems in a centralized economy. The Nepali Congress is wedded to the left-of-centre philosophy of Democratic Socialism. There is also a view within the Congress which seems to think that the state-controlled economy would address the country's socio-economic problems. The fact is that there is no dogmatic prescription to economic problems. The world is moving towards pragmatism which accords the principal role in business and economics to the market and in social and human development to the state. In a sense, it is a convergence of what works best under the two systems. B.P. Koirala's Democratic Socialism was mid-way between state-controlled socialism and a market-based capitalist economy. He believed in combining the social and judicial component of the state-controlled economy with the entrepreneurship and creativity of the Western countries, along with the democratic values of human dignity, self-respect, and political rights.

When the NC government started market-oriented economic reforms in the early 1990s, there was a barrage of criticisms for abandoning B.P. Koirala's Democratic Socialism. People had the nostalgia of post-colonial economic thinking when socialism was equated with every thing state-run, and state enterprises were deliberately promoted as an alternative to foreign private investment, which was often seen as symbol of colonial rule. State enterprises were also perceived as instruments of generating the surplus and profit required for investment in other priority areas. But such enterprises, instead of generating additional revenue for the government, turned out to be a net drain on the government treasury and administrative capacity. Such undertakings were blocking the growth of fair competition, and the resulting improvement in the quality of goods and services at competitive prices.

One unknown side of the privatization of public enterprises in Nepal is, unlike in other countries, it does not bring revenue to the state treasury. Normally, the PEs represent a net financial burden to the government, because of the huge unmet liabilities and the excessive staff which demand drastic retrenchment with attractive financial packages. This has to be met from the state treasury and delays in taking decisions would only add to future liability. In the Ministry of Finance, this author had personal experience of paying salaries of the staff of non-performing government-owned corporations, which in a competitive market would have been declared bankrupt long ago. But no government would venture to take such a decision for the social problems it would create. B.P. Koirala was aware of the limitations of the state's entrepreneurial role, and in the latter part of his political career, had become its critic. He used to give the example of the stagnation in Soviet agriculture under collective farming, in contrast to the booming productivity of privately managed kitchen gardens.

The essence of democratic socialism is social and economic justice, equal opportunities, human dignity, and removal of poverty. The modality of achieving this objective need not necessarily be the state at all levels. Over the years, the state has proven itself as the most inefficient manager in commerce, business and production. To quote Palkhiwala:

> State ownership is to social justice what ritual is to religion and dogma to truth. State ownership and state control are the shells of socialism that really intended to protect and promote the growth of the kernel; but rigid shells merely stunts its growth[16].

The state's appropriate role should be to create conditions for competition, innovation, and entrepreneurship in order to unleash the forces of creativity and production. At the same time, the state should also take the lead role in initiating programmes to reduce poverty, ensure economic justice, improve the living conditions of the backward and underdeveloped regions and communities, create infrastructure, protect the environment, and provide education and health services. There is a great degree of agreement on this approach throughout the world. Pragmatism rather than dogmatism is presently the accepted rule.

The preoccupation with non-economic issues has obstructed the Nepali regime from entering into serious dialogue with India in matters of vital national interest, like the use of water resources. Projects like the Karnali Multi-Purpose has been under discussion and study for about four decades, with tens of millions of US dollars already spent on it. The Mahakali Treaty was signed eight years ago and was hailed as a milestone in the use of water resources for mutual benefit of the two countries. Koshi High Dam and Kamala Diversion projects have been under discussion for almost two decades but none of them have moved an inch in terms of implementation. The Karnali Multi-Purpose is now under cold storage, while the Mahakali Treaty, after eight years of its signing has not yet seen the Detailed Project Report, which should have been completed within six months of signing. Differences in position between the two sides over a number of issues including: the location of the re-regulating dam (Rupaligadh or Poornagiri or somewhere else), ownership over the quantum of water in the post-Pancheswor scenario, prior-use of the Mahakali water in the command area of Lower Sarada over 160 kilometres downstream, and power pricing have hindered its progress. On the Saptakoshi High Dam, leading water resource experts are now expressing critical views on the project, after the two countries agreed to go ahead with the detailed study.[17] Territories on the Nepali side of the border have been suffering from inundation problems due to the construction of embankments on the Indian side.[18] So much so that Nepal's ability to tame some of its rivers like the Bagmati, Kankai, Babai, and Sikta for irrigation purpose with external assistance has met rough waters in view of the Indian position of 'prior consumptive use' of water across the border.[19] The result of this is that not a single major river irrigation project in the *tarai* has been approved for donor assistance in recent times. The support of major international agencies in Nepal's irrigation sector is now limited to ground water and farmers managed irrigation systems.

Mutual suspicion and mistrust between two neighbours with so much interdependence is most unfortunate. The use of Nepal's enormous water potential for her prosperity, not only through power generation, but also for consumptive use like irrigation, is practically impossible without proper understanding and cooperation between the two countries. For this, a climate of trust and confidence is a prerequisite. The not-so-happy experience with Koshi and Gandaki projects should not deter us from negotiating other projects in our national interest with an open mind. Looking at every proposed venture with suspicion reinforced by the compulsion of domestic politics, rather than on merit, will only harm Nepal's interest. Similarly, the Indian side should respect

Nepal's sensibilities and vital interest on this issue by not looking at Nepal's water product from the perspective of a monopsonist market with the bureaucratic mindset of out-foxing the Nepali side.

DISPARITY AND CENTRALIZATION

The market-oriented economic reforms have enhanced and expanded the private sector's role in the economy. This is visible in virtually all fields of business. Although our export sector is still heavily dependent on a few products and few countries, the ingenuity and enterprise shown by the private sector is remarkable. Consider the carpet industry. The raw wool is imported from the far Pacific and mixed with Tibetan wool and the final product using Nepali skills is sold in Atlantic countries. Even the momentary success of the *pashmina* shawl exports showed the capacity of the private business to capture emerging global fashion trends. The Nepali tourism industry is probably the most innovative and diversified in South Asia as it responds to a variety of tastes and interests ranging from adventure tourism like mountaineering, trekking, mountain biking, rafting, bungy jump and para-gliding, to wildlife safaris, and the showcasing of diverse cultures and archaeological monuments. Similarly, the remarkable strides made in air travel, banking, education, health services, media, real estate, and shopping is also due to private entrepreneurship.

Unfortunately, most of these activities are concentrated in Kathmandu and relatively well-off areas. This has accentuated disparities between the urban metropolis, particularly the Kathmandu valley, and the rest of the country. The NLSS II findings also clearly point out that although real income has increased for all income groups, regions and ecological belts, the households at the upper quintile have benefited more than others. Over the period of eight years since 1995/96, the real consumption expenditure per capita increased by 42 per cent. The bottom quintile of the population only saw an increase of 21 per cent, while the top quintile got a 64 per cent jump. The gap in the consumption shares across population has also become worse. Similarly, the increase in real per capita income for the bottom quintile of the households was 20 per cent during the same period, while it was 67 per cent for the richest quintile. Thus, the income disparity has clearly accentuated.

Despite some commercialization of the agricultural sector and increases in agricultural exports, this sector remains predominantly traditional and subsistence oriented. The share of agriculture in the national production has declined noticeably and there has also been a decline in the ratio of population engaged in this sector. However, the modernization of agriculture has not kept pace with the advancements made in other fields. The expanding industrial and trading activities have very low backward linkages. Major export industries depend largely on the imported raw materials. Increasing disparities in income and wealth is visible in the quality of life between rich and poor, towns and villages, the metropolis and the rest. The newly created income and wealth has been concentrated largely in the modern dynamic sectors —export, industry, tourism, finance, real estate, communications, aviation, etc.

A key factor blamed for these discrepancies is the centralized administration of Kathmandu, which has a monopoly over all national decision making. Much of the regional disparity, exclusion, and discrimination can also be attributed to Kathmandu and the skewed power that its pampered elites hold. An important foundation of the Maoist appeal is the spatially uneven development resulting in growing social inequality and centralization of resources. As indigenous people mostly inhabit the backward and oppressed regions, the regional discrimination manifests itself as national, cultural, and linguistic discrimination and oppression. The most backward and poorest regions of the country also happen to be the geographically most remote, and farthest from Kathmandu Valley. The status of Human Development Index across districts show that the farther the districts, particularly in the west, from the country's capital, the lower their HDI. Of the 20 districts with the lowest HDIs, 16 are in the mid and far-western regions. The four districts with highest HDI are located in the Kathmandu valley and Pokhara. The capital city, with its political power and the concentration of economic and social services, has attracted capital surplus from the rest of the country.

There is no doubt that the twelve years of democracy has brought about a redistribution of political power. This has caused a redirection in the flow of public resources towards rural areas resulting in visible improvements in social and economic services. But this has not been sufficient in relation to the rising aspirations created by democratic exercise and an awareness of poverty and deprivation. Deprived minorities and people living in far-flung and backward areas blame the political and administrative power exercised by Kathmandu as the root cause for their troubles. Incidentally, this reality came into sharp focus with the rise of Maoist insurgency. Relatively well-off people from all over the country started making Kathmandu their home as only the capital city was considered relatively safe. Needless to say, this has led to further disparity and inequality.

EDUCATIONAL DUALISM

The education sector is marked by rapid quantitative expansion. Increasing government investment, strong social demand, community participation, and a sizable mobilization of private capital have led to growths in literacy, enrolment, educated manpower, and educational institutions. The total number of students at primary and secondary levels expanded from 3.2 million in 1990 to 5.5 million in 2002. Similarly, the number of students in higher education increased from 95,000 to 153,000. Furthermore, we have already described the growth of private education in various technical fields such as medicine and engineering in prior chapters.

However, this quantitative expansion has been accompanied by low quality of inequity, and disparity resulting in a phenomenon of educational dualism. Those who are economically well-off send their children to fee-charging private schools, in institutions inside and outside the country. On the other hand, poor families are forced to dump their children in government-run schools which suffer from poor infrastructure, lack of educational materials, and an insufficient number of teachers. It is often said that teachers are more absent from schools than students, and the teaching schedule hardly exceeds three hours a day.[20] While the quality of education provided by private institutions is also a matter of debate, if the results from the SLC and the marketability of the school graduates is any guide, the products from the government schools have little access to decent jobs. The same phenomenon prevails in higher education. An educationalist writes:

> Academic standards in the campuses are mediocre, with teachers again, lacking dedication and scholarship. University classes consist of straight lectures that adhere to the text, or teaching notes prepared some years ago. Instruction is bookish, prescriptive and suffers from what Paulo Freire calls "narration sickness".
>
> Seminars, discussions and case studies are unheard of in Nepali higher education. Reading assignments, term papers, projects, and paper presentations are regarded as conventions from another planet. Tribhuvan provides neither the rigor nor the challenge of university life. Academic calendars do not exist: students leave early for vacation and return late. Unscheduled holidays, student meetings and teacher absenteeism frequently interrupt classes. College students probably spend less time in the classroom here than in any other country.[21]

An even more serious problem is the political malaise afflicting public sector educational institutions that account for more than two-third of the total education system. There is no control on university enrolment and colleges are swamped by an ever increasing number of students. Classrooms and furniture are inadequate and there has been no worthy capital investment for years. The tragic situation is further manifested in campus buildings with disheartening structures and "graffiti-filled corridors, dingy class rooms, broken furniture, blackened walls and whitened blackboards. In the libraries, books are in perpetual short supply and professional journals a luxury."[22] The result of all this is the production of poor quality human resources. About sixty per cent of some 200,000 students appearing in the annual SLC examination fail and most of the top scorers are from private schools. All this despite the fact that the public sector education expenditure has increased from 2.2 billion rupees in 1990/91, accounting for about 10 per cent of the government expenditure, to around 14 billion in 2003/04 accounting for 16 per cent of the government expenditure.[23]

These are only but symptoms of the educational malaise of the country and can be explained not only by defective policy, but also by the utter lack of proper planning and management. Prior to the introduction of the New Education Plan (NEP) in 1972, there used to be community ownership of education. All educational institutions, except a few, were run and managed by the community of parents, guardians, social workers, and leaders. By and large, education was uniform, and community participation ensured the best possible education with the resources available. Almost all the leaders of today in various fields including politics, public administration, education, and medicine are the products of that system. However, the top–down method of managing the education with the introduction of NEP changed all that. All educational institutions were nationalized, and their management came under state control. Teachers became government civil servants and were no longer accountable to the community. The system stunted community energy, initiative, and enterprise. The system was destined to fail not only because it was not financially sustainable, but because it was inefficient and the quality of education suffered. This led thousands to go to Indian cities and other places for education. Subsequently, private education was permitted, but the hugely expanded government system also continued.

Meanwhile, the slogan of free education up to secondary level became the political demand of all parties, without considering the financial, managerial, and other educational capabilities of the state to meet its requirements. The slogan of free education sounded egalitarian and attractive, but the government's inability to provide enough qualified teachers, proper infrastructure, education materials, and strong oversight, led to poor and inappropriate education system that was unable to meet the emerging needs. The system also took away the rights of the community and the parents to demand proper education for their children, without paying a minimum fee. This is the state of affairs in both school and university education. While Tribhuvan University suffers from a serious financial crunch, unable even to meet its operating cost because of inadequate annual grant from the government, students continue to pay an annual fee of a paltry 600 rupees (US $8) for university education. Any proposal for a fee hike could invite the risks of mass protest and strikes. The reform measures initiated in the early nineties towards cost recovery in higher education unfortunately could not be sustained under pressure of popular politics.

The alternative is private education at exorbitant cost, beyond the means of the average Nepali. There has been rapid but unplanned proliferation of private educational centres, mainly in urban areas. Most of these institutions have been established with commercial motives and with limited government oversight and regulation but some of them do offer quality education. The result is the development of a dualistic education regime—a large public sector education of abysmal quality for the poor, and the expensive private education for the rich. The manpower thus created will further accentuate the existing inequity and disparity in future. The already educated and the privileged class will further enhance their position through better education while the poor will continue to languish with low human capital. What is missing is the space for community support and ownership in this field. This is perhaps the only way one could save the publicly funded education, with an element of cost sharing from students and parents. Free education should be confined only to those who are desperately poor and below the poverty line. Only that can rescue government education from sliding further downhill. In this regard, the recently introduced scheme of handing over schools to community is a small step towards correcting the malaise. But in view of the huge damage already done by the past policy, reviving the old community spirit and partial cost recovery from the beneficiaries will be an uphill task for some time to come.

DONOR DEPENDENCE

The importance of external finance in Nepal's economic development is beyond question. Over the course of the history of concerted development efforts, the nature of foreign assistance has also expanded and diversified. It now includes programme-and-budgetary support, in addition to project assistance of the past. The rise of Maoist insurgency and the consequent pressure of security budget have made this inevitable. This dependence is accompanied by increasing external influence in domestic policies. The weakening of domestic institutions, insurgency situation, governance problems, and political instability, together with a changing approach of the aid community towards issues like governance, corruption, domestic policies, social engineering, and human rights have created space for the international community to have a greater say even on internal policy matters. In-built donor imposed conditionalities are now part of most project assistance and many such conditions are economically justified to ensure financial discipline and sustainability. Most governments in developing countries come to power with promises that are beyond the country's financial capacity and Nepal is no exception to this. But policy reforms require hard decisions beyond and contrary to electoral promises, and are therefore not undertaken for risk of losing popular support.

But all donor conditions do not make economic and social sense; they also impose alien principles distorting internal values and practices. For example, land acquisition for road building in rural Nepal normally does not involve cost, as people are willing to contribute the land voluntarily[24] in view of the new economic benefit and opportunity the road construction brings about. But once the road building becomes a donor-assisted project, adequate compensation for land becomes a prerequisite involving a huge budget, which is normally beyond the government's financial capacity. In various donor-funded roads, claims for compensation are a major problem. This also creates a discriminatory practice within the country, where land is acquired free in internally funded road projects, but handsomely paid for in externally funded ones.

The traditional IMF-supported Extended Structural Adjustment Fund has now been re-christened as Poverty Reduction and Growth Facility (PRGF) for a more humane look, but the basic nature and thrust of the programme remains the same. One of the conditions of this project is the phasing out of the Priority Sector Lending provision by commercial banks. This provision earlier required the commercial banks to allocate a portion of their lending to 'small priority sector', defined by the Nepal Rastra Bank, with the view to ensure a reasonable flow of bank funds to often neglected areas. Conditions like this may be understandable to allow unrestrained competition between banks to maximize profit for the shareholders without consideration to social responsibility. But the implication of such conditionality in terms of 'reducing poverty' in rural areas is questionable. The government's weak institutional capability to resist donor advice, the desperate need for external funds, and fear of losing assistance in hand, are some of the compelling factors to accept assistance even when tied with 'donor-imposed conditions'.

In addition, a further concern is the increasing dependency of foreign aid in practically every field. The areas of external assistance, instead of shrinking with improvement in domestic capabilities, have now been expanding.

> It is one thing to depend upon foreign aid for development finance and another to depend upon foreign aid for development itself. More aid does not necessarily translate into greater external dependence. It becomes so when aid does not lead to corresponding enhancement of the development capacity of the recipient nation, and leads to some erosion in it instead, and when it develops a tendency to fuel the greed of some in the name of the need for many.[25]

Similarly, the accountability aspect that normally should accompany the donor-imposed values and practices, and the negative fallouts of such values, is becoming a matter of debate.[26] Donor-assisted projects are generally criticized for over-capitalization and high expatriate components. A multi-modal transport project completed two years back, with World Bank credit of US $23 billion has constructed a massive modern inland container depot at Sirsiya Birgunj with a railway yard comprising 6 full lines, a huge stacking yard with a concrete pavement of 87,000 square metres, and commensurate container freight station, shed, and goods platform. The complex also includes 4 reach stackers each with capacity of 45 metric ton for handling 40-foot ISO containers.[27] Hardly 10 per cent of the capacity of this massive facility is being used at present and the prospect of attaining even one-third of the capacity utilization looks remote in the foreseeable future. In another Financial Sector Reform Project, the annual cost of professional services for the management of the two public sector commercial banks (Nepal Bank Ltd and Rastriya Banijya Bank) is about US $4.5 million financed mainly by loan money. The high professional cost of the project proved disruptive to the local job market and salary structure.

There are also reports of donor preferences in matters of individual appointments. Unfortunately, there is now a rush to avail foreign aid from practically every organ of the government, from the Prime Minister's Office to the Supreme Court, the parliament, and ministries to do routine things like drafting legislation, which was being done internally in the past. The donors are willing to assist in these traditionally 'off-limit' territories in the name of 'governance improvement' and the recipient institutions are all too eager for such assistance, because of some extra benefits to their offices that donor-funded projects normally bring about.

The civil society and non-government institutions are the new vehicles of development assistance. In view of the inadequacy of the state, this is a right direction and in the spirit of a plural and liberal approach for development. However, there is an absence of a strong regulatory and supervisory capacity to oversee their functioning, resulting in the mushrooming of non-governmental institutions with little accountability and transparency in their performance. The growth and expansion of this sector has been too rapid and extensive for the institutional capability of both the donors and the recipient to effectively regulate and monitor.

Development assistance is now spread to areas like capacity building, conflict-resolution, empowerment of the poor, and social mobilization. Most of these activities are tied to the overall goal of poverty alleviation. But the outcome of such projects in poverty reduction in relation to the investment made is rather questionable. There are an increasing number of projects on subjects like democracy, governance, peace and human rights, as if democracy and peace needs to be nurtured with expert advice and training if it is to take roots. With the outbreak of violent insurgency, Nepal is fast emerging as an attractive venue for various models of 'peace experiment'. 'The more elusive peace becomes, the more it seems to become an industry', wrote *The Nepali Times* referring to the swarming of conflict resolution experts all over the capital, some of them rubbing shoulders with arms merchants in hotel lobbies.[28] Dozens of peace organizations including the government-established Peace Secretariat and the high-level Peace Committee have sprung up. Scores of donors have been spending millions of dollars hiring a slew of experts and consultants to advise on the 'conflict mitigation', 'conflict prevention and resolution', capacity building, research and analysis of conflict situation, and promoting peace. While peace objective of these initiatives is laudable, it is highly questionable whether they will have any impact whatsoever in addressing the problem of violent conflict with an undiluted political agenda. The opportunity cost of such investment in a country suffering from rampant poverty is too high to be easily ignored. Furthermore, despite the plethora of such peace-building initiatives, both sides in the conflict are relying increasingly on military means to achieve their respective goals.

LOW PRODUCTIVITY

In today's globalized world, a nation's prosperity depends on how efficiently it can produce goods and services and sell them in the global market. For a small and poor country like Nepal with a limited domestic market, it is even more important to create a strong export sector to raise national income and economic prosperity. This becomes possible only by being competitive and productive. Productivity is a function of various factors including transaction costs, technology, management, labour efficiency, and overall business climate. Nepal's labour cost is one of the lowest in Asia. But this clear advantage is more than offset by lower productivity, resulting in higher unit cost. Nepal's unit labour cost is among the highest in nine Asian countries studied by UNIDO. The cost competetiveness index in 1999 shows the unit labour cost in Nepal at a 100 level, compared to 81 in India, and 90 in Bangladesh. There was some improvement in the 1990s, when the unit cost of labour declined by 3 per cent annually, which was one per cent faster than that of India. This improved competitiveness was, however, due to lower wage growth compared to other countries.[29] Nepal's low labour productivity remains an important constraint for future competitiveness.

A study on the trend of long-term total factor productivity, which combines the effect of all factors of production of firm efficiency shows that the Nepali economy carries large inefficiencies at the firm level. The average level of firm productivity in Nepal is only 53 per cent (measured as percentage of the most efficient benchmark), as compared to the 60 to 70 per cent found in the studies from other developing and developed countries. Factor markets are not efficient enough to reallocate capital and labour from inefficient to efficient sectors. The study attributes the overall low productivity to rigidities in the labour markets, inadequate provisions for bankruptcy and foreclosure, and the exit of inefficient firms. The inefficient financial sector has also contributed to maintain inefficient firms by constraining the growth of efficient ones. A lack of adequate mechanism for technology transfer, untrained human capital, poor infrastructure, and unfriendly business atmosphere are other factors responsible for keeping the productivity low.[30]

The low productivity is not limited to industrial sector. Because Nepal missed the green revolution that took place in most parts of South Asia in the 1970s and 1980s, agricultural productivity here remains low compared to the neighbouring Indian states and Bangladesh.[31] Limited availability of and inefficient use of irrigation facilities and other agricultural inputs including technology, fertilizer, improved seeds and poor extension services contribute to this. The agriculture system in the difficult hill and mountain terrain of the country has little to practically no access to irrigation. The use of modern inputs is also difficult and costly in the absence of transportation network.

NOTES

1. Maurice Zenkin, *Development for Free Asia*, p. 82 cited in Gunnar Myrdal, *Asian Drama: An Enquiry Into the Poverty of Nationsm vol. II*, New Delhi : Kalyani Publishers, 1992. p. 895.
2. The World Bank, *Financial Accountability in Nepal,* Chapter 3, 2002.
3. Gunnar Myrdal , *The Asian Drama*, New Delhi: Kalyani Publishers 1992, p. 896–897.
4. See an interesting article by Ratnakar Adhikari, 'Lessons from Sugar Crisis', *The Kathmandu Post*, 11 November 2004.
5. Nani Palkhivala, *We The People,* New Delhi: UBSPD, 2003, p. 25.
6. The large-scale civil service retrenchment under the first NC government 1n 1992 to reduce the size of bureaucracy, the wholesale transfer and penalizing the civil servants partisan consideration under the first UML minority Government in 1994 are some of the examples.
7. Bimal Koirala and Damodar Gautam, 'The Practice of Good Governance in the Present Nepalese Situation', in *Byabasthapan*, February, 1998 Kathmandu: Management Association of Nepal.
8. See the budget speech for the year 2001/002.
9. The only exceptions were K.P. Bhattarai and L.B. Chand. G.P. Koirala did it twice. The first one was challenged at the Supreme Court but was upheld. The second one announced with the consensus of other parties, therefore not questioned. Man Mohan Adhikary's decision to recommend the dissolution when faced with a Vote of No Confidence was upturned by the Court. The king on judicial advice rejected Surya Bahabur Thapa's recommendation. The latest dissolution by Deuba was challenged at the Court, but was upheld by it. But he himself could not hold the election, and was sacked by the king on that ground on a questionable move.
10. Ram S. Mahat, 'Security and Political Environment' in *India–Nepal Relations: The Challenges Ahead*, 2004. p.10. New Delhi: Rupa.
11. Lok Raj Baral,'The Unclear Roadmap: Parties and the Parliamentary Practice' in *Political Parties and Parliament,* 2004, New Delhi: Adroit.
12. Lok Raj Baral (2004) p.18, op. cit.
13. Krishna Khanal, 'Parliament and Governance' in *Political Parties and Parliament* (2004), op. cit. The author makes reference to the reported resentment expressed by King Birendra in 1991with the then Leader of the Opposition Man Mohan Adhikari, against the public statements by Communist leaders against the Monarchy, even after he had accepted a limited role. The king is also reported to have told if this continued, he would take power and hold referendum on the issue of monarchy.
14. The king sought the Supreme Court's opinion on Surya Bahadur Thapa's recommendation to dissolve the House of Representatives in 1998. Similarly, he referred the Citizenship Act passed by the parliament in 2001 to the Supreme Court.
15. Mahbub ul Haque (1997), Chapter 3, *Human Development in South Asia,* Chapter 3, op. cit.

16. Palkhiwala, op. cit. p. 61.
17. Deepak Gyawali, a former Minister and an water resource expert, launching a study report, said: the dam will be disastrous for Nepal, as it will inundate 150 VDCs of Okhaldhunga, Ramechhap, Taplejung and Sankhuwasabha districts of eastern Nepal. *The Kathmandu Post,* 2 January 2005.
18. The most recent embankments cases are: the Laxmanpur barrage in Baharaich district in India near the Banke district of Nepal, and the Khurdalotan Raisawal Embankment across the Marchawar area of Nepal causing widespread inundation of the Nepalese territory including the sacred Lumbini area.
19. International agencies like the World Bank and the ADB require no-objection from the lower riparian country before financing such projects. Donor interest to support irrigation projects like Kankai, Babai, Bagmati, and Sikta were, later on withdrawn, in the face of India's objection. The ADB withdrew from the Kankai Multi purpose Project when the project was at the last stage of financing agreement.
20. Mathema, Kedar Mathema, 'Cheating Our Children', in *Himal,* May–June 1990.
21. Ibid.
22. Ibid.
23. Based on figures published in *Economic Survey* reports.
24. Unless it involves sacrificing a major portion of their land. In that case reasonable compensation is made.
25. D.R. Pandey, Managing Development Aid for Greater Effectiveness, in *Chairman's Report on the Proceedings, NDF 2002.*
26. Foreign assistance which has been with us for the national development journey of more than half a century, but rarely will you find introspection among agencies as to their share of the blame in Nepal's continued backwardness...foreign aid has depoliticized civil society, converted our feminists into gender specialists, our activists into service delivery professionals, and our scholars into well paid consultants that do not even cry in the wilderness. Kanak Dixit, 'Diplomat, Donor and Democracy' in *The Kathmandu Post,* 3 January 2005.
27. See *Progress Report of Nepal Multi-modal Transit and Trade Facilitation Project*, September 2003.
28. See Navin Singh Khadka's report Peace Industry in *The Nepali Times*, 12–18 November 2004.
29. HMG (2004), Nepal: *Trade and Competitiveness Study*, Chapter 4.
30. Ibid.
31. World Bank (2004). p. 43.

Chapter Seventeen

Bottom Line and the Future

In 1992 when a Thai Airbus crashed over the Talukasheri hill of Nuwakot district killing 139 passengers, a section of the overly enterprising Nepali press quickly blamed the air traffic control of the Tribhuvan International airport. A team of high-level professionals including the ICAO representative that subsequently investigated the incident attributed the error to the side of airline pilots for this disaster. This author happened to be in Bangkok reading newspapers when the report came in. An editorial of a Thai daily was questioning the probe finding, citing Nepali newspapers which had faulted the poor employees of the TIA's air traffic control system.

These real-life reactions to a great human tragedy are the reflections of the thinking process and culture of the two societies. Nepali society suffers from a culture of negativism. Part of the trait and character of the nation's urban elite is the pleasure it takes in glorifying the merits of others, while denigrating one's own. This becomes obvious if one listens to the chattering at cocktails and coffee houses, high society living rooms, and public discourses. It has become a habit and culture to see failure all around—in our social and political institutions, and in our progress that others would consider reasonable. There is a tendency to exaggerate our weakness and minimize our strength.

The opinions expressed with respect to Nepal's post-1990 democratic order are not always favourable and betray the symptoms of this malaise. Regular attempts are being made to paint the period dark as if everything went wrong under democratic dispensation. Real and concrete socio-economic achievements are easily glossed over or taken for granted as natural developments. The main emphasis here is on the failure and weakness of the system. The Royal Proclamation of February 2005 was itself a strong indictment against the democratic exercise of the period. This negative trait is not confined to the

Kathmandu valley and Nepali towns, but to a part of the Nepali diaspora outside the country.[1] While some are trying to smear the period dark to make a case for authoritarian rule, some others are forwarding the Maoist solution as a panacea for all ills that afflict our society and governance. While one can also sense in this phenomenon some genuine expression of frustration because of the system's inability to meet popular expectations, it also reflects a culture of negativism and part of the premeditated propaganda.

NOT A LOST PERIOD

The twelve years of democracy was not a lost period. The statistics presented in Part II of the book offer adequate proof of this. The post-1990 political order gave the people not only their rights—including those to choose their own rulers—but also some socio-economic benefits that enhanced the quality of their lives. Despite the growing Maoist violence and terror, the first twelve years of the democratic Nepal made satisfactory economic progress. The growth rate improved in relation to the previous decades and became comparable with the South Asian norm and pattern. Even amidst the trials and tribulations of tumultuous politics, the economic reforms were swift and far-reaching, and created new opportunity and space for all sections of the society to unleash their energy and enterprise. Macroeconomic stability was maintained throughout the period. Fiscal deficit was controlled. Public debt policy was prudent and sustainable. External sector registered a robust growth, with the trade/GDP ratio reaching around 50 per cent compared to 24 per cent in the late eighties, indicating higher integration with the global economy. Export to GDP ratio almost trebled. Significant structural transformation took place in the economy. Agriculture's role declined both in national income and employment, with corresponding growth in the contribution from non-agricultural sectors—industry, trade, tourism, banking, services and other modern and dynamic sectors. The country started attracting foreign capital in industry, tourism and hydropower. Although still very low, productivity increased both in farm and factories. Unlike in previous decades, the production growth in agriculture was the result of productivity rise, not acreage expansion.

Nepal's international relations expanded and diversified. The democratic image of the country attracted new partners offering development assistance. Nordic countries like Norway, Finland and Denmark made new entries. Other bilateral agencies like the USA, UK and Germany increased their normal assistance. A number of multilateral agencies of the UN family and others made Kathmandu their regional headquarters. Foreign investment started increasing. The vibrant civil society and local self government was another significant byproduct of democratic Nepal. The dramatic growth and progress in the media and free flow of information and ideas breathed vigour in civic life. The growth, and increasing maturity and sophistication of the print and electronic media including the FM radios, and television channels contributed to better inform, educate, enlighten and entertain the people. The rise of private sector and the civil society, NGOs and voluntary organizations offered additional mechanisms to carry out development and social works that previously were considered largely the prerogative of the not-so-efficient public sector bureaucracy. The local bodies received more power and resources to carry out development activities in their respective fields and locations. In many places, the municipalities, DDCs, and VDCs showed exemplary initiatives in resource mobilization and innovative development activities.

Nepal's position in the global ranking of human development has undergone satisfactory progress. The nation now spends more on education, health, drinking water, and other fields of basic human well-being. People are more literate, live longer, have more income and consume more. Significant progress was made in other human indicators like maternal and infant mortality, family planning practices and female literacy. People have better and improved access to infrastructural and economic services like roads, bridges, drinking water, irrigation, banking and other economic services. The country's road network increased by 130 per cent while the number of people with access to electricity grew by five times during the democratic years. Similarly, noticeable progress has been witnessed in rural ecology. Nepal's image as an environmental hotspot with denuded forests, frequent landslides, and erosion under demographic pressures presented about two decades ago,[2] is no longer valid. Instead, Nepali hills are now marked by growing trees and thick foliage. Visible changes are seen in the quality of rural life. As a result of all this, the poverty profile of the country underwent significant change. Poverty declined at all levels and across all regions and ecological belts in various degrees.

The most significant development of the democratic era was the empowerment of the rural masses. This segment of the population had always been at the receiving end in the past. If one reviews 240 years of Nepal's political history, the twelve years after 1990 was the only period which was marked by the assertion of popular voice, people's power, and tangible reforms and improvements in living conditions. In the early years of nation building, the rural poor provided the economic foundation for the geo-political consolidation. It was the burden borne and sacrifices made by rural Nepal and its impoverished peasantry that made the country's territorial expansion and national unification possible. But the poor were voiceless and silently bore not only the cost of expansion, but also the systemic exploitation by the nobility, their agents, and officials. The end of expansionary drive after 1816 did not bring much relief to the poor people. The size of the military superstructure, whose cost the poor peasantry met, did not diminish. The Rana regime was marked by the consolidation of political power by the family oligarchy under the protective umbrella of the British. The century of Rana autocracy was marked by the serving of the British interest externally, the consolidation of power through internal suppression, and the exploitation of national wealth for family enrichment. All dissenting voices were ruthlessly controlled and the country and its people were effectively shielded from modern and progressive influences. Throughout these periods, the people had no control over their destiny.

People felt some relief after the end of the Rana rule. Expectations of the people shored up and democracy, liberal values, and progressive thinking made their influence. The creative impulse and the new thinking found their expressions in various fields including art, culture, education, literature, and politics. But increasing political instability, frequent changes of government, and the dilution of the principal outcome of the revolution left very little time and energy for economic development programmes to improve people's lives. The first general election in 1959 brought new hopes. An able and visionary political leadership made a promising start with a progressive agenda. But the charisma of the leadership and the progressiveness of the agenda it espoused themselves became the cause of its downfall. An era of authoritarian rule was ushered towards the end of 1960 and it lasted for some three decades. Despite the catchy and progressive slogans to mask the autocratic character of the regime, and its declared raison d'etre of economic development, the *Panchayat* era could not bring tangible improvements in the lives of the people.

The post-1990 era is the only period in Nepal's history when people felt empowered politically and economically for more than a decade. The twelve years is the longest period in Nepal's history when the people were ruled neither by an absolute monarch nor by a family oligarchy, but by their elected representatives. Under this dispensation, rural Nepal provided the foundation of the country's political power. At no point in Nepal's history did the rural community felt more empowered with resources and authority. Part of the negativism of the urban elite towards politics and politicians under democracy is also explained by the emergence of this rural power, represented by leaders with middle and lower middle class backgrounds. A section of the intelligentsia perhaps is not reconciled with the rural folks running the show in the country's capital.

Despite the relatively better developmental record of this period, it was far short of the country's potential and popular expectation. The market-led reforms brought about dynamism and economic growth in various sectors, but the growth was not sufficiently broad-based and pro-poor to make a serious dent on the country's poverty and disparities. Weak regulatory mechanism created new problems and distortions. Economic disparity increased, with market-led activities largely confined to urban metropolis. New employment opportunities were inadequate to meet the requirements of the job seekers that enter the labour market every year. Weak governance and the absence of social discipline hindered the potential performance. Voices of the nationalities and sub-nationalities suppressed and ignored for centuries started to be heard. Awareness of exclusion and discrimination based on region, ethnicity, and gender increased. Fault-lines hitherto unseen or unappreciated surfaced. The unprecedented communications revolution, the frequent democratic exercised raised the awareness and aspirations of the masses to new heights. The actual performance and delivery were short of these expectations. Inefficiencies, malpractices and corruption did not result in the best utilization of limited resources. News of scandals and corrupt practices made headlines particularly during the time of turbulent and unstable politics. All these helped to strengthen the negativism of the elite, often bordering on cynicism.

History shows that such phenomenon is not uncommon in democracies at their early stages. Democracy shows weaknesses and will take time and efforts to attain maturity. However, the system does have the ability for self-correction. In Nepal, the last few years have also seen enactments of various reform bills such as those relating to the regulation of political parties and the empowerment of anti-graft bodies. These reforms have no parallel in this sub-continent and are expected to go a long way in controlling malpractices and political distortions. Political consensus is also emerging on a reform agenda to address the issue of exclusion and deprivation of traditionally neglected communities.

DEMOCRACY AND 'DEMOCRATIZATION'

The remedy to the growing pains of democracy lies in reforms and improvements and not in its substitute. Substitutes, even if they exist, would be much worse in every respect. Authoritarian and violent means will only complicate the problem. They can bring neither peace nor democracy. They bring only pain, agony and further poverty. The solution to tricky political problems can be found only in a functioning and vibrant democracy, and not in the strangulation of its process and decimation of its vital institutions. Winston Churchill's famous quip—"democracy is the worst form of political system, except for all those that have already been tried"—is equally valid in Nepal's case. The country has witnessed various forms of autocracy and democracy in its history but no system has proven even remotely close to the democratic regime in terms of delivery to the common masses and overall development performance.

There are some who see advantages of an authoritarian regime for the sake of economic development. Arguments are made in support of "technocratic and efficient" government insulated from the compulsions electoral politics to pursue prudent and bold economic policies. They are usually the proponents of the 'development first and democracy later' argument. A historical review of Nepal's political economy proves them wrong. The experience elsewhere—particularly the abysmal record of military rulers in Latin America, the "strong men regimes" of Africa and communist rules in Soviet Union and east Europe—have proven them wrong. The theory of authoritarian advantage for development has now been thoroughly demolished. A very illuminating study by three American academics based on the comparative economic performance of democratic and autocratic regimes of developing countries concludes that democracies have outperformed autocratic regimes in every aspect over the past four decades[3]. They have asserted that a development-first strategy perpetuates a deadly cycle of poverty, conflict, and oppression. Democratic regimes are also more competent to cope with natural calamities and humanitarian emergencies. Nobel laureate Amartya Sen's thesis that democratic institutions and processes provide strong incentives to avert famines has now been universally acclaimed. No country with a free press has ever experienced a famine. He says 2–3 million Indians died during the Bengal Famine of 1943, but there have been no famine deaths after democratic and independent rule despite serious crop failures at different times. On the other hand, famines in China during 1958–61 killed nearly 30 million people.[4]

Why do democratic regimes perform better? The advantages of

democracies over autocracies are many. Unlike in autocratic patronage- and clan-based politics where political monopoly converts itself to economic monopoly, powers are widely shared in democratic regimes and they encourage openness and adaptability. Democratic leaders have incentives to respond to the needs of common men. Debates here move from economic growth to broader measures of human well-being. The free flow of ideas fosters efficient and effective policies. Openness reduces the scope of corruption. The gaze of the opposition forces, independent and investigative media will force greater transparency and disclosures regarding the potential conflict of interests. In view of the fundamental role played by democratic regimes to spur development, a case was made to amend the articles of the Bretton Woods institutions to enable the democratic countries to qualify for higher levels of funding[5]. At present these institutions are prohibited from using political criteria in aid decisions.

Strict adherence to the rule of law, respect for universally accepted human rights, functioning democratic institutions, openness, transparency and accountability to the people are not luxuries only the rich nations can afford, but the very pre-requisites for peace, social justice, and economic progress for poor countries. The image of political leaders in Nepal may have suffered in the eyes of common men. This is a familiar phenomenon both in developing and developed societies. But this has not dented popular faith in the democratic system and its institutions. A nation-wide opinion poll conducted in recent months by an international agency shows that an overwhelming majority of the Nepali citizens (77 per cent) still view democracy as the best polity for Nepal, with a strong preference (60 per cent) for a constitutional monarch. Only 2 per cent of the people support an absolute monarch, while 17 per cent support a republican polity[6].

The Royal actions of 4th October 2002 and 1st February 2005 came as setbacks to democracy and were in contravention to the agreement between the Monarch and the popular forces reached after the 1990 Peoples' Movement. The king has reiterated his commitment to the system of constitutional monarchy time and again, but his actions do not fall under the norm of constitutional monarchy as it is generally understood. The Nepali people want to see their monarch beyond controversies—as a symbol of unity and stability, acting as a guardian and protector of democracy. He could use his moral authority to counsel, alert, guide, and correct the political leaders when they go astray. He can be firm with a Prime Minister and his ministers when power is abused and misused for personal and partisan purposes. He could encourage progressive measures for the cause of the downtrodden and deprived communities and act as a source of inspiration for modernizing values—rational, austere, and developmental. All these can be done through exercise of moral authority and guidance without offsetting the established democratic practices and subverting the constitutional process.

At the same time, the success of multi-party democratic polity will also depend on the strength of political institutions and the quality of governance. The crisis of democracy, according to Anthony Giddens, comes from not being democratic enough[7]. Faced with democratic derailment, there is an urgent need for 'democratizing democracy' through innovative solutions in Nepal. In the ultimate analysis, a democratic political system can sustain itself on the strength of effective delivery and strong performance, and by a demonstrated ability to address weaknesses and handle the emerging problems—violence, weak state, corruption, poverty, disparities and unemployment—with competence and effectiveness. Failure in this regard will prevent democracy from taking root and continue to provide fertile ground for conflict. Such conditions provide the alibi for authoritarian rule with promise for economic growth, good governance, social progress, and stability.

The 'democratization' process should involve reforms in the political structure to address the aspirations of diverse communities and regions, with built-in constitutional provisions for equitable power sharing that reflects the country's plurality. Affirmative actions until the time the neglected and excluded communities are brought at par with other communities, need immediate attention and priority. Meritocracy and 'equality of opportunity' is not sufficient, as they tend to favour the already better off. Similarly, a decentralized regional approach of governance is necessary to break Kathmandu's monopoly over political and economic power. Education is a great equalizer because of its ability to redistribute opportunities from the rich to those with talents. Unless reforms are introduced urgently to make public education more responsive to emerging needs, the prospect of better future for the under-privileged will be remote. This will accentuate the disparity further.

'Democratizing' democracy does not stop here. Multi-party democracy will require strong, and efficient political parties to succeed. The preoccupation with power politics should not distract the political parties from their ultimate commitment to the general masses and to basic parliamentary practices and processes. Politics is not just a game of power but a mechanism of social service. Political parties have no choice but to reengineer themselves, dedicate to high standards of integrity and be subjected to a strong code of conduct. Such a code would include internal democracy and transparency in finances, term limit to leadership positions, financial disclosure of individual party leaders, adequate representation of women and other disadvantaged groups, and commitment to keeping education and civil service institutions out of politics. Above all, the renouncement of all methods which will harm the economy and the interest of the ordinary people is an imperative[8].

Ten years of Maoist violence has proved painful, costly, and devastating for the nation. It has weakened the country economically, pushed militarism to unprecedented levels, and brought further misery and human costs. Tired of violence and anarchy, some may justify the authoritarian rule to clear the mess. But the experience of world history and Nepal's own past shows that authoritarianism does not coexist with peace, human dignity, and welfare. Democracy offers the best hope for finding a non-violent solution to conflict. Autocracy and militarism cannot address the problem of insurgency. Any illusion which existed in the minds of a section of our society that the royal regime would prove more effective in dealing with the country's problems, particularly the insurgency, has largely been demolished with the post-October four experience. There is no ground to believe that the direct rule could be any better. No trade-off exists between democracy and development.

The Maoists should understand that nobody in modern times is prepared to accept a philosophy enforced through violence. The violent methods may have given the Maoists some tactical advantage from where to negotiate with any government whose primary obligation is to protect the life and property of its citizens, but this has not endeared them to the people. Whatever initial sympathy that may have existed for the Maoists' cause has been declining because of their brutal methods. This is evidenced from the news of popular resistance and uprisings reported from different parts of the country. No political philosophy can sustain itself for long simply on the strength of terror. A philosophy that has been discarded all over the world has no chance of succeeding in Nepal, although the country's poverty and unequal development provided a fertile environment for its appeal. If the Maoist objective is to guarantee people-based sovereignty and equity to the neglected communities and regions, a political consensus can be built on the form, content, and modality of the political arrangement. But violence must be discarded for good. The solution lies in the middle ground—inclusive, decentralized, and democratic—based on the principles of social justice, liberal values, and people's sovereignty expressed through elected representatives. This is the middle way between the right authoritarianism and left extremism.

ECONOMIC AGENDA

Together with democracy, economy should be the central national agenda. Only a national preoccupation with economic issues can lead the nation to the path of prosperity for a better life to its citizens. The order of the day is pragmatism rather than a doctrinaire approach to face new realities and challenges. The forces of globalization and market power, non-governmental organizations, rise of sub-national and sub-regional identities, declining faith on government institutions make it necessary to make pragmatic adjustments on traditional postulates. The issue is not whether more or less government, but an effective government and where it can deliver. The people's reluctance to trust the government in Nepal, as elsewhere, arises because of the government's cumbersome size, inflexibility, and inability to respond to change.

Even for a market economy to succeed, state institutions must be capable of enforcing laws, ensuring fair play, regulating markets, and administrating public. A capable state is as important as right policy instruments to generate success. For this reinventing of government and government institutions is necessary, even with market based solutions where necessary. Corruption and abuse of authority erode public trust and hamper development and growth. New safeguards are necessary to control this problem. There is, however, no real basis for the perception of higher corruption under democracy. The perception has occurred not because corruption necessarily increased, but the political environment in which it occurs has changed[9]. Democracy ensures greater scrutiny and powerful information mechanisms.

Foreign assistance has been an important source of investment for Nepal's development, and has helped in creating the foundation for the country's physical and human infrastructure. However, its scope, instead of shrinking over time, has expanded and diversified to a wider arena. With this, external influence in public policy has also increased. Donor-driven values sometimes create anomalies and distortions as aid priorities, its modalities, and accompanying policy prescriptions are determined by the mandates of foreign decision-making bodies. Despite the partnership nature of external assistance, recipient countries like Nepal, in desperate need for assistance and suffering from weak institutional capacity, have limited influence over the aid package.

The answer to this problem lies only in strong domestic performance and well-defined priorities under a capable government. A better development delivery and a demonstrated ability to attract private investment will not only reduce counterproductive foreign influence but also attract external assistance on domestic terms. There is a natural eagerness on the part of the donor community to be partner in success stories. An efficient civil service, insulated from political interventions and not prone to corrupt practices, is essential for this.

Nepal's factor endowments offer distinct comparative advantages in certain areas for international trade. Tourism and hydropower are two acknowledged areas of potential advantage, which can make this country a tourist haven and an energy export house. The extraordinary biodiversity of the country made possible by a variety of agro-climatic zones offers exciting possibilities for development in agriculture and forestry. With proper know-how, technology, capital investment, and business environment, bio-diversity can be an engine for Nepal's future prosperity and is capable of transforming the lives of the millions who have traditionally relied on farming for their livelihood. Even the most economically backward and underdeveloped Karnali area has the potential of offering exciting economic opportunity. But it requires proper management and conservation of its high value of herbal species. Dolpa district alone has 286 plants and 375 kinds of herbs used in traditional Tibetan and Nepalese medicines including the valuable 'Himalayan gold' *Yarshagunbu* (cordyceps *sinensis).*[10] The economic potential of these bio products is very high. It is pity that in a country with one third of its territory under forest cover, forestry contributes less than two per cent to the country's GDP. The potential for the country becoming an education, health and an outdoor sports hub, in view of the perfect setting offered by its pleasant climate, unique hospitality, and unspoilt natural beauty is yet another area that can be exploited.

But the comparative advantage based on natural resource endowment, in itself, is no guarantee for the country's economic success. As Lester Thurow says—for all practical purposes, natural resources have dropped out of the competitive equation: having them is neither necessary nor sufficient condition to becoming rich. Japan does not possess them, but is rich. Argentina possesses them, but is not rich.[11] If resource endowment in itself were sufficient to assure economic prosperity, countries with abundant resources, and not resource-poor countries like Singapore, Korea, Hong Kong, and Taiwan, would have been the fastest growing economies in recent economic history. Resource endowment can certainly help but only under the right policy and a facilitating economic environment. Proper public policy that rewards entrepreneurship and innovation, coupled with quality education and training that produces first-rate human capital are the ultimate weapons. With these assets in place, capital can flow anywhere and a low saving rate will not be a constraint.

This is also the age of knowledge-based industry. The fastest growing economies in the world are those which have excelled in brainpower and knowledge-based industries. This requires high quality education capable of meeting emerging demands; and that is where national priorities should lie. A lot of fast-growing industries including information technology, financial services, biotechnology, microcomputer, and telecommunications can be located anywhere where these assets are available.

Market access is yet another important contributor to growth and prosperity. The world has entered into the WTO regime. This has opened unlimited access to global markets, provided one can be competitive. Nepal's low factor productivity is a serious constraint for its competitiveness as evidenced by some of the export industries, such as textiles, that are already facing this crisis. Increasing productivity is a time-taking process. Productivity grows with new investments, fresh technologies and know-how that bring and produce better skills. The rapidly growing economies of the neighbouring countries, particularly India, can be an advantage to spur industrial expansion and growth. The preferential treatment that Nepali products enjoy in the Indian market should be used as an opportunity. Various products that meet the minimum value-addition criteria are already enjoying the quota and duty free access to the Indian market. Further external investment, including third country investment, must be attracted with an eye to the Indian markets to benefit from this provision. Similarly, Nepal's LDC status that qualifies if for Every Thing But Arms (EBA) export to European Union will be an attraction for capital from India and elsewhere. Last, Nepal's much hyped hydropower potential will remain only a pipe dream unless we de-link it from politics and deal with the matter in a rational and business-like matter.

The last decade has left us with some achievements on which the foundations for a higher growth path can be laid. A series of economic reforms resulting in decontrolling and deregulating investment, trade, foreign exchange regimes, improvements in the tax and tariff regime, a hugely expanded role of the private and non-government sectors have helped in transforming and diversifying a number of areas. These include a few manufacturing industries, export trade, banking and finance, tourism, aviation, hydropower, and health sectors. Modern institutions of governance including laws and regulations to ensure accountability and transparency, with checks and balances have been created and operationalized. The decentralization of authority to local levels and the periodic democratic exercises at local and national levels have empowered the people and heightened their awareness and level of participation in governance. Importantly, the international community continues to be sympathetic to Nepal's needs and aspirations.

Effective interventions are immediately needed to meet the concerns of the people at the margin, bypassed by the government and the market forces. The redistribution of public investment towards backward rural regions must be given further momentum with emphasis on efficiency and effectiveness in use. Mere transfer of resources without strong regulatory and accountability mechanisms could lead to wastage, leakage, and corruption. In order to eliminate poverty and backwardness, there is no alternative to generating higher but equitable and broad-based growth accompanied by effective population control strategies. Increased investment to spur agricultural growth and rural development is the key to the strategy of broad-based and equitable growth.

The smallholdings of inferior and marginal farmlands are a major reason behind Nepal's rural poverty. Farm income, even with more fertilizer, irrigation, and extension services, will be inadequate to lift the vast majority of the rural poor above the poverty line. It is only the development of rural infrastructure with greater investment in public works that will provide the much needed safety net. In fact, the improvement in the poverty profile seen in the recent past is mainly attributed to the expansion on non-farm income, particularly from the public works, the urban-based industrial and service jobs, and remittance income. Higher public spending on roads, irrigation, bridges, and other schemes will have two positive impacts. First, it will increase rural income immediately through employment creation, and second, it will build the foundation for agricultural development.

Development also requires a culture and value system that rewards productivity and where economic considerations trump other matters. Increasing factor productivity is the key to economic success and wastage in any form is unacceptable. The success of democracy depends on social discipline, hard work, strong institutions, and respect for the rule of law. Economic growth is the sum-total of individual efforts and higher growth and prosperity is only possible with the harnessing of the energy and talents of all citizens and putting them to optimum use. This will only be possible in a liberal, decentralized, and inclusive governance, which encourages initiative and enterprise.

Peace is the prerequisite for all this. Countries with violent conflicts are not the preferred locations for investment—public and private, internal and external, human and capital. The 'country risk' factor will lock them out of investment opportunities. The cost of increasing violence has been grievous and devastating to Nepal. It has put a brake on new investment and diverted resources from fields of economic and social concerns to physical security. The socio-economic gains made earlier are being reversed. It is difficult for a society suffering from threats to personal security, social trauma, agony, and economic dislocation to offer immediate economic prospects. Therefore, putting an end to the violent conflict and restoration of democracy should be an urgent national agenda.

NOTES

1. An example of the academic negativism is Nanda Shrestha's book, *In the Name of Development,* where one finds everything degrading and negative in Nepal. Combining the philosophies of Marx, Gandhi, Mao Tse-tung and the Green environmentalists as his frame of reference, he condemns the ruling elite for all round failure. Nanda also refers to the opposition charge against me as Finance Minister in 1996 for maintaining an 'illegal' foreign exchange account in New York Chemical Bank. He has refuted the explanation I gave in the Parliament—that the deposit represented my savings during my stint as UNDP international staff. He has alleged that the deposit was made during the time I was the Finance Minister. I challenge Nanda Shrestha to prove his point, or he should withdraw his baseless allegation. I stand by my statement, which also said: I would renounce public life if proven otherwise.
2. Report on the forestry sector prepared by the World Bank in 1989 had predicted that Nepal's accessible forests would be wiped out in 20 years at the prevailing rate of tree felling. A widely published English television film Fragile Mountain highlighted the serious environmental degradation caused by rapid depletion of forest cover.
3. Joseph Siegle, Michael Weinstein, and Morton Halperin, 'Why Democracies Excel' in *Foreign Affairs*,vol.83.no.5, September/October 2004. USA.
4. Cited in UNDP, Human Development Report 2002, pp.57–58.
5. Seigle et al.
6. This was one of the findings of a poll conducted by National Democratic Institute with the help of AC Neilsen/ ORGMARG and the US-based Greenberg Quinlan, Rosner Research based on the survey of 3,200 randomly selected individuals in 60 districts in January 2005. See NDI/Nepal, Working to Strengthen And Expand Democracy, Kathmandu,15 April 2005.
7. Anthony Giddens, *The Third Way: The Renewal of Social Democracy,* Cambridge: Polity Press, 1988. Chapter 3.

8. Kul C. Gautam outlines an 11-point stringent code of conduct for the political parties. See, his contribution 'Mistakes, Miscalculations and the Search for Middle Ground: An Exit Strategy for Nepal, in Nepal Study Centre: http://www.unm.edu~bohara.
9. Greater openness creates an impression that corruption is increasing. A study the Transparency International in Kenya showed that the perception of corruption was worse in 2003, the first year of democratically elected government, than in the late nineties under an authoritarian rule. but the same organization found that Kenyans paid an average of nine bribes in 2003, down from 23 in 2002, saving roughly 10 per cent of their annual income. Cited in Siegle, and et al.op,cit.
10. Even without proper policy, crude method of collection, and exploitation by various level of middlemen, the net economic benefit from Yarsagunbu alone to Dolpa was equivalent to US $ 3 million in 2004. See Nagendra Budathoki, 'Karnali Region: Not a Burden, but an Opportunity', a paper presented at the CNI-organized Stakeholders Symposium to Partnership Summit - Can Nepal Achieve a Double Digit Growth?, 15 August 2004.
11. Lester Thurow *Head to Head*. London: Nicholas Brealey Publishing, 1992, pp. 42–43.

Select Bibliography

A World to Win (2001). 28 May 2001.

Acharya, Nilambar (2004). 'People and Parliament', *The Kathmandu Post.* Kathmandu, 29 November.

Adhikari, Hari Prashad, (2003). "Sons of Soil in Southern Bhutan" in *Bhutan Political Problem,* R.B. Basnet and D.N.S. Dhakal (eds).

Adhikari, Ratnakar (2004). 'Lessons from Sugar Crisis', *The Kathmandu Post, Post (Daily).* Kathmandu, 11 November.

Agrawal, Hem Narayan (1976). *The Administrative System of Nepal.* Vikas Publishing House, New Delhi.

Agriculture Development Council (ADC)(2004). *Renewable Energy Data of Nepal, 2003.* Kathmandu.

ANZDEC Limited, New Zealand (2002). *Nepal Agriculture Sector Performance Review* (ADB TA No.3536-NEP). Manila.

APROSC and John Mellor Associates (1995). *Nepal Agricultural Perspective Plan Main Document.* Kathmandu.

Asian Development Bank (ADB) (2004). *Nepal 2005–2009: Country Strategy and Programme.* ADB, Manila.

Asian Development Bank(1985). Privatization; Policies, Methods and Procedures. Asian Development Bank, Manila.

Aslam, Abid (1999). 'Asian Military spending Unscathed by financial crisis'. *Asia Times.* 23 June 1999.

Baral, Lok Raj (2001). 'Governance and Security in Plural Society: The Case of Nepal' in P.R. Chari (ed.) (2001) *Security and Governance in South Asia.* Regional Centre For Strategic Studies, Colombo.

Baral, Lok Raj (2004). 'Security, Democracy and Pluralism: The Case of Nepal' a paper presented at NCCS Regional Seminar, 16–17 November. Kathmandu.

Baral, Lok Raj (2004). 'The Unclear Roadmap: Parties and the Parliamentary Practice', in Lok Raj Baral (ed.) *Political Parties and Parliament* (2004). Adroit Publishers, New Delhi.

Baskota, Narottam Prashad (1981). *Indo-Nepal Trade and Economic Relations.* B.R. Publishing Corporation, Delhi.

Besley, Timothy & Roberto Zagha (ed) (2005). *Development Challenges in the 1990s: Leading Policy Makers Speak from Experience.* A Copublication of the World Bank and Oxford University Press.

Bhattachan, Krishna *B. (2002).* "Challenges of Ethnonationalism in South Asia" *Journal of Contemporary Studies,* Kathmandu, Vol 1, No. 2, Sept.

Bhattarai, Babu Ram (2003). 'The Political Economy of People's War', in Arjun Karki and David Seddon (ed.) *People's War In Nepal: Left Perspective.* Adriot Publications, New Delhi.

Bhattarai, Babu Ram (2003). 'A Rejoinder on Current Issues' in Arjun Karki and David Seddon (ed.) *The People's War in Nepal: Left Perspectives.* Adroit Publications, New Delhi.

Bista, Dor Bahadur (1993). *Fatalism and Development.* Orient Longman, New Delhi.

Blaike, P.M., John Cameron and John David Seddon (1980). *Nepal In Crisis: Growth and Stagnation in the Periphery.* Clarendon Press, Oxford.

Blaikie, P.M, John Cameron, and David Seddon (2001). *Nepal in Crisis: Growth and Stagnation At The Periphery* (Revised and Enlarged Edition). Adroit Publishers, New Delhi.

Borja, Luis Arce (2003). 'Criticisms of the Peace Negotiations', Brussels.

Budathoki, Nagendra (2004). *Karnali Zone: Not a Burden, but an Opportunity.* Paper presented at the Seminar on Can Neapl achieve Double Digit Growth? organized by CNI on 15 August 2004. Kathmandu.

Central Bureau Of Statistics/NPC (2004). *Nepal Living Standard Survey 2003/04, Volume One and Volume Two, CBS/NPCS, HMG/N. Kathmandu.*

Chandrasekharan, S. (2003).'Bhutanese Brand of Ethnic Cleansing' in *Bhutan Political Problem,* R.B.Basnet and D.N.S. Dhakal (eds).

Collins and Associates (1996). *A Financial Future For Nepal: Creating an International Services Center.* Boston: Collins and Associates.

Collins and Associates (1999). *International Banking Legislation for Nepal: Principles and Draft Texts.* Study sponsored by Nepal Rastra Bank.

Community Awareness and Development Centre (2003). *Renewable Energy Data of Nepal.* Kathmandu.

Dahal, Dilli R. (2002). Madhese, Regionalism and National Integration: A Case of the Nepal Tarai in *Nepal Journal of Contemporary Studies.* Vol. 2 No. 1. March 2, 2002. Nepal Centre For Contemporary Studies, Kathmandu.

Dahal, Kirti Bikram (2004). 'Micro Finance in Nepal' in *Mirmire,* an NRB publication No. 217, (2060).

Dahal, Madan, Keshav Acharya and Dev Raj Dahal (1999). *Development Challanges for Nepal.* NEFAS/FINNIDA, Kathmandu.

Dangol, Sanu Bhai (1999). *The Palace in Nepalese Politics.* Ratna Pustak Bhandar. Kathmandu.

Dasgupta, Swapan (2005).' Kingly Faith', *The Telegraph* (Daily). Calcutta, 11 February.

Department of Archeology (2054). Ministry of Youth, Sports and Culture, *Prithvi Narayan Shahko Dibyopadesh.*

Department of Information, Ministry of Information, Communication and Broadcasting, HMG/N. *Prithvi Narayan Shah's Dibyopadesh.* Kathmandu.

Devkota, Subash and Sarad Adhikari (2061). A Report ' Paribartan Ko Batomaa' in *Samaya,* (Nepali weekly), Marg 10.

Dixit, Kanak in *The Nepali Times* (weekly). 16–22 May 2003, Kathmandu.

Dixit, Kanak "Kunda Dixit 's Report" (2004). *The Nepali Times*, 29 October 4, November. Kathmandu.

Dixit, Kanak (2004).'Exit Strategy, Nepal Quagmire' *The Kathmandu Post* (Daily), 30 October. Kathmandu.

Dixit, Kanak (2005), 'Diplomat, Donor and Democracy' *The Kathmandu Post,* (Daily) June. Kathmandu.

Dixit, Praveen M. (1995). 'Economic Reforms in Nepal: A Cursory Assessment'. Paper presented at the Seminar On Fiscal and Monetary Policy in Nepal. 8 March, Organized by CEDA, Kathmandu.

Gautam, Puskar (2004). "Tunnel Vision", in *Nepali Times (weekly),* #220 5–11 November.

George, Paul. 'Defense Expenditures In the 1990s: Budget and Fiscal Policy Issues for Developing Countries'. Conference paper on Converting Defence resources to Human development organized by Bonn International centre for Conversion. www.bicc.de/general/events/devcon/george.html.

Gersony, Robert (2003). *Sowing the Wind: History and Dynamics of the Maoist Revolt in Nepal's Rapti Hills* a report submitted to Mercy Corps International.

Ghai and Raman (1979). *Rural Poverty and Small Farmers Development Programme in Nepal,* ILO.

Giddins, Anthony (1998). *The Third Way: Renewal of Social Democracy.* Blackwell Publishers, Cambridge, UK.

Group of International Solidarity (1998). *Bhutan: South Asia Conference on Bhutan.* Kathmandu:

Gupta, Bhabani Sen (1999). *Bhutan: Towards a Grassroot Participatory Polity* Konark Publications, New Delhi.

Gurung, Harka (2002). 'General Election–1999 in *Nepali Journal of Contemporary Studies* Vol. 1. No. 2, September 2002. Kathmandu.

Gurung, Harka (1999). *Nepal: Social Demography and Expressions.* New Era, Kathmandu.

Gurung, Harka (2003). 'Trident and Thunderbolt' in *Cultural Dynamics and Nepalese Politics.* M.C.Regmi Memorial Lecture, Kathmandu.

Gyawali, Dipak and Koponen, Juhani, (2004). 'Missionary Zeal on Retreat' in *AID Uunder Stress.* Himal Books, Kathmandu, Nepal:

Hachhethu, Krishna (2004). "Parties in Parliament: The Role of the Prime

Minister"in L. R.. Baral (ed) *Political Parties and Parliament.* Adroit Publishers, New Delhi.

Hachhethu, Krishna (2004). *State of Democracy in Nepal.* State of Democracy in South Asia/ Nepal Chapter. Indreni Offset Press, Kathmandu.

Haque, Mahbub ul (1997). *Human Development in South Asia.* The Human Development Centre, Karachi.

Hayward, Ruth Finney (2000), *Breaking the Earthernware Jar: Lessons of South Asia to End Violence against Women and Girls.* UNICEF Regional Office for South Asia, Kathmandu.

HMG/Environment Protection Council (1993). *Nepal Environmental Policy and Action Plan.* Kathmandu.

HMG/World Bank/SAPROS (2000), *Delivery of Rural Development Services, SAPROS.* Kathmandu.

Huntington, Samuel P. (2004). *Who We Are? America's Great Debate.* Penguin Books, New Delhi.

ICIMOD and Central Bureau of Statistics (2003). *Mapping Nepal Census Indicators 2001 & Trends.* ICIMOD, Kathmandu

ILO (1976). *Nepal Rural Household Study.* ARTEP.

ILO (1980). *Poverty and Landlessness in Rural Asia.* Geneva.

IMF (2004). *International Financial Statistics,* Year Book 2002. Washington, D.C.

IMF (2004a). *Nepal: First Review of the Three Year Arrangement on the PRGF,* October 2004. Washington, D.C. (Internal Document).

IMF (2003). *Nepal: Request for Three Year Arrangement Under PRGF,* November 2003. Washington, D.C. (Internal Document).

IMF (2003a). *World Economic Outlook,* September 2003. Washington, D.C..

IMF/The World Bank (2004). *Debt Sustainability In Low Income Countries: Further Consideration On an Operational Framework and Policy Implications.* Washington, D.C, September (Internal Document).

Informal Sector Service Centre(2004). Nepal *Human Rights Yearbook 2004.* Indreni Offset Press. Kathmandu.

Institute of Foreign Affairs(2005). *Trade Facilitation: Nepal's Prioriries.* IFA, Kathmandu.

International Crisis Group (2005). *Nepal's Royal Coup: Making a Bad Situation Worse.* Asia Report No. 91, 9 February.

International IDEA (1998). *Democracy and Deep-Rooted Conflict: Options for Negotiators.* Peter Harris and Ben Reilly (ed). Stockholm: IDEA.

Islam et. al. (1982). *Employment and Development in Nepal.* ILO/ARTEP, Bangkok.

Islam, Rizwanul (1985) 'Poverty and Income Distribution in Rural Nepal' in *Poverty in Rural Asia.* ILO, Bangkok.

Jack D. Key note address at Interlaken, Switzerland.

Jackson, Howell E. and William W. Park. *An International Financial Service Center in Nepal: The Legal foundation. The Selective Incorporation of Legal Systems*. Boston: Collins and Associates.

Joshi, Bhuban Lal and Leo Rose (1966). *Democratic Innovations in Nepal: A Case Study of Political Acculturation*. Berkely: University of California Press.

Kantipur (Nepali Daily),12 November 2004. Kathmandu.

Kelly, Thomas 's Online Interview with King Gyanendra for *Time*, 26 January, 2004.

Khadka, Rup (2001). *Income Tax in Nepal: Retrospect and Prospect.* Ratna Pustak Bhandar, Kathmandu.

Khadka, Rup (2001a). 'Value Added Tax: The Concept, International Experience and Its Application in Nepal' in Rup Khadka (ed) *Value Added Tax: Four Years of Implementation,* Katmandu.

Khadka, Rup (2004). *Tax Reform in Nepal: A Unique Experience.*

Khadka, Rup (1994). *Nepalese Taxation: A Path for Reform*. Marburg Consult, Marburg.

Khan, Azizur Rehman and Eddy Lee (Eds) (1984). *Poverty and Rural Asia*. ILO / ARTEP, Bangkok.

Khanal, Krishna (2004). 'Parliament and Governance' in L.R.Baral (ed). *Political Parties and Parliament.* Adroit Publishers, New Delhi.

Khatri, Sridhar (2004). *What is the 'New' Security Agenda for South Asia?*, A paper presented in NCCS Seminar in Kathmandu, 16–17 November.

King Gyanendra's Royal Proclamation on 1 February 2005.

Koirala, Bimal and Damodar Gautam(1998 .) 'The Practice of Good Governance in the Present Nepalese Situation' in *Byabasthapan*, February. Management Association of Nepal, Kathmandu.

Kumar, Dhruba (2003). 'The Necessity of Choice: Demobilization, Demilitarization and Democratization in Nepal'. *Journal of Contemporary Studies*, March. Kathmandu.

Kumar, Dhruba (2004), *Trenches of Violence: Militancy, Militarism and Militarization of Social Sphere in Nepal*. A paper presented in Seminar on Non-traditional Security in South Asia by NCCST on 16–17 November. Kathmandu.

Landon, Perceval (2001). *History of Nepal,* Vol 1 and 2 Adarsa Enterprises. Delhi.

Lawati, Mahendra (2002). 'Defining Minorities' in *Nepal Journal of Contemporary Studies*, March 2002. Kathmandu,

Lawati, Mahendra (2003). "Maoist and Minorities : Overlap of Interests or A Case of Exploitation?" in *Studies in Nepali History and Society*. June. Mandala Book Point, Kathmandu.

Mahat, Ram S. (1994). *Press Statement on the Revision of National Accounts,* June 24. Kathmandu.

Mahat, Ram S. (2003). 'Nepalese Elite and Negative Syndrome', *The Kathmandu Post*, 16 October. Kathmandu.

Mahat, Ram S. (2004), "Security and Political Environment: A Nepalese Perspective" in *India- Nepal Relations: The Challenge Ahead.* Rupa in association with Observer Research Foundation. New Delhi..

Mahat, Ram S. (2004). 'Peace Mantra and Maoists' *The Kathmandu Post* 7–8 January. Kathmandu.

Mahat, Ram S. (2004). 'The Development Denominator' *The Kathmandu Post,* 15–16 March. Kathmandu.

Mahat, Ram S. (2004). 'Political Stand-off'. *The Kathmandu Post,* 7 April 2004.

Mahat, Ram S. (1978). 'Peasantry as a Revolutionary Force in a Proletarian Revolution: A Possibility' in *Arthavijnan,* June, Gokhale Institute of Politics and Economics. Poona.

Mahat, Ram S. (1993). "Prospects and Issues in Nepal–India Economic Cooperation in the Context of New Democratic Order and Economic Openness". A Paper presented at a Colloquium Indo-Nepal Relations sponsored by B.P.Koirala Foundation on November 24–25, 1993 Kathmandu, Nepal.

Mahat, Ram S. (1994). Statement at the Conference on Hydropower and Environment, Oslo, Norway. 12–14 September 1994.

Mahat, Ram S. (2003) *"Democracy in A Plural Society; A Case of Nepal."A* paper presented at the Conference on Pluralism, Democracy and Conflict Resolution: A Search for Stability in South Asia after 9/11 organized by Observer Research Foundation, New Delhi in association with the Rosa Luxemberg Foundation, Berlin. February 20–21. New Delhi.

Mahat, Ram S. (2003). 'Mice enter the barn'. 9 April 2004. *The Kathmandu Post.*

Mahat, Ram S. (2004) 'UN Mediation for Peace ?' *The Kathmandu Post,* 19–20 April. Kathmandu.

Mahat, Ram S. (2004), "Double Digit Growth ?" *The Kathmandu Post,* 20–21 August, Kathmandu.

Mahat, Ram S. (2004). "Corruption Perception" *The Kathmandu Post,* 29–30 July, Kathmandu.

Mahat, Ram S. (2004). 'Dynamics of Maoist War in Nepal'. Paper presented at the Conference on Economic Growth and Security organized by Delhi Policy Group in collaboration with Lahore University of Management Science and Union Bank in Lahore. October 8–9, 2004.

Mahat, Ram S. (2004). 'New Peace Bid', *The Himalayan Times*, 29 September 2004.

Mahat, Ram S. (2004). 'Economic Dimensions of Conflicts in South Asia: A Case of Nepal' in *Comprehensive Security: Economic Perspectives from India.* Seminar Proceedings, Delhi Policy Group. New Delhi.

Mahat, Ram S. 'The Refugee Impasse' *The Kathmandu Post,* 15 February 2004. Kathmandu.

Mann, Arthur (2004). *Nepal: A Feasibility Study for the Establishment of a Semi-autonomous Revenue Authority* (unpublished report).

Manandhar, Narayan (1998). *Public Enterprise and Privatization.* Kathmandu: Indreni Offset.

Mathema, Kedar (1990) 'Cheating Our Children', in *Himal*, (weekly) May–June. Kathmandu.

Mathema, Kedar. (2003). "Nepalese Elite and Negative Syndrome" *The Kathmandu Post*, 16 October. Kathmandu.

Mihaly, Eugene Bramer (2002). *Foreign Aid and Politics in Nepal.* Himal Books, Kathmandu.

Ministry of Economic Planning, HMG/N (1965). *The Third Plan 1965–70.* HMG/N, Kathmandu.

Ministry of Finance (2001). *Budget Speech of the Fiscal Year 2001–02.* HMG/N, Kathmandu.

Ministry of Finance (2002). *Chairman's Report on the Proceedings*, National Development Forum (NDF). HMG/N, Kathmandu.

Ministry of Finance (2002). *Foreign Aid Policy*. HMG/N, Kathmandu.

Ministry of Finance (2004). *Targets and Performance of Public Enterprises (FY 2002/2003–2004/05).* HMG/N, Kathmandu.

Ministry of Finance, Budget Speeches of Different Years. HMG, Kathmandu.

Ministry of Finance, *Economic Survey Reports* for different Years, HMG/N, Kathmandu.

Ministry of Finance, His Majesty's Government/Nepal (HMG/N) (2004). *Economic Survey, 2003/0.*, HMG/N, Kathmandu.

Ministry of Industry, Commerce and Supplies, *(2003). Progress Report of Nepal Multi-modal Transit and Trade Facilitation Project. HMG/N,* Kathmandu.

Ministry of Industry, Commerce and Supplies, HMG/N (2004). Nepal: *Trade and Competitiveness Study*. HMG/N, Kathmandu..

Ministry of Law and Justice, (1952). *Nepal Gazette*, 3 February, Nepal Sarkar Printing Press. HMG/N, Kathmandu.

Ministry of Trade, Commerce and Supplies (2004). *Nepal Trade and Competitive Study,* HMG/N, Kathmandu.

Muni, S.D (2004). *Human Security in South Asia. A* paper presented at NCCS Seminar, 16–17 November. Kathmandu.

Myrdal, Gunnar (1992).*The Asian Drama.* Kalyani Publishers. New Delhi.

Nath, Tribhuvan (1975). *The Nepalese Dilemma*. Sterling Printers, New Delhi..

National Planning Commission (1997). *The Ninth Plan(1997–2002).* NPC, HMG/N, Kathmandu.

National Planning Commission (1992) *The Eighth Plan, (1992–97. Draft Approach Paper.* NPC, HMG/N, Kathmandu.

National Planning Commission (1992). *The Eighth Plan*, (1992–97), NPC, HMG/N. Kathmandu.

National Planning Commission (1995). *Perspective Energy Plan For Nepal,* NPC, HMG/N. Kathmandu.

National Planning Commission, HMG/N (2003).*The Tenth Plan (2002–2007) Summary.* NPC, HMG/N, Kathmandu.

Nepal Development Forum (2002). *NDF Bulletins—1,2 and 3*. MOF, HMG/N Kathmandu.

NDI/Nepal (2005). *Working to Strengthen and Expand Democracy*. 15 April 2005. Kathmandu. (Summary findings of an opinion poll).

Nepal Peace Campaign (2004). *The Costs of War in Nepal*. Bisnu Sapkota (ed). Kathmandu.

Nepal Rastra Bank (2004). *Financial Sector Reform*. A paper submitted to the Nepal Development Forum. Kathmandu.

Nepal Samacharpatra, (Daily), 19 August 2001.

Nepal South Asia Centre (1998). *Nepal Human Development Report 1998*. NESAC Kathmandu.

Nepali Times (Weekly), #209 13–19 August, 2004.

Nepal's national daily newspapers on 5 February, 2005.

Neupane, Govinda (2000). *Nepalko Jatiya Prasna,* Kathmandu.

NGO delegation to the 27th ADB Annual Meeting in Nice, France.May 1994

NPC (1965). *Third Plan*. HMG, Kathmandu.

NPC (1970). *The Fourth* Plan *(1970-75*. NPC, HMG/N, Kathmandu.

Onesto Li (2000). Interview with Prachanda *The Revolutionary Worker*, 20 February 2000.

Palkhiwala, Nani (2003). *We The People,* UBSPD. New Delhi.

Pandey, D.R.(1999). *Nepal's Failed Development: Reflections On the Missions and Maladies*. Nepal South Asia Centre, Kathmandu.

Pandey, D.R.(20002). "Managing Development Aid for Greater Effectiveness," in *Chairman's Report on the Proceedings, NDF 200*. MOF, HMG/N, Kathmandu.

Pandey, Sardar Bhim Bahadur (1982). *Tyas Bakhat Ko Nepal*. CNAS, Tribhuvan University. Kathmandu.

Pant, Raghab Dhoj (1991). *Nepal: Towards a New Development Policy*. Institute of Developing Economies, Tokyo.

Pant, Y.P.Pant. (1982). *Economic Development of Nepal*. Kitab Mahal, Allahabad.

Papows, Jeff (1998). *enterprise.com: market leadership in the information age*. London: Nicholas Brealey Publishing.

Pokhrel Durga (2003). Issues and Opportunities for Women's Advancements in Nepal. Nepal Women's Commission.Kathmandu. May 2003. (unpublished).

Pokhrel, Bharat (2003). 'Commissions, Kickbacks, and Bribes in Nepal' in (2003) in D.B.Gurung (ed) *Nepal Tomorrow Voices and Visions*. Koselee Prakashan, Kathmandu.

Pokhrel, Durga (2003). Eyewitness report on field visits to insurgency-affected areas (unpublished).

Prachanda's press statement of 1 February, 2005.

Pradhan, K.L (2001). *Brian Hogdson at the Kathmandu Residency*. Spectrum Publications, Delhi.

Prashashan Shudhar Ayog. *Prashashan Sudhar Ko Pratibedan 2048*. Mudran Tatha Prakashan Bivaag. Kathmandu.

Press release of 4 August 1995 by International River Network.

Public Expenditure Review Commission 2000/2001 Report. 3 March 2001 (Unofficial translation by DFID).

Rana, Pravakar, Pashupati S.J.B.Rana and Gautam Rana (2002). *The Ranas in Nepal*. NAEF, Geneva.

Regmi, D.R. (1961), *Modern Nepal.* Firma K.L. Mukhopadhyaya, Calcutta.

Regmi, M.C. (1971). *A Study in Nepali Economic History 1768–1846*. Manjusri Publishing House, New Delhi.

Regmi, D.R.(1950). *A Century Of Family Autocracy in Nepal.* Nepali National Congress, Banaras.

Regmi, M.C. (1978). Land Tenure and Taxation in Nepal. Ratna Pustak Bhandar, Kathmandu.

Rizal, Tek Nath (2004). *Bhutan: The Other Side of the Shangrila.* Sap-Publishing House, Kathmandu.

SAARC(1992). *Meeting the Challenge. Report of the South Asian Commission on Poverty Alleviation.* SAARC, Kathmandu.

Sachs, Jeffrey D. (2005). *The End of Poverty: Economic Possibilities For Our Time.* USA: The Penguin Press.

Sakya, Sujita (2003). "The Maoist Movement in Nepal, An Analysis from Women Perspective" in Arjun Karki and David Seddon (ed.) *People's War in Nepal Left Perspective,* Adroit Publications, New Delhi.

Sanwal, B.D. (1965). *Nepal and the East India Company.* Asia Publishing House, Bombay.

Seddon David, Jagannath Adhikari, Ganesh Gurung (2001). *The New Lahures: Foreign Employment and Remittance Economy of Nepal.* Institute of Develoments Studies (NIDS), Kathmandu.

Seddon, David (1987). *Nepal A State of Poverty.* Vikas Publishing House, New Delhi.

Sen, Jahar (1977). *Indo-Nepal Trade in the Ninteenth Century.* Firma KLM, Calcutta.

Shah, Sadip (2004). A presentation in the IIC conference in New Delhi on Democracy and Peace in Nepal 6–7 December.

Shaha, Rishikesh (1982). *Essays in the Practice of Government in Nepal*. Manohar, New Delhi.

Shaha, Rishikesh (1993), *Politics in Nepal 1980–1991.* Manohar, New Delhi.

Shaha, Rishikesh (1996). *Modern Nepal,* Vol. 1 and 2. Manohar, New Delhi.

Shaha, Rishikesh, (2000) *Privatization in Nepal: An Independent Review of the Privatization Program in Nepal,* A report to Department for International Development (DFID in collaboration with Gopal Ghimire and Lana Kinley) Kathmandu.

Shakya, Rabindra Kumar (2002). *Development Policies and Institutions and Their Impact on SID*. A report submitted to UNDP/UNCTAD, Kathmandu.

Shakya, Rabindra Kumar (1994). "Social Dimensions of Economic Reforms in Nepal" in *Social Dimensions of Economic Reforms in Asia,* Rizwanul Islam (ed). International Labour Organisation, South Asia Multidisciplinary Advisory Team (SAAT). May 1994. New Delhi.

Shakya, Rabindra Kumar (1999). *Productivity and Labor Cost in Manufacturing: Policy Issues in Nepal.* A study undertaken for International Labor Organization (ILO), Kathmandu.

Sharma, Prayag Raj (1986). 'Values in the Doldrums: Does the West meet the East in Nepal?' Paper presented at a seminar on Political development and Social Change in Nepal. 7–11 December, 1986, Kathmandu.

Sharma, Shalik Ram (2003). 'Microfinance Against Poverty' in *Economic Review Occassional Paper,* No. 15. Nepal Rastra Bank, Kathmandu.

Shrestha, B.P. (1981). *The Economy of Nepal,* Ratna Pustak Bhandar, Kathmandu.

Shrestha, B.P. (1964). *The Economy of Nepal.* Bombay: Vora & Co. Publishers.

Shrestha, Bihari K. (2002), 'Conflict Resolution Through Governance Effectiveness' in *Conflict Resolution and Governance in Nepal.* NEFAS, Kathmandu.

Shrestha, D.P. 'Trends, Patterns and Structure of Economically Active Population' in *Population Monograph of Nepal,* Vol. I Central Bureau of Statistics, Kathmandu.

Shrestha, M.K. (1965). *A Handbook of Public Administration in Nepal,* Kathmandu.

Siegle, Weisten and Halperin. Democracy and Development in *Foreign Affairs* September/October 2004.USA.

Singh, Naresh Man (1957). *Nepal's First Five Year Pla.* Nepal Council of Asian Relations and World Affairs. Kathmandu.

SIPRI (2002) *Yearbook 2002.*

Solidarity International (2002). *A Decade long Bhutanese refugee crisis: Soliciting international support and solidarity.* Vol.11. No. 1&2. GRINSO-Nepal. Kathmandu.

Spotlight, 8–17 October, 2004.

Stiller, Ludwig F. (1995). *The Rise of the House of Gorkha.* Human Resource Development Research Centre, Nepal.

Stiller, Ludwig F. (1976), *The Silent Cry.* Sahayogi Prakashan, Kathmandu.

Stiller, Ludwig F. and Ram Prakash Yadav (1979). *Planning For People.* Sahayogi Prakashan, Kathmandu .

Stockholm International Peace Research Centre(SIPRI) (2002). 'Recent trends in military expenditure'. http://projects.sipri.se/milex/mex trends. Also, // projects sipri. se/milex/mex major spenders.html html.// projects sipri. se/ milex/mex share gdb.html

Stockholm International Peace Research Institute (SIPRI). *Yearbook 2002.* Stockholm.

Thapa, B.B. (1967), *Planning For Development in Nepal: A Perspective for 1965-80,* Claremont Graduate School, California.

Thapa, Deepak with Sijapati, Bandita (2003). *A Kingdom Under Seize.* The Print House, Kathmandu.

Thapa, Manjushree (2005). *The New York Times*, 12 February 2005.

The CBS/NPC (1994). *The Revised GDP Series of Nepal (1984/5-1993/94)*. HMG, Kathmandu.

The Central Bureau of Statistics (2003). *Population Monograph of Nepal*. NPC/ CBS, Kathmandu.

The Central Bureau of Statistics and ICIMOD (2003), District of Nepal, "Indicators of Development", ICIMOD, Kathmandu.

The Central Bureau of Statistics and ICIMOD(2003). *Districts of Nepal: Indicators of development Update 2003*. ICIMOD, Kathmandu.

The Central Bureau Of Statistics and ICIMOD(2003). *Mapping Nepal Census Indicators 2001 and Trends*. Kathmandu: ICIMOD.

The Central Bureau of Statistics and The World Bank (2004). *Measuring Poverty in Nepal: Results from NLSS I and NLSS II*. CBS,NPCS,HMG/N, Kathmandu.

The Centre For Bhutan Studies (1999). *Gross National Happiness: Discussion Papers*. The Centre For Bhutan Studies, Thimpu.

The Himalayan Times 18 January, 2005.

The Himalayan Times, 1 February, 2005.

The Himalayan Times, 25 November, 2004.

The Himalayan Times, 28 February, 2005.

The Himalayan Times, 26 December, 2004.

The Kathmandu Post (Daily), 13 December 2004, Kathmandu.

The Kathmandu Post, 11 January, 7 April 2005.

The Kathmandu Post, 13 November, 2004.

The Kathmandu Post, 18 February, 2005.

The Kathmandu Post, 18 November, 2004.

The Kathmandu Post, 19 to 23 November.

The Kathmandu Post, 2 January, 2005.

The *Kathmandu Post*, 27 January, 2005.

The Kathmandu Post, 29 November, 2004.

The Kathmandu Post, 3 September, 2004.

The *Kathmandu Post*, 6 November 2004

The Kathmandu Post, 6 November 2004.

The Nepali Times, 11–17 February, 2005.

The Nepali Times, 12–18 November, 2004.

The Nepali Times, 19–25 November, 2004

The World Bank (1993). *Nepal Expenditures in the Road Sector*, Washington, D.C.

The World Bank (1994). *Staff Appraisal Report, Arun Three Hydro Electric Project. 29 August*, Washington, D.C.

The World Bank (1995). *News Release No.96/Soo8*. August 3, Washington, D.C.

The World Bank (1996). *The East Asian Miracle: Economic Growth and Public*

Policy. Oxford University Press, New York.

The World Bank (1997). *World Development Report 1997*. Oxford University Press, New York.

The World Bank (1999). *Nepal: Poverty at the Turn of the Twenty First Century*, Washington, D.C.

The World Bank (2001). World Development Report 2000–2001. Washington, D.C.

The World Bank (2002). *Financial Accountability in Nepal*. Washington, D.C.

The World Bank (2004), *Nepal Development Policy Review: Restarting Growth and Poverty Reduction*. Washington, D.C.

The World Bank (2004). *Nepal: Country Assistance Strategy 2004–2007*. Washington, D.C.

The World Bank (2004). *The World Development Report 2004*, Washington, D.C.

The World Bank(1997). *Helping Countries Combat Corruption: The Role of the World Bank*. Poverty Reduction and Economic Management. PREM Network.

The World Bank, (1996). *Sustainable Transport Sector Review and Lessons of Experience*. Washington, D.C.

The World Bank, (1999). Project Appraisal Report on *Road Maintenance and Development Project*. Washington, D.C.

The World Bank: Various World Development Reports.

Thurow, Lester (1992), *Head to Head*. Nicholas Brealey Publishing, London.

Thurow, Lester (1996). *The Future of Capitalism*. Nicholas Brailey, London,

Timsina, C.L (2003) 'Option for Peaceful Bhutan', in Basnet and Dhakal (ed.) *Bhutan Political Problem*.

Transparency International (2002). *Corruption in South Asia: Insights and Benchmarks from Citizen Feedback Surveys in Five Countries*. December 2002.

Transparency International (2004). *Corruption Perception Index 2004*, Berlin.

UNDP (2004). *The Macroeconomics of Poverty Reduction: The Case of Nepal*. Kathmandu.

UNDP (2001). *Nepal Human Development Report* 2001.

UNDP (2002, 2003, 2004). *Human Development Report*. Oxford University Press, New York.

UNDP (2004). *Nepal Human Development Report 2004*, (Draft), Kathmandu.

UNDP. (1994,1996,1997,1998, 2001). *Human Development Report*. Oxford University Press, New York.

United Nations (2002). *Financing For Development: A Critical Global Cooperation*. Document prepared by the Secretary-General to Preparatory Committee of the International Conference on Financing for Development. Monterry, Mexico, March 18–22, 2002.

Index

K

L